D0590231

Feeding Frenzy

Feeding Frenzy

WILL SELF

VIKING
an imprint of
PENGUIN BOOKS

For Suzanne, Patrick and family

VIKING

Published by the Penguin Group
Penguin Books Ltd, 80 Strand, London WC2R ORL, England
Penguin Putnam Inc., 375 Hudson Street, New York, New York 10014, USA
Penguin Books Australia Ltd, Ringwood, Victoria, Australia
Penguin Books Canada Ltd, 10 Alcorn Avenue, Toronto, Ontario, Canada M4V 3B2
Penguin Books India (P) Ltd, 11 Community Centre,
Panchsheel Park, New Delhi – 110 017, India
Penguin Books (NZ) Ltd, Cnr Rosedale and Airborne Roads,
Albany, Auckland, New Zealand
Penguin Books (South Africa) (Pty) Ltd, 24 Sturdee Avenue,
Rosebank 2196, South Africa

www.penguin.com

This collection first published 2001
2

Copyright © Will Self, 2001

The moral right of the author has been asserted

The publishers would like to thank Faber & Faber
for permission to quote from 'The Waste Land' from
Collected Poems 1909–1962 by T. S. Eliot.

Set in 11/13.75 pt Monotype Bembo
Typeset by Rowland Phototypesetting Ltd, Bury St Edmunds, Suffolk
Printed in Great Britain by Clays Ltd, St Ives plc

A CIP catalogue record for this book is available from the British Library

ISBN 0-670-88995-4

Introduction

My wife, Deborah Orr, suggested the title for this collection of my journalism and occasional writings. The pieces were written and published (and sometimes not published) over the period 1995–2001, and represent a selection that, although by no means exhaustive, none the less constitutes an obese volume. What apology can I possibly offer to the reader for this hypertrophy of verbiage? This painstaking restoration of yesterday's fish 'n' chip papers? Save to observe that I have never considered myself to be anything other than a writer, a person who mediates the world through his language, curry-combing reality with his sentences, winnowing out the truth with his words. The world is my brine – I am an oyster: a literary bivalve, cemented to the sea-bed, extracting whatever nutriment I can from the ebb and flow of the popular unconscious.

Deborah felt that 'Feeding Frenzy' did justice to this collection because it not only carries an implication of my propensity for writing/feeding too much, but also gives a nod to my tenure as the *Observer*'s restaurant critic from 1995 to 1997. While this was a comparatively short time to be 'in irons' (as we professional forkers term it), the restaurant gig furnished me with a certain notoriety, as well as providing me with an opportunity to carp, ridicule and generally excoriate contemporary British culture that for a satirist seemed heaven-sent.

Looking back from a new millennium in which the phenomena of the celebrity egg-flipper and the *echt* eatery are so fully digested that they seem always to have been before us, it's worth remembering that this high table of decadence was really only laid in the last decade or so. True, both fatuous foodies and fashionable restaurants are perennial features of the urban scape, but it was only in the 1990s that the Michelin stars began seriously to invade the kingdom of the carbohydrate, and undermine the suzerainty of stodge. Further, it was only in the 1990s that new restaurants began to be fully 'styled', presenting themselves not simply as attractive environments within which to ingest, but as gustatory temples, with décor, servitor, clientele and menu in a fully reciprocal relationship with one another; an achieved, mutual masticatory masturbation. It was only in the 1990s that those soupy dragons, the Delias, the Nigellas and the Jamies, burst through the double doors from their steamy lairs to become not simply local heroes of the urban middle class, but tabloid-bestriding ogres of popular culture. I think it fair to say that the last decade of the twentieth century will be remembered not so much for its wars, its mass murders or its scientific advances, as for being that era of human progress in which, at last, focaccia became available in the Fens.

In line with this democratisation of the dinner came a British government that enshrined the dictum: you are where you eat. We'd do well to recall at this point that it was Blair and his merry confrères who planned their ascent to power at a fashionable Islington restaurant; and it was Blair who, with his own impeccably modulated mediocrity, seemed to enshrine a new cultural manifesto for the burgeoning bourgeoisie. No longer need you wade through reams of writing, or scrutinise acres of canvas, or watch many metres of film in order to affirm your status as someone *au fait* with Italian culture. Simply sup at the River Café and holiday in Tuscany, and your credentials are assured.

I had the good fortune to be a restaurant critic (and I say 'restaurant' rather than 'food' advisedly – I've never cared substantially more about what enters my body than about what leaves it) during just that period when these changes were under way. I can't make any great claims to have punctured the pachyderm of pretension that these bogus values constitute, but I had my moments. In 1996, I heard it on good authority that a secret cabal of restaurateurs had met up to deliberate how to be rid of their troublesome critic. Within a month or so there was sinister confirmation of the forces ranged against me, when a tabloid newspaper called Deborah to inform her that the proprietor of a restaurant I had recently slagged off was accusing me of having tried to score cocaine off the doorman.

The preposterousness of this (who needs to solicit coke from a London restaurant doorman, when so many of them will offer it unasked?) leads me to the third reason for the title of this collection, namely my sacking from the *Observer* in April 1997, following my own admission that I had taken heroin on John Major's election jet. The background to these events has long been in the public domain; suffice to say: no, it wasn't a gonzo journalism stunt in emulation of Hunter Thompson; yes, I did have a heroin habit at the time; and yes, I do regret the whole incident, which was damaging and distressing for my family and friends. But what remains pertinent is that I myself then became the human bait for a media feeding frenzy.

Deborah characterised this at the time as an example of a new kind of story in the British press, the 'broadsheet tabloid story'. This she defined as a story that should have been of interest only to tabloid readers, but was blown out of all proportion by broadsheet journalists behaving like gutter hacks. A precursor of my own imbroglio was the *brouhaha* surrounding my friend Martin Amis's new teeth; a more recent example is the furore over what the Poet Laureate does with his butt of sack. However my own media monstering may have affected me personally, what's of wider note is that the broadsheet tabloid story – like the *echt* eatery and the celebrity egg-flipper – is an important cultural marker of the 1990s. Its coming of age was paralleled by developments in the whole character of British newspapers, and in the relationship between the fourth and the other estates.

Some small recompense for the grotesque way in which Alan Rusbridger and Rosie Boycott behaved during the affair has been to witness their subsequent slide into the red-top gutter. Rusbridger, as executive editor of the *Observer*, was at least notionally in accord with mast-head slogans on the paper, which had informed readers in the run-up to the election-jet débâcle that I was 'Back on Drugs Again'. When pressure from a hack on the *Express* led the kind and decent Will Hutton (then the *Observer*'s editor) to ask me to sign an affidavit denying that the drug-taking had occurred, having no wish to perjure myself, or widen the ambit of the witch hunt, I confessed. Rusbridger summarily fired me, and made it difficult for me to gain another contract. This also made things extremely uncomfortable for Deborah – who at that time was one of his senior editors, in his capacity as editor of the *Guardian* – to continue in her post; feeling sidelined, she eventually left the newspaper.

But Rusbridger, having inherited a noble, campaigning left-liberal newspaper from the redoubtable Peter Preston, has in the latter part of the 1990s presided over its slide into being little more than the lickspittle house journal of New Labour. The *Guardian* is now a tabloid-broadsheet, a *Daily Mail* for the dumbed-down and deracinated, who'd rather read easy-to-swallow gobbets about Dolce & Gabbana than the kind of serious, campaigning articles that characterised the paper in its heyday. As for Boycott, who manipulated me and Deborah and finessed a confessional 'scoop' out of me, at a time in our lives of maximum vulnerability, she too has reaped. The last four years have seen her slide from nobly campaigning for the right to spliff up (in her capacity as editor of the *Independent on Sunday*), to purveying celebrity tittle-tattle in the *Daily Express*, to accepting a handsome pay-off from a pornographer. One can only assume that her ennoblement by Blair will be not long coming.

But it's the Blair-Mandelson-Campbell troika – this ephemeral triangle

– that represents the true nexus of the tabloid-broadsheet phenomenon: a Prime Minister who believed (and continues to believe) that only the tabloids can guarantee his election; an *éminence grise* who slid up and down the greasy pole with seemingly effortless lubrication; and a press secretary whose pop-eyed, dry-drunk control-freakery has been the story about the Government for the past four years. Never before has the press's agenda been so much about what the Government's . . . err, press agenda is. Never before has so much been written about so little. Never before has style so fantastically glossed substance. Pop ate itself years ago – and for the last half-decade we've merely been listening to it burp.

I'd like to claim a little foresight about all of this, which is why the first piece in this collection concerns my adoption, in 1995, of Tony Blair as my 'villain', for the last of the 'Heroes & Villains' columns to appear in the *Independent*. True, I got it wrong about him losing the election for Labour (and that was only a hortatory trope anyway), but I suspect that the majority of socialists must by now be feeling that this was the most Pyrrhic victory since Pyrrhus himself whopped those global capitalists of the ancient world, the Romans. Blair recurs throughout these pieces as a kind of bogy-man of blandness – the Anti-Self, if you will – and is equalled in igniting my antipathy only by the Tampon Apparent and his sad, dead clothes-horse of a wife, and the rest of the absurd, biscuit-tin monarchy we still needs must endure.

I'd like to be able to say that the tendency towards shorter pieces in this volume, as against my 1995 collection of journalism *Junk Mail*, is a reflection of my genuine unwillingness to write at great length – but this would not be true. It's rather that the broadsheet-tabloids have little inclination to print anything much over 3,000 words that isn't pegged on fifteen minutes of fame, or some such extraordinary popular delusion. I have been driven to conciseness, and apart from a couple of travel pieces, a brace of interviews, an art-catalogue blurb of uncompromising weirdness, and a long meditation on my relationship with London (an irresistible commission from Granta), by far the majority of the pieces in this collection are columns of what might be termed 'cultural criticism'.

I make no apology for preoccupying myself with architecture, television, conceptual art, restaurants and Jane Asher's cakes. I've never altogether understood this very English idea that a novelist who is also a critic should confine himself to criticising fiction. It's in line with the notion that what you need to be a working novelist are a couple of good leather elbow patches and a degree in English literature. It's a workaday vision of the novelist as artisan – or, worse, as hobbyist. The last thing I want to do after a hard day spent suspending my own disbelief – like a seal balancing a ball on its nose – is to watch some other poor sap attempt it. For years now I've read very little fiction – and as a result I tend to eschew criticising it.

One of my problems as a person (and I hope strengths as a writer) is that I really have no interests whatsoever to speak of; no interests, that is, but interest itself. So this collection betrays as many different preoccupations as there are pieces – and there are well over a hundred of those. In the introduction to *Junk Mail* I admitted to an abiding interest in the work of Adam Phillips, William Burroughs and Thomas Szasz. Since then I've been 'psychoanalysed' by Phillips – and I'd like my money back. Burroughs has died, and I fear I now think of him more as a superannuated Gap advertisement and uxoricide than as the great writer he undoubtedly remains. As for Szasz, I picked up on him as the most lucid advocate of the full legalisation of drugs. He was, but since I myself have now stopped taking drugs altogether, my wish for their legalisation, while enduring, has shifted from the highly personal ('I want more drugs now, damn it!') to the rather more dispassionately political.

A few words are needed about how to approach *Feeding Frenzy*. A contents list for a cornucopia such as this is as potentially abusive – and revolting – as a 1990s restaurant menu *nouveau*, with its talk of tossing, searing and drizzling with *jus*. There also seemed little point in exhaustively reproducing the titles these pieces received on publication, since these were entirely composed by subs, and almost always neither apposite nor amusing. Instead, the pieces are simply numbered rather than titled, the date and publication appearing at the end; and they are arranged in no particular order, nor are they categorised.

If this gives the text a certain agglutinative quality, I hope that it's aerated by the provision of a more than usually fluffy index. This covers not only people, places and things, but also ideas, obsessions and my own irritating stylistic tics. I like to think that if, dear reader, you should have an abiding desire to read about – for example – Tony Blair, you will simply turn to the back, jot down the page numbers and then turn to the relevant articles.

This approach to *Feeding Frenzy* is in line with my interpretations of the title itself. You can snack, you can brunch, you can gorge until you puke. You can sip phrases delicately, carefully selecting them to accompany word dishes of more solid fare, or you can relentlessly chomp your way through the book, like a compulsive eater at a midnight fridge-opening. All I ask is that you enjoy.

This collection owes its birth as much to the thorough and sensitive editing of Penny Phillips as it does to my own rather more broad-brush abilities. It was Penny who made the selection, Penny who hunted down the publication details, Penny who comprehensively re-edited the copy. In almost all instances she has worked from my original text rather than the published version, retaining jokes, observations and *aperçus* that were cut either because of failures in editorial sense of humour, or because of feeble political and moral sensibilities. She has punctiliously checked all spellings, facts, coinages and quotes; she has laboured diligently to reduce my repetitions, stylistic tics and syntactical infelicities to a minimum. In short, she has done everything she can to raise ephemera to the status of something worth preserving in book form. Let her receive her fair share of whatever odium attaches to the enterprise.

As for those editors (newspaper, magazine and broadcast) who have worked with me over the past five years, thankfully I've fallen out with a good many of them. But there are still some individuals whose willingness to commission me should, by rights, place them in the firing line of opprobrium: Lindsay Baker, Jason Cowley, Laura Cumming, Marcus Field, Michael Hainey, Mark Jones, Nick Lezard, Rod Liddle, Gill Morgan, Alex Renton, Louise Rogers and Inigo Thomas. Special mention should also be made of Victoria Hull, who acted as a perfect foil for much of the restaurant criticism.

However, in the last analysis, if you find yourself at the end of my *Feeding Frenzy* bored and groaning, I suggest you blame not me, but yourself. I only work here.

W. W. S.

London, May 2001

I'll give Tony Blair a 'sound bite'! I'll run right across the floor of the House of Commons, sideswipe the Master of Arms, and take a bite out of one of his copious ears; then we'll hear the Leader of the Labour Party really sound off.

Because I think that's what it'll take to get an authentic noise out of this poetaster of the glib, this walking autocue in a sensible suit. Tony Blair is my villain all right, but such is the vacuousness of his projected image (all we ever have to go on with a politician, for once they're dead and the 'truth' comes out, we're too bored and too relieved to be bothered to read it) that I've had to take a series of biopsies on what-he-is-not, to definitively establish why it is that he gets right up my nose.

But for starters, take last week and the death of Lord Harold Wilson. Tone has a gift opportunity to say something intelligent, something clever, something that fully expresses the twisted legacy of Lord Kagan's favourite mac-wearer. He bounces up, and with that prefectorial gait hops to the dispatch box, his mouth opens and what does he chime up with? 'Harold Wilson was to politics what the Beatles were to popular culture – he dominated the era.' Oh no, I don't think so, Tony, I think you're too absorbed in trying to concoct one of your bites here – the right-sounding comparative phrase – to notice that (a) it isn't true, and (b) nobody cares that much anyway.

By the time we reached the *Ten o'Clock News*, Harold's demise had been knocked back to the second lead item. You should suck on that, Tone, because I fear it's the shape of things to come as far as you're concerned. Even the ridiculous John Major, that avatar of the grey, had it nearer to the truth (although probably inadvertently) when he said that Wilson and he belonged 'nominally' to different parties.

I'm fed up with politicians who belong 'nominally' to different parties; for how much longer will Butskellism rear its Siamese head? And I'm utterly sick of 'devoutly Christian' politicians who cut their ideological cloth to fit their electoral communion dress. Perhaps it's something to do with your training in advocacy, this ability to make one kind of statement sound so completely like another? It's all in the tone, Tone, isn't that right?

Of course, I don't know you personally; I'm sure you're a 'really nice man'. I'm sure that's pretty much *all* you are, too. How could you be anything else? The path to electability is a greasy runnel, slick with niceness: there's no way of turning back, and the only way forward is by being nicer and nicer and nicer, until we're all drowning in the saccharin of your happy marriage, your family home, your bourgeois bloody values.

I read politics at your alma mater, Tone. I only missed running into you on Magdalen Bridge by a year or four, but you're worlds away from me. I had hoped that your advent might provoke some late surge in political interest on my part, but no. I should say the Blair year has engendered a terminal decline in my engagement with contemporary political events. The minute I hear your voice, or cop a view of your ridiculous quasi-seventies haircut – which looks to the future, but is spray-mounted by the past – I feel a deep sense of enervation come over me. Religion may or may not be the opium of the people, but under Blair, politics is becoming our Largactil.

No, Tony, Labour is not the natural party of law and order, nor is it the party of 'family values'; Labour is the party of trade unionism and the 'labour movement', as any fool knows. I particularly object to your rap about the family. I don't want some pol like you telling me that I represent social disintegration because I'm separated from my wife and children. Mind your own bloody business. See if you can do something about the budget deficit, the dependence of our economy on arms exports, the moral pusillanimity of the western European countries' response to the Balkan conflict, the destruction of the environment and so on, and so on, before you come waggling your ditsy ethical concerns in my face.

You're representing something that doesn't really exist, Tone. Your party is riven over issues of sovereignty, just as the Tories are. Europe and electoral reform are the only real issues in our polity; everything else is a displacement activity. I suppose it would be a bit much to expect you to fess up to this, yank that fragile consensus from under your sensibly-shod feet. But it's not too much to expect from someone with an ounce of real political courage.

You say that you want to 'see Labour reach out to the ten million people who did not vote in 1992'. You say that 'non-participation on such a scale is a symptom of social disintegration which threatens the health of our democracy'. You call for parliamentary and electoral reform, but the rhetoric you bring to bear is so suffused with the jargon of the very system you are attempting to impact upon that it is void before it's passed your lips. You are a past master of what Theodor Adorno typified as 'the jargon of authenticity'.

Stop saying words like 'promote', 'include' and 'provide'. Stop wittering on about 'political renewal power' and the 'Christian concept of community'. It was said of you when you acceded to the leadership that you had no 'ideological baggage'. Too right. You checked it in at the left-luggage office of ambition and have conveniently forgotten the ticket.

You are an absence, not a presence, Tone. We need someone who is unafraid to dump rhetoric and speak with genuine flair. Someone who acknowledges that when the heir to the throne and defender of the faith is entering the mind-set of a tampon via the method, it's time to disestablish the Church. Quite clearly you aren't our man. I think it's distinctly possible that if you don't buck up, and rethink your entire approach, the Tories may win the next election. I'd tell you to go to the dustbin of history, if you weren't already standing in it.

Independent, June 1995

2

The most fundamental – and the most difficult – task for the creative artist is to get their audience to suspend disbelief. It doesn't matter whether you're a conjuror or an abstract expressionist – the key thing is that rabbits are seen to appear from hats, and emotional epiphanies are summoned from splatters of pigment. I myself have worked in several different media over the years – literary fiction, journalism, television, performance – and in all of them suspension of disbelief has proved hard. My analogy is that it's like a performing seal having to keep a ball balanced on its nose all day; if you manage it you're 'clever', and if you fail you're just another seal.

But then I've never had to suspend disbelief in cake – which is just as well. The very nice woman at Jane Asher Party Cakes told me in no uncertain terms that 'you can't suspend cake', and I could see her point entirely. I'd been examining some five hundred different photographs of custom-designed cakes in a Jane Asher Party Cakes (henceforth JAPC) portfolio, searching for the ideal model for a cake for my son's eighth birthday party.

There were cakes done as football fields, secret gardens, Havana cigars, Tiffany clutch bags, mobile phones, Po of *Teletubbies* fame, and, in one astonishing *coup de théâtre*, a life-size one-year-old African child. This latter cake in particular failed to suspend my disbelief. Whereas some – presumably the adoring parents – must have seen an uncanny likeness, almost breathing, of their adored one, I saw simply a big mound of roughly toddler-shaped sponge, covered with black icing.

I'd got the wrong end of the spatula though, because the nice cake woman went on, 'Take a rampant horse, for example – we just can't do that, you'd have to suspend cake.' That was it, she was talking about *literally*, rather than metaphorically, suspending cake; the business of the verisimilitude of the cakescape, its correspondence to the real world, didn't even obtrude.

I felt suitably humbled. Indeed, my whole trip to the Jane Asher empire in Chelsea proved to be a humbling experience. I'd set out from Sloane Square quite blithely, happy in the knowledge that at last I was tilting at a proper satirical target. After all, in the last few weeks we've seen the elevation to sainthood of a woman who championed Quorn burgers – surely there would be an open season on other McCartney significant others, especially those who design cakes?

And Jane Asher! I mean to say, what a fragrant, floral, ultimate Laura Ashley of a woman; her underwear is probably swagged and ruched, and her cosmetic surgeon – if she has one – has undoubtedly replaced her lower intestine with several bowls of pot-pourri. Furthermore, to go from hanging out with Paul and the Maharishi to designing party cakes off the King's Road – clearly such a thing could only ever happen in a nation devoid of the remotest scintilla of cool.

All right, granted Ms Asher appears in *Men Behaving Badly*, but has it ever occurred to you that putatively the *worst* thing Martin Clunes et al. are engaged in is lusting after a woman old enough to be their mother? These mean thoughts jostled in my sick brow as I trod through the esplanades of expensive chi-chi vendors that constitute commercial Chelsea. When I got to the cake shop – and its attendant tea shop – I was fulsomely reassured. The window was full of cakes it was impossible to suspend disbelief in, competing for merchandising space with other Asher productions: *Good Living*, the book of her daytime TV lifestyle show; *The Longing*, her 'critically well-received' novel; and examples of the Jane

Asher Collection of cake decorations. Confidently sneering, I strode in . . .

. . . Only to bottle out – at least initially. I asked the nice woman whether she had ever been asked to design a cake that was too *risqué* or disturbing. She thought for a while before answering, 'No, I don't think so.' Chastened, I ordered a perfectly normal, football-shaped cake for my eight-year-old. The only extraordinary thing about the cake was its price – £85. Bearing in mind that this was a cake for fifteen people, this worked out at around £5.70 a slice. Marie Antoinette should be living in such an age!

In the tea shop I watched superannuated upper-middle-class people reading copies of *Hello!* and brooded over my Earl Grey. Eventually, nauseated by my own pusillanimity I locked antlers with the nice woman once more: 'Erm . . . when I said that stuff about *risqué* cakes I wasn't altogether speaking theoretically –'

'Really?'

'Yes, you see I've got a friend who would like a rather unusual cake made.'

'What would they like?'

'Um, well, he's just had a successful triple heart-bypass operation and he'd like a cake that sort of . . . well, *depicts* the surgery –'

'We did do a heart once . . . let me see, where is it . . .' She leafed through the JAPC portfolio, until coming upon a glossy Polaroid of a glossy heart, complete in every detail – aorta, valves, arteries etc. – nestling on a cake plate.

'Wow!' I exclaimed, disbelief dangling. 'Is that a cake?'

'Oh yes,' replied the nice young man who had served me in the tea shop, 'it's just sponge and icing, but the photo doesn't do it justice.'

'So you could manage my friend's bypass – he's got some photos of the surgery taking place.'

'Just get him to bring them in,' the nice woman said firmly – and then she went on about suspending cake.

I left in a daze, but not before buying a copy of *Good Living*. Who knows, I thought as I shuffled off down the road, perhaps if the novel is dead, the future of fiction lies in the cake?

The Times, May 1998

3

There are many places that you go to and hope, often devoutly, not to return to. In my category of such destinations I include Victoria Coach Station, Agra in India, and for some obscure reason Rio de Janeiro. But equally there are places you go to, perhaps only for a few days, and find yourself falling for. The atmosphere in these places penetrates your mind; you begin to construct an alternative history for yourself, one in which this place has played a significant role. One such place – for me – is the island of Rousay in Orkney.

I first went there at Easter in 1992, to stay for a week with an English friend who has owned a house on Rousay for many years. I found the wind omnipresent, a combination of zephyr and sprite that managed to infiltrate itself into every nook and cranny. Even in April, to a southerner, the cold was gripping. But despite this I found myself so in thrall to the landscape of round, green isles, set in a turbulent sea, that I knew I would return.

I am a great believer in the idea that seascapes exert some kind of lunar pull on the imagination. Often, just being close to bodies of water in motion can have a direct effect on the content of my dreamlife. As much of my literary work is based on surrealist techniques, I prize dreams almost more than waking notions. Those few days I spent on Rousay visited me with amazing dream fodder and I was inspired to start writing a second draft of what was to become my first novel, *My Idea of Fun.*

At the end of last year I found myself in several kinds of impasse down south. Work was not going well, I hated the poky little flat I was living in in Islington. The tawdry round of drinking and cynical socialising, which so often seems to characterise London literary life, appeared even more vapid than usual. I had a strong intimation that if I stayed in the Smoke for the winter, I would end up creating little more than an enlarged liver. I decided to rent the house on Rousay where I had spent Easter the previous year, and see how I would cope with an isolated winter in the far north.

It took me four days to pilot my decrepit Citroën up through England and Scotland, to the ferry port at Scrabster. The further I got, the more quixotic the journey seemed. Breakfasting in splendid isolation in the echoing dining room of a mouldering hotel on the lunar Caithness coast, I almost sprayed the Wilton with Rice Krispies when the proprietor came and asked me how I had 'heard about' his hostelry. It was, after all, the only one for miles around.

On a storm-tossed *St Ola*, crossing the Pentland Firth, I moodily sipped McEwan's and listened to an impenetrable dialogue between two young Orcadian men, which seemed to consist entirely of the word 'fuck' interspersed with glottal stops and weird diphthongs.

But then I wasn't coming to be with people – or so I thought. I was intent on experiencing isolation, rigour, and the psychic strangeness of a remote place that had (*circa* 3500 BC) been the most populated part of the British Isles other than Salisbury Plain.

I'm not a great fan of the new-age obsession with neolithic monuments. I have no crystals about my person save for the one in my digital watch, and the only reason I ever pass by Stonehenge is to avoid the traffic jams on the M4. Nevertheless, something about the sheer density and magnificence of the neolithic remains in Orkney had got to me.

Rousay itself is known as 'Little Egypt' on account of the tremendous density of neolithic monuments. The house where I spent the winter was built near on the site of a Pictish brough. When I came out of the front door every morning, I would look up to the brow of the hill and see the imposing eminence of the Knowe of Yarso, a chamber tomb that has had the best south-facing views on the island since long before Tutankhamun buffed up his head-dress.

Something about this: the fact that the evidence of neolithic settlement in Orkney is almost as salient as that of the current age leads one to contemplate theories of temporal simultaneity (the idea that all events are in some sense happening at once). For a writer of fiction, who is intent on summoning up alternative realities, such an idea has enormous appeal. I wouldn't go so far as to say that I saw the hunter-gatherers of Orkney's neolithic past processing through my sitting room on stormy nights, but it didn't take too much squinting of the eyes, and too many drams of Highland Park, to convince myself that I might!

However, for the first few weeks on Rousay it wasn't the psychic atmosphere that preoccupied me, but the more prosaic issue of the air temperature. The house I was renting had once been that of the Laird's agent, employed by the notorious General Traill-Burroughs, who in the 1860s launched one of the few clearance schemes in Orkney. I don't know whether this bad vibe had persisted, but the place was extremely hard to heat.

For a city boy such as myself, getting an Aga to work is as potentially difficult as ploughing a field, or baiting a lobster-pot. I tried lighting it in different ways, cleaning it, adjusting all its knobs, all to no avail. The house remained icy.

Of an evening, I would nudge the conversation in the Taversoe Hotel (Rousay's premier hostelry) round to issues of domestic heating. And that, I suppose, is how I gained some small toehold in the local community: through that time-honoured form of oral literature, the Orkney Aga Saga. Haltingly at first, but then with greater dispatch, I was offered advice on the operation of my Aga. Eventually people came down from the pub and examined the beast, prodded it, and then got it to work.

In some ways this was a disappointment. With the house heated, my excuse for spending most of my evenings working my way through the unrivalled collection of single malts in the Taversoe Hotel was in part gone. I had already gained the impression that the Taversoe was a kind of Institute of the North. I had spent evenings there discussing hypnotism with the local doctor and schoolteacher, and philosophy with sundry fish farmers.

But on other nights the landlady, Diana Preston, and I would be the only human presence in the bar, quietly supping and listening to the wind howl around the eaves.

In order to counter possible SAD (seasonal affective disorder), I made a point of getting out of the house for at least three hours every day. Wrapped up like a Michelin man I would patrol the upper reaches of the island. From the top of Rousay, you can see most of the southern Orkney islands, all the way to the high, snowy ground of Hoy, where the hares turn white in winter.

No matter how gloomy and lonely I felt, the sight of the twin lochs in the middle of Rousay – Peedie Water and Muckle Water – like silver mirrors, and then the silver of the sea surrounding the land, was uplifting. The proximity of so much water was also having the desired effect. By the time Christmas came I had shucked off most of my southern *Weltsch-merz* and was writing again, with great speed.

Gradually I began to feel my sense of geography shifting. I was becoming Rousay-centric. England and the south was an impossibly tropical and decadent region; the Faeroes began to take on the aura of a possible holiday destination, Reykjavik to seem a plausible cultural centre. As I walked to the Taversoe in the gloaming, I could see the lights of Kirkwall twinkling across the water, twelve miles to the south-east. 'Ah!' I would think to myself, disapprovingly, 'there's that Gomorrah of a place, full of distraction and debauchery.'

Up until Christmas I had met some of the islanders, but had little social contact with them. I wasn't on Rousay to socialise but to work. I wanted – like a rather hairy and unwashed Garbo – to be alone. In the new year things changed. Having missed the first-footing, I returned from the flesh pots of London with a rather unpleasant bout of blood-poisoning, which put me flat on my back in Kirkwall Hospital for a week.

There's nothing like spending time in an institution for getting the measure of a community. From the doctors and nurses I learned all about the politics of local social-security issues, and heard much more about the social history of the islands. In Orkney the most oft-used adjective is a diminutive, 'peedie'. Perhaps you could make out a case for all small places being fixated by diminutives, as a function of their geography.

In Orkney almost everything is 'peedie', as in 'You'll have a peedie dram?' (In practice this means a large tumbler of Highland Park.) I think the apogee was reached when a young man was admitted to the medical ward looking as if a dolmen had been dropped on his face. 'What's wrong with him?' I asked the starchily efficient sister. 'Och, him,' she replied, 'he's just had a peedie car crash.'

Diana Preston sent her daughter Naomi up to the hospital with cigarettes for me, when I had run out. And when I was discharged, Jean Harris, who runs the best bed and breakfast on Rousay, came to take me home to convalesce.

After that, if not exactly enfolded in the bosom of the community, I started to see more people. As an Englishman I was far more acceptable in Orkney than I would have been on the mainland; the islands are, after all, half populated by English immigrants, and the native Orcadians have a very strong sense of not being Scottish. One Scottish friend, who had lived on Rousay for a number of years, had at first committed the solecism of wearing a kilt – until, that is, his nickname 'Jock the Frock' became a tad too galling.

My last few months on Rousay were altogether more comfortable. I had the measure of the Aga and I felt the isolation increasingly as a balm. My book was writing itself. Although it is not directly concerned with Orkney I was amused to see, when I came to edit it, how many of the names of local people, and their physical characteristics, had managed to infiltrate the text.

I began to feel out – in my own mind – the possibility of staying for longer. The communications really aren't that bad. Three flights south a day, and at least one ferry even in winter. I had almost grown used to the people at Kirkwall Airport check-in telling me, 'The plane will take off as soon as there's only two millimetres of ice on the runway.' While my kind of writing isn't exactly in tune with the oral traditions of the islands, perhaps over the years I would adapt and begin to resemble a cut-rate George Mackay Brown?

What stopped me – in addition to all my commitments down south – was the sense that while I might be accepted to some extent, I would never really feel that I belonged. The Human Genome Project visited Orkney while I was there and took blood samples. The results seemed to show that the native Orcadians are one of the longest-extant populations in Europe. It's no wonder that I felt such a strong sense of temporal simultaneity on Rousay: some of the people propping up the bar in the Taversoe are the lineal descendants of the builders of the Knowe of Yarso.

Many English people have made a good life in Orkney, and arguably they have helped prevent some of the island from becoming depopulated. But I knew that I would never feel altogether rooted. The paradoxical effect of my sojourn was to make me feel more English than I ever have before – so it was back to accidie, ennui and bilious conversations in the Groucho Club. But when it all gets too much again, I'll know the solution: head north.

Scotland on Sunday, January 1995

4

Book review: Design for Dying *by Timothy Leary
with R. U. Sirius (Thorsons)*

At the back of this quintessentially Learyesque, adolescent, stoned rap session of a book we reach an appendix that offers the accounts of those who attended upon the great put-on artist in the final days before his 'deanimation'. Among them were west-coast semi-Satanist and detached philosopher Robert Anton Wilson. Contributors were asked to offer their favourite memory of Leary and an account of the most important lesson to be drawn from his very public and unashamed mode of death. Wilson writes, '. . . right now I guess my favorite *favorite* would be the email I got from him a month after his passing. It said: "Robert how is everything? Greetings from the other side . . . It's not what I expected. Nice but crowded . . . Hope you're well. Love Timothy".'

Now Wilson – the cybercultural doyen and all-round twerp R. U. Sirius describes him elsewhere as 'the most intelligent man in the world' (*sans* Leary) – takes this to be a great joke. But I wouldn't see it that way at all. In truth Leary's final months, during which he railed against the morbidity of our current attitudes towards death, and plundered the wilder fringes of contemporary scientific thought for the furniture of an afterlife, can be read as a perverse return to the lonely, strict Catholic boyhood that really made him what he was.

This is the sad current that lies beneath *Design for Dying*, a book that on the surface is a studied reprise of all of Leary's crankiness. When 'Mademoiselle Cancer moved in to share [his] body' in January 1995, Leary – ostensibly – decided to use this as an opportunity rather than a defeat. He posted a sign on his door proclaiming an ongoing party, and decided to die with as much barnstorming razzmatazz as he had displayed during his thirty-five-odd years of counter-cultural rebellion.

In the death zone Leary continued to haunt the Internet, creating his own home page with the assistance of a number of young cybernauts. The Leary home page features a tour of Timothy's house which allows you to visit his 'Drug Room'. Fine if you want to clutter up the hard drive of your computer with the thousands of megabytes it takes to download the QVTR programme from the Web. Leary would have you believe, in his bowdlerised Californian *Book of the Dead*, that this is exactly what he would hope for. Leary takes us in this manual of moribundity on a *tour d'horizon* of just about every fringe theory concerning the interface between biological and machine intelligence.

One of the theories Leary enthusiastically endorses is that of Richard Dawkins's 'memes' – the notion that human evolution is now being advanced in the form of culturally transmitted, self-replicating code mechanisms, rather than old-fashioned RNA and DNA. Leary twists this a bit to let you know that when you take a trip round his drug room, you may in some elliptical sense be gifting him a shot at sentience from beyond the grave.

But this isn't his only stab at immortality. In *Design for Dying*, far from providing us with a heroic, stoical depiction of a Zen practitioner contemplating an infinity of the Dharma body, Leary rather puts me in mind of someone desperately thrashing round for a good old-fashioned afterlife. Leary may detail the latest theories of cyborgisation, cryonics and nanotechnology. He may contemplate his soul, sentience, the possibilities of being encrypted in DNA, transmitted through his works, or saved by his brain being frozen; but in the end it's quite clear that what he really doesn't want to contemplate is being Timothy Leary (not).

The book displays all Leary's egregiousness to dazzling effect. There seems to be an odd axiom at work that wherever a writer gets too close to these sorts of 'frontiers', her (or 'hir' as Leary rather more ponderously puts the possessive pronoun) prose style gets shot to shit. Aldous Huxley said of Leary, 'If only Tim wasn't such a silly ass,' but it has to be said that after Huxley himself opened the doors of perception, his prose style plunged into a veritable coal bunker of obscurantism.

It's a shame, because much of what Leary has to say could, potentially, be of interest; if only he wouldn't freight his text with wilfully crap coinages and hideously convoluted clusters of dense, neologistic verbiage. There's that, and there's also those bloody drugs. While I wouldn't argue with anybody's right to go out of this world in a blizzard of uppers, downers, twisters and multicoloured screamers, I can't help feeling that Leary's willingness to do so wasn't so much the hallmark of his sincerity as the guarantor of his status as this century's Great Adolescent.

He ushered in the era of the permanent teenager in the sixties; and he was still writing and acting like one well into his seventies and our nineties. He was still chasing teenage totty right up until he toppled into the grave. Like his confrère William Burroughs he survived the suicide/ deaths of both partners and children. You can't help feeling that it is this that provokes the tide of quite relentless desperation which flows through all of these final antics; and that while Leary wanted us to believe he was dying as he had lived, the truth was that he wouldn't have minded a crumb of good old-fashioned absolution when it came to the crunch.

New Statesman, September 1997

5

Restaurant review: Garfunkel's, 43 Charing Cross Road,
London WC2

Who is or was Garfunkel? We may never know. I phoned Garfunkel's
head office and they palmed me off on to some subsidiary office where
allegedly there was a marketing department. Well, not a department, a
marketing executive (which, as anyone who has worked in public
relations knows full well, is in all probability a school leaver who spends
most of their time popping bubble wrap). But the marketing executive
was 'on holiday'. The receptionist suggested her secretary, but Yolanda
was 'at lunch' and the following day she was 'sick'.

'Sick'. Ha! I don't think so. I picture Yolanda and the marketing
executive skipping with Garfunkel around a kidney-shaped swimming
pool, probably somewhere in Surrey. Garfunkel wears threads of uncompromising naffness: flared, patched jeans; a cheesecloth shirt. He has chest
but no head hair, and a moustache that looks as if a hank had been
retrieved from the plug hole and glued to his upper lip. The marketing
team are in matching bubble-wrap bikinis.

This matter of Garfunkel's provenance, age and identity is of some
interest because Garfunkel's, the chain of restaurants that bears his name,
has that peculiar air of persistence through both space and time that makes
me feel it has always been part of my life. Perhaps it's what Freudians
term a 'screen memory', but I'm certain I once clashed teeth with a fellow
teenager, awkwardly crouching on a vinyl banquette in Garfunkel's while
we shared a knickerbocker glory, *circa* 1976.

And I have another, more plangent memory of Garfunkel's, which
inspired me to eat there again. I'm not making great claims for my
apolitical status, but the fact remains that one sunny spring day in 1990, I
went into the West End to see a film, and on quitting Leicester Square
tube station I found myself in the very epicentre of the poll-tax riot.
Various Class War and anarchist types had – I learned later – just breached
the police line at the top of Trafalgar Square and, as I watched, a phalanx
of the Met's finest were retreating up Charing Cross Road under a hail
of bottles and bricks.

13

I was pressed up against a plate-glass window and as I observed the police regrouping outside the Porcupine, I became aware of browsing noises to my rear. I turned to contemplate a large Dutchman, sitting in Garfunkel's ingurgitating some coleslaw and apparently blissfully unaware of the street theatre going on some twenty feet away from him.

What greater recommendation could a chain of restaurants have? You can imagine the advertising slogan: 'Visit Garfunkel's and Miss Out on History in the Making!' I vowed at that moment to return.

On this occasion there was no riot in Charing Cross Road, just the wraiths of the city tottering around, pressed down by the louring sky. There was hardly anyone in Garfunkel's to watch a riot anyway. I had hoped to do a vox pop on some tourists, because, after all, Garfunkel's and its ilk are very likely the first encounter foreign *hoi polloi* have with what passes for English cuisine.

And English restaurant interiors for that matter. What must they think of us on entering Garfunkel's? Here, in full flood, is that style of décor for which the term 'Corporate Umbrian' was undoubtedly invented. The walls had been not so much rag-rolled as subjected to some form of dirty protest by prisoners armed with a lot of umber paint. A *trompe-l'oeil* mural of stone windows gave an umber view of umber fields, umber houses and umber trees. There were tiles in evidence; ersatz *fin-de-siècle* adverts; and in the window, shelves full of Chianti bottles, balsamic vinegar bottles, olive-oil bottles and the inevitable mock sacklets stencilled 'café'.

Naturally the manageress – who attended us – appeared to be a Filipino. It was all rather disorientating and I would have turned tail and run at this stage had it not been for seeing something so solid, so imposing in its quiddity that I was resolutely earthed. The salad bar! This crouched beneath the window, looking for all the world like one of the life-support sarcophagi on the spaceship in the film *2001*. Contemplating the array of different salads embedded in its umber concavity, I found it easy to imagine that the real purpose of this thing was to transport twenty portions of grated carrot to another galaxy.

The menus arrived and they were heavy on things like frozen yoghurt, cheesecake 'favourites' and giant banana splits. I was home. My companion opted for the potato skins with cheese. She pronounced them 'tasteless, yet inoffensive'. But really, when you think about it, the notion of potato skins is the most astonishing rip-off. The idea of flogging people a staple as if it were a titbit could only have been arrived at in a decadent society. You can't imagine people in Somalia flocking to Sorghum-U-Like.

I had melon balls to start. Frightening really, melon balls: the very sight of them makes you envision the implement that must have been used to create them. What if some psychopath got hold of one? 'They found Pendleton in the culvert. His buttocks had been horrifically mutilated with a melon-baller.'

A glass of wine appeared on the table and my companion sipped it. 'It's perfectly quaffable,' she said. 'It could be a slush of all the wines in the world.' Her penne arrived, together with a sauce boasting extra chillies. I tasted one and they were a tad on the rigid side. Indeed, these pasta quills might have been used literally rather than metaphorically – perhaps to write a note to Garfunkel himself, concerning the plight of the painters on the dirty protest.

I had a burger and a beer. Both were splendidly replete; in the Heideggerian formulation they were 'standing into being'. I have no doubt that as the 'forms' were carried past the mouth of the cave in Plato's famous simile, a burger and beer from Garfunkel's were among them.

And that – so to speak – was that. The bill came to a modest £20, plus tip. We didn't have time for the frozen yoghurt and I wasn't able to obtain a copy of the menu, so as to give you a more comprehensive idea of what Garfunkel's has to offer. The manageress told me that it was 'against company policy'. That's her story, but I suspect the truth is that there's a burgeoning black market for the things. I picture shadowy men lurking in alleys off the Charing Cross Road: 'Psst . . . Wanna buy a Garfunkel's menu?' After all, as we all know, kidney-shaped swimming pools require considerable upkeep.

Observer, October 1995

6

Restaurant review: Yetman's, 37 Norwich Road, Holt, Norfolk

In the week when statistics have been published showing a doubling over the last ten years of the numbers of obese people in this country, I feel that the time has come to offer my own observations on this weighty matter.

My predecessor as the *Observer* restaurant critic, that noted *incorruptible* John Lanchester, maintained his sylph-like figure by abjuring all desserts during his tenure. Not so much as a nougat glacé passed his shapely lips in over two years. When confronted with a passion-fruit coulis, the Lunchmaster (as he is popularly known) would say, 'I do not know you.'

So successful was this policy that John has since become a highly-paid catwalk model, despite being in his mid-thirties. However, I'm afraid I lack John's iron self-control and commendable narcissism, and over the last year have – to put it mildly – 'filled out'. My formerly smooth edifice of a body has been redeveloped with great balustrades and tiers of near-lithic fat. My feet have become but distant provinces, Datias and Hibernias, no longer answerable to the edicts issued by my mad Nero of a head. I require the assistance of a crowbar to pass through conventional doorways.

But in the very depths of my portly predicament, I have providentially found deliverance, and it is this – I believe sure-fire – cure for overeating that I wish to share with you. In order to pursue my métier I have been driven to consulting *The Good Food Guide*. Not, you understand, in order to find places to eat (nowadays you can shake a tree and a new restaurant will fall out of it), but to discover whether or not a given establishment allows for wheelchair (or in my case either motorised-trolley or winch) access.

Reading through the potted restaurant reviews, I chanced upon a novel form of aversion therapy. Ignore all the stuff about décor, service, starters, main courses and wine, and move straight to the desserts. After ploughing your way through page after page of chocolate marquise with coffee-bean sauce, apple crumble with warm butterscotch sauce, and vibrant sorbets garnished with myrtle syrup, I guarantee you'll never look so much as a wafer-thin mint in the eye again. However, despite my still colossal (although waning) bulk, I did just manage to squeeze myself into Yetman's restaurant in Holt last week, on the final leg of my annual prandial pilgrimage.

The Significant Other had been fairly worried about Yetman's. In the guide entry it did say there was wheelchair access, but with the bracketed proviso 'one step'. In the event she managed to lever me over the threshold with the assistance of three stalwart Norfolk agricultural labourers and a block and tackle.

A charming young man with a mop-top of curly brown hair seated the SO and sited me in a small sitting room abutting the main dining room. We ordered bloody Marys and consulted the menu. The drinks arrived quickly and were mixed properly, with a fair whack of lemon juice and Tabasco. When I asked whether there was a public phone available (I needed to call my tailor, who nowadays is engaged on altering my suits on a more or less constant basis), the mop-top very kindly let me use the house portable.

Call completed, I turned my attention to the décor. This was, to say the least, on the bright side. In the sitting room the chairs were blue, the carpet grey and the walls white. On a shelf there were various cutesy cards, one depicting Basil Fawlty; another, the Tory Party's shamelessly populist new party chairmen, Wallace and Gromit.

I ordered a soufflé to start, and followed up with the local pork. The SO decided on the crab cakes, followed by lobster thermidor. Her appetite for the dubious bounty of the North Sea was apparently unblunted after last week's sojourn at the Hoste Arms. A bottle of Saint-Aubin Burgundy was also called for.

In due course the Leo Sayer lookalike conducted us to our table. It was a Sunday evening, and until our advent Yetman's had been devoid of custom except for one lugubrious, moustached couple who were chomping in a corner. In some parts of rural Norfolk sexual dimorphism hasn't quite developed yet.

Moving me into the dining room necessitated a lot of cheerful pushing and shoving by all parties concerned, and the humping of this thigh and heaving of that buttock seemed to bring all of us closer together. The dining room was low-ceilinged, beamed, and very, very fresh-feeling. The mantelpieces at either end were painted bright white, as were the walls. The three chairs I sat on were done up in those odd, bag-like covers – though whether this was a permanent, decorative feature, or simply for my benefit, I couldn't be sure.

On the mantelpieces there were collections of little piggies (presumably local) and electric lamps. On all the tables there were glass vases full of marvellous fresh-cut flowers: pink lilies, carnations and sweet peas.

The wine arrived. It was great: light, rounded, with bags of flower (pink lilies, carnations and sweet peas, to be precise). My soufflé was a tiny little itsy-bitsy baby of a thing. It was made using goat's cheese and this gave it a novel flavour. It also arrived on quite an aggressive bed of gem lettuce and frisée that looked a bit like the kind of forest you have to hack your way through to reach Sleeping Beauty. The SO's crab cakes were truly flavoursome and came accompanied with some samphire grass. I love samphire grass. It's the most friendly of seaweeds for the neophyte. I first ate it as a teenager, in a stew of run-over rabbit and sliced puffball, cooked by the time-honoured method of a biscuit tin buried beneath a beach fire. The chef was a diminutive Scottish hippie called Bob, who a year or so later took an astral trip from which he never returned.

Ah! When to the sessions of sweet silent thought we summon up remembrance of things past! I began to snuffle somewhat, recalling the carefree days of my youth, before I acquired the body form of a Weddell seal. The SO thoughtfully ordered a bottle of Chorey-lès-Beaune 1993 (Lite) to dilute my mood. This was fine, although a fly had insinuated itself into the bottle and rapidly adapted to its new environment by growing a minuscule tweed suit and joining the Garrick Club.

The main courses hove into view. My pork was very good indeed: pink, succulent and apple-tarty. There was also a gargantuan truckle of vegetables, featuring both big and baby carrots, flat-leaf Italian parsley, broccoli, broad beans and enough boiled potatoes to ballast a catamaran.

I wasn't so sure about the SO's lobster thermidor. If God had intended the lobster to be slathered with cheese, He would have made it a ruminant. We rounded off with espressos to fortify us for the long walk to the three-and-a-half-ton flat-bed truck we currently drive. The bill was £75.

I liked Yetman's, despite its rather ditsy decorative scheme. As the truck, with the SO at the wheel, bucketed down the A11 towards London, I lay on the flat bed staring up at the stars and fantasising about what I would do once I'd got my weight down to triple figures. Wait for me, Thierry! Wait for me, Jean-Paul!

Observer, August 1996

7

We don't really want people to ask us to be wholly consistent in our beliefs, now do we? When I was a student of sinistral persuasion in the early eighties, one of the gags we used to like to pull was to ask some dextral dickhead whether he or she would have supported the Tories on every single political issue they had fought over the past hundred and fifty years. After a bit of jockeying you could usually engineer them into blustering that they would have, whereupon you would cry: that means you would have opposed both Reform Acts, female suffrage, the National Health Service – and so on until the victim was exposed as a hopelessly reactionary bigot.

The same sort of polarisation can easily be forced on anyone who espouses environmental beliefs. You are opposed to more road-building? Then how far are you prepared to go – or not? No driving to anti-road demos? No driving at all? No consumption of fossil fuels whatsoever? Total non-involvement in the mighty economic infrastructure that chomps up the world in order to support the scurf of humanity? Do you want to live in a yurt, in a field, honking a didgeridoo and existing by virtue of photosynthesis?

The same arguments can be piled on the heads of the animal-rights lobby. If it's bad to keep veal calves in crates, is it any better to rear them in the nursery, give them a name and then after years of family life introduce the notion of a 'humane' slaughtering? Of course, many members of the broad coalition of environmentalists are considerably more sophisticated and pluralist in their thinking than this. But I believe there is an inherent conflict between the spirit of the new environmentalism – which I take to be broadly pantheistic – and the highly rational tactics required to check the Moloch of technology.

At its most absurd level this conflict summons up the spectacle of animal-rights supporters actively espousing the use of violence against humans for retributive purposes. Is this any worse than any other form of revolutionary violence? Yes. While even soft-left sixties radicals went some way towards backing 'liberation' movements of all stripes, there's an important sense in which the Marxist appeal to revolutionary violence was constrained by rational thought. The appeal was to harness the consciousness of the proletariat, and for action to take place within a definedly human, social context.

The new environmentalism is often only too willing to borrow from the bank of unreason and pay in the coin of emotion, and the way that this transaction is mediated makes a mockery of the very real gains that have been made in the overall quality of life for the majority of people. Paradoxically, by attempting to subsume humanity once more and assign it the status of just one part of the Gaian biosphere, environmental theorists are giving humanity a specious importance. Really it's a kind of cosmic tit-beating: oh, we're so awful, we've screwed up the ecology, we must do penance. This self-flagellation is nothing new; when I was a teenager it was exactly the kind of rhetoric that was applied to Third

World poverty, and which burgeoned into the astonishing ethical posturing of Live Aid.

But with environmental issues – as with feminism, interestingly – the lurch towards arational thinking is far more pernicious, because in unseating humanity from the apex of the evolutionary pyramid people are only too willing to take flight into all kinds of magical thinking. I don't view all the 'alternative' modes of thought, therapy and life that are pullulating at the moment as benign evidence of a healthy broadening of society; I see them as indicators of a degeneracy and decadence of thought, of an inability to develop the will to constructively engage with the very real problems we face. The very people who should be giving their full attention to the ramifications of contemporary technological developments that affect who we are in the most basic and compelling sense – such as genetic engineering and artificial intelligence – are off in some wigwam dangling crystals over each other's tummies.

There's an essential defeatism in thinking about environmental issues that derives from distancing ourselves from the mentality that – we assume – created the very physical reality of the world we are living in. We are the sons and daughters of the people who built the motorway system, designed Concorde, synthesised antibiotics. The environmentalist tendency is to say: look at all this shit we've done, and really we're just like a monkey tied to the top of a firework. Wrong. We're superintelligent monkeys who have built up an entire infrastructure dedicated to the production of such rockets, and we really ought to take responsibility for it on our own terms – because there are no others.

I love motorway driving – but fear what the car is doing to our environment. I'm glad I love motorway driving, because if I didn't I'm sure I'd find myself down some hole on a diet of pulses. I'm as keen to look for certainty at the cost of painful deliberation as the next anthropoid. A flight into single-issue politics is an abrogation of the responsibility to engage totally with the situation we're in; it represents a tendency to say: a pox on all your houses, and I'm just going to squat righteously here in this hut.

I can no more understand the mentality of someone who dresses up in a red coat, tootles a little horn, and urges a horse on to chase a fox across hill and dale, than I can that of someone who sets out to obstruct this sport. The fact of the matter is that the fox would have been extinct in this country by the end of the sixteenth century were it not for hunting. That's what neither side seems to be able to acknowledge. Both wish to pose as the guardians of the environment; both are really very ignorant about what the realities of that environment are.

It's a great truth of humanity that bigotry is always based on fear. The problem we are now facing is that we're frightened of our own minds – and that's a recipe for a fascist disaster the like of which we've never seen before.

Big Issue, March 1997

8

Over the last ten days I've covered the waterfront without going any-where near the sea. Last weekend saw me in Motherwell in Lanarkshire, taking the same walk I always take with my father-in-law. We pick our way out of the estate full of vertically clapboarded houses where he lives, bisect the zone of bigotry which lies between the opposing Modernist disasters of the Catholic and Protestant churches, traverse the ridge studded with tower-block dolmens (which are still only half-way towards post-modernism, some freshly panelled, others still weeping concrete), and plod down the track to the banks of the Clyde. Here we stand and my father-in-law mutters at the spectacle of the rapid return to nature of the ruins of the Ravenscraig Steel Works pumping station, then we plod back again.

That afternoon saw me at the Spiegeltent (I kid you not), a giant yurt, tricked out to resemble a Victorian boozer, which is erected each year in one of the fine squares of the Edinburgh New Town grid, so that literary types can give and receive readings in it. I gave while the rain drummed on the roof. Quitting the circle in the square, I dined with Alex Linklater. Aware of my status as an architectural lean-to, he began to fulminate about Piers Gough's new TV series *The Shock of the Old*. 'He keeps talking about the Romans and the Britons, but I ask you, isn't that an anachronism? I mean, when did the Britons become the Britons? And another thing, he implies that there was no grid-pattern city built in this country between the end of Roman rule and Milton Keynes in the 1970s. What about Glasgow? What about Edinburgh?' Warming to his theme, Alex went on to ask, 'Why is it that no one, absolutely no one, can do architecture on television properly?'

In the week I made a point of watching a tape of Gough's programme.

21

Nope, he didn't imply there was no grid-pattern city built in Britain between the third and the twentieth centuries; and no, Alex, there's nothing anachronistic about describing the turn-of-the-last-millennium inhabitants of these isles as 'Britons' – that's what the Romans dubbed them; and no, Alex, some people can 'do' architecture on television properly – it's just that as yet (give the guy a break), Gough doesn't appear to be among them.

In truth, the problem of presenting architecture on television is that there's too great a synergy between the structures and the medium for the latter to adequately convey the meaning and importance of the former. I would argue that the existence of the television camera itself presupposes ways of seeing that themselves derive from the built environment. It's only in the last few years that the micro video cameras installed in birds, worms, beetles and fish have brought us non-anthropomorphic views of the environment. Prior to this the only places to locate cameras were in relation to human structures. Sure, you can make films in the great outdoors, but isn't it noteworthy that the vast majority of westerns had to have a scene shot in Monument Valley? It isn't so much that it's difficult to present architecture on television, it's that television is principally about architecture to begin with.

What would *EastEnders* be about if it weren't for Albert Square? Is *Brookside* or *Coronation Street* conceivable without the attendant Barratt and back-to-back *mise-en-scène*? Look how badly wrong things went for *News at Ten* when they abandoned the credit sequence in which an alien eye zooms down into the London conurbation and alights on Big Ben. The perfect architecture programme on television at the moment (which is also the best piece of drama, documentary and reportage) is, of course, *Big Brother*. With its fusion of CCTV surveillance and unchanging rooms, we can tune in day after day and witness the incredible spectacle of apparently living, breathing and vaguely rational human beings who're prepared to be incarcerated in a prison designed by Ikea. All other architectural television programmes are ludicrously recherché.

Still, if you want a suggestion from me, TV production people, sod travels with Pevsner, or gambolling with Gough; simply implant any old opinionated bastard with a camcorder and turn them loose – with one proviso: that they don't know they've got it on them. Then, just maybe, we'd get some angles on the built environment that appear neither hackneyed nor otherwise scripted.

Building Design, August 2000

9

It's ten in the morning at Le Carousel, that portion of the Louvre that has been customised and given over to the peculiar razzmatazz that is the Paris fashion shows. Flooding down the stone stairs and packed into this Babylonian vestibule is a seething, flying wedge of bodies. Some hundreds of fashion photographers, fashion journalists and fashion buyers are all chattering and yammering as they press towards the PR people who decide whether or not admission will be granted.

It's clear that nothing short of push and shove can secure me my seat for the Chloé show. For fashion is a business of paradoxes, and here is one of the greatest: that in order to participate in an event that is all about 'the look', I must immerse myself in the touch.

The fashion clan are in a ripping, snorting mood, pawing at the back of one another's coats. Most have already had a week in Milan, racing from show to party to hotel, then back to another show; and now they've got another week of the same in Paris to contend with, before the survivors limp on to London and then drag themselves to New York for the final *schmutterdämmerung*.

Even at this early hour there's an atmosphere of frayed neurones, of eyes that have been open for too long, bodies that have been upright too long. Someone said to me, 'Forget about the double "C" of Chanel, the three "C"'s that really matter in this business are cocaine, cigarettes and coffee.' And it's easy to believe this as the mass presses forward. Because there's something simultaneously frenzied and yet asexual about this throng, something rodentine, rather than human.

Konrad Lorenz, the founder of modern ethology, wrote of the brown rat as a 'contact animal', and described the ceremony of friendly contact as 'creeping under' performed by younger animals, and 'creeping over' performed by the older animals. This seems to hold for the fashion pack who, as they smarm over and under one another, also display another rat-like characteristic: 'Within the pack there is a quick news system functioning by mood transmission.'

Then we're in! The hall itself is like a scaled-down Wembley Arena, tiers of seats either side of the long tongue of the catwalk, at the far end of which is a battery of telephoto lenses. These style gunners have taped out their pitches earlier, jockeying for the best angle from which to shoot their pulchritudinous prey.

There's Steven Miesel, in his trademark little black hat, in prime position. A photographer so powerful he can make or break a collection. And there's Suzy Menkes, the doyenne of fashion correspondents, wearing an eau-de-Nil chiffon scarf and an eau-de-Nil expression. Alongside her (she would never, ever be seen to the rear) is the stern visage of Anna Wintour, fashion editor of American *Vogue*, whose nickname within the pack is Nuclear Wintour, because of her allegedly relentless frigidity.

There are other odd characteristics the pack shares with the social animals. Although we're about to feast our eyes on young women whose lineaments are allegedly exactly congruent with those of desire, our body-types are about as non-standard as you can get. Yet, fat, thin, tall, short, all of us are wearing the ubiquitous fur of expensive, tailored clothing.

Furthermore, our positioning in the hall is as much determined by our sexuality as by our political or economic importance. Homosexual buyers are up front; behind them are tiers of neutered females; the photographers are almost certainly heterosexual. And all of us are about to witness the flower of young womanhood strutting its stuff.

The previous night, as I lay desultorily partaking of the two 'B's (beer and bad television) in my eau-de-Nil hotel bedroom, I tried to imagine this moment: would I be able to read the show as a text or would its exegesis be obscured? Channel 6 chose that moment to run a squib on the *prêt-à-porter* collections. Two Japanese designers were interviewed, their remarks intercut with bewildering images of emaciated girls being sewn into hessian sacks. The camera zoomed in on one reticulated niblet of a body. 'I'm an innocent missionary,' she mouthed. 'Me too!' I wanted to say. But was I so innocent? Or was I, like everyone else, a bit of a psychic voyeur when it came to fashion? I did not want to see it, but I needed to know it was going on. Without it the world would be a duller place.

The music begins to thrum and jar. It's loud, very loud. It's 'Armed and Extremely Dangerous'. From behind the twenty-foot-high letters, which in Popsicle pastels spell out 'Chloé', come the mannequins (always referred to as 'the girls' in the business). This is the moment I've been waiting for; will it be a turn-on, or a turn-off? Will I long to take their designer threads off with my teeth, or long to take them home for a much-needed bowl of chicken soup and a solo tuck-up in bed?

Here they come! Walking flat-footed, and swivel-hipped. Linda, Kate, Helena, Jodie and Nadja. Their gait is somewhat unnatural, as if they've recently staged a mass escape from the Island of Dr Moreau. But other than that, what's most shocking is that they – like us – are non-standard too. Some are undoubtedly candidates for chicken soup, and a stiff lecture on the three 'C's; others – like Linda – look positively matronly, as if they're on their way to return some library books.

There's also a confusion in scale. Our received photographic images of the catwalk are of Brobdingnagian figures swathed in cloth and ataraxy; a live view poses the incongruity of tiny Kate passing towering Cecilia, both clad in the same filmy mini-dresses, both with floaty hair, but one a full head taller than the other. It gives the impression that you've accidentally flicked from size eight to size twelve on the rail.

What about the clothes? I hear you ask. Isn't that what it's all about? Maybe, but since I've only just had the notion of a bias cut explained to me, and am still wrestling with its semantic incongruities, I don't think I'm in a position to comment. This show is held to be irredeemably 'bourgeois', one of six big collections that Karl Lagerfeld (a.k.a. The Big Ponytail) cranks out with Teutonic efficiency each year. This show, like many others, is as much a vehicle for the Chloé range of fragrances – which is vastly more important in terms of revenue – as for the clothes themselves.

There is a hiatus. The girls have effected a staggered withdrawal from the catwalk. The PA hisses, 'This is a Magnum .45, the most powerful handgun in the world . . .' They've wheeled in Dirty Harry to sell dresses. Such is the strange semiology of the fashion show: to somehow equate the deployment of lethal force with the notion of fatal attraction. The whole set-up teases me with a hard, binary opposition: this is sexy/this is not sexy. This is a Scottish widow, tripping towards me, grey-cowled, demure. She turns, and it appears that someone has let a vent into the back of her dress to better effect rear entry.

To paraphrase Levi-Strauss on abstract painting: the fashion show is a school of art, in which designers, stylists and models struggle to express the kind of sexuality that they would have, were they in fact to have any at all.

But then it would be tendentious and unfair to take altogether at face value something that expressly presents itself in just that way. The latent meaning of this is money, and lots of it. As we sit and watch dresses undulate up and down, here yellow, there aquamarine, over there iri-descent, *les Grands Fromages* of the industry are involved in something altogether more serious. In the salons and lobbies of the big Parisian hotels, deals have already been struck predicated on this collection.

See that big buyer over there? He handles the budget for a Fifth Avenue emporium. He's the biggest of cheeses, and his sculpted blond hairdo and sculpted pink face must not be creased by the merest of reactions to what we are seeing. His is a polka-dot face, designed for retail gambling.

It's the Americans and the Japanese who dominate these shows, with their huge buying power and smoothly organised industries. Take any high-street up-market clothing outlet in Britain, and you can be more or less certain that there are ten times that number of the same in Japan. British designers are held in high esteem in the international marketplace, but somehow by the time they've got there they've ceased in some sense to be British.

The season's avant-garde hits were Galliano and Vivienne Westwood. The pack transmitted the information that a consignment of Westwood's rocking-horse, ankle-high, pink fetish boots was on its way over. But I turned tail and ran, for this was the fashion show as existential, ephemeral 'happening'. What I had witnessed was an excavation of decadences. Appropriate, that is, for taking a biopsy from this dummy tissue.

But it's wrong to castigate the fashion industry for decadence, for it is by its very nature always in the mode of ten years after. Nevertheless, the Nino Cerruti show had to take the decadent biscuit. The highlight of this extravaganza was the swivel-hipped girls, marching out as a posse, in chalk-striped, double-breasted men's suits. There was a round of applause and someone said, 'That's a statement!' 'Yeah, welcome back to 1985,' I muttered.

But it still ill behoves us here in London to bite the evening glove that feeds us. 'Retail services' constitute a huge part of our invisible earnings, and an important part of that is clothes design. We may not have big buying power, or be the most sartorially advanced of nations; but it's sobering to reflect that just as it is said that in London you are never – on average – more than ten feet away from a brown rat, by the same token you are probably never more than ten feet away from a fashion designer.

Observer, October 1996

They're down there as I write – having the fun that rightfully belongs to me. They're ranged along the quayside, staring across the dancing, azure wavelets of the River Dart at the villas and cottages on the Kingswear shore. There's a peaceful burble of chatter, broken only by the occasional plash as a sinker hits the water; but now and again there'll be a flutter of activity – someone is reeling in: 'It's heavy . . . it's really heavy – my line must be caught. No it isn't! It's coming up! Oh! I've got loads – or it's a really big one. It *is* a big one! Look at that – it's *the* big one! He's coming up . . . Aww! He's fallen off!' The greenish, barnacled shell slides obliquely into the local depths just as the baited hook breaks the surface. It's left for the disappointed fisherman to intone, 'He's got my bacon' – and reach for the bargain pack of streaky.

Yes, they're down there crab fishing, and I would sooner be there with them than in any other cultural milieu. You can lower the curtain on the world of the performing arts; you can spike the Western canon – all I want is to go crabbing in Dartmouth.

I admit it, initially I was sceptical when Dr 'Big' McFee, my neurologist (and near constant companion), proposed that I spend my summer holiday being 're-parented' in a family-oriented resort town in south Devon. I had thought to repeat the total relaxation of last year's sojourn, which I spent fighting for control of the world opium trade against the Shan tribespeople of the Indo-Chinese hinterland. Or, alternatively, why not attempt the Cresta Run on a drinks coaster? It'd been weeks since the last time.

But McFee was adamant. 'You need to recapture some of the abandon of childhood,' he adjured me. 'All of your current problems – your inability to put a face to a name, or vice versa; your insomnia; *and* your refusal to allow human rights to men with goatees – they all have their origins in your repression of your childhood self. Believe me, a couple of weeks at the seaside, doing traditional, wholesome, child-centred things, will see a significant amelioration of your condition.'

Things went well to begin with. A friend of McFee's lent us a pleasant little cottage *and* I managed to remember my swimming trunks. On the first morning we were up bright and early and took a stroll through the delightfully picturesque streets of Dartmouth, a town that has remained virtually unchanged since the *Mayflower* and the *Speedwell* put in here for repairs – apart from the construction of a second pasty shop. Many seventeenth-century merchants' houses remain intact, clustered around the dinky dock, their bulging façades of plaster and lath supported on carved stone pillars.

I was quite prepared to spend the morning sauntering, and making snobbish cracks about other people's taste in leisure wear, but McFee had other ideas. 'Look at all those kids crabbing,' he gestured at the rows of chubby little legs dangling over the quay. 'That's what we should be doing.'

'Come off it!' I was incredulous. 'We're grown men, someone will have us arrested – and what if I'm recognised?'

'Nonsense,' he snapped back. 'There are plenty of adults crabbing; and as for being recognised, isn't it about time you dropped this pretence of celebrity?'

He dragged me to a shop where we purchased a net, a bucket and two crab lines; then to another where streaky bacon was contracted for. Back on the quay we found a pitch in between well-established crabbers. To our right was a family of three males. The father had a savagely layered haircut which made his blond thatch look like a divot; he was naked save for Nike trainers and tight, striped trunks. His sons were prepubescent and pubescent versions of the same. All of them were baiting hooks with globs of squid, putting down their lines and hauling them up again with remorseless efficiency. Their crab lines were of industrial tensility and their net looked as if it could land a basking shark. Needless to say, their bucket seethed with crustacea.

To the left, two small girls hovered around a bucket shaped like an inverted sandcastle, within which one little crab skittered. McFee baited the hooks; I tried to look as if I were a passer-by, paused to watch. 'Come on!' said McFee. 'Get hold of your line.' I took the line with its bacon bait. At that moment, one of the ferrymen who was piloting a launch past us, on his way to Dartmouth Castle, shouted up, 'I can't say I altogether agree with your views on Quentin Tarantino!' I'd been spotted: a cultural critic crab fishing.

McFee got five of the little bleeders on his first reel down, but I didn't catch any for ages. McFee became a tyrant in the cause of crabbing – shouting for the net, the bucket, more bacon. He caught twice as many crabs as I. I can't conceive that this was anything to do with his knowledge of the brain; after all, there is absolutely no skill involved in it – you simply reel down and then reel up a few minutes later to see what you've caught.

Be that as it may, crabbing unlocks some deep, atavistic compartment in the British mind, some phylogenetic fishing memory. All along the quay, grown men would approach one another's buckets and say things like 'Oooh! You've got a lot – what bait are you using?' And then there was the myth of the Big One That Got Away. Sometimes it got away from my hook, at other times from McFee's. Needless to say, neither of us ever saw the other's monster near-catch.

At the end of the morning McFee had caught twenty-two crabs and I'd managed a mere fifteen. I felt marvellously innocent, abandoned and youthful. I celebrated by having a big sulk and then a crying row with McFee. He had to buy me a lolly to calm me down.

The Times, August 1998

I I

It sometimes seems to me that London doesn't have an awful lot to recommend it as a city – in a social sense, that is. People often talk about 'village London', referring to the supposed interlinked 'villages' that constitute its urban fabric. But when I think about 'village London', I think about the 'villages' of gossip, whether media, literary, business or entertainment. I think about ears on stalks, craned necks, and snide remarks falling from twisted lips.

But I will say one thing in favour of this village London: just as the villagers like to snipe behind one another's backs, so they are deeply circumspect when actually in view. So it was that Salman Rushdie and I were able to eat lunch together, for two and a half hours, in a highly fashionable central London restaurant, without once seeing anybody in the place give us so much as a second glance.

Of course, I suppose the other diners may well have been speculating as to what it was we were discussing, what tortured aspect of the internally-exiled author's predicament we were chewing over, along with our oysters and gnocchi. Well, it may surprise them to learn that we were talking about literature, talking about what is involved in writing fiction seriously; and talking in particular about Rushdie's new novel – his first since *The Satanic Verses* – *The Moor's Last Sigh*.

I often seem to have occasion, in these pieces about people who have been demonised by the media and popular perceptions, to have to drag things back down to the most basic of grounds. No, Rushdie is not arrogant or supercilious in conversation. On the contrary, he is quietly-spoken, thoughtful and deliberate. No, Rushdie is not saturnine, diabolic, or physically creepy in the flesh. On the contrary, in grey piped sweater and jeans, his beard neatly trimmed, he is distinctly cuddly.

The new novel is set, once again, in the city of Rushdie's birth, Bombay. And, like *Midnight's Children*, *The Moor's Last Sigh* is a braiding together of the realistic, the fabulous, the sensual and the philosophic, to produce a cloth of metaphoric gold; which in its lustre seems to reflect the very richness of India's pluralism.

The novel is full of evocations of smells, sights, tastes and sensations. The pivotal scene of the first part of the book (set in Cochin, the south Indian statelet, which became part of Kerala after independence) has Aurora da Gama, the beautiful and fiery mother of 'the Moor' who is the novel's narrator, seducing her husband-to-be on top of bags of spices in the family godown. Had, I wondered, this novel been a feat of Proustian recall, an attempt to link sensual memories of childhood to an overview of consciousness?

'I think that *Midnight's Children* was the novel that grew out of childhood. And the vision of the city and the country in that novel comes from trying to recall how I perceived things as a child. This novel grows out of the sense of the city and the country I've developed as an adult. And then to my horror I found myself exiled from it, and that has made a change of relationship.

'In the year before the fatwah I must have spent six months in India. It was always a big shot in the arm for me to go back there. I still have family and friends there – I love the place. I never felt before that that I was writing from exile. If you live in one country and go and visit another and write about it, that isn't writing from exile, it's just a choice. The fact is I haven't been to India now for seven years, so in this novel I have had to recapture a lost place, a lost thing.'

Midnight's Children – albeit in a fantastical way – did seem to contain strong elements of autobiography, particularly in the evocation of the central family. Not much is written about Rushdie's own childhood nowadays. Were there, I wondered, autobiographical elements in the new novel? Particularly in the characterisation of Aurora Zogoiby (née da Gama), the larger-than-life matriarch and visionary painter, who is the novel's protagonist?

'The family in this novel is not at all like my family. In a way, that's why the family is the way it is. My family was a middle-class business family, not at all involved in the arts, high society, or bohemia. We did have distant connections with the film industry, and I had schoolfriends who came from that kind of family.

'But really the family in this novel reflects a truth about Bombay society in the past thirty or so years, which is that the rich have got very much richer and the poor very much poorer.'

What, I asked Rushdie, about the strangely Oedipal relationship between the Moor and Aurora? Did this reflect elements of his own relationship with his mother? 'No, no, this is all to do with the idea of the mother being associated with the idea of the nation. This was a notion that Indira Gandhi deliberately cultivated. She used the mythology of the mother goddess to enhance her own legitimacy.'

In the novel mothers are, therefore, peculiarly dominant (although as it transpires – without any wish to give the plot away – the fathers have been up to quite a lot on their own account as well). One of the ways the matriarchal influence is most clearly evinced is that Aurora, her mother and her daughters all speak a peculiar kind of idiolect. This is at one and the same time like the way that some Indian people speak English – with lots of 'o' endings and banjaxed noun/verb forms – and completely idiosyncratic.

What, I asked Rushdie, was going on? 'Well, it is an idiolect. What I was trying to show was the way that families develop their own private language. And of course this is passed down through the maternal line. Another element comes from Cochin and south India. I didn't go to southern India for the first time until 1982, and for someone from northern India it is as radically different as the Mediterranean would be for someone from Britain. In the south, people are far more resistant to speaking Hindi than they are to speaking English.

'And any novel that takes place over a large canvas in India will cross a lot of linguistic frontiers all the time. I've thought this since *Midnight's Children*: you can't afford to have your reader wondering all the time what language the characters are speaking.'

Midnight's Children did, of course, represent a new kind of Indian novel in that it made it possible for Indian writers not to write in standard English. In conversation this is something that Rushdie is highly aware of. And although he feels that his work has in some senses formed a bridge between the 'classical' works of Desai and Narayan and the younger, post-*Midnight's Children*, polyglottists, he is no way absolutist about the way the 'Indian' novel should be approached, having considerable praise for what he terms Vikram Seth's 'Balzacian project'.

But I don't wish to give the impression that *The Moor's Last Sigh* is a novel that beats you around the head with its linguistic games and innovations. Far from it, what comes across most clearly is the sheer power of imaginative visualisation that Rushdie possesses as a writer. Did he, I wondered, pay much attention to such surrealist techniques as dream transcription?

'I do, and there are several things in this novel that arose directly out of dreams. There's a dream that the narrator has, which I had. And in this he is swimming underwater, but he has the sensation that he is swimming under land, that he can't gain the surface because there's a sort of lid on top. And in this predicament the phrase that comes to him is "I must swim beyond the limit of my breath." I found this a particularly powerful image.'

Rushdie didn't choose to elaborate on why this image should be so powerful for him, but I think I have an idea. What is most notable for the informed reader of his new novel is how unsubdued Rushdie has been by the refusal in certain quarters to judge his work on its own merits, and to conflate both his personality and his novel with political events well beyond his control, or his imagination.

In *The Moor's Last Sigh*, Rushdie is still absolutely prepared – as any conscientious writer must be – to point out those aspects of the society he describes that he finds unpalatable. Fanatics of all stripes will find little comfort here in his depiction of the ways in which fundamentalisms queer the pitch of democracy. He is, he told me, 'uncowed'.

But more than that, like the Moor's mother, the 'bird of paradise' Aurora, painter and salonnière at the heart of a polymorphously perverse depiction of India since independence, Rushdie is a true artist. And perhaps artistry always consists in being willing to swim beyond the limit of your breath, no matter how weighty the hand that clamps you from above.

Out of deference and respect for Rushdie, I had decided purposely not to talk to him about the consequences of the fatwah for his day-to-day life. I figured that he gets plenty of that anyway, and would rather talk about the work. But there was another reason behind my not wanting to discuss it. I, personally, am fed up to the back teeth with listening to people cavil about the protection the British State is giving to one of its own citizens, threatened with death by a foreign power. It's a cavilling that all too often has an unpleasant, quasi-racist edge to it.

I often wonder how those very people would respond were anything to happen to him. My guess is that there would be a torrent of *explicitly* racist outrage aimed against Muslims both here and abroad. Now, that's a rather strange irony, isn't it? Even for a country that prides itself on an ironic perspective.

Or, as Salman Rushdie himself put it to me, rather wearily, 'I get treated more seriously as a writer in Iran than I do here.'

Evening Standard, September 1995

12

It's strange how some individuals always manage to sow the seeds of their own destruction, while others avoid the slings and arrows of outrageous fortune as blithely as the roadrunner skirts obstacles in the long-running cartoon of the same name.

Strictly in the former category is my now quondam neurologist Dr 'Big' McFee of the Glasgow Royal Infirmary. It's been a number of months since I first began to have my misgivings about him. Over this period the courses of therapy he recommended for me became increasingly bizarre: crab fishing gave way to Tantric sex, which in turn was supplanted by oxygen re-breathing. Then there were the little things he'd say – like 'I wonder what happens when your heart spring winds down?' – which led me to believe that his medical knowledge, if he ever had any, was becoming inundated by the sands of time.

I'd never been exactly sure what it was McFee did at the Infirmary, but then a friend encountered him there, in the lobby area, doing a convincing impression of someone running a sweet stall. When I confronted McFee with this evidence of perfidy he became incandescent with rage. 'You think you know it all!' he expostulated. 'You think you don't need me! Let me tell you – you're in *denial*. Just you try lasting a few days without my healing influence; then we'll see what a sick

33

bunnykins you become – ha!' And he stormed from the room, in his haste leaving behind a gross of Tunnocks Tea Cakes.

I managed a day, my mind a vortex of anxiety, sucking up fears from the ether. I lasted a second day, tormented by both agoraphobia and claustrophobia, unable to do anything but hover on the doormat. On the morning of the third day I cracked, enVolvoed, and headed for Alexandra Palace in north London, where the 1998 Annual Festival of Mind, Body and Spirit was under way. Surely, from among over a hundred exhibitors, whose expertise ranges across the entire compass of the healing arts, I would be able to find a substitute for the crazed Scottish confectioner?

Just driving up to Ally Pally put me in a better frame of mind. I went past the site of the ABC Cinema in Muswell Hill where in 1970, while watching the film *Zeppelin*, I was subjected to a half-chewed-toffee attack by some tough boys in the circle. I sat transfixed. On screen, mustard gas clotted the lungs of the Tommies; in the stalls, toffee clotted the collar-length hair of the prepubescent Self. I couldn't believe the calculated monstrousness of such warfare; if I tried to get the thing out it became still more gummily ensnared. Suddenly I had a brain wave: there was a ladies' hairdresser next to the cinema. Within seconds kind, capable fingers were freeing the recalcitrant bob-bon. I was back in the stalls before the gas had been blown from the battlefield.

With pleasing memories of my own capacity for self-help to sustain me, I parked up in the lee of the giant old pile. It was here in the late twenties that the first television pictures were transmitted to a thrilled nation. (Although they were conned, because it later transpired that the pictures were repeats.) And it was here in the early seventies that I went roller-skating. With such an auspicious history, surely this was the place to find salvation?

My first impressions of the festival were far from reassuring. I paid my modest entrance fee and wandered about the immense hall. At the far end, a nauseous pastel banner welcomed the Age of Aquarius, while underneath, a new-age trio – didgeridoo, guitar and keening – serenaded the collected psyches. What to choose or whom? Should I buy a crystal from Aphrodite's Rocks, or even a Bio-Electrical Shield? This, its marketers claim, protects you from the harmful rays of – among other things – electronic devices such as message pagers; which is presumably why Cherie Blair ports one. Or should I opt for some spiritualist healing? The sign at the front of the National Federation of Spiritualist Healers was direct in its appeal: 'Queue Here for Healing', it baldly stated. Now if only the NHS would adopt such a can-do attitude . . .

What about iridologists? They diagnose and treat by measuring the iris of the eye; and those Ayurveda people, they know their way around acne and psoriasis (some of them appear to have both); and why not essay the philosophy of Bruno Groning, 'I love so that mankind will be able to continue living . . .'? Pity he's dead.

My anxiety levels began to mount as I surveyed the mêlée of tie-dye T-shirt wearers, white-coated wallies and assorted children of the compost. Ferchrissakes! Had nothing alternative happened to the world of alternative therapy in the last thirty years?

And then I met him, my nemesis. He was standing outside a small corner stall with a sign saying 'The Farago Clinic' leaning against it. On the lapel of his smart, neutral suit was a name badge which read 'Robert Farago, Hypnotist'. I nearly ran into him, but stopped, collected myself and said, 'Don't you find it hard to get people to take you seriously as a hypnotist with a name like that?'

Farago didn't miss a beat. 'What,' he rasped in confident, American tones, 'you mean because it means a medley, hotchpotch, or confused group, as derived from the Latin word for mixed fodder?'

'Um – yuh, I guess so –'

'No!' he unhypnotically snapped. 'First, because that has two "r"s; and second, because no one knows what it means! No one can define it! Can you define it?' He swivelled to face the pretty, dark woman from Lotions & Potions who was beside us.

'Um . . . no –'

'You?' He rounded on a middle-aged security guard.

'Iss like . . . that sex thingy, innit?'

'Not *Vi*agra,' I snapped – I was catching Farago's style.

'Anyway,' he snapped again, 'the fact is I'll give you twenty pounds right here and now if you can find me anyone in this hall, in the next twenty minutes, who can define "farrago". Twenty pounds!'

I didn't take him up on it. Instead I watched him hypnotise the Lotions & Potions woman. He was brilliant at it – no question. I know nothing about hypnotism but Farago tells me that he's the best in the country. He says that whereas most hypnotists pretend that you can't hypnotise people against their will, he knows damn well that you can – and he does. He says that through hypnosis he can help people to deal with almost all the ills that afflict them. He says he can help me – and I believe him. His voice has such a thrilling, commanding quality. He drives a new Ferrari. He has a clinic in Windsor. I will dedicate my entire column next week to him. I will obey. On the way home in the car I nearly listened to the

Deep Sleep tape he sold me, especially since it warns you not to while driving.

I love Robert Farago; he has none of McFee's posing Scottish pretensions, none of McFee's woolly Celtic mysticism. And best of all there's Farago's name – which is so much sillier.

The Times, September 1998

13

From where I lie, I can't see much of the world, save for a projecting wall of my own house still fringed by green wisteria, the grey slate line of the next row of houses, and beyond this, the pill-box hat of one of the council blocks on the Wandsworth Road. Of course, if I sat up, I could get a bearing on at least a small part of iconic London – I could see the very tips of two of Battersea Power Station's stacks nestling same-sized amongst closer chimneys. And from this angle I'd also be able to see the gardens of this terrace, below and to my right; long strips of urban verdancy, most with their own dinky hut, sawn lawn and dwarf terrace: *urbs in rure in urbe in rure.*

Levi-Strauss said that all world cities are constructed on an east-to-west schema, with the poor in the east and the rich in the west. Some ascribe this to the prevalent winds; the poor, as it were, being swept into the gutter. I think Claude saw it as a deeper structural phenomenon than this; humanity displaying some of the instinctive, orienting behaviour of the social insects. But I've never experienced London in Levi-Strauss terms. I inhabit a city within which, no matter where I look, or in which direction I turn, I still find myself hideously oriented. I suffer from a kind of claustro-agoraphobia, if such a thing is possible. I fear going outside in London because it is so cramped and confining.

When you grow up in a great city (and by great I mean a city that is not readily geographically encompassed, even by an adult with mature visuo-spatial abilities), your sense of it is at first straightforwardly crazy – like a film with appalling continuity. (Characters turn the corner of St James's and find themselves standing, grinning foolishly, on the

Aldwych.) 'Daddy,' asks my eight-year-old as we drive past Clissold Park, 'is that Battersea Park?' Poor dog, nodding his way into comprehension, as the jump-cut scenes of the city are projected at him through the windscreen.

Then comes the integration, the coalescence of the two hundred billion neurones that will comprise the city-brain. The *faux* villages of London – the tiny zones around friends' houses, or known haunts – spread over a grey waste of overpopulation, strung out along ribbon developments of short-term memory. And then, in adult life, there is the long, long shading in of the rest, the even adumbration which constitutes regular experience. Even ten years ago, and certainly fifteen, I could patrol central London and still avoid my past self when I saw him coming in the opposite direction. I could take alternative routes to avoid the districts of failed love affairs, I knew short cuts that would circumvent the neighbourhood of an abandoned friendship, I had only to swerve to miss the precincts of a snubbing acquaintance. But now the city is filled in with narratives, which have been extruded like psychic mastic into its fissures. There is no road I haven't fought on, no cul-de-sac I haven't ended it all in, and no alley I haven't done it down. To traverse central London today, even in a car, even on autopilot, is still to run over a hundred memoirs.

The irregular, cracked flags of the driveway outside my childhood home in N2 have remained exactly the same for four decades. I know this, because I've been home. Not often, but a few times since the house was sold in the late seventies. Most recently, after a gap of a decade or so, I took my own children there and was amazed at the continuities of the topiary and the bricolage, set against the transitoriness of my own feelings. Of course, my last bitter memories of this house and its environs are of an insufferably stuffy, ultimate *ur*-suburb; Kate Greenaway on Largactil; the sort of place that could grow a J. G. Ballard out of the mildest and least imaginative of psyches. But that's because I was seventeen when I left here. Now, with my own kids chucking each other into the hedges and running on the wide, grass-bordered pavements, all I can see is how green it is; all I can hear is how quiet it is, the soundlessness of the suburbs.

It was on this driveway that we trundled our toys, small-scale precursors of the commuters we would become. It was here that we constructed rooms on the outside, cosy dens containing little stories; here we picked up the trails of our first narratives, worming in the crannies and clefts alongside virulent moss. In my childhood home, how many days would I spend, stowed in the hold of the upstairs back bedroom, imagining the oceanic city all around. There – or here, it makes no difference. In either place and time I have the same sense of residing in a permanent mid-morning, of avoiding the workaday world, of being marooned by the audience drain from Radio 4. Beached, here or there, on a grainy mattress, while outside the city hums and beeps and bumps and grinds and pulses and pullulates with a crazed sense of its own capacity to ceaselessly mutate, its fanatical ability to construct stories out of its rooms and its streets, its vestibules and its courtyards, its cars and its discarded fag packets. Any object the eye pursues becomes a story, another track scored in time. Any person is a potential Medusa, Gorgon-headed with writhing, serpentine tales.

Which is why I lie here in the spare room, safely barricaded by other people's stories, the tales of other cities. This refuge is almost completely lined with books, most of which have little to do with London. The wall opposite the sunny window is tiled with the spines of some 1,600 battered paperbacks. They are umber, grey, brown and blue, they are as pleasingly textured and involving to the eye as the robes of the couple in Klimt's *The Kiss*, a reproduction of which hangs on the wall opposite me. Their battered backs are a mnemonic of my own history. Despite the gearing of my own book collection into that of my wife, this impression has been enhanced, rather than diminished. It must be because we are both the same kind of trampish bibliophagists. Unlike other, more fastidious types, our collecting instinct is akin to the spirit in which homeless people acquire shopping trolleys, then use them to mass everything the verge, the bin and the gutter have to offer, creating small mobile monuments to obsolescence.

Thus we have all the books no one else wanted – as well as most of the ones we did. That's why we have Tony Buzan's *Memory: How to Improve It*, as well as *Extracts From Gramsci's Prison Notebooks*; that's why there are all of my dead mother's Viragos, and the family Penguins, Pelicans and Puffins, paperback generics which have come together in chunks, after generation upon generation of packing them into cardboard boxes, resulting in the evolution of a crude librarianism. But only very crude. J. K. Galbraith still abuts C. S. Lewis abutting Arthur C. Clarke, who in turn leans on *Zen Comics* and a collection of *Helpful Hints* compiled by some upper-class supernumerary. Good cladding – and an entirely suitable housing within which to stay firmly at home. In fact, it *is* my childhood home – or more like anywhere else could ever be like it again. And looking to the wall outside, its particular pocks, chips and coarseness of mortar, I am oppressed by the notion that the bricks may be texts as well, the spines of buried tablets, covered in cuneiform script, which bear, etched into the very mucilaginous matter of the city, the histories of all who live here now, lived here then, or could ever live here.

I can't believe this is exclusively a writer's problem. Consciousness is, after all, simply another story, another string of metaphors, another gag. I think all of us Londoners are like the young schizophrenic man who knocked on the door of my Shepherd's Bush house on a dull winter evening in 1989: 'Could you lend me £13.27,' he said, his voice jagged with the fateful snicker-snack of psychosis, 'and drive me to Leytonstone?'

'All right,' I replied, keen as ever to experience a random act of senseless generosity. As we were scooting under the Euston Road underpass, and his delusional babble was mounting in volume and intensity, I decided that I'd better check out his destination. I pulled over. 'Show me,' I said to him, opening the *A–Z* to the relevant page, 'exactly where it is you want to go in Leytonstone.'

He looked at me warily. 'Come on, man,' he said, 'you know as well as I do that the *A–Z* is a plan of a city – it hasn't been built yet.'

The *A–Z*, the colouring book of London. Some of us live in this plan more than we do in the physical reality of London. Some of us even live more in the diagram of the tube than we do in the physical reality of London. After all, the tube imparts a sense of the city that is not unlike the child's unintegrated vision described above: you disappear down a hole in the Mile End Road and then pop out of another one in Chalk Farm. Some people's whole lives must be like that, with no coherent sense of the city's geography; they must find it impossible to circumvent old lovers, evade defunct friendships.

Of course, I've been orienting myself for a lifetime, which is why it's so hideous, but it wasn't until the mid-eighties that I had my first epiphany, the first coming-together of all these disordered ideas and impressions and imaginings of London. I was standing in Hill Street, Mayfair, on a warm, early summer morning, when the realisation came that I had never been to the mouth of the river that ran through the city of my birth. You couldn't have had more solid confirmation of the fact that London's geography remained, for me, exclusively emotional. What would you think of a peasant who had farmed all his life on the banks of a river if he told you he had never been to where that river meets the sea, some thirty miles away? You'd think he was a very ignorant, very insular, very landlocked peasant. There are millions of peasants like that in London; in imagining themselves to be at the very navel of the world, Londoners have forgotten the rest of their anatomy.

I got in the car and drove east. I had an idea, a visual image even, of Southend, the town on the northern bank of the estuary, though it was someone else's image, smuggled into my memory by photograph or film. But the south bank was unknown, and so potentially the more exciting, although in common with the other peasants, I was certain there was nothing there, only mudflats and defunct industries.

The Isle of Grain, the southernmost extremity of the Thames, was the provider of a parallax, a point of reference that allowed me to sense the overall shape of the city and its peculiar cosmology. Once you've spotted one parallax, you begin to apprehend more and more. Central London may seem curiously flat, but if you drive up the Bayswater Road towards Marble Arch and focus on the very tips of those same iconic, twin chimneys which you can see poking up from behind the green swell of Hyde Park to your right, you'll be able to realise the overall shape of the city moving beneath you. Or walk east across Wormwood Scrubs, under the machine eyes of the prison security cameras, but keep your eyes firmly fixed on the Trellick Tower, the block that dominates Notting Hill: you'll have the same sensation. I've now taken so many bearings that I am paralysed, ensnared by my own earlier sightings, lost in a tangled undergrowth of points of view. It took several more years and several more acts of geographic foolhardiness (the worst of which was undoubtedly making a film about the M25) before I could acknowledge the full extent of my own sense of confinement.

I adopted two stratagems to deal with the problem of being a small metropolis boy. The first was to take purposeless walks across the city; the second was to write fictions. The walks, in order to be purposeless, had to unite two parts of London that could not in any way be construed as bearing a functional relationship to each other; they were lines drawn on the *A–Z*: Perivale to Acton; Wood Green to Wandsworth; Hammersmith to Hackney.

This sense of confinement was enhanced by the fact that I was commuting at the time from Shepherd's Bush in the west to Southwark in the south-east. It was the first – and last – proper office job. It came with a company car, a Ford Sierra so new that there was wrapping paper on the accelerator and the interior smelled the way I remember new bicycle brakes smelling when I was a child. The temporal margins within which I had to operate were astonishingly narrow: five minutes too late leaving in the morning could mean another twenty on the journey time. Twenty minutes of giving children asthma, smoking cigarettes, merging with the collective ulcer. Twenty more minutes pinned like some automotive butterfly on the card of the Westway flyover, or the Gray's Inn Road or Blackfriars Bridge. When there were tube strikes – and there were a lot around then – the journey could last three hours.

I was overwhelmed by a sense of the totality of the traffic in the city, and of its complete interconnection. I began to imagine it might be possible to analyse it on a purely physical level, and from this to derive a complete knowledge of traffic flows throughout an entire built-up area. It would be like having an awesomely powered Trafficator computer – but inside your head.

I started work on a story that expressed this idea of a metaphoric meta-jam; this world of driverless cars, of ultimate claustrophobia. Soon I was getting up at six-thirty in the morning, rushing through London by car in order to sit down and write about it. I began to work on other stories in parallel – and I began to see their ontogeny, and to see that they were all about London. By this I don't mean simply that they were all set in London, I mean that the city was the main – and possibly the only – protagonist.

Although it seemed as if the city had sucked me in, it was a consummation I had no will to resist. For in order to avoid the massive and destructive sense of irony that I felt whenever I came to the act of writing fiction, I *had* to write about something I knew very well indeed. I was forced on my subject – and it was forced on me. We were locked up together, tapping the monotonous, plastic piano.

Needless to say, my stratagems didn't work. London wasn't going away. Now I was a writer, I thought I needn't actually live in the place. It might be nice to live in the country, to write about London from a position of rural reclusion, or even not write about London at all. What a fool. The country was crowded, noisy and polluted. My infant son's asthma got worse. At night the sky was bruised with the massive explosion of halogen, forty miles away to the south. In the day I fancied I could hear the distant rumble of the Great Wen's traffic, mocking my bucolic idyll. I began writing a novel, most of which was set in London. It was disturbing and involving, and I didn't want to get into it. We took a holiday in Morocco and as a piece of *jeu d'esprit* I wrote a novella, a light thing about a woman who grows a penis and uses it to rape her husband. Naturally this takes place in Muswell Hill, another theoretically anonymous north London suburb. I scrawled away, with the shouts of Berbers hawking in the Djemaa el Fna ringing in my ears, describing a pedestrian narrative around familiar precincts.

Eventually I forced myself back to the novel. The London it was set

41

in was a bewildering place containing many different levels of reality: my protagonist really could turn the corner of St James's and find himself mysteriously in the Aldwych. The city, once again, had usurped the tale, stolen the narrative. In the novel it was 'a mighty ergot fungus, erupting from the very crust of the earth; a growing, mutating thing, capable of taking on the most fantastic profusion of shapes. The people who live in this hallucinogenic development partake of its tryptamines, and so it bends itself to the secret dreams of its beholders.' This was, in fact, my own dark view. It was now not simply a matter of being in a confined, well-known place, it was like being in a confined space with a brooding, potentially violent presence.

My marriage broke up. I moved to the far north of Scotland. I wrote a collection of short stories, most of which were set in the M40 corridor. London was an enormous absence in these stories, but it was there, beyond the horizon, like a giant lodestone, attracting the cars down the motorway and then aligning them like iron filings around the M25.

I moved to Suffolk. It was a tired, eroded landscape which I walked ceaselessly, attempting to map it, but my subject matter, when I did manage to write at all, was exile. My protagonists were all writers who had left the city. I reached a point where my life and my writing life horribly intersected. I started to know people in the locale, there were invitations to gatherings of stultifying chit-chat. I was obliged to 'look in' at the craft shop. After four years, it was over in two days. A van was hired, a house was rented. I went home.

Initially I found myself to be pleasingly disorientated, occasionally even lost. My internal *A–Z* had faded with desuetude. But soon it was back, and worse than ever. The city was punishing me for my defection. Before I left, my fictionalised London might have been banjaxed and strange, but it exhibited no more anachronism than the real thing. Now this sinisterly altered. I began to perceive the city as not simply filled with my own lifelines and storylines, but choked with those of everyone else as well. I began to write stories set in a London where the opium den that Dorian Gray frequented in Limehouse was still mysteriously open, despite being shadowed by the Legoland of Canary Wharf Tower. This was a predictably more claustrophobic city than the one that had preceded it. It swarmed with humankind: humans running, humans walking, humans scratching, belching, farting, like a pack of apes. I decided to write a novel set in a London entirely populated by chimpanzees. My protagonist found the city to be about two-thirds to scale with the London he knew. That, and the way in which the chimps would ceaselessly and publicly copulate, served to make him feel overpoweringly claustrophobic.

I remarried and we bought this house in Vauxhall, closer to the centre of town than I've ever lived before. The great paperback miscegenation took place. My claustrophobia was now so complete that in some strange way it wasn't really claustrophobia any longer, more a case of my own partaking of too many London tryptamines: a bit of a bad trip. In the past I would welcome that sensation, familiar to all city dwellers, of suddenly noticing a building that I'd never paid any attention to before, even though it had been in my purview many thousands of times. Now I'm afflicted by a more ominous but related sensation, which involves suddenly noticing a new building and not being able to remember what it's replaced. This is unpleasant. This is like conceptualist burglars breaking into your house during the night and millimetrically realigning all the furniture.

There's only one way to arrest this entropy of the city – keep writing about it. I've learned to accept London as my muse. Initially, there I was, sitting on the tube, when she came in: filthy, raddled, smelly, old and drunk. Like everyone else I wanted to get up and move to the next carriage, especially when she elected to sit down right next to me. But now we're inseparable, going round and around the Circle Line, arm in arm, perhaps for eternity.

The measure of my acceptance is that I'm now prepared to fictionalise an area as soon as I move into it – like a dog marking its territory. I've set a short story in Vauxhall already, and to celebrate the hideousness of my orientation the climax takes place in the hot-air balloon that has recently been tethered here. Tourists pay a tenner to rise up four hundred feet over London. On a clear day you can see almost the entire city spread out beneath you. When I did my research ascent, I was struck anew by the immensity of the urban hinterland to the south; it needs a big book, a really long novel. The Great South London Novel has a ring to it – I think.

In conclusion: when I was a child my unhappily married parents would drive us, almost every weekend, to Brighton, where we would stay with my grandparents. My parents would argue all the way there and all the way back; the trip was synonymous with misery for me. In time I came to associate any leaving of London with this wrenching sadness. I began to conceive of the city itself as a kind of loving parent, vast but womb-like and surmounted by an overarching dome. By accepting the city as a source of fictional inspiration I've made this dome a reality – for me. My only wish now is that everyone else should experience the same peculiar sense of interiority, of being in London, that I have. So, my only objection to the Millennium Dome is that it should have been far, far bigger – and I could have told them what to put in it.

Granta 65, Spring 1999

14

Restaurant review: The Terrace Restaurant, London Stadium, London E1

A Polish friend just returned from Cracow tells me that you can buy anything there. The Russian mafia are flooding over the border bearing drugs, firearms, Fabergé Easter eggs – anything that's portable. Gullible people have been sold odd-looking puppies, which they were told were 'Siberian sheepdogs'. Carefully hand-reared, the 'puppies' grow prodigiously and turn into polar bears.

I mention this in passing, because the concept of the 'ringer', or substitute dog, is part of greyhound-racing lore. Not that you could replace a greyhound with a polar bear; the traps are far too small. Even if you could cram one in, when the traps opened and the other runners went for the lure, the bear would probably amble over to the terraces and scarf up a couple of bookies.

I've always had a soft spot for greyhound racing. To my way of thinking it's vastly superior to the so-called sport of kings. For a start, in an average evening's programme there are anything up to fifteen races; one every ten minutes or so. This means the adrenalin hit induced by placing your bet, egging on your dog and kissing – or tearing up – your betting slip has barely subsided when it's time to place the next.

Some years ago, I had part-ownership of a whippet. This scaled-down greyhound was pedigree to the nth degree. Dams and sires on both sides could be traced back to portrayals of ancestral dogs gambolling in the middle distance of Gainsborough paintings. The poor animal was so highly-bred that she looked as if her genes were about to undergo fission, sending strings of DNA and RNA shooting through the air like ticker tape. She shivered constantly. I was intrigued by the way you could see daylight and a tracery of veins through the taut skin of her back legs.

We took her to a race meeting once – a tiny, rural affair in a lumpy meadow. The lure was a rag tied to a length of rope that was reeled in by a small petrol engine. Our neurotic whippet wouldn't even get out of the car. She stayed huddled in her blanket, her muzzle emerging occasionally to quest the abhorred fresh air.

But she would have been right at home the other night in Hackney, at one of the most urbane greyhound meets it has ever been my pleasure to attend. Besides the intermittent tachycardia, greyhound racing has another strong selling point: many of the stadiums have restaurants built into the stands, so that you can match bet with bite.

We booked a table at the Terrace Restaurant, London Stadium, and negotiated our way there through the hinterland of motorway spurs, railway lines and warehousing units to the south of Hackney Marsh. The stadium has been completely rebuilt, and was reopened last October. It's now a great wedge of bluish brick, plate glass and corrugated-aluminium siding which wouldn't look out of place understudying Stansted Airport. We paid four quid entrance and took the lift up to the first level.

The vista that confronted us here was pure futurism: a four-storey-high sheet of glass enclosed three enormous, descending tiers of tables. There were television monitors mounted on blue-and-yellow columns, and acres of industrial-strength carpeting. Both the monitors and the carpet were badly afflicted with the jagged lines and pointillist dots of interference – but in the case of the carpet I think it was part of the design. In the distance, the NatWest Tower was burnished by the setting sun, a nice reminder of the follies of Mammon – as if we needed one.

Our table was on the lowest tier, and we had our own mini-monitor which flashed up the odds and pictures of the races. A waiter appeared bearing heavy, acrylic-backed menus and sporting the inevitable goatee. (I've had occasion before to remark on the disturbing spread of this chin-borne disease. Thank God for the Goatee Support Group, or GoatAnon as it's now known. Once sufferers admit that their facial hair is unmanageable, they can seek the help of a Higher Power, namely a razor.)

In the wake of the waiter came the bet-collector, another great feature of the dog track. Having bets collected from the table means that you have no fewer than two servitors in attendance, which has to be a bonus in a society as rabidly egalitarian as our own. The second race was about to begin, so we quickly slapped a fiver to win on Dutch Meadow. Needless to say, it limped home fourth out of six runners.

It was the first of about twenty losers we picked in an evening that would have driven Dostoyevsky straight to the bingo hall. It's true that the programme provides you with a complete record of each dog's form, but by the time you've deciphered this and correlated it with any of the betting combinations (reversed forecasts, trios, straights), the dogs are being given a post-race rub-down. You need to have either inside information or very good luck.

We had neither. The Significant Other – who's taken to drinking cider in the naïve belief that it's non-alcoholic – confessed that she had never picked a winner in her life. And this despite the fact that her father once owned two racing greyhounds. We turned our attention to the food, while all around us young women with drowned hair and young men with stripy shirts ululated their good fortune.

There was no pussyfooting around the beef crisis at the Terrace Restaurant. There were eight- and twelve-ounce steaks on offer, as well as veal and tournedos Rossini. They haven't bothered with any of that guff about the beef coming from organic herds; for all we knew the cattle had been fed on greyhounds. There was also the somewhat tactless inclusion of rabbit (albeit in terrine form with prunes and orange), which reminded me of a sign I once saw in a butcher's window: '*Watership Down* – you've seen the movie, now eat the cast!'

I had a minestrone soup which was putatively home-made and boasted dumplings, although mine – like Hitler's – was singular. Cider Woman had the watercress salad with 'warmed' Somerset Brie, hazelnut dressing and parsnip chips. The several acres of plate glass mightily refracted the sun's rays, so that the 'warmed' Brie floated in a pool of its own cheesy sweat. At the next table they'd commandeered a fan.

The main courses were all right. I had the monkfish, Cider Woman some duck. But nothing could cheer us up as we picked dogs who got trapped on the rails, dogs who ignored the lure, and dogs who would've been happier on a croquet lawn than on a race track. While all around us was an excitable sea, we were islanded by dolour.

I picked moodily at the label on my Labatt Ice lager. If I were lucky, the reverse would inform me that I'd won an 'Ultimate Weekend' in Canada. As the result was revealed, my heart skipped a beat – I'd won! 'Quick,' I said to Cider Woman, 'we must get back and tell our polar-bear cub the good news – he's going home!'

Observer, July 1996

15

Restaurant review: Mortimer's on the Quay, Wherry Quay, Ipswich

It wasn't until the waitress at Mortimer's said there were no oysters that I realised that that was exactly what I wanted. But it was more than that, it was a Zen moment, because the negative mollusc response hit me like a form of enlightenment: I am always in a state of desiring oysters and perhaps the only way for me to attain nirvana is to enter all fish restaurants in a posture of not wanting them, or 'ostracising', as the etymologically-inclined might term it.

Mortimer's on the Quay is an eponymous hero of a restaurant. However, this is no cobbled promontory, mounded with floats and netting. Instead a reef of brickwork, home to a species of resolutely uncolourful office-dwellers, runs alongside the dank pit of the Orwell River. On the far side are yachts, smallish ships and those modern cranes that look somewhat like the Martian invaders from H. G. Wells's *War of the Worlds*.

Mortimer's is a long, high, wedgy establishment, rather like a sub-atrium. It has spider plants, it has chequered table-cloths, it has various fish transfixed on the walls and many many more listed on the menu. In short, it is a real fish restaurant. Above our table a red mullet looked lugubrious and sexually rejected, while above it a marlin arched its back, the very image of piscine priapism.

My dad – who was my companion for the evening – has had a compulsion to state the obvious ever since a car crash in 1967, involving himself, four Irish MPs and a bottle of Power's whiskey. 'Mmm,' he pronounced, looking around him, 'this is a *real* fish restaurant.' Before he could get going, I began to spoon an excellent bottle of Mâcon-Lugny Laroche 1994 down his neck.

Daddy had the fish soup to start and I went for the lobster cocktail. The lobster was excellent, the flesh fresh and firm. But I was surprised to find the goblet it came in generously coped with Thousand Island-style dressing, which quite overlaid the taste of the lobster. Daddy's fish soup was good. Someone really knew how to do a fish stock in the kitchen and there was no trace of greasiness in this well-modulated broth.

'There's really nothing to restaurant criticism,' said Daddy, as I visual-ised the patricide scene in Pasolini's *Oedipus Rex*. 'Mind you, we used to have Raymond Postgate's *Good Food Guide* when you were a boy – terribly bourgeois, I suppose.' He paused for a moment, spoon *en route*. 'Of course, they say fish is good for the brain.'

'Who says fish is good for the brain?' I snapped.

'P. G. Wodehouse.'

We lapsed into silence. I regarded our fellow diners. They were a robust, chunky lot. At the table next to ours, seven men with moustaches were fishing out. Ipswich has had strong American connections since the war, and what with the décor, the waitresses dressed as waitresses and the empty quay outside, the impression of being Stateside was strong.

Daddy opted for the char-grilled marlin with garlic butter, and I, propitiating our tutelary spirit, decided on the grilled whole mullet with dill and melon. We shared a side salad. The salad was a tightly furled bunch of rather hard leaves. The impression it gave was that the chef had once had an extremely unhappy affair with a cabbage and was trying to forget it. Both fish were garnished with more leaves and a clutch of those distinctly penile-looking new potatoes.

My mullet was a charming fish: delightful figure, and just the right size. As with all my favourite creatures, its body fell open upon being pressed in the right places, to reveal firm flesh with a slightly woody bouquet. I was ravishing this when Daddy came up with his conversational bombshell of the evening: 'You know,' he said, eyeing me over a forkful of marlin, 'I had a peripheral part in the expansion of Ipswich.'

You can depend on Daddy to say things like this. He's an academic who specialises in the theory and practice of urban regional development, and it's fair to say that wherever you eat in south-east England, you won't be far from a Daddy-influenced conurbation. Yes, you could tuck into roast pork in Peterborough, masticate mangetout in Milton Keynes or nosh Neufchâtel in Northampton, safe in the knowledge that my daddy has had – no matter how peripheral – an input into the local environment.

Daddy went on to discourse about the cusp of new town development in the late sixties. I was disconcerted: while clumsy in almost every aspect of manual operations (his doctoral students have been known to tie his shoelaces for him), when at trough Daddy's hands almost blur with speed. I just managed to swipe the last chunk of the marlin before it was ingested. It was worth it. Marlin has dark, heavy flesh and unless it's grilled to perfection it can become either rigid or exhausted. But the chef at

Mortimer's had this fish's number, and it was now playing a peripheral part in Daddy's development.

Mortimer's offers an extensive menu. On the night Daddy and I were there, there were six specials on the board, and the à la carte runs to a couple of pages. The wine list is fairly predictable, but if our Laroche was anything to go by this is no bar to excellence.

We had no time for dessert – Daddy had a train to catch. Slightly insipid filter coffee came with the bill and a little menagerie of white chocolate animals. The service throughout was courteous and the bill was somewhere in the late fifties. Not bad for a real fish restaurant.

Observer, October 1995

16

We were walking along the incredibly vertiginous bank of shingle that constitutes the shoreline at Dungeness – my wife, toddling son and I. Behind us we could see a number of JCBs and earth-moving trucks hard at work scraping up the beach. On the far side of Dungeness nuclear power station we could see where this ongoing exercise in earth-moving was leading: they were dumping it all over there.

I explained the irrationale behind it: 'You see, they were warned when they planned to build the power station here that the erosion would constantly threaten its foundations, but they didn't listen. So now, they have to expend vast amounts of energy and labour to ensure that it isn't washed away, by moving this bit of the beach over there.'

As we scrunched on, she remarked that it sounded like a good subject for a *Building Design* column. Trouble was, I told her, that I was almost certain I'd written about this colossal example of civil-engineering folly before. That's the trouble with being a columnist over a long period of time; almost invariably you find yourself having come full circle, like a cat attempting to catch sight of his tail in the mirror, so that he can write a few hundred words about it.

But in fairness to me, the last time I wrote about Dungeness I hadn't actually visited the place for some time. What inspired me this time is that our friends Mark and Sam have bought a shack there, and they'd told me about the shingle-go-round. I've always had a pronounced liking for places like Dungeness where the influence of humanity on the natural environment is, at one and the same time, tremendous – and insignificant. There's absolutely no gainsaying the enormous impact of the power station itself, which, unlike say Dounreay or Sizewell, presents itself as being akin to administrative, factory or public buildings erected during the same era. The former power stations are pure science fiction, but Dungeness looks like a chance meeting between Centre Point, an oil refinery and a brutalist housing estate on an architect's drawing board.

I've no idea whether the contribution it makes to the national grid justifies the ongoing earth-moving operation that prevents it from collapsing into the Channel (and what a disaster that would be, making Chernobyl look as apocalyptic as a chip-pan fire), but one thing you can say in its favour is that it's helped to create one of the most unusual landscapes in southern England.

The most famous of the shacks that litter the lea of the power station is Prospect Cottage, formerly owned by the avant-garde film director Derek Jarman. Jarman created a bizarre garden in front of his creosoted, clapboarded shack. Obviously not even the hardiest of perennials can stand up to the salt winds, nor find purchase in the stony soil, so instead he planted cacti and samphire grass, and created odd sculptures out of driftwood. I had heard that since the film director's death the garden had been subject if not to vandalism, at any rate to the removal of various items by so-called 'fans', but on this visit I was pleased to see that it's still intact.

The Dungeness shacks straggle out along the shoreline in no discernible pattern. They were there, of course, before the steam-belching behemoth was built, but I can't help feeling that they gain their ambience of total eccentricity, complete rejection of the pretensions of civilisation, from their proximity to this technological white elephant.

There are shacks that have been bought out of catalogues, which would look more at home in suburban gardens; there are shacks that have been converted into dwellings out of World War II Nissen huts; and there are others that have evolved into permanent dwellings because that's where the caravan's wheels happened to be replaced with piles of bricks.

Our friends' shack is as comfy and as four-square as it's possible for a shack to be. The great advantage of such a tiny dwelling is that one wood stove in the corner is sufficient to get it delightfully cosy within minutes of lighting. We arrived in darkness, grounding the car in a shingle bank and puncturing a back tyre simultaneously. Once inside we had one of the most spectacular nighttime views it's ever been my pleasure to witness: the oblong window above the sink in the tiny kitchenette exactly framed the bulk of the power station, which, in the stygian blackness of this remote coast, appeared like the spaceship in *Close Encounters of the Third Kind*. But there was better – the pane of glass in the door also exactly framed the lighthouse. I don't think I've ever witnessed a better, or more extempore, light show.

Building Design, February 1999

17

So, back in dirty old London, as my nine-year-old used to so amusingly remark before the rest of the family took it up as a catch-phrase and destroyed it. Truly, as Wilde so wisely said, wit is the epitaph of an emotion.

And back to anxieties on behalf of nice David Marks and his millennium wheel. Yup, the London Eye is still resolutely horizontal, filmed over by the glaucous waves of the Thames. We went down to Victory Gardens on Sunday afternoon for a game of footie (Family Self invariably selects the most shit-bedizened, trash-maculated and generally polluted terrains for its sporting activities), and there was the wheel lying on its side in the river. From the air it must present a fantastic figuration of the year zero, not that this will provide a scintilla of consolation for Marks et al. When accosted, a site worker told us that the HSE had been down on the original Vertical Day and halted the winch; and that the second attempt – which had been scheduled for that very afternoon – was also subject to delay by said Executive.

I digress to hate, but I once played cricket against the Health and Safety Executive. I remember it well because even at the time there was a hint of absurdity about the gig. The ground was a dismal scarified patch off the Great North Road, and I was appearing ('playing' is not a term applicable to my appalling endeavours) on behalf of the *New Statesman*. We were fielding such luminaries as Julian Barnes, the novelist, who majestically bestraddled the crease like Sweeney: 'broad-bottomed, pink from nape to base'. The HSE, on the other hand, were a squitty little bunch of Aertex-swaddled minor-public-schoolboys and scholars from Manchester Grammar.

There was a rank unseemliness about the way these players made a tolerable effort to have a reasonable game of cricket, while the *Statesman* XI lounged about the outfield, discussing the destiny of entire nations from the absorbing perspective of a minor parochial left-wing periodical. (Or, in my case, making yet another attempt at a daisy chain. Ah! *Où sont les colliers floraux d'antan?*) Unbelievably, at one point in the afternoon, there was such a deep hiatus in the *Statesman*'s game, I was actually asked to bowl. Rising manfully to a task for which nature has ill equipped me (the physique of the freak spider baby, and not so much a wall eye as an eye wall), I galumphed an approach and unleashed the ball into the fume-laden air. It described a protoparabola prior to the dawn of physics: straight up – and then straight down again. Straight down on top of the HSE batsman, who staggered to avoid the leather bomb and collapsed atop his wicket. How we socialistic types chortled – or at any rate I did.

I suppose ironies are often 'delicious', because there's something gusta-tory about the way they repeat on you. Irony definitely unites tastes of all kinds. But the irony of near-maiming a member of the Health and Safety Executive is as nought (there it is again; not present in Europe until the year 1000 which so obviously demanded it, and now wholly ubiquitous) when set against the sand-into-rubble saga that, it transpires, has been the reality of the recent Turkish economic boom.

I may have sojourned in Orkney, the Scilly Isles (silly isles – insane prices) and the Scottish Lowlands this summer, but night after night I've spent trawling the wreckage of Istanbul, Izmit and Adapazari, courtesy of the new rolling-news format of the BBC World Service. Not that I've wanted to indulge in this aural catastrophilia, it's just that that's what was happening – and I've been an insomniac all my life. As the corrupt building contractors who'd cut their concrete with beach sand fled the country, and the wreckage of their phoney endeavours was ploughed under with corpses and disinfectant, there was plenty of time to speculate on the whys and wherefores of what had happened.

We heard from politicos and pundits of all stripes, and plenty of gobbets of despair from the victims of this criminal deconstruction spree. There was a whole heap of wreckage – both on camera and in the studio. What was lacking, however – at least in any of the coverage I heard or saw – was the presence of the Turkish HSE, or its equivalent. No busybody

Turkish planning officers were on hand either. Granted, we heard from a fair few Turkish equivalents of the *Statesman*-like characters I used to bandy bats with, but it's useless having a functioning fourth estate if your house has just been destroyed in an earthquake.

Building Design, January 2000

18

I watched the prime ministerial broadcast on the Queen's Speech the other night with an admiration that bordered on sycophancy. At last here was someone in authority who was prepared to speak out on the issues and concerns that affect real, hard-working, tax-paying voters such as myself; voters who, with some justification, think of ourselves as the very spleen of middle England. There he was, this elegant, young, yet firmly-spoken man, this man of steel in an Armani glove, his rear end propped on the corner of a desk, while behind him a bank of CCTV screens displayed the reality of life on the no-longer-so-mean streets of his beloved County Durham.

Who among us, with at least a scintilla of moral fibre, could fail to hearken to his call? He told us – with great modesty – that under his administration 'crime has fallen', while under that of his predecessors it had, quite simply, 'doubled'. He told us that he would see to it that the drunken louts who make our streets unsafe and our lives a misery would soon be subject to on-the-spot cash fines. He reminded us of something we're all sickened by – the way in which drug barons flaunt their evil profits by driving around shamelessly in expensive cars. But also, in a week that saw the nation shocked and revolted by the murder of a young boy, he instructed us – quite rightly – that it was the responsibility of all of us to tackle crime. We should not turn away, or cross the street, when we see a violent incident; we should not shirk from our duty as citizens.

As the credits of this fine ethical infomercial rolled, I was pleased to see that we were being encouraged to do our bit immediately, by calling the national Crimestoppers line if we had any intelligence that might lead to the apprehension of someone we suspect of criminal activities. Without more ado I picked up the phone and spoke to a kind, engaged, sympathetic woman at a call centre in Perthshire. 'The situation is this,' I told her. 'I live in Vauxhall in south London, and just across the river from me, in a district called Westminster, there's a man who shows all the signs of being a major trafficker in narcotics.

'He lives in a heavily fortified compound in a nondescript street. He is guarded around the clock by men with guns. He only ever comes out of his compound being driven in a flashy Jaguar. He regularly entertains a coterie of show-business types, who, so gullible are they, hang on his every word. To my certain knowledge he is operating a protection racket whereby he uses his goons to intimidate young men the worse for wear for drink into coughing up cash. But worst of all, he peddles a drug so insidious and vile that most of the people he sells it to don't even realise they're addicted. He and his henchmen call this drug "policy", and they push it relentlessly, telling their "electorate" that it is this "policy" that's making them feel so good, and that with a bit more "policy" they'll feel still better. I understand that they smuggle a lot of this raw "policy" in from America, and then refine it in laboratories called "policy units" before selling it on in the form of packs of five easy-to-swallow catch-phrases.'

The woman in the call centre took my fears seriously. She told me she'd pass them on to the relevant authorities and they would then begin surveillance of the man. I didn't trouble to voice my worst suspicion, which is that despite the fact that this man is already under near-constant surveillance – he's still getting away with it.

Today, BBC Radio 4, December 2000

19

Book review: What Remains to Be Discovered
by John Maddox (Macmillan)

It was Benjamin Franklin – a natural scientist *manqué* if ever there was one – who observed, 'But in this world nothing can be said to be certain, except death and taxes.' And it's John Maddox's aim in this splendid book to modify the opinion in a novel way. According to Maddox, if I've read him right, nothing much is certain in this universe save for the Second Law of Thermodynamics (i.e. death), and the lack of available fiscal appropriation for scientists who wish to study the Second Law of Thermodynamics (i.e. taxes).

It's entirely suitable that it is Maddox (who, in his capacity as the long-serving editor of *Nature*, has for so many years been an editorial nursemaid to important scientific discovery) who should be the person to take this compelling tour of the current frontiers of our knowledge of pure science *and* the possibilities for their rapid extension into the hinterland of ignorance. What is altogether more surprising is how lucid – and indeed readable – this tour turns out to be.

Half a century ago C. P. Snow defined the 'two nations' of the arts- and science-educated graduates who comprise the British establishment, and remarked that these particular nations find it impossible to speak unto each other. While I think it fair to continue to level this accusation against the arts lot, in recent decades the scientists have been doing their very best to get through to us. In the fields of evolutionary biology (Richard Dawkins and Stephen Jay Gould), cognitive theory (Daniel Dennett) and particle physics (Stephen Hawking), commendably clear pedagogues have stepped forward to make their fields surprisingly intelligible to a wider audience. I fear this transmission has not occurred in the opposite direction; all too often scientists find artists' incorporation of their recent discoveries into scenarios and motifs, tropes and metaphors, simplistic – if not absurd.

There's nothing simplistic about Maddox's work, but I have to say that it's the first book that made me – as an arts graduate – feel that I understood twentieth-century particle physics with any depth at all. With Hawking's *A Brief History of Time*, despite his use of only one piece of mathematical notation in the entire text (or, more likely, because of it), I found myself grappling with his paragraphs. No wonder this was the widest-bought and least read book of all time. It is Maddox who deserves Hawking's sales. Somehow he manages, through clear and careful writing, to lead his readers deeper and deeper into the paradoxical worlds described by contemporary physics.

Of course, for the literary-minded this is an exciting realm. Ever since Murray Gell-Mann, at Caltech in the fifties, seized upon the Joycean 'quark', to describe unstable, subatomic particles, science has become a remarkable source of new coinages. But it isn't just his analysis of 'solitons', 'hadrons', 'skyrmions' and 'gluons' that makes Maddox's approach so entrancing; it's his ability to make you visualise them. I suddenly realised, reading this book, that when physicists talk of subatomic particles having a 'right-angled spin', they mean this *quite literally*. And that the best way of comprehending this is to imagine yourself in the kind of brightly coloured, topsy-turvy, arsy-versy cosmos depicted in old Marvel comics. Yes, looked at through these Stan Lee lenses, the paradoxical nature of our universe becomes a lot easier to grasp.

I only harp on about this because it was quite an epiphany, and one that stayed with me through the sections on genetics and molecular biology as well. Given his ability to provoke vivid pictures in his readers' minds, these parts of Maddox's book became like that film *Fantastic Voyage*, where the scientists are miniaturised and injected into a human bloodstream. With such a competent helmsman I found myself able to cruise into the human genome, side-swing strings of *Alus* – or genetic 'junk' – and tie up to the essential nucleotides.

Maddox is careful in his analysis of the 'arrogance' involved in the search for GUT and TOE (respectively the 'Grand Universal Theory' and the 'Theory of Everything'), seeing them as blind alleys which the pace of discovery has drawn scientists into; but with cellular biology and genetics he is more forceful. Both, he argues, have set themselves up as in a position to offer total explanation – whereas all that they are currently capable of is increasingly thorough description.

Maddox's remarks on the current prospects for genetic engineering are equally compelling. It may interest lay people to learn that while a cure for cancer may be relatively close, the possibility of selecting for favourable heritable characteristics among humans remains remote. The 'eugenics scare' – according to Maddox – is still just that.

When it comes to his own descriptions, Maddox doesn't eschew the proper language of science – mathematical notation – but by golly he makes it work for the ignorant. In his section on artificial intelligence he explained to me the following: the algorithmic basis of computer science; Fermat's Last Theorem; and Gödel's Conjecture – *and* he was addressing a reader with a flat 'C' in O Level maths.

What Remains to Be Discovered is a fighting title if ever I heard one, and Maddox works to make it prevail by consistently referring back to the kind of forecasts scientists made on the brink of our century. He shows how scientific discovery continually throws up the unexpected, and he makes powerful arguments against the Luddite thinking that drives lay people into imagining that a restriction in the 'pace' of such discovery will somehow make for a better world.

From the exciting search for the point of our own origin as a species, to the philosophically queasy notion of the 'beginnings' of our own consciousness, to the truth or otherwise of global warming – this book is an invaluable guide. And if anyone requires further confirmation that Maddox's long years beneath the green eyeshade have made him expert at holding the front page, while I was actually reading this book, two of the areas he identifies as ripe for new discoveries – the synthesis of human flesh, and the discovery of 'missing mass' in the cosmos – witnessed them. Now that's a promise fulfilled!

New Statesman, November 1998

20

There's one indispensable item that you really need in 1996 if you're going to accessorise, if you're going to have a good opportunity to buy all those little nylon bags, foldaway wheeled gizmos and Velcro-fastened garments. Not only that, the accessories for this must-have item are so *damn cute*. They all have patterns on them, hearts, flowers, Hanna-Barbera cartoon characters; and they all have a pleasingly chunky aspect – practical, yet friendly.

You may have thought your other hobbies and pastimes gave you enough in the way of accessory action. But whether it be photography or grouse-stalking, astronomy or gut-barging, the truth is that the accessories are only really updated from time to time, in line with some specious technological advance. With *this* addition to your portfolio of durables, you'll have gone one better. For this is an item the possession of which requires new accessories not just every year, but every month. Even – if you're especially zealous – every day.

Not only that, but this handy thing – which can weigh in at purchase at as little as five pounds – is in and of itself a tremendous accessory. Men and women alike will find their lives immeasurably enriched by it. Prop it on your arm and you'll look sensitive, caring, concerned. Throw it in the air and you'll look full of *joie de vivre*, impulsive, devil-may-care. Lie naked with it supine on your chest, and you'll appear – *without any further effort being required* – incredibly sensual and in tune with your body and your environment. Dress it up in the same kit as you're wearing, and you'll look like the founder of a dynasty. An accessory dynasty.

Perhaps that's the direction the baby has travelled in the past twenty years: from being an accessory before the fact of having a family, to being an accessory to its murder.

In the late seventies babies weren't exactly seen and not heard, but their role in the culture was both more ambiguous and more defined. The old Victorian verities were still in place for the upper classes: along with baby came Norland nanny. For the middle classes male childcare was coming in, but it was still a novelty, segueing on from the more outrageous social experiments of the sixties, rather than acting as a faithful harbinger of the egalitarian society to come. And the working classes? As they teetered on the edge of being extinguished, shot by both sides of the political divide, their babies remained embryonic, although long past term.

In 1976 Madonna, the quondam pop star, was possibly a babe – now she has one. But really it was the eighties that saw the rise and rise of the baby as accessory. With birth-rates still declining, and more and more women of child-bearing age realising that that's all there would be to it – a demographic category – the baby became decoupled from its traditional romping ground, the family, and went crawling for more action.

It found it in the form of fashion. The baby looked good in clothes, and it looked good in clothes when being toted, flirted with, dandled and hugged by models who couldn't possibly have borne it for much longer than an F-stop. Yes, it was sharp, that eighties baby, sharp as a razor, and like a razor the best that some men could get.

Is it too fanciful to suggest that this commoditification of the baby, this reduction of its status from person-of-the-future to handbag-of-the-now, was a darkly ironic counterpoint to the other things that were happening to it? For by the end of the decade we were looking at the baby in crisis once more.

All those babies conceived in the white-hot glare of the flashcubes, and the unsteady frame of the camcorder, were coming of age. They were beginning to talk and to articulate their dissatisfaction with their accessorising parents, parents who in two-thirds of instances could stay conjoined only just long enough for sperm to swim to egg.

The Victorians were notoriously sentimental about babies and child-hood in their books, their songs and their pictures. And they were also cruel to them in the flesh. But whatever the hypocrisies embodied in such attitudes, they did know one thing: babies were babies and adults were adults, and never the twain should meet.

But we're in touch with our inner child; we pet and cuddle the babies within one another. Our national airline is advertised by visualisations that portray porcine businessmen morphed back to infancy and cradled in giant, protective arms. Like the jet-setters we are, we have babies and move on, and have more babies and move on again. Every other weekend we swap our babies back and forth, so that they – like us – are engaged in enormous sleep-over parties that last for days and float around the town. Yes, we're all babies now, cuddling under a gigantic duvet that swaddles the empyrean.

You have only to pick up any magazine aimed at the people who do the job of actually squeezing them out, to see that babies aren't natural any more. They're the product of *in vitro* fertilisation, or a rational decision; they're coldly arrived at for reasons of benefit fraud, or hotly conceived with the same irresponsible result. The one thing they absolutely cannot pretend to be is – that animate contradiction in terms – a love child.

Is it any wonder that having created the baby as accessory and created so many accessories for it, we now find ourselves – both men and women, mothers and fathers – racking our brains for where to find that most indispensable of baby accessories: the grown-up.

Observer, January 1996

21

I love that line 'That was business . . . but this is personal.' It's so true to life. If I ever go out on an exclusively business-oriented gig, it inevitably winds up being horribly personal. Granted, last night's foray into the land of new experiences was freighted with tea-chests full of irony, but even I never expected the caravan to get stranded in this peculiar a mirage.

I'd never been to a literary reading before. Leastways, I'd only ever been to a literary reading before when it was me who was doing the reading. It's like the novel my friend Dave is writing about his theatrical dynasty of a family, entitled *Me, Me, Me!* But last night it wasn't me, it was P. P. Hartnett who was in the driving lectern at Waterstone's, Charing Cross Road.

For the professional writer Waterstone's isn't merely a chain of bookshops – it's the Vatican, Qom and Microsoft rolled into one great big ball of importance. Their monopoly on selling books means that we grovel round them like ants circumnavigating a munificent pork pie. Waterstone's threw a Christmas party last year which they grandly announced as being in the flash, minimalist hotel The Hempel. But when I turned up it transpired that it wasn't in The Hempel itself, it was in the annexe. Have you ever been in a minimalist annexe? Especially with a hundred novelists and indifferent canapés – and Sartre said hell was other people.

Which is all by way of saying that I reverence their premises and wish to reside for ever amongst their solid shelves, and bed down for eternity upon their burgundy carpets.

The advantage of being part of the audience for a literary reading was that I finally got a go at dishing out the punishment rather than receiving it. I also got to see up close the cast of superannuated postgraduates, aspirant photographers and other heterogeneous, existential inhabitants of the inner city who make up the audience for these kinds of gig. P. P. Hartnett is an aggressively gay, extremist writer who deals with child abuse, prostitution and serial killing, and who is currently involved in editing the memoirs of the serial killer Dennis Nilsen. Yet the audience who breathed appreciatively through Hartnett's recitation of the seduction of a thirteen-year-old Japanese boy by his mother wouldn't have looked altogether out of place at a Joanna Trollope event.

To be fair to Hartnett – and God knows nobody else is going to be – he did read well. He eschewed the tactic adopted by many a novice reader of attempting to bed the audience into the text with an introduction. This never works – instead of suspending their disbelief, it simply brings it crashing to the floor as they realise you're just another nervous nerd with a Biro and a power complex. Hartnett walked to the lectern, looking slim and stylish in black jeans, a light-green check shirt and highly shined Doc Marten shoes. Every inch the non-threatening suede-head. He had good mike control and attractively draped himself and a large Styrofoam beaker across the lectern. He also read for a short period of time. All of modernity is concerned with abbreviation. In the next millennium everyone will have fingernail computers displaying one word of text.

The trouble began – as it always does – with the question-and-answer session. Nowadays I get round these by the simple expedient of telling the audience that I don't have any answers, but Hartnett, the poor sap, had all too many. I'd only gone to the gig because Paul Burston, the editor of the gay section of the London listings magazine *Time Out*, had recommended it. Paul's a personal friend. Hartnett described him during the Q&A as a 'turd journalist'. Well, I mean to say, you just can't call anyone a turd journalist – a *shit* journalist, granted, but not a turd journalist. It just doesn't add up.

But that was the least of it. I can't see a block without wanting to put my neck on it, and the case of Nilsen has always beguiled me because I – unconsciously – met him, when he worked in Professional and Executive Recruitment at the Kentish Town Job Centre in the early eighties. When I read Brian Masters's genre-setting account of Nilsen's slaughter, *Killing for Company*, I realised that the *danse macabre* intersected with my own north London life in all too many ways.

I set the ball rolling by asking Hartnett whether it was true about the Nilsen biography, and when he got going – questions provoked in Hartnett an effluvial response; if you asked him to pass the salt he'd probably regale you with a four-hour disquisition on Turkmenistan – he informed us that he wasn't interested in Nilsen because of his past crimes.

Well, excuse me, but there really isn't anything interesting about Nilsen besides the fact that he's a serial killer. Arguably, that's *why* he was a serial killer. I mean, what else could you say about Des? That he liked the theme from *Harry's Game* by Clannad? That he wore tweed jackets? That he was a minor civil servant? That he had a dog called Buzz? That he drank vodka and Coke? I mean to say, none of it adds up to *This Is Your Life* without the nine or so murders.

Still, that doesn't concern Hartnett, who sees the more rounded man. Possibly people are going to see this editorial project as a piece of cheap publicity-seeking on both their parts – but not I. When Hartnett was reading from his new novel, *I Want to Fuck You*, I saw up there at the lectern not him, but Gitta Sereny.

But then I am mad.

The Times, May 1998

22

For some years now I've been waging a blatant campaign, in print, to have Mr Richard Branson give me a lifetime upgrade to first class on every single transportation system he owns. Actually, why limit myself to travel? I could usefully employ his financial services, his entertainment superstores, his condoms, his vodka and – a concern I've only recently learned that he owns – his 'strong Cheddar and onion' crisps.

Frankly, I don't know what it is I have to do to secure Branson's attention. I've taken every opportunity presented to me to give him free puff in the newspapers. (I even used that word 'puff' because of his love of ballooning.) Then, two years ago – although admittedly in a small-circulation magazine – I offered to go round to his barge in Little Venice and perform an unsavoury sex act with him. Still no joy.

Well, all that's going to end now. I admit that I was sceptical at first about the privatisation of Britain's railways. I don't know what it was – some niggling little doubts about whether competition would adequately operate in favour of the consumer in a market not so much defined as constituted by the Government being hand in gear-stick with the motor lobby . . . Ah well! Silly old me – but now I've seen the results I'm completely in sympathy with Mr Blair holding firm on this vital plank of economic policy.

Anyway, the other week Family Self – a large, heterogeneous group of people, who most closely resemble superannuated extras from *Byker Grove* – boarded the Virgin east-coast service from London Euston at 12.25 p.m. The train was scheduled to arrive at our destination, Glasgow, at 5.55 p.m., and it did. This is momentous enough – I mean to say, regimes have been actively promoted *simply* for getting the trains to run on time, ours can do that *and* build a giant dome to commemorate the millennium as well! – but there's far better to come.

Now, as any fool knows, the way industrial designers proceed with two-class transit systems is to design the first class first and then make second class worse. This was evident on the old British Rail, where the lighting in first class was just about tolerable and the lighting in second modulated so as to provoke an epileptic seizure in every third passenger. Branson has kept the faith, although as yet only the thinnest veneer of

Virgin has been applied to the east-coast line – a red chevron here, some liverish livery there, and the word itself appliquéd to the antimacassars.

This is because we're all awaiting the delivery of Virgin's amazing new flotilla of 'balloon-trains'. The balloon-trains are conventional enough trains tethered to vast balloons travelling in the jet stream. The balloons both tilt and pull the trains, vastly reducing journey times *and* ridding the world of filth. Truly, we will all be virgins once more.

But for now it's business as usual: the same slopping puddles of urine in the toilets; the same desultory figures staggering through the carriages imperfectly emptying the bins; and, of course, the same wounded burgers for sale in the buffet car. I say 'wounded', because only on trains do they come with a dear little piece of gauze dressing. Alongside the burgers were the most astonishing chips I've ever seen in my life. They came in a compact box with three tiers of perfectly regular chips, each imprisoned in its own little cardboard runnel. The overall impression this graticule of reconstituted potato powder gave me was: this is the future. But then I was knocking the things back with the correct, traditional beverage – lashings of Virgin vodka.

By the time we were nearing Crewe, my enthusiasm for Virgin snack foods was waning; not only that, but the baby needed several pounds of rank ordure scraped off him. I went in search of nappy-changing facilities, only to find that there were none. Still, I suppose it made sense – on a Virgin train there couldn't possibly be babies, unless they were the result of some immaculate conception.

That was the outward journey. In the interests of research I had upgraded myself to first class, while leaving the rest of Family Self to fend for themselves (at least three of them have to travel in the guard's van on any given train trip). However, on the way back to London I braved second class. Instantly I began to miss that little extra sixty-five pounds' worth of elbow room. It's often observed that first-class train travel is ludicrously overpriced, and that more often than not the carriages are three-quarters empty. How, these doubters opine, can this be profitable? But the whole point of paying to travel first class is that you're paying to keep the masses out. Isolation is what we first-class types crave.

It's a craving that I'm sure I share with that charismatic Renaissance man Richard Branson. People might imagine that the ambition to fly a balloon non-stop round the world is an intrinsically competitive and macho one. Not so. I have it on good authority that whenever Branson climbs into that capsule he is in a state of sheer bliss at the prospect of being entirely alone. I know he has that Norwegian bloke along with him, but he doesn't really count – he's merely there to handle the controls, leaving Richard (I feel I can call him 'Richard' now) free to embrace isolation.

Yes, as the giant balloon is whizzing through the upper reaches of the atmosphere, he is thinking great thoughts, profound thoughts, like 'Why don't I start a chain of Virgin pizza restaurants? The pizzas could have really thin crusts . . .'

I'm up there with you, Richard – in spirit. I think we're perhaps a little bit more alike than you imagine. We're both free spirits, mavericks and yet with a sensitive side to our natures; so please, please do me the kindness of that lifetime upgrade . . . because if you don't, I may find myself compelled to begin taking the piss out of you.

The Times, March 1998

23

Restaurant review: Bridge End Restaurant, 7 Church Street, Hayfield, Derbyshire

The Vale of Edale was wan in the mid-morning light of midwinter. We stopped at the post office-cum-general store to provision. The only rolls available were described – on the label – as 'Tasty Baps'. After another three hours and a 1,000ft ascent followed by some fairly rough walking, we stopped to eat them in the lee of an outcropping of curiously-shaped rocks. They were as far from being tasty as it's possible to conceive. Indeed, if these baps *were* tasty, I would think it not unlikely that Escoffier was alive and well, and working at Big Un's Ribs in Leicester Square.

As for the outcropping of curiously-shaped rocks, the truth is that the whole of Kinder Scout, the moor-sized mountain that looms over Edale, is castellated with curiously-shaped rocks. There are rocks in the shape of butterflies (the Butterfly Stone); in the shape of a chair (Pym Chair); in the shape of a stool (Noe Stool); and most famously in the shape of the North Country footballing father-and-son combo (the Cloughs).

We proceeded haltingly. My companion was labouring under the weight of several tea-chests full of Kendal mint cake (we have a relationship of domination-submission; this week it was her turn to be 'mule') and the wind battered her about. But as I strode along, unhampered, I felt invigorated by the fresh air, the soaring prospects and the sight of so much Gore-Tex in one place.

Eventually we descended, following the old pack-horse route that winds down past the medieval Edale Cross, into Birch Vale. The small town of Hayfield was spick and span in the gloaming. There was a bright splash of colour against the dark fronts of the houses, an array of fresh vegetable produce courtesy of Derbyshire & Son, Greengrocers.

I had had the good sense to telephone ahead for a short-term let on a room at the Bridge End (there's a small guest house attached to the restaurant) and a stall for Mulie. I gave her a bit of a rub-down, but the poor wee beast was shivering when I went up for my nap, and still shivering when I came down three hours later for dinner.

Outside, the Bridge End Restaurant has the darkly-weathered air of a traditional, Peak District-style weaver's cottage, but inside all is piny and tasteful. The tables were blond wood; the wine rack was blond wood; the chairs were blond wood; the woodwork was blond wood. 'Wow,' I thought, 'blond on blond.' A sheaf of dried plants was affixed – with the utmost taste – to the wall next to our table, prominent among them a fine example of *Papaver somniferum*. Nice touch. I always warm to an establishment that uses narcotics in its decorative scheme.

A delicious glass of house white quickly arrived, and I reneged on our arrangement to the extent of allowing Mulie to loosen the straps of her nosebag so as to have a sip. Some home-baked rolls cropped up as well, flavoured with chunks of hazelnut, apricot and poppy seed (ha!). These were good, although it was obviously tricky to get them to bake consistently when – as in the case of the hazelnut variety – there were large chunks of matter in the dough.

The menu at Bridge End was both adjectival (hot, crispy, sun-dried, wild) and more unusually verbal: 'cheese melting on top of a pastry tart'. The house salad was charmingly described as 'a jumble of salad leaves'. Now, there's not a lot of salads you can say that about.

We opted for the soup of the day – mushroom – and the fish hotpot, with monkfish, salmon, prawns, halibut and dumplings. Both went down our necks faster than you can say 'sump oil' and were superb. The hotpot broth was full and lemony; the dumplings, dear little bollocks of flavour; and the mushroom soup had hints of Cognac and coriander seed in it.

A decent bottle of Crozes Hermitage in the fifteen-quid range manifested itself on our table and I generously allowed Mulie a glass. The place was beginning to fill up, mostly with couples. Couples in cardigans, couples in pullovers, couples in woollies. I began to wonder if we were in one of those Mandatory Lanolin establishments. There was also an entire family whose existence proved that not only ophthalmic dysfunctions, but eyewear styles, can be inherited.

We did for another bottle of Hermitage. The main courses arrived. The Mulester was on roast saddle of rabbit with a tarragon-mustard sauce, garnished with pasta. Probably irritated by the things hopping around her shanks all day, she'd decided on revenge. This was rabbit the like of which neither of us had ever tasted before. The flesh very white, very light, no hint of oiliness. It was like idealised poussin.

Both of us experienced a bat's squeak of revulsion. I wrinkled up my nose. 'Hippity-hoppity,' I said, 'it feels just like a bunny lolloped on to your tongue, doesn't it?' She put her fork to one side, her nosebag charmingly puckered with distaste. 'Chill, Muleini,' I chided her. 'After all, I'm eating Bambi's mother.'

Actually the venison was fine. Top hole. Which was where it went. We had a dessert, but frankly by now I was giving up all pretence of taking notes and making the bad mistake of listening to the background music: 'My old man,' warbled Tracy Chapman, 'devil with the bottle – that's all he is/Someone's got to take care of him/So I quit school and that's what I did.'

Cool, I internally slurred as a brandy arrived with the bill. Both were big. In the cab we talked food. The cabbie was an *habitué* of an establishment called The Druid, somewhere in the vicinity of Matlock. 'It's bloody brilliant,' he said. 'You get a proper-size saddle of beef. I mean, proper size. Two pieces, on a plate, each one twelve inches long by two inches thick by two-and-a-half inches wide. The vegetables have to be brought on a separate plate! And you get a proper prawn cocktail up front. Heaps of grapes and passion fruit, but on a *small* bed of lettuce. Twenty-five quid for the lot, including wine!'

I instructed him to make course for Matlock, but in vain. Midnight had struck. My companion passed me the halter and the bridle, while relieving me of the goad. Ho-hum. Hee-haw.

Observer, February 1996

24

Restaurant review: The Ark, 122 Palace Gardens Terrace, London W8

The Ark has more good reasons for its name than any restaurant I know. Not only does it look ark-like – a pine-boarded hutment, crouching on the smutty bank of one of west London's busiest one-way systems – but it is also ark-like in its somewhat sham air, looking, as it does, as if a Creationist-inspired hoaxer has knocked the place together no more than a couple of months previously, preparatory to filming a television documentary which will seek to establish that Notting Hill Gate is, in fact, Mount Ararat.

This having been noted, it would be unfair – and inaccurate – to say that the Ark is Old Testament in its cooking. You'll find no pre-Leviticus dishes here. No solham, hargol and hagab locusts in their several kinds, cooked in their several ways. No gecko sorbet or goujons of koah grace the menu. No, the Ark is another kind of vessel altogether. For in this modest assemblage of superannuated saunas, grounded on a paved bluff for some thirty years, is preserved, like a neolithic human in a peat bog, Homo Bourgeois *circa* 1974. He (and she) are apparently frozen at the very moment they were entombed: uncomfortably seated on narrow pew benches, next to a little wooden shelf with a few gewgaws on it, a pot plant dangling by them, and about to tuck in to a candle-lit repast.

To enter this trendoid time capsule is to immerse yourself in a vanished civilisation, a forgotten culture. Here the word 'Dordogne' is still uttered with a certain *frisson*; and you half expect the supping couples to start discussing Malcolm Bradbury's *The History Man*, or Tom Stoppard's *Travesties* – the first run. The moribund ship is hushed with an atmosphere of humane interpersonality, which one expects may, in the blink of an eye, switch to tense histrionics.

Indeed, I have had the odd tense, histrionic lunch at the Ark myself. It's perfectly placed for such occasions, located as it is in a mystical position: exactly equidistant from the homes of any two people having an unhappy affair anywhere in west London.

That's as may be, but the Ark has other reasons to be proud. In a

Notting Hill currently dominated by barn-like eateries (upper-middle-class canteens where epicene sub-aristos and pensioned-off actors masticate their way through tons of lettuce, as if in search of a final, adaptive, snail-like trait), what a relief to opt out, or rather opt back, to a time when gazpacho, radicchio and just about anything that ends with 'o' carried a sophisticated cachet.

Yes, at the Ark you need not be ashamed of your beard, your poncho, your mid-length skirt that looks like a patched denim pouffe. At the Ark you can relax with others of your kind, before heading home, two by two, to repopulate the world with warm, caring, collarless-shirt-wearing offspring who know nothing of Judge Dredd or ketamine.

The Ark is also at the core of another important nexus. It represents the logical mid-point of a graph demonstrating an axiom of my own invention, the Law of Pulchritude. This axiom (which is expressed symbolically as a quadratic equation) states that the quality of a restaurant's cooking is a function of a single variable. Not the chef, not the management, not staff in general; not location, ingredients or décor can overrule the Law.

This sole important factor is the ratio of staff-to-customer pulchritude. In many, many years of restaurant-going, from Freak Street pie shops in Kathmandu to Michelin three-stars on the Rhône, I have seen this law illustrated time and again: the greater the disparity between the style, appearance and general *tenue* of the two moieties, the better the food. This can go either way: beautiful staff – ugly customers; or lumpen servitors and sylph-like snackers. The quadratic relation means that the nearer these two tend towards a mean, the worse the food will become. At the Ark, where staff and customers are of consummately average appearance, effectively interchangeable, the food is bound (according to the Law) to be shite.

It could be that, or it could be that it was an off-night for eating. London had been heating up remorselessly all day, like a concrete pan full of indescribable leftovers. By the time evening came, the metropolis was choking on its own nacreous exhalations. The staff at the Ark could have gone out to the adjacent bus stop, scooped up a bowl of the leaden atmosphere and brought it frothing to the table, a soufflé of emissions.

In such conditions an entrée of sliced black pudding, with apple and potato, was clearly beyond the pale. In fact, *tout le monde* went for the gazpacho, just proving that they wished they'd never stopped going to Camden Lock. It was serviceable, cool enough, but puréed in that way that betrays a finger pressured by tedium on the button of the Moulinex.

I opted for the sardines with chilli sauce from the main menu, and found them both greasy and depressed. Depressed, yes, ground down by the sardine's lot, the poor opportunities, the lousy environment; but for all that not despairing, not like the lemon sole I had for my main course.

This poor fish tasted of despair, of skull-flattening gusts of some clinical malaise. It appeared to have eased itself on to my plate, using a sinister lime sauce as a lubricant, and lay there enjoining me to schizophrenically incorporate its misery. Which I duly did.

My guests stuck with the plats du jour and covered the waterfront. There was sadness here, empty lives and lost loves, but not the micro-Broadmoor my sole and I were committed to. The medallions of lamb with carrot purée and radicchio was mushy and unresolved. The supreme of chicken with a yellow pepper sauce was . . . well, Jim, who had it, assured me it was 'OK', but to me personally the pepper sauce looked like some sort of hideous, brightly-coloured ichor, which the chicken had ejaculated on dying in order to scare off predators.

I say 'covered the waterfront', but they couldn't quite stomach the warm, poached salmon with grilled courgettes, tomato *concassé*, basil and olive oil. It's the 'warm' that queered things here. (Well, the 'warm' and the '*concassé*'. I'm not mad about tomatoes in the first place, something to do with their floating, their refusal to vote for either fruit or vegetable status. They are the Liberal Democrats of the leguminous polity. But to subject them to flaying and castration and then expect them to taste any better is clearly ridiculous.) On an evening when everything was warm from the off, to eat something wilfully designated 'warm' was like asking for a tongue shot of Novocaine . . . with grilled courgettes, tomato *concassé*, basil and olive oil. But an acquaintance at another table – I think we attended an InterAction workshop at the ICA together in 1972 – said he'd had it and it was 'fantastic'.

There was a certain tension towards the dessert course. One of our party had been having the *pot au chocolat* at the Ark since an early and traumatic weaning – Spock was still top childcare guru when the restaurant was grounded. She was seeking a Proustian fugue, a marriage of past and present in the sweet mousse of the present. No dice. It was, she said, 'rather Dairy Milky in aftertaste'.

The rest of the desserts were, however, fine, and the coffee plentiful if overdone. Throughout the meal the service was antediluvian in its courtesy and good humour, and if the nosh itself was disappointing, all I can say is you pays your money and you takes you choice. At the Ark a three-course dinner, with lots of bog-standard veg and plentiful quantities of chilled rosé Sancerre, will set you back at most twenty-five quid a head.

Not only that, but you're removed from the sort of preening and the little ripples of fatuity that course across most Notting Hill establishments. No, the Ark is free from such distractions. There's just cosy surroundings, uncomfortable furniture, inedible food and – as John Glashan would say – 'absolutely *real* people'. When did you say that deluge was due?

Observer, August 1995

25

Book review: My Education: A Book of Dreams *by William S. Burroughs (Picador);* Ghost of Chance *by William S. Burroughs (High Risk Books)*

How stands it with Burroughs? As we limp-dick it towards the third millennium after Christ, what is the condition of the last great avatar of literary modernism? On the face of it, his continuing Nietzschean will to produce looks grim. In the last few years we have seen the publication of Ted Morgan's biography, *Literary Outlaw*, and the voluminous *Correspondence 1945–1959*. There has also been David Cronenberg's 'adaptation' of *The Naked Lunch*, and sundry off-beat musical, graphic and animated sallies.

Fair enough for a writer in his eighties, whose CV is the history of the counter-culture. But to go on attempting to grind out original work? Surely this is tempting fate, just asking to end up a castle-bound, Daliesque figure, your hand being guided across the page by assistants with posterity-vision and pecuniary concerns? No, not necessarily; and furthermore, far from representing some awful, senile decline into irrelevant muttering and mournful reprise, the two new productions from Burroughs Inc. actually add significantly to the corpus of his work, and go some way towards plotting the hypercast of the *maître*'s overheated mind.

I have not been alone among readers of Burroughs in seeking to locate an 'epistemological break' in his work. There are the three great 'lucid' novels *Junky*, *Queer* and *The Naked Lunch*, all written – if not published – before notoriety hatched in the early sixties. And, more importantly, all written before the frightening year he spent with Brion Gysin in the so-called Beat Hotel, in Paris, at the fag-end of the fifties. It was during this time, when Burroughs fell under Gysin's spell, that the two experimented with various kinds of table-turning, and scrying, and also developed the methods of 'cut up' and 'fold in' which were to distort the more chaotic novels of his mature period.

In *My Education*, Burroughs pays homage to his old mentor: 'Brion Gysin was the only man I have ever respected,' he writes; and in many of the dreams here recorded, Gysin appears, together with a gallery of other eccentrics in the hypnogogic realm Burroughs dubs the Land of the Dead.

It was always a surprise to Burroughs's contemporaries that he saw anything in Gysin, who, apart from sharing with Antonin Artaud (and many, many others) the distinction of having been expelled by André Breton from the Surrealist movement, had little to recommend him as either artist or author (an execrable novel, *The Process*, is subject to turning up on rotating racks in the most remote petrol stations).

But for Burroughs, Gysin was the hierophant, the decoder of the auguries. When they plunged into the noumenal world together, Burroughs found there ample confirmation of all the magical suppositions he had always had. It was at this odd juncture that he ceased to be in any way a conventional writer and started to become something far more interesting. For Burroughs is a writer who, instead of living with the phenomenology of commonplace perception and taking occasional sallies into the world of imagination, has taken on a ninety-nine-year lease in the collective unconscious, and deigned to send us back a series of datelined, bylined reports.

On the face of it *My Education* is a horrific conceit. At what point could anyone become sufficiently unhinged to imagine that his or her dream jottings were palatable fare for the general public? What maundering egotism could give rise to a conviction of the importance of such minutiae? The answer comes early on: 'The conventional dream, approved by the psychoanalyst, clearly, or by obvious association, refers to the dreamer's waking life, the people and places he knows, his desires, wishes and obsessions. Such dreams radiate a special disinterest. They are as boring and commonplace as the average dreamer.'

Paraphrasing De Quincey is very much Burroughs's style: 'If a man who tends oxen should eat opium, he will dream of oxen'; but more importantly Burroughs is setting up his entire *modus operandi* here, as an assault on one reading of the Freudian project. He has always had a sublime ambivalence to the psychoanalytic project. This dates back at least as far as his own wartime analysis in New York. After having learned the trick, Burroughs 'analysed' Kerouac and Ginsberg, driving the latter to ego-death.

Given that he has managed this feat of fully incorporating the perspective of the other, it's no surprise to learn that the dreams that interest Burroughs are lucid, or pre-lucid dreams, dreams in which the dreamer has some control of the context, of dream-action and dream desire. They are also dreams in which the dreamer possesses insight, and therefore short-circuits the possibility of interpretation by anyone else: 'How are shifts made in a dream? How does one get, say, from one room to another? By shifting the context you are in.'

This tendency towards the right hemisphere of the brain, which neurology informs us is the locus of non-sequential, non-rational cogitation, becomes explicit in a footnote to the novella *Ghost of Chance*: 'Those who have heard voices from the non-dominant brain hemisphere remark on the absolute authority of the voice. They know they are hearing the Truth. The fact that no evidence is adduced and that the voice may be talking utter nonsense is irrelevant. That is what Truth *is*.'

Burroughs has always been a sort of science groupie, peppering his texts with the latest gleanings of his now octogenarian autodidacticism, but who is to say that he isn't – in some specialised way – right? Burroughs, I like to think, is a writer who has given his psyche to literature to be used as a strange test-bed, a petri dish full of neural matter in which the most frightening viral nightmares have been allowed to culture. Looked at in this way, his odd politics – enthusiasm for firearms, militant homosexuality, cranky misogyny, crankier environmentalism – are sinisterly accurate reflections of our own current collective obsessions.

My Education: A Book of Dreams is laid out in a series of short gobbets. The ontological status of the dreams recounted travels the gamut from unreflective (conventional dream), through partially insightful (what psychologists term 'pre-lucid dreams'), to fully insightful (lucid dreams), and then on into the wilder shores of prescience, precognition and even alien abductions. These latter categories also seem to tip the *maître* into some of his familiar rants on the War on Drugs, and other idiocies of the global thought police, rants that slide from the lucid dream – to the uneasily lucid. *No one* reads *The Nigger of the 'Narcissus'* in a lucid dream – though some have attempted *Nostromo*.

While the act of writing the dreams down ensures that they will have a certain literary feel, there is no doubting Burroughs's commitment to their own logic. The Land of the Dead, a dream location where Burroughs's dead friends and acquaintances disport themselves, is described thus: 'The usual mixture of rooms and squares and streets that is the mark of the Land of the Dead. Streets lead into kitchens and bedrooms, so no area is completely private or completely public.' This is what we would expect, given research that shows lucid dreaming as coincident with higher right-hemisphere EEG readings. The right hemisphere is also implicated in 'envisioning' – constructing the 3-D world out of the mulch of sense data. This is research Burroughs is undoubtedly aware of.

But while we may cavil with Burroughs's precognition claims – 'Obviously, the strangely-colored cats I dreamed about on Saturday night were precognitions of the animals I saw last night in the book' – there is no doubting his seriousness. Burroughs has in spades what we might call, in Adam Phillips's formulation, 'the courage of his own perversions'. For many this has always been an act. Burroughs is after all the hard, hetty boys' favourite queer.

And yet it must be this courage that makes him capable of still churning out more inspired *aperçus*, apophthegms, riffs and tropes in any given ten pages than most writers manage in an entire volume. Who but Burroughs would come up with the following: '*Does sex have anything to do with sex?* The whole ritual of sex, courtship, desire itself, the panting and sweating and positions, a sham, while the actual buttons are pushed offstage?' Or a description at once so quotidian and so revolting as this: 'On a wooden shelf about four feet off the floor, a man is laid out. He looks like he is made from excrement, fired and glazed, with cracks at the shoulder and elbows, a dark brownish color with a slight glassiness to it, the face smooth, the eyes a pus-yellow color. Is it alive?' Or this! 'I see a centipede, about three feet long, coming into the room. It rubs against the doorjamb like a cat and spreads its pincers and makes an indescribable sound of insect ingratiation.'

My Education may be retailed by its British publishers as 'the closest to a memoir we may get', but it's a memoir of the fictional footprints of a spirit, not a record of sequential impressions and causal relations. There are odd hints here of long-incubated personal horrors, specifically the deaths of his wife Joan and his son Billy, but those wishing for a commonplace description would do better to look at Ted Morgan's biography, which Burroughs himself dismisses as follows: 'Ted Morgan's biography starts with a basic misconception. *Literary Outlaw*. To be an outlaw you must first have a base in law to reject and get out of. I never had such a base. I never had a place I could call home that meant any more than a key to a house, apartment, or hotel room.' Hence, presumably, the importance to him of what Burroughs terms 'packing dreams'.

But while such plainting on his 'mission', and the wilful impaction of art and life throughout the text, may grate on the uninitiated, to followers of the project *My Education* points the way forward.

Ghost of Chance is a short novella, published in this country by Serpent's Tail under their aptly-named High Risk imprint. It appeared originally in the USA some five years ago in a special edition, and one can't help but suspect that the reproduction of Burroughs's own paintings, which illustrate the text, was considerably better. At any rate they can't have appeared quite as turd-like as they do in this volume, the use of attractive monotone rendering what must have been dim daubs at the outset wholly murky.

If the illustrations are dim, they do at least serve to point up the luminous quality of Burroughs's prose, which has lost nothing of its range or sparkle. *Ghost of Chance* returns us to territory familiar from the *Cities of the Red Night* trilogy. We are in Libertatia, a Utopian colony of ex-pirates set up on the west coast of Madagascar. Here Captain Mission has established a community of free spirits: 'There would be no capital punishment, no slavery, no imprisonment for debt, and no interference with religion or sexuality.'

While Burroughs may claim that this scenario has a basis in historical fact, it is clear early on that the generative force for the narrative (such as it is) comes from the author's own preoccupations with global environ-mental catastrophe. Schopenhauer remarked, 'The more I love mankind, the less I love men.' For Burroughs this should read 'The more I hate mankind, the more I love . . . lemurs.' Or cats, or just about any other animal species. What happened to the committed cat-throttler of *Junky*?

The 'ghost' of the title is the Madagascan lemur Captain Mission seeks to protect from an agent of the Board, a sinister committee dedicated to the propagation of the Big Lie (the superiority of humanity, or at any rate the Cartesian line on the lack of an animal soul), which rather aptly – given current events – seems to have its base in England.

Captain Mission's trip – literal on two counts – to the heart of the island gives Burroughs an opportunity to reprise some of his finest fictional fixations with global pandemic and strange chimeras. Mission encounters the Garden of Lost Biological Chances, wherein 'The last Tasmanian wolf limps through a blue twilight, one leg shattered by a hunter's bullet.

As do the almosts, the might-have-beens who had one chance in a billion and lost.' He also, inadvertently, sets up a chain of events that leads to the cracking open of the Museum of Lost Species, which contains a frightening ecological revenge on upstart humanity, in the form of quasi-Biblical plagues such as 'the hair': 'With a cry he rushes into the bathroom: his face is completely covered; great clusters of hair sprout from his ears, from the palms of his hands, from the bottoms of his feet. And the hairs are *alive*, all writhing and twisting with separate life. The hairs have grown through his cheeks and palate into his mouth and throat.'

Grand Guignol doesn't get much grander. Or does it? There is also 'the Christ sickness': 'The Literalists – or "Lits", as they came to be known – actually put the words of Christ into disastrous practice. Now Christ says if some son of a bitch takes half your clothes, give him the other half. Accordingly Lits stalk the streets looking for muggers and strip themselves mother naked at the sight of one. Many unfortunate muggers were crushed under scrimmage pile-ups of half-naked Lits.'

In his attack on Christianity, Burroughs is making greater common cause with Nietzsche than ever before: 'The teachings of Christ make sense on a virus level. What does your virus do with enemies? It makes enemies unto itself. If he hasn't caught it from the first cheek, turn the other cheek.' But his kinship with Nietzsche exists at another important level. Like the Prussian dyspeptic, Burroughs is a describer in the guise of a prescriber.

Taken as a genuinely-held philosophic position, much of what Burroughs says in the lively and idiosyncratic footnotes to this text is hideously unpalatable – not so much politically as existentially non-correct, receiving an ethical lecture from Burroughs being something in the manner of a category mistake. But seen as another experimental bloom on the neuronic culture it makes perfect sense. This is the disordered realm of ideas that we actually inhabit, and Burroughs has offered us his own psyche as a biopsy.

Towards the back end of this volume Burroughs reprises the ideas of Count Korzybski (he also crops up in the Land of the Dead), one of the writer's earliest and most consistent influences with his doctrine of 'Factualism': 'Korzybski would begin a lecture by thumping on a desk and saying, "Whatever this may be, it *is not* a desk or table." That is, the object is not the label.' On the same page we are reminded of Brion Gysin's dictum, the motto of the cut-up: '*Rub out the word.*'

Burroughs is almost unique among contemporary writers lauded for their 'genius' in not having forgotten the full impact of twentieth-century ideas – and specifically linguistic philosophy – on the practice of fiction. His determination to rub out the word may make for an awkward text, and infrequent attendance at PEN meetings, but then as he says himself, 'Writers do tend to be bad luck. No trouble . . . no story.'

Guardian, September 1995

26

Conceivably the most obvious alternative profession for a philosopher would be architecture. Or at least, the most logical for a philosopher who, in the traditional, European fashion, was engaged in constructing a conceptual architectonic intended to mirror the structure of reason itself. It's quite possible to say of a building that it has Hegelian, Kantian, or even Marxian characteristics (although this latter would require the edifice to be 'turned on its head' in the same way that Marx upended Hegel's phenomenology). The philosophies of Spinoza or Leibniz, with their systematic conceptions of the relation between individual consciousness and the world, would undoubtedly afford elegant opportunities for the spirited builder. I myself once wrote an essay on Spinoza's *Ethics*, which was laid out on the page in the form of a spiral of script, like a queered cabbala. If I could've added a third dimension I would've.

The sceptics are altogether a more difficult proposition. A Lockean building is imaginable, but what about a Humean, or a Berkeleian one? Weird. Is there any connection, I wonder, between Descartes's avowed intention to doubt the very grounds of his own sense perception, and the fact that he composed his *Meditations* after spending an entire winter sitting in a defunct wood-burning stove? The philosopher as heating engineer – discuss.

Undoubtedly the most influential philosopher of the twentieth century was Ludwig Wittgenstein. He was also one of the few world-class philosophers to have actually had headed notepaper printed describing him as an architect. In 1926, Wittgenstein, together with his friend Paul Engelmann, designed a house for Wittgenstein's sister Gretl, which was subsequently built in Vienna's Third District.

The house was – and is – exceedingly stark. Boxy and completely devoid of external decoration. It makes the Bauhaus look positively rococo. Wittgenstein's contribution to the design was the windows, doors, window-locks and radiators. However, as his biographer, Ray Monk, says, 'This is not as marginal as it may first appear, for it is precisely these details that lend what is otherwise a rather plain, even ugly, house its distinctive beauty.'

God was in the detail, and Wittgenstein displayed characteristic fanaticism when it came to the practical end of things. Perhaps not that surprising when one appreciates that he had trained as an engineer himself, and was responsible for a pioneering – and patented – design for a jet-engine propeller. When a locksmith who was working on the windows asked, 'Tell me, Herr Ingenieur, does a millimetre here or there really matter so much to you?' Wittgenstein had roared, 'Yes!' before the man had even stopped speaking. He drove other contractors to tears with his savage precision. And nothing better illustrates the lengths he was prepared to go to, than that he had one of the ceilings of the rooms raised by three centimetres just as work was nearing completion.

To the contemporary sensibility the house sounds *echt* beyond belief, with its floors of dark polished stone; walls and ceilings painted dark ochre; unpainted metal windows, door handles and radiators; and rooms lit by exposed light bulbs. But although Wittgenstein's client loved the house, most contemporaries found its chilly clarity a little too hard to take. This was indeed a house conceived of as an embodied system of logic. But then is it any wonder, for the Wittgenstein who designed it was the same man who had fought his way through the hell of the Eastern Front during World War I, while internally composing the glacially pure propositions of the *Tractatus Logico-philosophicus*. This was the Wittgenstein who still conceived of the philosophic project in classical terms as – at least in the main part – being a descriptive exercise: the structure of reality itself as derivable from a number of core logical propositions.

What, one wonders, would a house designed by the later Wittgenstein have been like; the Wittgenstein of the *Philosophical Investigations*, or even the *Remarks on Colour*? This was the philosopher who came to view language itself as a purely functional semiotics, the meanings of words deriving from their use in ordinary life. This was the philosopher who came to view metaphysical questions themselves as aspects of confused thinking, and philosophy – as ordinarily understood – to be more in the manner of a therapy than a kind of conceptual *grand projet*.

Perhaps it's unfair, but the fate of the house on Kundmanngasse, which ended up with its rooms L-shaped by dividers, its walls and ceilings painted white, and the hall carpeted and wood-panelled, might well be seen as the logical result of Wittgenstein's own philosophical development. After all, as Ray Monk so sagely says, 'It's quite possible he would have preferred it to be demolished.'

Building Design, February 2000

27

The Islington Building Design Centre sounds almost tautologous, just as a Chingford Business Design Centre would be positively oxymoronic. This ever-so-*echt* conversion of the old Royal Agricultural Hall in Our Leader's former patch has given us a beautiful exhibition facility which combines elements of the old – the fine, barrel-vaulted glass ceiling – with the new – trendy emporia selling light fitments and desks. The overall effect is a chance meeting between a computer notepad and an antique Victrolla on a drawing board. For now, it's the perfect venue for an event like the London Contemporary Art Fair, but come the restoration it should be handed over to King Tony and Queen Cherie by a grateful nation. It'll make a perfect palace for them.

The Art Fair has been going for ten years now and it's grown bigger and bigger and bigger, until this year, when you can't so much as swing a palette in the vicinity of Upper Street without KOing five anorectic gallery girls. There are now some seventy-plus galleries presenting work for sale, and a host of art-affiliated publications and bodies who come and set their stalls up too. The whole gig presents the ordinary punter with a number of teasing opportunities. You can wander around making an assay of what's being shown in British contemporary galleries; or you can piss yourself laughing at the outrageous prices being charged for works that have the aesthetic merits of a used nappy. Alternatively, you can simply amuse yourself by counting how many men there are wearing suits made from fabric with the texture of carpet underlay, and how many women there are who've cut up their curtains.

I decided to style myself as a modest high-roller, and after a conversation with my fictional broker, agreed on a spending limit of a mere fifteen thousand. First off, I went straight to the stand occupied by Jay Jopling's White Cube Gallery. Jopling is the dealer at the core of the new wave in British conceptualism, and if I wanted to build a collection with its feet firmly in the here and now, I had to at least try to bag a Damien Hirst or an Antony Gormley.

Outside the stand there was a Gormley waiting for me; a scaled-down version of the artist's controversial *Angel of the North*. This angel was a mere six feet high with a wingspan of about ten, but it still made an impressive chunk of metal. The gallery girl told me it cost a cool £140,000, plus, of course, VAT. I can tell you it was the VAT that really put me off. The other White Cube artists were similarly out of my range: a Marc Quinn sculpture weighs in at the £20K mark, a Damien Hirst spin painting at £35K. Even a modest Gavin Turk – the charming imposition of the word 'Gavin' on a host of glued polystyrene balls – will set you back ten grand.

Better to slide to the next stand, occupied by Marlborough Fine Arts and featuring an impressive selection of Lucien Freud etchings. *Reflection*, 1996, from an edition of thirty-six, weighed in at a modest enough sixteen thousand, and the one next to it, *Bella in her Pluto T-Shirt*, 1995, was well within range at £7,250. I asked the gallery woman – this was a more mature outfit – how business was. 'Brisk,' she succinctly replied, summoning up a vision of people pushing shopping trolleys full of Freud etchings.

The White Cube people had already told me that their stand had been 'packed out' the previous day, and within a couple more minutes I met a buyer who confirmed the fair's status as an art supermarket. 'I haven't bought anything yet this year,' this elderly lady told me, 'although I have my eye on a nice Emma Ridpath painting for £1,950. Last year I got a very nice print for £120 – you see I came late and I'd already been to Sainsbury's that afternoon . . .'

I suspect that this woman was more representative of the bulk of the people who visit the fair to buy the plethora of cheap and cheerful stuff there is available for under £200. And really, as I took a speedy trawl through these thousands of pictures, it occurred to me that the real price point of pretentiousness in contemporary art is £2,000. Below two grand nobody cares much about anything – this will be purchasing not to impress, but to please. But paintings like Ian Robertson's *Primitives* – offered for sale by a gallery who should be ashamed of themselves – which is really a series of lurid, badly daubed geometric figures, demand a heavy financial outlay, along with the mortgaging of whatever passes for your sensibility.

Of course, you can get your art on the instalment plan. A very jolly gentleman called Mr Caxton, working for the Jill George Gallery, told me that he would be happy to make such an arrangement; he also told me that he'd once taken a $10,000 cash payment for an artwork from a mobster, and had to count the bills in front of him – but that was in Chicago. Mr Caxton happened to have his mitts on the best remotely affordable works I saw on sale. These were three collages by David Mach, depicting mutated scenes of London: the environs of Battersea Power Station turned into the Garden of Earthly Delights; Hampstead Heath bizarrely mated with *Hunters in the Snow*; the Hayward Gallery transformed into the Hanging Gardens of Babylon.

They were five grand a pop – an absolute steal. I was on the point of slamming down the notional cash when Mr Caxton vouchsafed that he'd already sold two of them and the third was on reserve. 'What?' I queried. 'You mean someone bought two, but not the third of the series?' He nodded mutely. 'Cheapskate bastard!' I snapped. After all, what could this person have done with his remaining five thousand, save for buy an atrocity by the likes of Ian Robertson?

The Times, January 1998

28

Gore Vidal famously remarked on leaving Australia, 'I have seen the past – and it works.' This is what I tend to feel about that most – allegedly – futuristic of contemporary communications systems, the so-called Global Information Superhighway. Or, put succinctly: the net.

I don't know how I can gently break the news to all those frenzied keyboard-tappers out there, but there's nothing intrinsically new about the net. When you think about it, the invention of the telegraph and the telephone occurred before the beginning of this century. Which is by way of saying that the twentieth century has really been *defined* by the possibilities of near-instantaneous transmission of the spoken word and the written text. If you think globally communicated panic is a new phenomenon, just place yourself figuratively on the floor of the New York Stock Exchange during the fateful hours of the 1927 stock-market crash: you would have seen the surfers of the day crashing to the deck in a psychotic spume of ticker tape.

If the telephone and the telegraph admit of the possibility of such instinctual, collective reactions among millions of people, then what would happen if the net were to crash? It might generate a form of emotional panic among all those who've over committed themselves to a virtual life. All those people who for the past few years have only chatted in chat rooms, all those who've only taken in entertainment, or information, or shopping via their home computers, would find themselves terminally homeless, banished from electronic space. With the net crashed we'd see them wandering the streets, their fingers twitching spasmodically, victims of repetitive brain syndrome.

This is not a fate I wish for myself, so I've always been circumspect about using the net. I've got all the gear, of course, I've had it for ages. In the eighties I even used to interest myself in technical specifications, but realising at the time of my last upgrade that I now have on my desk sufficient computing power to manage the Cuban missile crisis, I've given up on the theory. It's as specious as a monkey knowing the precise thrust of the rocket he's tied to.

No, I leave all of that stuff up to Toby, my computer consultant. Every couple of months he'll come by, 'clean' my hard disk ('Ve had to vash your brain – because it vas dirty!'), then take me for a giddy little whirl around the hyperspace. He'll push that mouse about like a cat and riffle those keys like David Helfgott. He'll whip me from some sordid exhibition of human deformities, to the University of Missouri home page, to a European currency news group, then dump me back in the smoky torpor of my study without so much as a hair out of place. 'See!' he'll proclaim on these occasions. 'Surfing's easy enough – you just have to get a feel for it, try it for yourself.'

But I don't want to do it for myself, I want a boy to do it for me. This strikes me as the most atavistic aspect of the net: that nobody who's in a genuine hurry has any time to wally about on it. What I wish for is a timeless relation of apprenticeship. I sit in a high-backed armchair reading Montaigne's essays and eating toast slathered with Oxford marmalade, while my net flunkey sits in the corner surfing. *De temps en temps* I will lean over and say something like 'Why don't you check out Timothy Leary's site, I hear you can take a virtual tour of his drug room?' and the net flunkey will get tapping. This will deliver me from the tedium of all those keystrokes, and from having to witness all the execrable graphics that dominate the net.

Yes, the Internet is clearly the last refuge of the graphically inept. This is where the people who used to cut and paste *Reveille* and *Tit Bits* have gone to ether. The average website is as full of clichéd 'design' elements as the company report of a design consultancy. But there's worse – far worse. Whenever I set out to surf I inevitably have the same experience in virtual reality as I do in 'real' reality. Either the waves I catch dump me unceremoniously, or else they turn out to be ludicrously febrile, mere plashes that deposit me panting in the shallows.

If I set out on a mission of genuine research, swinging from site to site, a great chest-beating ape of an electronic voyager in search of the hard facts, I invariably find myself perching on the home page of some spotty dweeb in middle America: 'Hi! I'm Carter and welcome to my world. My favourite TV show is *Friends* and my favourite dorrito is mesquite hot!' And if I set out for entertainment I run up against my own timorousness.

I've heard it said that the vast majority of 'recreational' hits on the net are on pornographic websites; indeed, further, that the net was actually developed so that the members of the American military-industrial complex could send one another dirty pics. But whenever I've got close to these tacky regions I've found them ringed with dragon's teeth. I mean, who in their right mind would actually consign their credit-card number to the net? Not me. I'd sooner hand it to a convicted embezzler and whisper my PIN in his ear. Even if I could stomach this, I still can't cope with the technical side of accessing these sites. When it flashes up that I will require two gigabytes of free hard-disk space I start to sweat: what if I try to download something and there simply isn't room? Will my computer start to bulge ominously, before exploding and showering me with digitised crotch shots?

No, it simply isn't worth the risk just to see a picture of Nick Berry without his underpants on. I mean, I'd stand a better chance if I simply asked him out to dinner.

The Times, February 1998

29

In the desert the dawn of the third millennium breaks in a pale, thin smile, which lengthens and lengthens until the skull-cap of the night peels away from the circumference of the horizon. The features of the landscape swim out of the haze and yet again the world reveals its primordial character, devoid of the diminishing presence of man. The gigantic bulk of Uluru, the largest single lithic outcropping in the world, emerges from the darkness, first charcoal grey, then purple, then a throb-bing, dark red. The Rock is isolated in this waste of scrub and scree; the only other eminences are similarly vast formations rearing up from the crepuscular terrain. Einstein said that 'God does not play dice', but as you look upon these stupendous chunks of the world littering the desert floor, it's difficult to resist the thought that this *is* the aftermath of some divine game of chance, and these are the abandoned counters.

Certainly the locals are in little doubt about the spiritual significance of Uluru, just as they equally revere the thirty-six rock domes of Kata Tjuta, which rise a thousand metres out of the earth forty kilometres to the west. But the Aboriginal world view, which regards the consciousness of humans as the reverie of the earth's very ecology, fits these monuments into a quite different kind of cosmology. Some are the petrified bodies of mighty animals; beings who once moved over the surface of the earth during a protean period called – in English – 'the Dreamtime'. Others – like Uluru itself – are monuments to great conflicts between the Dreamtime spirits. But for the Aboriginal individual this is a living past, a permanent now, the great antiquity of which – Aboriginal myth refers with consistency and accuracy to geological events that occurred tens of thousands of years ago – testifies to its importance.

Here, according to the Pitjantjara people, was once a flat expanse of land dominated by the Uluru water-hole and Mutitjilda Spring. This latter place was – and is – the abode of Wanambi, the Rainbow Snake. The Rainbow Snake is possibly the most ancient, but certainly the most widely known, of the Dreamtime spirits. To the original Australians, this amalgam of creature and natural phenomenon is the very cord that connects spirit and matter. When contemplating the mythology of Uluru it's better to think of the *Bhagavadgita* or the *Iliad* than any monotheistic tale. For the environs of where the Rock now looms were once the scene of a battle to rival any staged between Arjuna and Karna, under the gaze of Vishnu.

Most of the major indentations that form the 'wumbuluru' or shade side of the Rock (the south-west face) are petrified reminders of the conflict between the Kunia (or carpet-snake people) and the Mala (or hare-wallaby people). The point at which the dawning rays of the third millennium first strike is exactly where, in the wake of more trials and tribulations than there is space-time here to recall, the Kunia finally gathered together and sang themselves to death.

Yet as the desert floor begins to resonate beneath your feet, as if it were flexing itself in preparation for the pulverising heat of the day, you can see that you are not alone in the lee of this majestic massif. Far from alone: silhouetted against the rapidly blanching sky, inching its way up the gargantuan buttress, is an ant-like file of human figures. And as the busy, unruly sun mounts the empyrean, all around you on the desert floor are revealed the members of a mighty motorcade: coaches from the four corners of the continent; ditto camper vans; ditto cars; ditto motorcycles. There are even a few cyclists and walkers in amongst this throng, Mad Maxes who've pounded the eighteen kilometres of tarmac out from Yulara, the tourist resort beyond the border of the National Park.

It isn't, you now realise, the eerie rustling of a Dreamtime spirit that you can hear above the moan of the wind coming from the desert. It's the click, whirr and whine of a thousand thousand cameras – digital, camcorder, automatic – registering the first daylight of a new age. And that murmuring all around, it isn't – you acknowledge to your companion – the voices of the Pungalunga Men, on their way towards the west, where they'll transmogrify into the thirty-six rock domes of Kata Tjuta. Oh no. These are the voices of twenty-five thousand very real Japanese salarymen and their wives. These are the voices of thousands of others who have come to inaugurate their new era by snapping and snooping around the timeless grandeur of some other people's immemorial past.

Do I think there's anything wrong with visiting Uluru (or Ayers Rock, as it's known in the West)? No, not particularly. Would I climb the Rock itself? You've got to be joking – it's the psychic equivalent of pissing on the Wailing Wall or spreading a picnic out on the Kaaba. Would I go there on the eve of the millennium? Not even if you paid me a vast amount of money and fully insured me (in a weird, cosmic fashion) against eruptions of the Rainbow Snake, mass hysteria, or any other unsettling phenomenon that might occur.

Not that there's much chance of my going – or yours, for that matter. Unless, that is, you've taken the precaution of finalising your itinerary an aeon ago. Not only has the Yulara Resort long since been fully booked, but the flights into Australia itself have been full up for months now. Of course, you could get there – and stay there – if you really really wanted to be at Uluru for the millennium experience, but you have to ask yourself: what kind of people are likely to descend on an incredibly remote place, *en masse*, in order to simultaneously revere and profane the sacred beliefs of the people who own it? Tie-dye nutters is who; the patchouli and bangle mob; types who think the Rainbow Snake is a clothes shop in London's Knightsbridge. Yes, them, the tofu-heads and the Tantrically incorrect.

Actually, to say that the Pitjantjara 'own' Uluru is a reversal of the real state of affairs. It is rather the land that owns the people; and this land is the omphalos, the very navel of the body that is their world. To trample upon it has to be a mistake, especially in the midst of the odd psychic maelstrom generated by partying like it's 1999 (because it *is*). It's not that I'm superstitious, it's simply that I have a slight acquaintance with the very periphery of the Aboriginals' world picture, so as to know better than to advance further – unless having respectfully requested permission.

These Pitjantjara, like many desert peoples, are ascetics, fanatics and magicians. Think of the same environment that nurtured successive waves of Sufi brotherhoods out of the fastnesses of the Sahara; and then imagine its impact on a people who've been profoundly culturally isolated since the Upper Palaeolithic period. These are people whose initiation rites include infibulation and subcision (a slit the length of the boy's urethra); whose *minor* punishments are spearings and beatings; and who regard all deaths as caused by some agency, human or otherwise. I well remember one friend of mine, who negotiated with mining companies on behalf of an Aboriginal mob, saying of his employers, 'When they say, "Jump," I ask, "How high?"'

And I too have had my fair share of odd experiences in the red centre, experiences which, while falling short of transgressing the laws of nature, certainly impressed upon me that they can be significantly warped. The first time I ever ventured there, I was thudding north to Alice Springs on a corrugated dirt road (at that time, in the early eighties, there was no sealed road across the continent), when the two Aboriginal men who had been sleeping (*sleeping!*) all the way from Port Augusta on the south coast – despite the fiendish jolting of the un-air-conditioned bus – awoke simultaneously, and walked to the front. They didn't say a word, but the driver pulled over. The Aboriginals got down and without so much as a backward glance disappeared into the Tanami Desert.

I subsequently learned that the majority of Aboriginal people – including the blind – have perfect orientation in this way. I suppose in an ordinary country, its inhabitants' familiarity with the land can be taken for granted. But here, in a continent the size of the USA, with a Westernised population of a mere fifteen million, living in densely populated cities on the coasts, the ability of a few scattered individuals to find their way unerringly around this oceanic interior seems little short of miraculous.

Particularly given that I myself, with all the comfort, ease and power afforded by technology teetering on the edge of the twenty-first century, was unable to make it the five hundred kilometres from Alice Springs to Uluru without getting lost. How, it is reasonable to ask, can anyone get lost in perfectly clear weather conditions, on a near-flat, straight route, which involves only one – right-hand – turning the whole way? The answer is: you miss the turning.

In fairness to me, I was intoxicated by the sheer scale of landscape and its brooding beauty. I was also pushing our rental Ford Falcon along at around the ton and savouring the sensation of the big car beneath me slicing its way through the turbid, hot air. I was also engaging in a slightly manic conversation with my wife, Deborah, our seventeen-month-old son Ivan, and a recently acquired hitch-hiker: Colin the Canadian. Nevertheless, to zip past the turning for the Lasseter Highway was one thing, but to continue for another hundred kilometres south, and still not realise our mistake, even when we'd gone well over the South Australian border, smacks of lunacy.

A literal lunacy, I suppose, because this, the oddest of the earth's inhabited continents, always seems – to me – like another world which has been inadequately terraformed. And it's always ultra-widescreen in the red centre; this is a vista that requires a 140-degree lens. And it's always very harsh in the red centre, whether the harshness be heat, or cold, or rain, or wind. Oh, and there was also the red-bird incident – enough to unsettle anybody.

It was just after we'd acquired Colin, and Ivan was getting a little fractious so Deborah began reading to him from a book called *Brown Bear*. This happy little fable involves the reader chanting, 'Brown Bear, Brown Bear, what do you see . . . ?' and then turning the page to reveal to the child the next animal in the sequence. She was on the verge of completing the couplet, '. . . I see a red bird looking at me,' when out of the red centre and smack into our widescreen windscreen flew a suicidal red bird. The impact was so loud I was certain it had shattered – but it was the bird. A grisly smear of feathers, blood and a single claw were the evidence. 'Phew!' Deborah exclaimed. 'That was close, the next animal in the book is a blue horse.'

I realise now that we were suffering from spatial shock, the result of having been standing in Sydney Airport only a few short hours before. Colin was more acclimatised by virtue of being young, Canadian, and having travelled overland to Alice on the Ghan – the railway line which, at the turn of the century, was forged through the desert from the south, by Afghan labourers using camel power. We were spaced out – Colin was spaced in. He didn't even bat an eyelid when, having discovered that he was an amiable computer nerd, I teased him that I had a satellite phone which he could link up to my laptop, so that he might spend the rest of the dull drive to Uluru surfing the net!

However, I think the majesty of our surroundings began to impinge upon him at last, when he realised how far off course we were. There were two hours of daylight remaining and we still had three hundred and fifty kilometres to go. Given that the wildlife – indigenous and otherwise – is subject to strolling towards the beams of oncoming headlights, this is not a situation you want to find yourself in in the red centre, unless your car is equipped with protective steel bumpers – 'roo bars', as they're known locally.

We kept on through the gloaming at a healthier 80 k.p.h. From nearly seventy kilometres away we could see the massive flat-topped bulk of Mount Cotter towering over the plain to the south-east. Apart from the gentle furrowing of the ranges to the north, it was the only thing we saw until, at last, the lights of the Yulara Resort showed in the stygian darkness. We dropped Colin at the campsite and went in search of a room at the inn.

The resort may have been designed so as to blend in with its desert surroundings, but despite its low, moulded bulk, its predominant colourings of sand and ochre, and its crenellation of rigid, sail-shaped awnings, it completely fails. It may not be as gauche as its counterpart in Nevada, but the Desert Sands Hotel is still a fanfare of cacophonous materialism in the ancient calm of the interior. There are four different hotels within the complex, and I'd been quite keen on trying out the most luxurious. While it may grate with the environment to the extent, frankly, of surrealism, it's well worth experiencing the contrast between Australia's – usually – tremendous infrastructure and its uninhabited hinterland.

However, the marble floors and acres of plate glass, the trilling reception-ists behind their reef-like desk and, most of all, the huge display of Aboriginal 'artefacts' – all conspired to make me feel like a member of the rat pack. And I'm not talking about a cool gang of sixties film stars here.

We settled for the second-best hotel, and spent a humid night enfolded in its modernity. Deborah and Ivan slept, while I read an account of the discovery of the last Aboriginal people to be brought out of the Western Desert. In 1986 an elderly Walpiri couple were brought out of the Tanami, after living there for thirty years in fear of tribal retribution, for having married across totemic groups. Right until the bitter end of their free existence, these people were living entirely off the land, and employing tools and equipment unchanged for many many millennia. I wondered what they would have made of the Desert Sands, with its minibars and swimming pools, and its rapid turnover of well-paid maids and porters, and its still more rapid turnover of the world's more prosaic travellers.

It was still dark when we awoke and dragged the somnolent baby along with us to the campsite, where we looped in the adorably clean-cut Colin. As we drove towards the Rock, the dawn came up as rapidly as if some Titan were yanking upon a solar dimmer switch. Each time I looked towards our destination, its colour, its size, its position – all had altered. It was sublime, the way this mammoth, granite entity hopped about the land. Less sublime was the apparatus of the National Park – cattle grids, admission charges, signs galore – and still less sublime were the rank upon rank of coaches and cars and tourists, all the panoply of humanity I evoked earlier.

We were at Uluru on a weekday morning in the off-season and there must have been five thousand-odd gawpers around the base of the Rock; how many more will there be come dawn on 1 January 2000? I shudder to think. Of course, there's no question that the creation of the National Park has helped to preserve the Rock, and Kata Tjuta (the Olgas) to the west. In the dark old days there were, I'm reliably informed, corrugated-iron 'hotels' which backed directly on to the Rock itself. I wonder what the Rainbow Snake made of that! But it's debatable whether any of the developments around Uluru will ultimately help to preserve the sacred sites, or simply hasten their erosion by myriad sightseers' feet.

No, we didn't climb the Rock. We had Ivan to think of, and respect for the site was neatly conjoined with indolence. Anyway, we could dispatch Colin, like a denim-trousered mountain goat, to do the hike for us. I think that had I been his age I would have gone with him. Not simply because of being more limber, but because when I was younger I felt the need to confront other peoples' belief systems – now I simply admire them from afar. Colin asked me whether I wanted him to take my camera up to the summit; I thought this the most amazing idea of tourism by proxy. Instead we repaired to the Desert Sands for a breakfast of cow's milk and reconstituted wheat granules.

To prove the point that the Aboriginal omphalos has become an Antipodean sink, down which package tourists disappear anticlockwise, later that morning we drove out to Kata Tjuta. Despite the fact that its bizarre rock formations are larger – and if anything more spectacular – than Uluru, there were no coaches, no synchronised snappers, no brouhaha. Puffing on a generous Havana (in my experience the best possible fly-spray for all concerned), I carried Ivan up into the awesome fissure that cuts through the core of this kilometre-high granite plug. And at the top of the track there was a wooden platform, from which we could stare back down the way we'd come, out from the shady verdancy and into the harsh irradiation of the noonday sun.

That evening we found ourselves a hundred kilometres to the north at the King's Canyon Resort. King's Canyon is a medium-sized gulch leading into the Petermann Ranges. There are cliffs and rock paintings there; an Edenic water pool and honeyeaters in the tangled undergrowth round about. At the resort itself there are the necessary mod cons – swimming pools, showers, air-conditioning – but none of the ersatz pizzazz of Yulara. And of course all around was the red centre. Plenty of it.

While Deborah slumbered I took Ivan for a roast dinner in the restaurant. One of the rather more endearing features of British colonialism in the Antipodes is this obstinate adherence to the culinary mores of a remote north-west corner of Europe. Great tranches of roast meat, potatoes and boiled greens are served up in 40° heat; food which was intended to have the internal effect of swallowing an immersion heater. Nevertheless, Ivan and I wolfed it down while pink travellers noshed all around. Afterwards we drove at a snail's pace around the adjacent camping ground. Under the massy stars of the southern hemisphere, every conceivable type of temporary mobile accommodation had been assembled into a compact little village. There were transparent tents with built-in barbecue areas; tiny igloo tents; enormous Winnebagos; and khaki army twenty-pounders. The quiet murmur of conversation floated through our open windows as we rolled by and on out of the tiny settlement. As we sat out in the bush, listening to the night sounds, I meditated on how much better it would be to see in the millennium at King's Canyon, with all these solid, calm families about. The Mad Maxes will be down at Uluru, screaming at the sun and invoking the Rainbow Snake, while the Sane Maxes will stop at King's Canyon, drinking from thermoses and eating the occasional sandwich.

It was the briefest of Centralian sojourns; the following day we headed back to Alice Springs. There, in the dried-out river-bed of the Todd River, were the usual seated groups of Aboriginals – some quietly erect, some drunkenly comatose, some out for the count. They were the first significant numbers of the Traditionally Owned we'd seen since leaving Alice two days earlier. There had been none in evidence at Uluru and just the one propping up the bar at King's Canyon. However, the bar at King's Canyon was also being run by a most distinctive-looking individual: burnished copper skin, shaven head, smooth features with a sharp, triangular nose; and big, very big.

He was a Maori, naturally. It's estimated that there are anything up to three-quarters of a million Maoris in Australia – a huge minority of the total world population. They do well there, working as barmen and bouncers. They're industrious and they stick together. It's said ruefully by white Australians: the Maoris are the indigenous people we wish we had – and the Aboriginals are the ones we've got.

Certainly this guy was running a beautifully efficient bar, and with his Hawaiian shirt and pressed chinos he looked right at home amongst his clientele; but out there in the red centre, set beside the awesome Uluru, he'd look just as out of place as all the rest of us.

High Life, June 1999

30

Some Bastard's Stolen My Face-Off: Remarks on the Sony XR-C500ORDS MD/CD Changer Control, as against the Sony XR-C550ORDS MD/CD Changer Control

When I went into the shop in Tottenham Court Road it was not to replace the face-off of my fine Sony in-car sound system. I actually thought this was the thing I could hang on to, because of course it hadn't been in the car when they smashed the quarterlight – probably with a flicked spark plug tied to a length of string – and ripped all the gubbins of the system out of the dash.

'Silly tossers,' I thought to myself. 'They've cost me hundreds, and what have they got? A £10 fucking wrap of smack.' I wheeled into town, looking at the leads trailing out of the ragged hole in the car's fascia, as if they were entrails. Auto theft always seems to involve some element of disembowelling.

The man in the shop was emphatic: 'You'll be upgrading to the XR-C550.'

'Is it the same?'

'Exactly the same – just without the Dolby.'

'Isn't that a bad thing? I mean – don't I *want* the Dolby?'

'Oh no, no, the Dolby doesn't really work so well in cars . . .' There followed a lucid and concise explanation of why it is that you don't need Dolby noise reduction in in-car sound systems, which I will omit for the simple reason that I couldn't actually hear it. Any technical information that's imparted to me doesn't so much go in one ear and out the other, as refuse to enter the auricular zone at all.

The new Dolby-less system turned out to have a new face-off. 'But what shall I do with my old face-off?' I pleaded. I really liked the old face-off. It was slim, light, beautifully modular to hold in the hand whether cased or unsheathed. It was easy to use in the car as well. The buttons for the ten different compact discs in the autochanger were ranged along the bottom of the face-off, and they were fingertip-friendly, as were the buttons on the left for sourcing the tape machine and the radio. The buttons for selecting the bass/treble/volume levels were also

91

large, lightly knobbled for greater purchase, and artfully composed for ease of access. As for the three buttons that were set on the right-hand side of the panel, the ones necessary for programming the radio, I didn't really care, the act of programming the system being well beyond me. (The book of words for this system ran to a good ninety pages.) However, I had managed to find out how to change the colour of the display (a decent-sized LCD 20mm high x 80mm wide). This could be either a lurid green or a funky rose, depending on your mood.

Yes, I liked the old face-off. I thought it looked very much state of the art, and complemented – with its large LCD displaying keen, black electronic digits and lettering – my conception of car interiors as being virtual recreations of the cosmos, the lights on the fascia becoming a sort of star map, a sidereal display.

The salesman looked at me very seriously. 'What you should do with the old face-off is take it home and smash it to pieces with a hammer; that way no one will ever be able to make use of it.' I goggled at him. This was inconceivable – and indeed, I have the thing on the desk in front of me as I write. Its poor, lifeless face is now off for ever.

The new face-off was altogether less pleasing than the old. It was the shock of the old. The carrying case was bigger, chunkier, less well moulded. When I opened the case I discovered that the display panel was the same. On the old face-off there had been no maw for cassette insertion; instead you put the cassettes in when the face-off was hinged, but not locked into place. But on the new one there was this deeply retro cassette hole, and as a result a far smaller LCD. This LCD is black, with light digits/lettering on it. If it can change colour I haven't discovered how yet.

The buttons on this display are also far harder to deal with, especially if – like me – you have large hands. To switch from one CD to another you need to manipulate two small + and – buttons, rather than having a button for each of the ten available. The volume controls, station controls and indeed every other button on the thing are smaller than on the old face-off. Overall, the 550 seems – to me – to be more anachronistic than its predecessor.

To be fair to Sony, they did introduce the new model for a good, practical reason. The old DIN plug on the 500 was wilfully inadequate and often resulted in the whole system either cutting out or not powering up. It was also bloody fiddly to get the face-off into its slot. As Martin Amis has described impotent copulation, 'It was like trying to fit an oyster into a parking meter.'

The other mitigation is more theoretical. Design does not move fluently forward, projecting a broad teleology of progress – and by implication modernity and even futurity. Rather there are always glitches, large and small. There is no reason at all why technological innovation shouldn't be placed into momentary, and even long-lasting, reversal. So-called 'cutting-edge' design often strives to achieve a notion of futurity, but is also very often eclipsed by the truth about what the future really does hold. What draws this out most clearly is the paradoxical fact that at some times in the past people have been better at imagining the future than we are now. Kubrick's *2001: A Space Odyssey* still, to my mind, looks like a better vision of the future than most that have been produced in the twenty-five years since it was made. (A technologically advanced future, that is.)

This is perhaps a better way of looking at the decadence of my new face-off. I'm like Yul Brynner in *Westworld* (1973), a mere robot gunslinger, built to resemble a human being for the amusement of others – but no one could tell until some bastard stole my face-off.

Privately commissioned by Dr Lorraine Gamman,
September 1997

31

Book review: St Kilda: Island on the Edge of the World
by Charles Maclean (Canongate Classics)

I first read this book in Viera Lodge, the house of my friend Christopher Bowerbank, on the island of Rousay in Orkney. It was Easter 1992 and the islands were encountering some unwelcome notoriety as a result of the accusations of satanic ritual abuse involving children from South Ronaldsay. My then wife and I had driven up from the south, through the Scottish Highlands, then taken the ferry from Scrabster across the stormy Pentland Firth, rounding the magnificent sea cliffs of Hoy, before landing at Stromness in the relative calm of Scapa Flow.

I didn't find Orkney at all to my taste. The islands were bare shading to stark, the vernacular architecture seemed austere to the point of brutality, the wind blew ceaselessly, and the Lodge – a very old house – let it in. We toured the megalithic tombs on Rousay, the plethora of which has meant that archaeologists have dubbed this seven-by-three-mile teardrop of turf and rock, adrift in the margins of the North Atlantic and the North Sea, 'Little Egypt'. I could appreciate the singular atmosphere of the great chambered tomb at Midhowe, but it didn't make me want to linger. When, after a week, we rolled south once more I was relieved to be going.

However, in retrospect there are two things I did during that week in Orkney that sowed the seed that would, over the subsequent years, germinate a revolution in the way that I viewed Britain and my work as a writer. The first was that I began my first novel at the Lodge. It wasn't that I found it a particularly conducive place to write, it was simply that I was driven, but writers are – in my experience – creatures of superstition and magical thinking, and when, a year later, my marriage broke down and I needed somewhere remote to recuperate and work, the house near the end of Britain seemed ideal. In the past seven years I've ended up writing a good proportion of all my books in that house, and if London with all its teeming urbanity has often seemed to play the part of my muse, it's only been in the slightly spooky solitude of Viera Lodge that she's been prepared to seriously dally with me awhile.

The second thing I did that week was to read Charles Maclean's *St Kilda: Island on the Edge of the World*, an account of the life and death of the remote Hebridean society of St Kilda. Maclean's book is by no means the only one to have been written on this strange community, which for over six hundred years survived almost entirely unknown on the outermost extremity of Britain, but it's a good one, it's the one I read first, and it's one I must have reread at least every year since. Maclean's vision of St Kilda as our own pre-lapsarian preserve of noble savages (in the nineteenth century, steamer trips to the island were advertised 'Come and See Britain's Modern Primitives') chimed with my own sense of fictional possibility. I was embarked on a project involving the construction of alternative worlds that both mirrored and refracted the reality of our own; in St Kilda I found a real-life version of one of my own fictions.

The St Kilda Maclean describes is a tiny world which never numbered much above two hundred inhabitants. They spoke their own dialect of Gaelic littered with Norse archaisms. They lived off of the fruits of the island, most notably the teeming seabirds – puffins, fulmars and gannets – which nest in the thousand-foot-high sea cliffs that fall away from the backless hills of Hirta, the main island in this tiny archipelago. Indeed, to be a good cragsman was the acme of any male St Kildan, and to prove himself worthy of a woman's hand in marriage he would have to perform a dangerous rite involving balancing on the edge of a cliff-face. Maclean's book abounds with descriptions of the odd harvesting of seabirds, every part of which was used locally or exported to the mainland – their oil for heat, light and medicinal purposes, their feathers for mattresses, their carcasses for food. The St Kildans themselves even made primitive shoes out of the necks of gannets. The demise of the community was also intimately bound up with the birds: the economy collapsed when the oil was no longer in demand, and Maclean hypothesises – with some evidence – that it may have been an ancient pagan ritual, whereby the navels of new-born babies were anointed with fulmar oil, that led to a devastating infant-mortality rate in the late-nineteenth century, and the eventual depopulation of the island. The last St Kildans were evacuated for ever in 1930.

With its own communistic political system centred on the 'Mod', or parliament, which determined work according to each family's abilities, and divided up the resources according to their needs; its own literature and mythology (necessarily oral – the islanders were illiterate until the twentieth century); and its own unique subspecies of wren and mouse (Maclean even suggests that the St Kildan men were adapted for climbing with prehensile toes); the island was truly a world unto itself. Maclean doesn't suggest that St Kilda was a paradise – the life was harsh and uncompromising – nor does he cling to any illusions that its fate could have been avoided. None the less, he does paint a chilling and pathetic picture of the depredations that came with civilisation in the nineteenth century, particularly in the form of a virulent strain of Presbyterianism and boatload after boatload of gawping tourists.

What the St Kildan story, as told by Maclean, did for me was to reawaken my awe at the strangeness of our world. Here, on our very doorstep, was a veritable singularity of human society, an expression of the limitless potential of humans to accommodate with their environment and circumstances. With St Kilda as an ultimate outlier I began to reorient my conception of the British Isles; a winter spent living in Orkney completed this literal revolution. Viewed from the north, Edinburgh became an immense southern city, London a near-equatorial Babylon.

New Statesman, November 2000

32

Television review

Wanted: seven million viewers, willing to be marooned for one year in the main stream of the television schedules, and prepared to undertake the building up of a community of interest out of the raw materials of crass tabloid voyeurism. Even if these weren't its avowed intentions, why am I surprised there were so many takers for the BBC1 docusoap series *Castaway*? After all, most of us fancy ourselves as decent sorts, ready and able to muck in with the rest of the community, and well-equipped to withstand the isolation of anything up to an hour spent staring fixedly at a screen, while sustained only by a nugatory diet of chocolate Hobnobs and cups of tea.

Trumpeted in the broadsheet press by its meretricious producers – and gullible participants – as a landmark of television as social think-tank, the first series of *Castaway* reveals that the whole conceit is indeed a ghastly synecdoche of British society in the year 2000. After allegedly rigorous trials, thirty-six 'castaways' were to be set ashore on the Outer Hebridean island of Taransay to live there for a year. But the real aim of the project is to provide easy watching for couch potatoes, titillating material for the tabloids, and dosh for the producers, Lion Television. The Prospero of Taransay, producer/director Chris Kelly, is in the process of becoming truly prosperous off the back of this useless farrago – and all power to him, for he's only holding the crazy mirror of bad television up to the truly loathsome society we have become.

I'd like to believe that Kelly and his cohorts at Lion set out deliberately to select the most incompatible and ineffectual of those who volunteered for the project. After all, they managed to sign up a totally neurotic doctor, a bibulous bricklayer, and a vet's son who was clearly raised as a dog. Perhaps the whole selection process was rigorous only in so far as it aimed rigorously to provide the right mix of 'castaways' for a subsequent mix of farce, fighting and futility. But I fear this isn't the case. Rather – who are these twerps who queue up for such a bogus undertaking? Joe and Josephine Ordinary British Public, that's who. They want to 'find themselves', while experiencing nature, and learning to live in a small community – but only so long as they're paid a decent whack and have the whole experience broadcast to an appreciative audience of millions.

It's grotesque. You poltroons! Any of you could have the potentially positive dividends of the *Castaway* project merely by pitching up. Anyone with a marketable skill is welcome in the Western Isles, which have suffered progressive depopulation throughout the last century. For Christ's sake, there are men up there who are dying merely in order to extract some fish from the sea – and you lot ponce in with your television crews and helicopter support, expecting to 'find' yourselves in nature. About the most poetic justice that could be expected from the whole gig would be for the mainland of Britain to be destroyed in some holocaust during the next year, leaving the Taransay 'castaways' to truly fend for themselves.

If you want to understand the sad comment that *Castaway* makes on our currently woeful level of commonality, it's that the presence of the television company – with their outlier hacks, snappers and assorted supernumeraries – has actually fomented a minor economic boom on the Isle of Lewis. The locals are getting a longed-for influx of hard cash. A second tourist officer is being appointed for this year, because of the anticipated demand that beautiful television pictures of the islands are expected to generate. Anyone listening there in the Government? Maybe this is the longed-for diversification that will solve our problem of British rural decline – simply send internal pilgrimages of urbanites into rural areas to resettle them with a view to selling the entire bloody nation as a television spectacle. Hell, as it stands the balance of payments is entirely held up – apart from arms sales – by our export of media services to the rest of the world. This Britain-as-*faux*-rural-community docusoap is only the next logical step.

If there were another reason – any reason – for the presence of the 'castaways' on Taransay, then the project would have some justification. I wouldn't care if they were building a weather station, or monitoring the island's deer herd, or producing a study of the environment, or even worshipping the bloody wind god, as long as there were a point to this 'community' beyond ego and television. Honestly, to hear this lot witter on about the difficulties of fending for themselves when they have fortnightly boatloads of supplies shipped in, booze and fags, livestock supplied, a satellite phone, and a budget for toshing the place up – well, it's a wonder civilisation ever got going in the first place.

These 'castaways' would've done well to have examined the history and prehistory of the Western Isles and noted that not only were there fully functioning communities there thousands of years ago, but also they managed, during their leisure time, to raise some of the most incredible megaliths ever seen. I wonder how many of the 'castaways' know anything of the history of St Kilda, the next island out in the Atlantic beyond the Outer Hebrides? This scrap of land supported a fully functioning community with its own dialect, poetry, building vernacular and spirituality for hundreds of years in almost total isolation. Of course, as contemporary sixteenth-century commentators noted, the St Kildans spoke in unison on those rare occasions when they visited the Laird of Lewis to pay their tithe. It wasn't until the island was finally evacuated in the thirties that any of them dreamed of selling their story to the tabloids.

If the *Castaway* programmes prove anything it's what we already know – that democracy was a late addition to human social organisation, not a precondition. It's once you've got the slaves and the women firmly integrated at the bottom of the heap that you've time to strut around the agora discoursing with Socrates. But this lot want it all and want it right away – how typical of our fetishistic society in which even peace of mind and pantheism are marketable commodities.

As for whether or not it makes good television, the answer must be that the most exploited person on Taransay is Tanya Cheadle, the twenty-six-year-old resident camerawoman. While she works hard to produce a reasonable record of what's going on, her efforts are completely traduced by the post-production. Soupy music is added, as is an illiterate and facile commentary. The programme-makers concentrate on such weighty issues as when and how the maverick brickie, Ray Bowyer, will sell his story to the tabloids (something anyone who reads the tabloids knows about already), a beard-growing competition, and who among the singles is going to get laid first.

Oh – and I almost forgot the puppies. Ah! The sweet ickle puppies. I'm living in a nation where seven million people want to watch a multimillion-pound televised social experiment to see who gets custody of a collie puppy. The sooner I'm marooned on an island the better – and all I want to take with me is my bile.

Independent on Sunday, April 2000

33

Restaurant review: The Magpie Room at St James' Park,
Newcastle upon Tyne

'Cheese football is coming home!' cried the small band of die-hard fanatics as I strode into the arrivals lounge of Newcastle International Airport. I patted a few bat-eared small boys on the head and signed the proffered menus and credit-card stubs. The press pressed forward: 'Mr Self, is it true that you intend to make the North East the centre for your new Cheese Football Fantasy League?' asked a battle-scarred old restaurant reviewer from the *Evening Chronicle.* 'That's one hundred per cent correct,' I snapped, 'and I'm no carpetbagger, picking up a vast amount of money for a couple of reviews and then shamelessly transferring my loyalty elsewhere. I intend to buy a house and move my family up here. Tyneside has always been close to my heart, ever since that September night in 1984 when I got shamelessly pissed on vodka at the Akbar Tandoori in Jesmond . . .'

In truth the similarities between me and Kenny Dalglish are rather more compelling than most people realise. All right, conventional football isn't exactly my speed. Throughout last year's European Championships I resisted all those exhortations to eat, sleep, drink and live football, although I did manage to smoke some on a couple of occasions. But like Dalglish I'm a spirited fighter with a history of being capped for my country (two porcelain and one gold), and I too have witnessed some of the most horrific disasters to occur in my professional field. I refer, of course, to the mass cafetière scalding at Just Lettuce in 1987, when Pru Leith and Fay Maschler had to be moved to a new setting.

Like Dalglish I take my status as a role model for the young seriously. This week I've been appalled by the comments of Brian Harvey, the lead singer of East 17, on ecstasy. Whatever this misguided young man thinks, it's a known fact that taking this drug can make you grow a goatee. Why, Harvey himself sports such an insidious chin garnish – is any more proof required? And this survey on alcopops; apparently 25 per cent of the eleven- to eighteen-year-olds questioned thought these beverages were purpose-designed for them. What's wrong with a whisky sour or a dry martini? They were good enough for me in my teens.

But it wasn't only cheese footballs that rolled me northwards this week. While Dalglish was winning the hearts and minds of fans, warming up with the players and canoodling with United supremo Sir John Hall, I was seeing whether or not I'd be able to push another Newcastle institution to the top of the league.

The Magpie Room at St James' (and don't ask me about the free-floating apostrophe – it's the way they spell it, not me) Park is one among a small number of football-stadium restaurants that are beginning to figure in gourmet guides. These eateries are determined to prove that their cuisine is the real thing, no mere Astro surf and turf. Armed only with a copy of *Understanding Soccer Tactics* by Konrad Lorenz (one of the only Nobel laureates to write convincingly on the subject), I headed for the ground, determined to wipe the dish clean.

It's just as well that the staff at the Magpie Room are so confident about their cooking, because unless you're the chief executive of Renault UK, or some similar corporate trouser press, you won't actually have the opportunity to witness the Magpies from their eponymous diner. The whole gaff is booked out for the season as a hospitality suite. The foot soldiers of the Toon Army can only munch on days when there aren't matches. Mind you, the manageress – a charming, hyperactive person in a pink jacket of uncommon tuftiness – was emphatic that they were 'very understanding' about the situation. I'm not surprised, as one of the waiters also told me that fans had been outside all day, posing for photographs in front of the new manager's designated parking-space. Such obsessional hero-worship is seldom seen in the world of restaurants, although I once queued all night to use a toilet stall that had been graced by Anton Mosimann.

The Magpie Room occupies the top right-hand corner of the stadium – as you look from the away goal. From the home end, on the other hand, you have a superb view of a McDonald's advert. Personally, I would find this a great incentive to score as I've always wanted to give the fast-food chain a big kick up its arches.

To reach the restaurant you ascend via the kind of lift exhibitionists have sex in, its glass wall providing you with a view first of bricks and then of the Newcastle Breweries complex, complete with achingly beautiful, blue five-pointed star. I have spent much of the past year staring at the New-castle skyline tucked neatly inside the star on the Newcastle Brown Ale bottle; now was my chance to stare at the bottle from inside the view.

When the lift door rolled back I entered a space that can only be described – in terms of Euclidean geometry – as curved. The walls curved, the floor curved, even the heavy green pelmets above the heavy green curtains were curved. Saving the fact that no one in the place was supine in a life-support sarcophagus, it rather reminded me of the Saturn probe in *2001*.

The manic manageress led me out through sliding doors on to the stand, and for a few minutes I savoured the immensity of the space. From where I was, someone standing on the opposite terraces would appear Nick Hornby-size. The floodlights were on and great swirls of mist were roiling overhead, as if the stadium were some enormous cauldron brewing up a fetid stock of sweat and tears, victory and defeat.

I was placed in the waiting area for a while where I had a two-two formation of Dalwhinnie whiskies. I perused the menu. It was essentially defensive with the emphasis on solid meat and fish dishes. Well, I mean to say, you can't imagine these tough Tynesiders tucking into a soufflé. The Toon Army would hardly march on a quiche. They were in evidence, these hard men, sitting in neatly pressed, short-sleeved shirts, the muscle bulging on the backs of their necks, and the glasses of heavy bulging in their fists. While I sipped my Scotch I heard one of them remark solemnly, 'Of course, the real problem is the back four . . .'

After consulting Lorenz I decided on the roulade of venison and chicken served on a tossed salad with a split-mustard dressing to front up, and for midfield the fillet steak with Orkney oysters. As for the back four, the obvious choice was banana toffee crumble with fruits-of-the-forest ice cream. And for the bevvy? Well, for such a home-coming it had to be champagne.

I ate in splendid isolation apart from the waiters coming by to take the piss – in a charming way – out of me for supporting Arsenal. My roulade was the rolliest roulade I've ever had in my life: tight little snails of dark and light meat studded atop a neat mound of lettuce. As for my steak, it was the size of one of my fellow-diners' fists, although I doubt they'd be as tender in the mouth. The Orkney oysters thickened the plot delightfully. So taken was I by the Magpie Room that I even ate all my dessert, despite its aggressively *nouveau* aspect – the chef had made free with his *jus*.

The bill came to fifty quid all in – not bad, considering the alcopop. Despite the fact that the refurbishment of St James' has only just been completed, Sir John has plans for a bigger stadium for the Magpies. During his incumbency Kevin Keegan boosted attendances from fifteen to thirty-five thousand; I can only hope that Kenny Dalglish manages to do the same – for the restaurant.

I wandered off into the night intent on emulating the activities of my favourite Tynesider hero – not Dalglish, but *Viz* magazine's the Brown Bottle. Like this mythical superhero, I ended my evening by entering a phone booth, drinking ten pints of Brown Ale, then emerging twenty minutes later with my underpants on over my trousers.

Observer, January 1997

34

Restaurant review: Coast, 26B Albemarle Street, London W1

My heart beat like a drum machine as the cab sped along the Westway. I was out on the town for the evening, meeting my friend John at the Sealink Club for a cocktail and then going to Coast, the new restaurant, the one on everyone's lips: 'Coast-Coast-Coast-Coast . . .' they were all murmuring. I began to murmur it in sympathy: 'Coast-Coast-Coast-Coast . . .' I synchronised my murmuring with my cardiac timpani.

'Wozzatyousay?' asked the cabbie.

'Oh nothing, just murmuring aloud . . . Coast-Coast-Coast-Coast . . .'

Charles Fontaine, chef, boulevardier, *homme sensuel*, was propping up the bar at the Sealink Club. 'I tell you what I done, Will.' He stared at me, a great, pink Minotaur of a man. 'I buy a piece of shit from an art gallery.'

'Is it good?' I asked.

Charles then gave a shrug of such extreme Gallic ataraxy that it included within it an entire compendium, a reprise of some tens of thousands of other shrugs. 'It's shit,' he concluded.

John showed up and we headed for 'Coast-Coast-Coast . . .' This hippermost venue turned out to be in Albemarle Street – not exactly a snappy strand at the best of times. One of those severe, dark streets leading north from Piccadilly, it has a workaday atmosphere primarily of heavy veneer, either for sale or to rent.

Coast has slid into this pool of urbanity without creating so much as a ripple. Why, from less than five yards away we didn't know the restaurant was there, because its huge, plate-glass façade darkly reflects the pillars of the institutional building across the way. There's that, and there are also the subtly engraved, corporate 'C's on the window imparting the impression that you are entering the sales office of an interplanetary travel company.

We rang a buzzer to one side, and a crack opened in the sky as a section of glass some 10ft by 20ft whoozed open. Inside, two tunicked space cadets greeted us from behind a black console. We were led back to the bar area. My eyes took in the place with a series of rapid saccades. Yea, truly, in a town where Modernist restaurant interiors seem to be *de rigueur*, Coast was achieving new heights of austerity. A great shoebox of a room housing some 120 covers was unadorned except for assorted, odd nodules protruding from wall and ceiling, some serving as light fitments, others merely pretending to. The nodule effect reminded me of nothing so much as those scenes in *Repulsion* where Catherine Deneuve hallucinates arms plunging out of the walls of her flat.

Most of the seating was fairly straightforward – round tables, chairs with a pre-school air – but there were also a few circular extrusions of banquette wholly encapsulating both table and diners. The floor was tan parquet; elsewhere umbers and greys predominated. The atmosphere was incredibly muted given that the place was packed with more suits than C&A. I couldn't figure it out; there was no obvious aural governor in the place, unlike that other great chomping warehouse the River Café, where what look like giant cheese-graters have been nailed to the ceiling in order – the sous-chef informed me – to absorb the diners' loquacity.

The wine rack behind the bar at Coast was so big that it looked capable of interplanetary travel all by itself: 'Roger, Houston, I have the Coast wine rack locked on beam, prepare for splash down, T minus 20 and counting . . .'

The barman handed me a vodka martini in a glass the size of an ornamental pond. I didn't know whether to drink the thing or dive in. And it was cold, this martini, dreadfully cold; I could feel my finger-tips beginning to lose all sensation. Cold, cold, so cold, and the great illimitable space we were in, the wastes of white and beige . . . 'I'm just going out for a short walk,' I muttered in John's direction. 'I may be some time . . .'

'Not so fast!' he snapped at me. 'Haven't you taken this place in? Look at it!' His eyes were starting in his head; his jaw was working. John used to be a Marxist at college. 'This gaff is so bland, so corporate, and these people – they've got no class. It's sickening.'

I could see his point. The aesthetic of Coast is as far removed from any of the sensuality of eating as it's possible to imagine. My initial impressions had been correct: this wasn't a restaurant, it was something new, something different, a food terminal for the twenty-first century.

A servitor arrived to conduct us to our table. Then another appeared at the table and did the napkins; a third happened by with the menus; and then a fourth with the wine list. Clearly Coast's corporate status implied a nit-picking division of labour. I wouldn't have been surprised if another waiter had popped up at this point, opened an attaché case, booted up his portable and offered to sell me a personal equity plan.

We ordered a bottle of Hermitage Bernard Fourie '89. It arrived at a fairly leisurely pace (presumably one waiter removed it from the rack, a second stood it upright, a third lifted it, etc., etc.). The menu was heavy on those double adjectival formulations that could give a stoic an aneurysm. The *pan-fried* scallops were bedded down on *soft* noodles; the *Oriental grilled* salmon came with 'Asian' greens (which are presumably what Asian mums feed to Asian babies).

I chose the Chinese beef broth with herb dumplings. John ceased his psychic metastasis just long enough to tussle with the head waiter (a foppish fellow desperately in need of the Goatee Support Group) over some seaweed. 'It has two distinct flavours,' claimed the tufted one, 'one of which is like asparagus . . .' 'Charred parsley is more like it!' John snapped back, the veins on his forehead writhing like anacondas.

In truth, as any fool knows, seaweed looks and tastes like the pubic hair of a Rhinemaiden, hence the scene in *Der Ring des Nibelungen* where the wily Wotan steals the gold Ladyshave of Alberich.

My broth was distinctly icky. The stock had a dishwater hue and texture, the dumplings were on the turgid side. John went down on his seaweed. I began to *feel* distinctly icky.

I felt that if we sat any longer in Coast truly unpleasant things would begin to happen. I might get sucked into the corporate atmosphere and find myself performing some mindless but essential role in the quality-control department, like looking up adjectival synonyms for tomorrow's menu. I peered at John. Was it a trick of the light or was he really beginning to grow a double-breasted suit jacket over his pullover?

The bill arrived at the same time as the main-course dishes. I'm not saying it was a big bill, but I've seen similar figures cited as salaries for middle management. John's calf's liver was superb but there was no

English mustard to be found on the entire littoral. My pigeon fluttered quickly into the Trafalgar Square of my stomach. John and I hit Albemarle Street at a brisk trot. We didn't really ease off until we were back in the Sealink Club. Charles Fontaine was still at the bar. 'You know what you should do with your artwork, Charles?' I said.

'No.' He did the shrug. 'What?'

'Take it down to Coast – they could do with some stuff on their walls.'

Observer, March 1996

35

The minute I pulled the car off the road, through the gates and on to the drive, I knew that I'd made a profound mistake. The sign said 'Shrublands Hall Health Clinic'. I turned to my wife: '*Clinic* – what the hell can that mean?'

'Well, I suppose it means it's a clinic.'

'But I thought it was a health *farm*.'

'Farm – clinic, what difference can it make?'

A lot is the answer. We were late on arriving – the car journey from central London to just north of Ipswich had taken a rear-end–numbing four hours – and were heavily expected. After parking the car in front of the ornate Palladian stately home that is Shrublands Hall, we were met in reception by a Sister Green, who was in full 'Carry On' regalia: 'You're due to see me right away, and then the doctor, and then Lady de Saumarez will see you, and then we have some treatments arranged for you this evening –'

'Treatments?! Whaddya mean treatments?'

'Well, there's a sauna and massage for you, and a facial for your wife –'

'What about something to eat? We've been driving for hours and we have to eat – my wife is breast-feeding, as you can see.' She certainly ought to have been able to see, for Ivan, aged three months, was wriggling frantically in his mother's arms, hunting around for an inexistent nipple.

'There'll be a light supper for you later – broth and some fruit.'

'That's not going to be enough for us – as you can see we're both *under-* rather than overweight. Are you going to be able to feed us up a bit here?' Sister Green wasn't certain that they could – although she herself had an impressive embonpoint.

The truth is that I'm obscurely attached to my own bad health practices: the unrecommended one hundred units of alcohol a week, the Formula One-sponsored gaspers, the tranches of red meat. Naturally I take little exercise – just the occasional jog to the ashtray – and I eschew rest and relaxation in favour of insomnia and tension. However, somehow it works. I'm not often ill, and I retain a resolutely sylph-like form. I thought I might be able to handle – for a couple of days – changing the habits of habit, as long as it was in a tolerant and non-judgemental environment. But all this talk of doctors and examinations made me want to scream.

We had a brief respite while we went and found our quarters. They'd decided to put us up in the 'Russian Lodge', an octagonal hut two hundred yards down the drive. This was probably wise – keep the journalistic contagion at a safe distance. The Lodge was also the place where guests with pets stay; and Shrublands serves the kind of class within which pets and babies are perceived as essentially the same kind of animal. Actually, after a night in the Lodge Ivan *did* look a bit like a pet, because the bed was full of black Labrador hair which stuck to his skin in an absolutely charming fashion.

Sister Green wanted to take an exhaustive medical history from me; I was unwilling. She wasn't to know it, but such were the peccadilloes of my youth that an exhaustive medical history would take about two hours to convey, and would include mention of more pharmaceutical compounds than an edition of the *British National Formulary*. I admitted to depression and allowed her to take my blood pressure, which surprised her by being absolutely fine.

Then there was the interview with the formidable proprietress of Shrublands Hall, Lady de Saumarez. Every 'guest' at Shrublands is inter-viewed by Lady de Saumarez; she is, she assured me, good at 'listening'. In truth this is where the snob element really tells – and this must be why people come to Shrublands: it's one part medical bogusness to one of old-fashioned class-consciousness. Yes, Tony and Peter may run the Government, and Liz may sit on the throne, but at the Clinic hierarchy is still the order of the day.

Lady de S was ineffably fragrant – a wafting old bit of posh spice, who was quite clearly used to being obeyed in matters of 'health', and deferred to by her 'inferiors'. Her office featured a small writing desk, a padded door, bottles of Ashbourne mineral water and an examination couch. She started off with the spiel about the evening treatments – I broke in, 'Look at the size of me! I haven't eaten today! I need more than broth – I need to eat! And now!' She steepled her fingers and looked at me with piercing, oik-seeking eyes: 'Are you prepared to undergo our treatment programme, Mr Self?'

We negotiated a compromise: no laying on of hands, no freaky medical consultations, but I would be open minded and fair; I would interview the staff and try to gain a balanced impression of the place. I was, however, negotiating in bad faith. I already hated Shrublands Hall, and was having real difficulty in not leaving forthwith. When I pushed the point about needing a decent meal, Lady de S eventually threw up her be-ringed hands and sighed, 'Well, I suppose you'd better go down to the pub.' Which was exactly what we did, after a desultory interview with one of the Clinic's 'specialist' doctors. (His speciality turned out to be obstetrics and gynaecology – hardly that relevant.)

The Sorrel Horse was a nice old country pub, heavy on beams and horse brasses. We slaked our thirst on Burton Ale and insulated our cavities with cottage pie and went to bed cursing our new, healthy lifestyle.

The phone rang at eight sharp the following morning – they were ready for me in the treatment suite. A nice, middle-aged man called Peter, clad in clinical white trousers and singlet, put me in the Turkish bath for fifteen minutes. After I'd had a good sweat, he ushered me into the plunge bath, and then, when I was truly chilled, dried my back and the backs of my legs. He was obviously used to working with guests who were unable to comfortably access the further reaches of their own bodies.

Then it was time for the underwater massage. Peter coaxed me into a tiled sarcophagus and proceeded to pummel my limbs with a high-powered hose. I suppose the sensation felt as agreeably unpleasant as it was meant to, but far more exciting was the moment when, while running the jet of water up my inner thigh, Peter gently cupped my testicles in his hand and said in a firm voice, 'I'll protect you.' Well, I mean to say, it's not every day you get such a forthrightly comforting offer. I felt tempted to ask him if he'd file my tax return for me and set me up in a small flat in Mayfair while he was at it.

But there was no time – I had to have 'the Blitz'. This consisted of my standing in a tiled cubicle while Peter directed two jets of ice-cold water at my back. This was all well and good, although this particular Londoner wasn't exactly burning to begin with.

Next it was on to the 'complete seaweed bath'. It was here that *I* began to suspect that Lady de S hadn't been negotiating in good faith. For, while all the other staff who attended to me were resolutely homely, Georgina, who was charged with rubbing seaweed gunk all over my naked body, was a dark-haired, olive-skinned beauty of around twenty-five. For her I even modelled a pair of paper pants!

In truth there was nothing in the least erotic about this experience. I don't see how there could be – unless you had a mermaid fetish – so pungent was the seaweed smell. It was pleasant enough being gunked, and then lying wrapped up in a protective covering while the whole messery was heated from below, but I can't honestly imagine it was doing me any good. Then Georgina did the same for my face – right down to two slices of cucumber over the eyes. And then it was back for another tête-à-tête with the Chatelaine.

We got on a little better this time. She told me how she had set up Shrublands thirty-one years ago, when the house became too expensive to maintain privately. It's very much a family business, with one of her twin sons, Eric, running the estate farm. Lady de S was eloquent about the benefits of the Shrublands regime, and sharp when I suggested that the place was chiefly known for its posher clientele: 'We get everybody here!' she trilled. 'From British royalty to barmaids.'

An hour later, having baled out from another broth lunch, I encountered the barmaid in question, Bridget Smith, licensee of the aforementioned Sorrel Horse. 'I hope you're not going to take the piss out of Shrublands,' she adjured me; 'I've stayed there and I had a great time. Everyone's equal there, everyone wears a dressing gown so you don't know whether they're posh or not.' I didn't like to point out to her that by the same token it means you don't know who *isn't* posh – presumably a great source of comfort to the *arriviste* hypochondriac.

I'm afraid, nice as she was, I took Bridget Smith's pro-Shrublands line with a pinch of salt. If you're running a pub hard against a two-thousand-acre privately-owned estate, it would ill behove you to slag off the owners. There was that, and there was also the fact that several of the estate staff were actually in the bar while we were talking.

But anyway, who am I to criticise the wealthy, the overweight and the hypochondriacal for wanting to pay for self-control rather than exercise it themselves? And who am I to attack people for wanting a few of the appurtenances of grand living while they sip their prune juice? And those appurtenances are quite something: marvellous big rooms with Adam ceilings, and one of the finest landscaped gardens in the country. Surely – and this is a figure of speech that Lady de S would appreciate –

it's a case of horses for courses? She had told me that around 70 per cent of her guests return, most regularly. Some even ensure that they come at the same time each year, so as to be with their pals. How cosy.

When I got home I called a wealthy, occasionally overweight, and slightly hypochondriacal person who I knew had visited Shrublands some years ago. I knew this because he is my brother, and the staff had kept insistently confusing us. I hoped that he would temper the acerbity of my vision. 'So, Shrublands, what did you think of the place?' There was a snort of laughter from the other end of the line: 'Killingly funny! The guy who massaged me was the old gamekeeper. I hated and loathed the whole thing – had to retreat to the village and get a stash of cheese and biscuits to keep in my room. The place was chock-full of either old nobs or the desperately *nouveau*. One old thing turned up with two dozen bottles of champagne in milk crates. I couldn't stand it – cut out after three days.'

So, there you have it, neither of the Self brothers will ever be welcome again at this redoubt of healthy feudalism. I'm not too upset about it – although I wouldn't have minded another pint at the Sorrel Horse.

The Times, December 1997

36

I well remember my interviews at Oxford University in 1979. I'd applied to three colleges, Balliol, Keble and Exeter. At Balliol, a gloomy pile of largely Victorian neo-Gothic, a smart, laconic American political scientist demolished my feeble edifice of ideology with a few well-placed dialectical charges in a matter of seconds. I knew at the time that my chance of a place was shot to pieces.

At Keble, an even gloomier neo-Gothic monstrosity, I was ushered into a crepuscular chamber where six dons languished in attitudes of seemingly terminal ennui. However, there was nothing languorous about the inquisition that followed. 'Which would you prefer to kill,' snapped a don, 'a human baby or an adult dolphin?' I hesitated for a few instants. 'Come on!' he barked. 'Which?!' I felt certain that if I demurred any longer a door would swing open, the putative victims would be wheeled in on trolleys, and I'd be handed a gun. Once more, I knew I wouldn't get a place.

Towards the end of the day I entered the back quad of Exeter, a dinky little college built from honeyed stone. Up a vertiginous staircase I was ushered into a cosy room, where a fire glowed in a grate. 'Do come in,' said a plump little don; 'I'm Lord Crowther-Hunt – and this is Mr Eltis.' Eltis wafted a hand from a wing armchair; he was, I knew, one of the mavens of the monetarist economics that dominated Thatcherite policy. As for Crowther-Hunt, he was a Labour peer and a political scientist. 'Sherry?' he asked rhetorically. We sipped our sherry and chatted about absolutely nothing of consequence for a few minutes. I felt my anxieties fade away, and it was absolutely no surprise to me when, as I headed for the door, Lord Crowther-Hunt said, 'Well, we'll look forward to seeing you next September then.' I was in.

When I came to analyse the reasons for my casual admission to these hallowed portals – and analyse them I did, for it seemed a most outrageous fluke – I had plenty of factors to batten on to, both positive and negative. There was I, a comprehensive-school student, already a high-achiever in delinquency, being welcomed with open arms. I must've written damn good entrance papers, or – and I shuddered to contemplate this – it was because of Dad. My father was, after all, a professor at the London School of Economics, personally known to all these dons. Could it be that I was an epigone of nepotism?

The truth is, I'm sure, that all of these factors played a part. And that's why the current attack by Gordon Brown on selection procedures at Oxford University is such a load of arrant rubbish. No matter that it's been accurately rebutted by the President of Magdalen (the college the Tyneside state-school female applicant was rejected by); the fact remains that Oxford is a university that very effectively turns the scions of provincial, lower-middle-class families on the make into future prime ministers (step forward T. Blair, M. Thatcher, and putatively W. Hague). It's absurd to castigate an élitist institution for aiming to produce élites. Apparently our pseudo-posh Prime Minister fully endorses Mr Brown's remarks; it's so easy to dispense with a privilege that you yourself have already enjoyed, isn't that so, Tony? No, Prime Minister, if this is the best attack on vested interests that you can come up with, I suggest that you take that paternity leave after all – and make it permanent.

Today, BBC Radio 4, May 2000

37

The Art of Sam Taylor-Wood Considered in Respect of the A3 Guildford Bypass, Summer 1996

Dylan [Thomas] talked copiously, then stopped.
'Somebody's boring me,' he said, 'I think it's me.'
Rayner Heppenstall, *Four Absentees* (1960)

The vinyl of the steering wheel clammy, buttock-like beneath his sweating hands. The asphalt of the road scintillating like frying bread. To the left a Microhard compound of irregular mirrored rhomboids, reflecting one another. In the stationary cars to the left of the carriageway they were playing middle-of-the-road music on their sound systems. In the stationary cars to the right of the carriageway they were playing middle-of-the-road music on their sound systems. In the central lane they were playing middle-of-the-road music on their sound systems. The grass on the central reservation was painful, viridian. He looked about at the three lanes of jammed traffic. He looked at Guildford on its hill. Surprising to see the lineaments of medievalism: castle and cathedral, university and market, drawn with red bricks and mortared crenellations. He looked at the Microhard compound and thought of the lives of the people who worked there. Did they still find the kidney-shaped lake, with its *faux* Japanese island, diverting? Did they still find anything diverting?

He knew there might be blue butterflies dancing amongst the grasses and weeds on the central reservation, and on the embankments of the road, beyond the endless fenders. He had heard floral friends proclaim that the median strips of the English roadways were paradoxical havens of unusual plants; but squinting at the exhaustive shading that drew the bottom halves of the cars, the road itself and the surrounding territory into a tight crosshatching, he doubted it.

And then gave up doubting it. Neither thesis nor antithesis was worthy of standing into being. Would the traffic ever flow again? Or would they remain thus: capsuled by a two-millimetre-thick layer of steel, artfully bent and shaped so as to resemble a car?

He turned to his companion. 'We're in Hell,' he said.

'Oh come on . . . it's just a traffic jam,' she replied artlessly.

'No, I mean it, we're in Hell. This *is* Hell, this . . . the Guildford bypass. We've died and gone to Hell. I know this with a deep certainty.'

She regarded him sceptically and asked, 'Do you know how we died? Was it in an accident on the way from London, or did we never leave town at all?'

'That I cannot say.'

'Cannot say – or do not wish to. Come on . . . it's you who're coming over all fucking omniscient.' There was appropriate bitterness in her tone.

'No, not omniscient. For example, I don't know if this is just our hell, or if it belongs to all these others as well –' he removed his hands from the steering wheel, each making a tangible 'flotch' of unsuction, in order to gesture; but as soon as he did so the car formation broke up a little. He grabbed the wheel once more and eased the car forward a few metres, then joined the re-formed unit. 'See! Hell. I bet if you attempt to get out of the car the traffic starts to move, but if you remain in the car it stays jammed.'

'Yeah!' She undid her seatbelt, opened the door on her side of the car, and swung both feet out. They were bare. 'Ow! This is hot.'

'Get back inside!' This he nearly barked. 'We're rolling.' They rolled another few metres.

'We're in Hell,' he said presently. 'Whatever we do we can't die – that's what's going to happen to us.'

'What?' Her eyes weren't laughing.

'Soon, when I've managed to convince you that this is the case, that we really have died and gone to Hell – and it won't take long: our inability to advance in relation to Guildford, and the sun's failure to traverse the sky, will pulverise your scepticism – we will drive hard into the car in front, try and impale ourselves on the steering column, or shred ourselves through the windscreen. But if we do so we'll merely find ourselves back here. Buckled in once more. The car intact. Our failure to find oblivion will be our particular terror. We will become poets of suicide. Perhaps for some years. Experiencing more and more ingenious forms of death – using our limited equipment. Death by anti-freeze. Death by windshield wiper. Death by eating car mats. Death from rubbing air freshener into exposed wounds. Perhaps combined with this, or during some later, later, later era, we will be driven into all kinds of bizarre experimentation in order to ward off – if only for a second – the numbing tentacles of oblivion that will descend upon us. We will, of course, commit unspeakable acts of brutality against each other; and undoubtedly we shall explore the uttermost extremities of sexual gratification. My love, nothing will compare to the titivations and excitations that we will produce in each other. Nothing, save the same titivations and excitations when – chillingly – we find ourselves experiencing them once more. We may attempt to enrich the illimitable dullness with the divine spark that remains, despite everything that has gone before, buried within us. During these aeons we shall tell each other everything we have ever done, said, or felt; impart the minutest and most ineffable characteristics of our subjectivities, with all the consummate eloquence that an eternity can allow you to acquire. Possibly this more humane approach to Hell will produce some happy results. Ironically – and over millennia the potential for irony is consummately vast – we may find ourselves in a less cerebral state. Then for centuries we could work at adapting the furnishings of the car with as much artistry as we can manage – given the limited materials at our disposal – so as to make it resemble the cockpit of a fighter plane, the bridge of a nuclear submarine, or the control centre of an alien spacecraft, or indeed some vehicle heretofore unimaginable. Then, when we have tired once more of our hands, and our teeth and our tits, no doubt we will recapitulate the vast storehouse of knowledge that our stretched, solitary existence has brought forth in us. They say that those who are marooned on desert islands for years find themselves able to remember all the books they have ever read, verbatim. Well, that will be nothing compared with the lost culture we will recover. Every piece of music that either of us has ever heard will come back, incontinently, eventually. And then manageably, in a controlled fashion, so that we will be able to subject it to scholarly analysis. The same will be true of every film we have ever seen. Every play or exhibition we have ever attended, and every building we have seen, ancient monument we have scaled, city we have strolled around. Right here in the car we shall assemble a treasure house of exegesis, that for sheer duration and ramification will make the Talmud or the Upanishads look like ad flyers. But not even that will save us. For, over the years, we will have come to dislike each other with a stupendous, awesome thoroughness. In milliseconds of communication between us myriad familiarities will be enjoined; and the contempt will match them, point for point. Paradoxically this hatred will be peculiarly painless, and with something like joy we will re-enter the era of attempted suicides. I will put the car in gear' – he put the car in gear – 'and once again drive hard into the car in front, try and impale us on the steering column, or shred us through the windscreen . . .' He drove the car a few metres forward, pulled up again, applied the handbrake, put the shift in neutral, turned to her and smiled. He squeezed her thigh.

She sat and looked at him, and at last agreed. She was, quite clearly, in Hell.

Sam Taylor-Wood exhibition catalogue, September 1997

38

Christmas isn't something I like at all. I'm not going to go through all that boo-hoo stuff again, but Tolstoy was right when he wrote that every unhappy family is unhappy in its own way. My family, when I was a child, specialised in unhappy Christmases. By the time I was nineteen I had seen Christmases disrupted by violence, acrimony, infidelity and mean-spiritedness – often all at the same time. Christmas dinners were frigid affairs, where everyone spent minutes examining the tines of their forks, just in case another family member made a lunge.

That's why I decided to spend the Christmas of 1980, my nineteenth, on my own. In fairness to the other members of my long-since exploded family, I was as bad as they were. On this particular Christmas they'd gone as far as possible towards emphasising this, by all leaving the country. My father was living in Australia – where he resides to this day. My mother had decided to go Spain for the winter and was living in Altea, on the Costa Blanca, where she found herself much exercised by a mouse phobia. I have no idea where my brother was.

The only possible haven I had for Christmas was my then girlfriend's family. Trouble was, they were too happy for my tastes. There would be good cheer, children, elderly relatives, parlour games, all of the crap I felt I couldn't stand to have around me, because, of course, I'd been denied it.

She put a lot of pressure on me to join them. On the day itself, they would be driving down from London to Cheltenham, where a grandmother lived. They could easily stop off in Oxford and pick me up – wouldn't I join them? No. I wouldn't. Instead I dedicated myself to a decadent, solitary Christmas. I resolved to take to my bed for the duration of the holiday. I would be entertained by my four-inch black-and-white television – a must for watching historical epics – and by my multicoloured drug collection. I also had one of the greatest novellas ever written – *Solaris* by Stanislaw Lem – to read. How could I possibly be unhappy?

Naturally I was miserable. At that time I lived in a shared house with five other students in a district of north Oxford called Jericho. Frankly, I wouldn't have minded if the walls of this gaff had been trumpeted down. It was an austere, warped, Victorian pile; and my room had the proportions – and the amenities – of a wind tunnel. My fellow lodgers were all the kind of vegetarians who eat vast amounts of aubergine and mushrooms. This is because what they all, unconsciously, really wanted to be doing was slavering over some juicy flesh. I had long since factored myself out of the catering equation and had taken to eating – when I did eat – exclusively the fastest of food. The result of this was that I'd developed a severe allergy to monosodium glutamate. Eat any of this noxious crap and I'd find myself wringing sweat out of the duvet in the small hours.

For my solo Christmas dinner I had, with predictable, stoned insouciance, bought a boil-in-the-bag curry that was – I realised with the hot gloop on the plate – absolutely chock-full of MSG. I remember with a horrific acuity how I felt scraping this muck into the bin. It was a cold winter; in a few weeks' time the Russians would use the cold to ease their occupation of Poland, as they repressed Solidarity. Standing in that kitchen, naked, stoned, miserable, I was in solidarity with no one. The Russians should have invaded me.

Then there was a knock at the door. It was my girlfriend, together with her parents and siblings. I wish I could tell you that I pulled myself together, got dressed and accompanied them to Cheltenham for an afternoon of good, warm cheer, but I can't. I'm not like that. Instead, after twenty awkward minutes of tea, I packed them off and retired to the damp pile of mattresses I laughably referred to as my bed.

And that was my most memorable Christmas. Most memorable, because with only a little backsliding when it's absolutely unavoidable, I've managed to ignore Christmas ever since. And now, I can say with some satisfaction, I've abandoned it altogether.

Elle, December 1997

39

Restaurant review: Una Restaurant Bar, 10 Russell Gardens, London W14

Years ago I formulated an axiom concerning the search for the right restaurant. You know those purposeless, circular discussions in which eatery after eatery is evoked and described only to be discarded. More often than not, the place initially proposed is the one you end up going to, after a lengthy tour of the bleak horizon. My axiom is as follows: the more you deliberate over where you're going to eat, the more you eliminate hunger itself. The recapitulation of the characteristics of so many different restaurants provokes a sensation of queasiness, biliousness and psychic indigestion.

All of this occurred to me the other night as we found ourselves tooling around the Olympia region of west London with dinner in mind. Should we stop off at the Iranian joint, located – allegedly – in a Portakabin off Russell Road? (No. We couldn't find it.) Or perhaps we could hazard Cibo, an up-market Italian which is allegedly Bryan Ferry's favourite snack bar? (No. They didn't have a table available.)

We had, unfortunately, lost our reservation at Le Cirque, the bizarre new spot located two storeys underneath Oxford Circus, so there seemed nothing for it but to undertake that most potentially disastrous of gastronomic risks: pot luck.

Opposite Cibo was a joint called Una. Whether this was because it was the only one of its kind, or because the proprietor has a fixation on the actress Uma Thurman but can't spell, we couldn't divine. From the outside it was unprepossessing in the extreme – heavy on the plate glass, the varnished wood and the 'aesthetic' vase full of twigs. It was also fairly empty.

Once we were seated, at a scalloped mahogany table with one leg two inches shorter than the other (something I didn't really mind; I like the opportunity to customise my own dining table from time to time – it makes me feel so well-rounded), the arrival of the menus didn't give much cause for hope. The wine selection was severely limited: one French, one Italian, the House, a Californian, a champagne, a dessert and something called 'Mad Fish Bay', an Australian dry red. Predictably we went for the latter. As for the victuals, there were certain key terms on this particular menu that are now so hackneyed within the lexicon of 'New British' cuisine that they invariably set alarm bells ringing.

'Pan frying' was happening and it involved 'filo' pastry; there was a 'balsamic' dressing in the offing; both bacon and noodles (although not in the same dish) were held to be 'crispy'; duck was to be 'honeyed'; pork, predictably, 'seared'; and the reputation of corn irretrievably 'blackened'.

I groaned throatily and resigned myself to one of those meals that is style without substance, idea without ideatum. Around us were an odd gaggle of people: Anthony Howard, the political commentator; and two tables largely dominated by men in stripy shirts and ties, who all looked uncannily like Mrs Thatcher's late lamented economic guru, Professor Alan Walters (not, I must say, a pretty sight). Dizzy Gillespie, or some other horn player, was emanating from a monolithic black speaker affixed to the wall.

This is all by way of saying appearances can be deceptive. The service was attentive and good-humoured. I chose the Caesar salad with fresh anchovies to start, while my companion risked the agnoletti of crab and coconut cream, despite this dish's involving the aforementioned pan-fried filo pastry. Neither of us was feeling that peckish, so we resolved on only one main course, the roast loin of lamb, with couscous, grilled vegetables, roast garlic and thyme *jus*. (Oh for the days when juice was juice and, in Hemingway's formulation, I felt 'juiced'!)

The Mad Fish was brought to the table. It was great – peppery, distinctive, with an afterburn like a Holden bucketing across the outback. My Caesar salad arrived. Despite the incongruity of large chunks of sliced Parmesan atop it, it was more than palatable. The fresh anchovies tasted a bit like soused herring to me, but then I really like soused herring. The dreaded agnoletti was good too: the pastry light, the crab and coconut cream well melded. It sat on the plate, as dainty and inviting as a small, edible pagoda.

The people at the next table were discussing the Public Sector Borrowing Requirement. Discussing it earnestly and with great attention to the detail of fiscal apportionment. I began to suspect that they might all, in fact, *be* clones of Alan Walters, sent out into the world by the Thatcher Foundation, in order to psychically destabilise people who habitually sit in restaurants listening to other people's conversations.

I was beginning to like Una, beginning to see myself as an Una type of person. I resolved that the very next day I would buy a Psion

Organiser and put a down payment on a Range Rover. There was only one problem with the place thus far: the lamb loin was taking its time joining us from the kitchen. Mind you, with the current preoccupation with ethically-reared meat, it wouldn't have surprised me to learn that the beast was being put through kindergarten.

Eventually it came, on a great, white plate. There were chunks of pink lamb, roundels of green courgette, ellipses and triangles of assorted red and yellow peppers, and beneath it all a stippling of couscous. The plate was piled high and it looked like nothing so much as an Arcimboldo painting – found food artfully arranged so as to depict a human face. I stared hard at the plate for some minutes trying to divine whose face it was, until the familiar, pensive features of Alan Walters began to emerge, whereupon I resolved to abjure hallucinogens until the next millennium.

The lamb was nicely *al dente* and the peppers and roast garlic sat well with it. As for the couscous, this was near-friable, rather than the soggy mush you so often get offered up under that name. All in all Una was turning out to be a darling little slice of pot luck. The bill was a modest £40 (although we didn't have dessert or coffee). I nodded to the monetarists, glad to do my bit in restricting the money supply, and we strode out into the windy night.

Observer, June 1996

40

Restaurant review: Franco's, Queen Elizabeth Road, Enniskillen, Fermanagh, Northern Ireland

The obelisk memorial to General Sir Galbraith Lowry Cole stood tall and white in the chill night air. Beneath it the town of Enniskillen huddled along the banks of the Erne. Carlo restrained me on the doorstep of Franco's, a warm ark of a restaurant pulled up on to the quayside. 'This place,' he hissed, 'is single-handedly responsible for the introduction of stripped pine to Fermanagh!'

We entered. It was true – there was a lot of pine in Franco's. Two large rooms full of it, in fact, as well as a conservatory-cum-bar where the stripped-pine culture had advanced so far as to produce complex artefacts such as those sublimely irritating, elbow-high tables which can either be sat at on high bar stools or else leant wearily against. Carlo, Tyga and I leant.

I sipped my glass of Guinness and meditated on the oft-retailed – but probably apocryphal – explanation for the difference in head-consistency between an English and an Irish glass of Guinness: namely that the Irish taps are slower-flowing, giving the beer its creamy finish. (Why is it that paint, beer and wine all have a 'finish', whereas relationships merely come to an end?)

If the streets of Enniskillen had seemed emptier than they perhaps ought to be on a Saturday night, all was now made clear: almost the entire population of the town was in Franco's. Old people, young people, families, couples – there wasn't a significant demographic group unrepresented. Why, later on in the evening, as if to demonstrate just how broad the church of Franco's is, the chef from the Indian restaurant next door wandered in and went for a chat with his fellows. As I watched, he propped himself up in a corner of the buzzing, clanging, partially exposed kitchen that's at the core of the establishment and assayed the crack.

'In my father's house are many mansions . . .' and Franco's offers 'progressive cooking', as well as seafood and a proper pizzeria. In the corner of one of the rooms there's a pine stage, and while we were there a man with a moustache and a guitar was knock-knock-knocking on heaven's door, quite innocuously.

The place caters to the tourist trade – much of which is of the angling variety, Loch Erne being the very natal cleft of Fermanagh – but really it has the feel of an inn strongly rooted in the local community. The staff were all young, bustly and smiley. A shift at Franco's is a rite of grafting passage for many in a town short on employment opportunities.

The only problem with the near-unrivalled popularity of Franco's (until recently it was the only restaurant in town) is that it leads to a certain laxity as far as uniting reservations with tables is concerned. Our little people-grouping remained embowered in the foliage of the conservatory bar for a full hour before a berth was found for us.

This gave me time to examine in some detail the cartoons from the *Weekly Fenian* framed on the walls. These showed rack-renters, bailiffs and croppies locked in the timeless turf war of local politics. Exhausted and starving men were cradled in the ample arms of emblematic Mother Irelands, while landlords absented themselves.

On a wall of one of the main restaurant rooms there was an even more revealing piece of pictorial allegory. Part mural, part painting, part bas-relief, it depicted, in a style somewhere between Paula Rego and Willie Rushton, a priest in a state of dishabille being disciplined by a nun in wimple and fish-net stockings. Hmm, I thought to myself, and they say the Anglican Church is broad.

Eventually we were guided to our table. We'd already ordered from an embarrassment of menus (one for each of the many mansions) and the food wasn't long in coming. My potato and leek soup was good: flavoursome, but not quite as bulky as a potato and leek soup can be. If you really push the boat out, you can fashion a potato and leek soup denser than a core metal with a consistency like steel wool. Carlo's baked cheese in filo pastry was more to the point. This was definitely at the progressive end of things, the hassock of lactose subsiding into an oval lappet of mango, plum and passion-fruit sauce.

Both Carlo and I had pizzas to follow. He, rather pedestrianly, chose a simple margherita, while I firmed up my credentials as a doddery juvenile delinquent by ordering something termed an 'antisocial'. This promised a riotous assembly of chillies and garlic, but although it was perfectly tasty it wasn't quite antisocial enough. Franco's is just too friendly an establishment to lay on a truly antisocial pizza. I feel certain that even if I'd eaten two or three antisocials, there still would have been a warm welcome.

Tyga was by now engaged with a turbot. 'It's a bit bland,' she said, as if describing its social attributes. 'It's meant to be with sorrel, but I don't know if it's even seen any.' This little speech conjured up in my mind an idea for yet another *nouvelle cuisine* – a kind of cooking so rarefied and purist that flavouring would be effected merely by allowing fish or fowl to view selected herbs and spices, rather than actually touching them. My reverie was shattered when Tyga protested, 'I wish I'd had the monkfish – it's better and fresher here than it is in the sea.'

The bill arrived. We'd stopped by the cash point on our way through town and I'd drawn out £100. 'Will this be enough?' I asked Carlo. 'Enough!' he expostulated. 'We could eat in Franco's for a week on that kind of money.' He was right; the bill was fantastically tiny. Why, in the Smoke you wouldn't get a hot wing and 5cc of lukewarm coleslaw for that kind of money. Even someone as antisocial as me was bowled over.

Observer, March 1996

41

According to Roger Scruton, whose philosophic works I've recently been perusing in an effort to increase my brain power and commensurate status, 'culture' is a pretty narrow field of endeavour. Certainly Scruton, who rides to hounds and doubtless listens to *Parsifal* on Bose Wavelength speakers, would give short shrift to the notion that taxation forms part of our culture. And yet the most cultured – and culturally perspicacious – person I know is an accountant. Not only that, but this accountant interprets the world almost solely through the lens of fiscal policy; he has, as it were, an accountancy *Weltanschauung*. I don't suppose for a second that Scruton would agree, but I bet some of you would. Especially the one million of you who're about to pay a £100 surcharge to the Revenue because you've failed to get your new, self-assessment tax forms in on time. You live in the same culture as I do – one of fear.

Yup, that's a cool one hundred million quid scored simply because of a stroke of a policy-maker's pen. I bet you regret not going into politics. Just think of it – simply attend myriad tedious meetings and you'll be able to screw up people's lives more than any multinational. Anyway, this brilliant, cultured accountant and I get together once a year to drink tiny cups of bitter coffee and have a serious chat about the culture of taxation. Now, neither he nor I wishes to be paranoid, but both of us felt that it would be a good idea to make it absolutely clear that he is NOT MY ACCOUNTANT. Not only that, but he is not my friend's accountant *either*. Indeed, I don't know anyone for whom he actually files tax returns – he's more of an accountant *manqué* than that, a sort of bohemian, underground accountant. So, if you're reading this out there in Faceless Bureaucrat Land, don't bother running your search engine.

My accountant (David Fishbein of Fishbein & Replicant) is utterly incompetent and for the last ten years has consistently paid more tax on my behalf than was required – so YOU OWE ME. I took him on initially because he had a piranha in a tank in his waiting room; and there was a sign on the tank reading 'Please Do Not Feed Me, I Only Eat Tax Inspectors'. Ha-bloody-ha, the piranha died a week later.

Now, Andrew X (of the long established X family) is not that kind of penny-ante customer at all. He has an altogether more sophisticated view of the entire field. When I met with him the other day, in a drab Bedouin tent in the Empty Quarter of Arabia, he was unequivocal: 'They go after the top 10 per cent of self-assessment earners in their district, and the bottom 10 per cent of earners. They go after people who make persistent errors in calculating their income. Their chief effort as a bureaucracy is channelled into chasing back-taxes and dealing with suspicious cases. They've got a cool one hundred million automatically at the end of this month, and then they get another 5 per cent surcharge in March. Given the current bank rate, if you can, you're better off borrowing it than owing it to the Revenue. Now, I wouldn't say the bureaucracy was lazy or incompetent for a second – but anyone can see that this is not the most sophisticated way of increasing tax. I suppose if they were called upon to justify it – in some existential fashion – they might say, "Well, you, the citizenry, have the right to limit your personal liability in business ventures; so we, the state, retain the right to similarly limit our liability." '

'Err, Andrew,' I gently interpolated, 'that sounds a little bit *Nineteen Eighty-Four*-ish . . . I mean, why did you go into accountancy in the first place? Do you have some kind of gut hatred of these people?'

'It's not a gut hatred, but I don't like being controlled, so I don't see why anyone else should. A lot of people who get into these positions become self-important bullies. They're unimaginative and they simply can't put themselves in the position of people who're trying to create something, whether it's a small business or a work of art. Now they're turning their attention to the Internet – believe it or not they're going to figure out a way of taxing trading on the net. They have so much computing power that they're able to do a full match between social-security fraud and any other kind of avoidance.'

'But Andrew, isn't that just a little paranoid? I mean to say, hasn't all of this resulted in increased revenues?'

'Absolutely. Increased revenues and declining costs. I know of one district office where they've slashed the work-force from fifty to fifteen – and two of them died last year from heart attacks. But their last twelve months' tax harvest was far higher than they expected – than anyone expected! And the fruits are all around us . . .'

'I'm sorry?'

'Nothing . . . nothing . . . just an old Bedouin saying. The fruits of this increased revenue are all around us – in increased representation, better schools, better hospitals, smarter bombs – all around us . . . all around us . . .'

And muttering these gnomic mutterings Andrew X took down his drab tent, packed it on to his drab camel, and disappeared into the drab distance; like generations of clever accountants before him he is intent on pursuing the old ways, and in maintaining a touching belief that progressive taxation is allied to democracy. Even if his way of life is vanishing – I'm convinced that he is a very great man.

The Times, January 1999

42

Through the courtesy of the *Guardian* newspaper, and along with a lot of other white liberals, I boogied down to the National Film Theatre the other evening to watch a black film made by a white capitalist man from Los Angeles. How we all laughed at the salty dialogue of those rough ghetto types. Every 'muthafucka', 'niggah' and 'asshole' drew an appreciative burble of merriment from our plump bellies; and each instance of indiscriminate violence, casual sex and gratuitous drug-taking engendered in us a warm sense of being there now.

After the screening of *Jackie Brown*, we were further blessed by the manifestation of the *auteur* himself, Mr Quentin Tarantino. According to Adrian Wootton, the programme director of the NFT, Mr Tarantino's schedule is *very* busy, so it was nothing short of saintly of him to agree to come to London for a few hours to promote his film. We were suitably humbled, with the possible exception of a black man in the audience who had the temerity to suggest to Mr Tarantino that he might have substituted a few more 'muthafucka's and 'asshole's for the profusion of 'niggah's in the film's script.

Mr Tarantino bridled. He had, he told us, grown up 'surrounded by black culture', and had attended an 'all-black school' in Los Angeles. This rather raised the question, did he himself have to black up in order to attend classes? At any rate this black saturation means that Mr Tarantino can address his black friends as 'niggah' with complete impunity, while we uptight British – whether black or white – are still enmired in asinine political correctness. When the black member of the audience pursued his point, suggesting that Mr Tarantino wouldn't 'get away' with this over here, the director threw his arms wide and proclaimed endearingly, 'But I do.' How we all chortled.

Another black man in the audience queried Mr Tarantino's championing of so-called 'blaxploitation' movies: 'Personally,' he said, 'I always found them rather vulgar and poorly made.' Mr Tarantino launched into a long and essentially vapid defence of the genre, in which the word 'vitality' kept popping up, as if it were in and of itself a validator of artistic integrity. Blaxploitation movies represented 'a gigantic wonderful black cinema movement' that had been 'cut down' by the black intelligentsia themselves. Deary me! Those unruly black intellectuals, they definitely need a white black man like Mr Tarantino to come along and resurrect their cinema.

In truth Mr Tarantino's film is a competent, workmanlike adaptation of an Elmore Leonard thriller, *Rum Punch*. The casting of Pam Grier in the title role was inspiring, not because she's a black middle-aged woman (although it is genuinely pleasing to see a lead character of this unusual kind), but because her dignified, controlled performance held the film together. The other stars – Robert De Niro, Michael Keaton, Robert Forster and Samuel L. Jackson – set around this jewel of a performance didn't shine nearly as much.

But to adapt the form of the *Guardian*'s own Pass Notes column, the thing Mr Tarantino is *least* likely to say is anything remotely modest or self-deprecating. According to him, Elmore Leonard on reading the script of *Jackie Brown* pronounced it 'the best adaptation ever' of one of his novels – and went even further, saying that it was 'the best script ever written', and that it was 'my novel'. This Mr Tarantino took to mean that his script had 'the weight of a novel'. One senses that there isn't a great deal of Dostoyevsky being read *chez* Tarantino; and as for Elmore Leonard, the poor man's memory and critical faculties must be seriously awry for him to prefer *Jackie Brown* over and above Barry Sonnenfeld's superb film adaptation of *Get Shorty*.

Mr Tarantino told us that his adaptation took a year to write; and that the process enables him to get in touch with a quality he's lacking in. He didn't tell us what this 'quality' was, but I venture to suggest that it's originality itself. For Mr Tarantino is essentially a *pasticheur* and an artistic fraud. His use of pop music for his soundtracks – 'I find the personality of the piece through the music' – is what confirms the status of his films as extended-play pop videos. These are deft promotions of the current generation's desire for unreflective entertainment, uncluttered by either ethics or purpose. His incorporation into his films of knowing little 'in' jokes about film (in *Jackie Brown* we have a character played by Bridget Fonda, watching a Peter Fonda film on television) is what confirms his status as a derivative and second-order filmmaker, rather than the Scorsese he would have us believe he is.

Mind you, this was the one Quentin Tarantino film I've ever managed to sit through. *Reservoir Dogs* got me puking into my popcorn during the torture sequence, and *Pulp Fiction* heading for the door after about an hour of pseudo-hip drug pornography. As for *Natural Born Killers*, I read Mr Tarantino's script and found it to be illiterate. I certainly hope he didn't spend a year writing that one.

There was some evidence the other evening that the Tarantino bubble is deflating. The last time there was one of these interviews at the NFT the crowds were enormous; this time they were merely big. I stuck out the question-and-answer session as long as I could, but when Pam Grier and Robert Forster came on stage to participate, it was time for this 'niggah' to head for home. After all, there's absolutely no point in asking an actor anything – unless they've already got a script.

The Times, January 1998

43

'Why a duck?' asks the bewildered Groucho in response to his brother Chico's plans for enhancing transport opportunities to their hotel, in the Marx Brothers' movie *Cocoanuts*. He never really gets to the heart of the matter, because, of course, Chico is saying, 'Viaduct.' It's an asinine exchange, which – if my recollection is correct – goes on for some minutes, and establishes more than anything else that the absurd humour of the Brothers was founded more than anything on their personifications of Melting Pot Americans. I mean to say, how could you have a family in which one brother was a Jewish wiseacre, a second an Italian shyster and a third a bizarre, blond-curled *idiot savant*?

Needless to say, the evocation of the viaduct is true to the Brothers' role as the quintessence of the American immigrant experience in the nineteenth and twentieth centuries. It's quite possible to imagine setting one of their movies in the context of almost any of the great civil engineering projects that undertook the steely conquest of the American wilds. Sod *A Day at the Races*, why not 'A Month at the Hoover Dam', or 'A Year at the Kinzua Viaduct'? The latter is particularly suitable for a Marx Brothers film, 'Kinzua' sounding so – how can I put it? – Marxian. The Kinzua Viaduct (1900) was built in a remote corner of Pennsylvania using the American iron style: a series of inclined cast-iron columns resting on stone pedestals, connected at the top by cast-iron arches, the whole system braced by wrought-iron ties. The Kinzua was big (92m high, 625m long), but easily eclipsed by the Lethbridge Viaduct (1909), on the Canadian Pacific Railroad in Alberta. This metal behemoth is over a kilometre and a half long, and is the heaviest in the world.

These American viaducts are great iron millipedes, crawling across the landscape. While they have a certain haunting presence, which makes me want to stuff a bottle in a brown bag and begin swigging from it while singing 'Hallelujah I'm a bum', they don't do it for me the way that a traditional viaduct will. I like my viaducts Romanesque, with multiple stone or brick arches, and piers to match. Frankly, I like my viaducts to be as near as possible to aqueducts.

Which is all by way of saying that I was up in Stockton the other day, and about the best part of my entire journey was the viaduct. I was disappointed on my return to discover that the Stockton Viaduct (1853) doesn't make it into any of the top-ten lists of notable viaducts (although a viaduct from the Stockton & Darlington line is so hip it's been put into a museum). I think it makes Stockton as a town. Granted, it doesn't have the sheer bulk of the Harrington Viaduct (1876), which is being considered as a World Heritage Bridge, but it has the virtue of being a working viaduct.

But why a duck? I hear you ask like Groucho; and the answer surely is that the stone-arched viaduct, more than any other structure, gives manifestation to our desire to smooth out the contours of the land, to reduce gradients, to facilitate inertia. Its arches provide prosceniums through which the built environment can be both viewed and subjected to a shifting parallax. We've just been subjected to many months of tedious electioneering here in London, much of it focusing on the vexed question of the tube system. But I'm fed up with the tube. I've gone down too many already to have much more stomach for it. Granted, the new stations on the Jubilee Line are beautifully designed, but they're not amenable to anyone who isn't prepared to travel on the thing.

No, what we want in the modern city is more viaducts. We don't even have to have trains on them – elevated walkways would be just the job. The motorway flyover is a brutal concretisation of a pollution-spewing past. Nowadays I only have to look at one of the things to vividly picture a fine spray of carbon monoxide falling from it like chemical rain. Anyway, they're too damn fast and their gradients are too steep.

If I had my way the new London Mayor would embark on a furious round of fiscal appropriation aimed at giving London the viaducts it needs for the twenty-first century. Failing that, he should buy up the Stockton Viaduct and have it transported brick by brick to the metropolis, thus severing ties with Manchester and depriving Richard Branson of income at one heavy swoop.

Building Design, May 2000

44

Currently on at the Victoria & Albert Museum in London is an exhibition of some of the one and a half million manuscripts, drawings and images being rehoused there from the RIBA archives. Prominent amongst these are a minuscule fraction of the 84,468 letters that passed between Sir Edwin Lutyens and his inamorata, Lady Emily Lytton, daughter of the Viceroy of India. In this correspondence Lutyens reveals himself as both commanding and whimsical; preoccupied by both the façade and the interior of things (and Lady Emily). We learn much of the man, and his profound love for Lady Emily comes as a tender corrective to the received view of Lutyens as an irascible old Edwardian goat, obsessed by red brick.

Take this, for example, from August 1896: 'My Dearest Emily, I miss you as the nut misses the bolt, the driver misses the screw, the hammer yearns for the nail. I wish we could be but sharp sand and cement to one another, inundated by the waters of time, until we were mortar. To think, my love, that we might serve as the glue for successive generations of little red children, rising up, tier after tier, until they form giant loggias of inheritance! Ah me!'

Within a couple of years Lutyens is on familiar terms with Lady Emily to instruct her in some of his views concerning architecture: 'My Dearest Emily, I have been working on the new country house in Surrey, and very important work it is too. I've often thought to myself that if only the great classical builders of yore could have had access to the right materials and locations, then they too might have built country houses in Surrey. Think of it! The Pantheon as a country house in Surrey! The Parthenon too! I would that the pyramids themselves might have been built near Redhill using red brick. If only the Hanging Gardens of Babylon had been closer to Coulsdon (and obviously, sunken rather than so dangling), then I warrant they might still be with us to this day!'

But despite the influence of the Arts and Crafts movement, Lutyens fell under the sway of classicism, abandoning country houses in favour of a series of romantic castles. In letter No. 21,967 (October 1906), we gain an insight into the master's obsession with detail, and his increasing frustration at the slow pace of his courtship. (By this stage, although they had been in regular and intense correspondence for thirteen years Lutyens and Lady Emily had still to meet, although he had once been allowed to fondle some of her toenail clippings.) 'My Dearest Emily, how cruel it is for one to yearn so, and in yearning to find so much more to yearn! I yearn not to yearn!

'I am hard at work on the furniture for Castle Wonga, the new home of Marchmont the pickled-herring tycoon. I have designed pleasingly robust furniture which sits well on the great herring-bone brick floor of the main reception rooms, but when the prototype chair arrived from the joiner yesterday it struck me as altogether *too* robust. I whipped out my pocketknife and in a frenzy whittled the thing down until it resembled an etiolated piece of Chippendale. Still unsatisfied, I went on whittling and whittling and whittling, until all that was left of the medieval throne was a splinter. This I poked myself in the leg with, hard enough to draw blood. The pain reminded me of the pain of being without you; the red blood reminded me of . . . red brick.'

In 1922, on his way to India, for more interminable work on the layout of New Delhi, Lutyens learned that Lady Emily was pregnant by him; and this despite the fact that he'd only brushed by her once in the corridor of the *Brighton Belle* (some Lutyens scholars dispute that the Master even knew it was Lady Emily he was brushing past). This letter (No. 56,719) shows us Lutyens at his most loopily endearing: 'My dearest, dearest Emily, when I think of the many miles that divide us how I weep! To celebrate our coming child, my dearest, I have decided to abandon all pomp and majesty in my work. From now on I shall devote myself solely to the designing of tiny buildings! Queen Mary has already given me a commission for a doll's house, and I look forward to more tininess. Yesterday I toured a specialist kiln and viewed some stock bricks no bigger than thimbles!'

Building Design, July 2000

45

Two a.m. in Soho, central London. It's been a drizzly late-autumn evening, but the narrow streets are still crowded with a bizarre gallimaufry of characters: gay clones pumped up on butyl nitrate and testosterone patrol the coffee bars of Old Compton Street; stocky African whores stand on the corners looking for business; crusty young beggars sit in doorways smashed on glue and extra-strength lager. Blanketing the whole scene are great processions of the straight by name and the straight by nature: phalanxes of suits heading home after post-theatre dinners, and bedraggled kids in from the sticks for a night of overpriced fun.

Behind the slickly nondescript doors of the Groucho Club, an evening of epic – and typical – egregiousness is grinding to a halt. In the main bar few are left, just the wrack that remains after the high tide of sociability has receded. Dotted around the overstuffed armchairs are the kind of embittered, ulcerated individuals who tend to frequent the joint. The Groucho is a very atelier of arrogance, a palace of preening. I've sat in here on many occasions, and watched A-list Hollywood celebrities struggle to get service from the staff. In the bar of the Groucho, Britishness puts its best and coolest foot forward, refusing to kowtow to any preconceived notions of success or celebrity.

There's this paradoxical, snobbish egalitarianism. There's also the fact that the ratio of 'names' to non-names at any given time is about one to one. But on this occasion, as I totter like a soused foal down the stairs from the upper bar and the games room, I notice a puncture in the atmosphere, a palpable heating up of the cool. Opting for my twentieth unit of alcohol for the evening, I amble to the downstairs bar and prop myself by a tall, dark-haired individual.

He's dressed in preposterously sharp garb. A lilac jacket of anachronistic cut, round-collared and flaring out over the hips. Down below are black drainpipe trousers and winkle-picker boots; up top are a mop of black hair and wraparound shades. I don't so much study the fellow as have his persona forced upon me. Waves of suspicion and hostility emanate from him like white noise from a television. His head jerks backwards and forwards, his fists nervously tense and clench. His entire upper body is like a whiplash aerial on a speeding car. If this guy isn't wired to the gills, then I'm the ghost of Lester Bangs, and Albert Goldman and the King are jamming together in purgatory.

But it isn't just the mutant mop-top's behaviour that's pumping things up in here. Even before the ludicrously pretty blonde in the satin halter top comes and drapes herself against him I notice something absolutely untoward: all the other people in the bar are looking at him! Blatantly regarding him! Have they no self-respect? If Christ himself walked in here he'd be utterly ignored, but this weirdo has everyone's attention.

When the blonde leads him away to the upright piano in the corner and pours herself across it in a pose strongly reminiscent of Michelle Pfeiffer in *The Fabulous Baker Boys*, it begins to dawn on me who they are. He languidly plays half a dozen chords, she essays a few notes. We're all transfixed. Who cares about Princess Di? Forget Tony and Cherie Blair. This is Liam and Patsy. This is the golden couple – the true home-grown and absolutely authentic face of stardom. She sings, he strums, they're islanded by our regard for a while . . . and then it ebbs away.

Oasis. I first heard them – over and over and over again – on my friend Mark Radcliffe's prime-time BBC radio show. Mark broadcasts from Manchester; he's known for catching whatever musical vibrations are resounding in this city of many-splendoured musical mutation. 'Maay-bay, I don' reely wanna know . . .' Liam Gallagher snarled over and over and over. I dug the rhythm – who couldn't? It was insistent, transmogrifying feet into sticks, carpet into drum – but it wasn't my thing. Too white, too guitar-band, too internally referential to rock music itself.

But when the press items and the rumours and the general babel began to overwhelm, I found myself intrigued. Noel claimed to have robbed a local shop at the age of thirteen. The band had threatened to burn a prominent club if didn't give them a gig. There'd been a mêlée on board a ferry. Oasis didn't just smash up hotel rooms, they filleted them. They proudly boasted of being bigger than the Beatles – the ultimate in pop hubris. And there were drugs – loads of drugs. And there were women – loads of women.

A month or so later I was back in the Groucho Club, playing snooker in a desultory fashion with some friends, when I noticed a row of holes along one wall. Big holes in the plaster, which looked like the impressions made by a number of large-calibre weapons of ineffectual ordnance. Initially, I thought they must be one of the generally indifferent works of conceptual art the Groucho insists on purchasing. But on looking closer I saw that they were a little ragged, even for a Damien Hirst. They were, I was told, the fruits of Liam and Patsy's first marital tiff – a savage volley of snooker balls unleashed by the Maddened Mancunian. Such is the awe in which Gallagher was at that time held, there was absolutely no question about censuring him. Indeed, I heard some wags say that the holes should be framed.

Later that evening, Liam was busted horning a line of coke in a shop doorway on Oxford Street. When the police released him with a caution, there was the predictable outcry. It was Jagger all over again, but Gallagher is the sort of butterfly who lifts up a wing and uses it to break you.

'D'You Know What I Mean?', the advance single from the Long-Awaited New Oasis Album, *Be Here Now*, hyped up all of my ambivalences. The track opens with a great grind of backward guitar noise, like the evacuation of the steel intestine of some mighty mechanical creature. Then Liam's whining, soaring threnody begins. But while the pay-off line is delivered with plenty of push, it's melodically not really there. And the lyric, instead of appearing as witty as it should ('D'ya know what I mean' is as ubiquitous in contemporary conversational English as 'actually' used to be), comes across as tired, threadbare. It all sounded alarmingly like the jangly, happy-time strumming associated with that late lamented (not) British subgenre: pub rock.

But no matter what I think of the music, there's a transcendent quality about Oasis. Noel Gallagher's songs, with their freightage of solipsistic, adolescent *aperçus*, are somehow the glass bricks of the *Zeitgeist*; the great screaming walls of guitar noise they're embedded in are as timeless as Sumerian ziggurats.

Before I got my hands on *Be Here Now*, I spent two weeks swooping around the crowded streets of London in a large turbocharged saloon equipped with a serious sound system. 'Shakermaker', 'Cigarettes & Alcohol', 'Live Forever' and 'Wonderwall' – all the 'classics', cranked up to the hilt. At times I felt as if the entire car were some vibrating puck being slammed around on a rink of guitar reverb. At times I felt carried away by it all, certain that I was in the refracted presence of genius; but at other times I felt buried beneath the dead, composting weight of pop decadence.

One minute the music is stirring me and all I want to do is wassail with the lads in a local blizzard of cocaine, under a heavy rain of Jack Daniel's and Coca-Cola; the next I'm finding the relentless harping on four chords a pain in the neck, and the posturing a pain in the arse.

Oasis sound best to me when I'm in a bad, self-indulgent mood ('I need to be myself/I can't be no one else'), when I'm rattling down the road intent on the stacked deck life has dealt me, and how no one understands. Then, the proscenium of crashing guitar chords that frame a ditty like 'Don't Look Back in Anger' capture a tale of pure, unalloyed romanticism. At moments like that, the plangent non-sequiturs of Noel Gallagher's lyrics sound almost Confucian: 'I'll start a revolution from my bed/'Cause you said the brains I had went to my head'. And the slight references to some kind of shared nationality, which the argot-heavy lyrics of Oasis are studded with (a 'morning glory' is the bladder-stopped wake-up call of a hard-on), can wrench a salt of sentimentality from my baggy old eye.

Liam Gallagher, with his birth date comfortably rooted in the seventies, isn't so much post-punk as entirely post-modern. And Oasis are the first global rock band to have their musical sensibilities defined within an atemporal sonic garden, free from the seasons of cultural change and the tempests of social revolution. Though ostensibly Brit-pop, the Gallagher brothers are actually second-generation Irish immigrants. Their musical sensibilities were formed as much by informal family ceilidhs in County Mayo as by the nihilistic antics of the Sex Pistols. Much has been made of the band's affinity with all things Beatle: they've always aimed to outshine their trichological forefathers; they've covered 'I Am the Walrus'; they're not immune to the harmonies; and – most importantly – there's something about the north-western English accent, whether Mancunian or Liverpudlian, that makes it particularly suitable for shouting the blues. But the truth is that the actual psychodynamic of Oasis owes far more to their poncy, aspirant-bohemian, southern progenitors – the original Satanic Majesties. Indeed: it's Jagger all over again.

Like the Rolling Stones, Oasis are a five-piece with an ineffably sexually charismatic frontman. Like the Stones, Oasis thrive on the psychosexual tension between their lead guitarist/songwriter and their frontman/style guru. In the case of Oasis, this is further cranked up by consanguinity. You only have to imagine what it might be like to hear your little brother singing about your sexual and emotional experiences to understand why songs like 'Wonderwall' and 'Don't Look Back in Anger' have such astonishing emotional resonance.

To push the psychoanalysis still further, if there is any parallel between Oasis and the Beatles, it's in the personalities of John Lennon and Liam Gallagher. Both endured difficult childhoods; both suffered the concomitant dislocation of self. Noel Gallagher has described his brother as 'living in his own little world', and averred that the essential effect of stardom has been to intensify the obliqueness of baby bro's relationship with sanity. I don't think you necessarily have to resort to pathologising or crude psychobabble in order to classify Liam Gallagher as a borderline personality; all things considered, it's a poetic judgement.

But unlike Lennon, the Gallagher brothers have never allowed themselves to be straitjacketed by the exigencies of commerce and image. Lennon was driven by cravenness to embrace his (initial) characterisation as lovable, void of class and (for the most part) of sexuality. The Gallagher brothers are inextricably linked to their working-class origins. To understand how important this is, as an American reader, you have to appreciate just how rigid British class distinctions still are.

In Britain, you can make the ascent from working to middle class in one generation, but you can't top out at the summit. If you have any kind of strong regional accent, you can't possibly be pukka. In Britain the industrial proletariat, particularly in the north, has long formed a masculine horde that on Saturday afternoons is dedicated to the fervent worship of soccer.

One of the most moving passages in Paolo Hewitt's procrustean biography of the band comes when Noel describes what these Saturday afternoons were like. The dads would leave their sons by the side of an enormous barrier that ran the length of the stands, while they sloped off to the bar. The Gallagher brothers sat there irradiated by the sound and colour that is a British soccer match in full cry. And then the singing would begin. It's this soccer-crowd bellowing that provides the strongly anthemic feel of so many Oasis tracks: they are purpose-built for mass chanting.

Another important part of the Oasis aesthetic – or anti-aesthetic – that comes direct from soccer culture is their 'casual' fashion stance. The Casuals were the lineal successors of the Mod aesthetic of the late sixties and early seventies who gained their inspiration from chain-store standardisation. Oasis, with their off-the-peg windcheaters and sloppy training shoes or sneakers, exemplify a bizarre hinterland between the amphetamine-fuelled dancers of all-night soul raves and the razor-toting hooligans who blighted British soccer matches in the eighties.

This, in a nutshell (with a healthy dose of whoring, drugging and wholesale bad behaviour), is the post-everything, post-label character of Oasis. This is why, with their hotel-room trashing and sibling pummelling and record-company baiting, they are so deliciously and deliriously iconic.

And the evidence bears this out: in the United Kingdom, *Definitely Maybe*, the band's début album, sold 100,000 copies in the first four days of its release; by the end of that year it had topped three-quarters of a million. The second album, *What's the Story (Morning Glory)?*, has sold more copies in the UK than any Beatles album – and gone twelve times platinum. Last year's mammoth gigs at Knebworth achieved a ludicrous, overcapacity attendance of 250,000. Pre-sales of the new album (and the new single 'D'You Know What I Mean?') are among the highest for any band ever. Who knows what sort of business *Be Here Now* will drum up. The mind boggles.

The assignment finally came to bed late last night during another visit to the Groucho. I'd stopped in for a drink, not in search of Oasis, but it transpired that Liam Gallagher was in the club again. He sauntered past me huddled up in his hood, flanked by discreetly tough and manifestly casual bodyguards. Patsy was nowhere to be seen. Liam was with a close friend who's also an acquaintance of mine. 'What's the story?' I asked. 'Oh, nothing really. I think Liam's leaving – there was a bit of bother at Ronnie Scott's earlier on.' Apparently, there'd been a showcase for another Creation Records band and Liam had been in an ugly mood. 'Do the two of you still go to Browns any more?' 'Nah – he was barred from there months ago. He just can't seem to behave.' My inner-circle friend walked away through the thicket of drinkers with their burning tobacco foliage.

I asked one of the club managers whether Liam was still in the building. 'No,' she snapped. 'And I hope we never see him again – he's a pain in the arse!' How the Mighty was beginning to lose his burnish. And this just a day after Noel had made another of his legendarily contentious remarks in an interview with the *New Musical Express*.

It had been in response to the question 'Do you think that Oasis are more important to the youth of today than God?' 'I would have to say,' he averred, 'without a shadow of doubt that that is true.' There it was – the final act of Beatle-aspirant blasphemy. Noel also spoke to the *NME* about the new album. He said he was increasingly interested in studio-based work, and had been hanging out with Goldie, the flamboyant British jungle star and mix-down supremo. Together they twiddle knobs, sample things and twist rhythms out of the mixing desk.

This may be the future for the band's creative powerhouse. If Oasis are going to develop a career anything like that of their fellow gods (the three other band members no one ever mentions are sort of clandestine demigods), Noel will need to sop up some profoundly new and eclectic source material. And at the moment, techno, drum 'n' bass and all that other computer-generated dance music are certainly what Britain does best.

Gallagher seems particularly vulnerable to accusations that his band hasn't evolved. In truth, when *Be Here Now* finally arrived – this afternoon – some of these anxieties proved justified. Suitably enough, I was listlessly hanging out at the elegant, high-bohemian townhouse of Blur's Damon Albarn and Elastica's Justine Frischmann when the courier knocked on the door. Only half of the Other Couple was in residence at the time. Justine unleashed a fairly pithy volley of her own at the Manchester men and their music. 'Utterly derivative' and 'They aren't even trying' were some of her less purple points.

The new tracks I listened to didn't exactly drive me wild, either. But then again, I wasn't in a bad, self-pitying mood. 'Stand By Me' repeats familiar anthemic patterns; on 'My Big Mouth', Noel offers his own, honed, second me-generation apophthegms: 'I'll have my way/I'll have my say', and so on. Elsewhere some McCartneyesque emotional insight is groped for, when Noel – through his mouthpiece – gives the trenchant advice 'Get your shit together, girl' over a background of softly jangling guitars. Predictably this ditty is entitled 'The Girl in the Dirty Shirt'. Presumably, unlike McCartney and Noel, she can't afford a new one. The mix itself is a bit more adventurous: NWA samples, backward noises, and psychedelic guitar accompany the title track, even as we're once again preached a cliché.

I don't know if *Be Here Now* will do everything its creators hope for. I'll have to hear it on a tinny radio while waiting at a sandwich counter before I crack that egg. I do have sympathy for these potentially vulnerable young men and their wives. They are locked into a considerable whirlpool of hype and scrutiny. The British press can be deceitful, vicious and unscrupulous. The Gallaghers' harassment has epitomised this: non-stop paparazzi, total stake-out.

But as far as their image and their music are concerned, I can only echo the words of another British bad boy of rock 'n' roll, Pete Townshend; I really do hope – in terms of the intense tradition they represent – they die before they get old.

Details, September 1997

135

46

King Kong is due for rehabilitation. For far too long we have uncritically accepted his demonisation. His actions have been wilfully misinterpreted, his motives impugned and his feelings disregarded. Enough is enough.

I wish to reclaim King Kong (or 'Kong' as I, more familiarly, refer to him) as a hero of the primal, the natural, the embodiment – as it were – of embodiment itself.

The Kong image that lies at the core of the 1933 film of which he is the eponymous anti-hero can be read in two countervailing ways. On the one view, we see a giant, gorilla-like creature, standing on top of the Empire State Building, batting biplanes out of the sky and threatening the lives of all the humans in the vicinity. But on the Self view, Kong is engaged here in his finest hour; and the scene is a *Götterdämmerung*, in which a godlike figure protests against the hideous alienation of the urban scape in the most potent way imaginable.

But this alternative role for Kong as an early proponent of direct action, a road protester *manqué*, is only one strand of my argument. There is also Kong the great lover. As the titles of the movie come up we are treated to an Arabian proverb: 'And lo, the beast looked upon the face of beauty and stayed its hand from killing/And from that day it was as one dead.'

Granted, he doesn't altogether stay his hand from killing – there is the young woman he somewhat precipitately claws out of her apartment when he goes on the rampage in New York (and which of us hasn't felt a little like doing that when on the rampage in New York); but that's as nothing when set against the poignant tenderness of his feelings towards 'Ann Darrow', played by Fay Wray.

Kong and Fay are in fact made for each other: she, a poor young woman, picked up off the streets by the exploitative film director Carl Denham (whose speciality is the kind of film that destroys nature in order to portray it); he, a poor ape-colossus, of indeterminate age, who is being exploited by the same man. It is one of the great tragedies of modern cinema that their romance is thwarted.

Not only that, but the whole action of the film is also misinterpreted, actually within the context of the film itself. One of the aspects of the film that I most profoundly disagree with is the business of the giant wall that separates Kong, and his Edenic realm of dinosaurs and rain forest, from the islanders who worship him.

In the film it is uncritically asserted that the islanders have built this wall to keep Kong out. On this interpretation, Denham and his film crew are delivering the simple islanders (who are meant to be of Melanesian Aboriginal stock, but whose appearance owes more to central casting) from evil, and thus represent the beneficent face of white imperialism. But you only have to take a cool look at the giant wall to see how patently absurd this is. It's obviously too big for the islanders to have built – each stone must weigh many, many tons. No, my theory is that the wall was built by Kong *himself* in order to keep humans out. All he wishes is to be free of interference.

And what does he get? A gang of dreadful American supremacists, trampling over the fragile peace that exists between Kong and the indigenes. What is the first action of Denham's party upon entering Kong's realm? To let fly with all their guns at a perfectly harmless stegosaurus. After that, can it be any surprise that Kong tries with all his might to repel Denham and his crew? But what damages his effectiveness is the *coup de foudre* – this Fay Wray thing.

Now, while I do not wish in any way to condone male violence towards women, or suggest that when a woman says 'No' to the possibility of sexual congress with a giant ape, she really means 'Yes', none the less, it is notable that when Kong gets Fay – literally – in his grasp, he doesn't crush her to death, or abuse her, but rather, very, very gently, with teasing and delicate eroticism, he removes her skirt.

In this Kong encapsulates the paradox that is human sexuality. He is both 'the beast' that makes two backs – a defiantly animal act which you don't have to be a Freudian to believe manifests aggression in the pursuit of ecstasy – and, at one and the same time, the refined and courteous lover.

I venture to suggest that had Kong and Fay been left alone for a while, and given the opportunity to get to know each other a little better, she might have come round.

But, as it transpires, Kong is dragged back to New York by Denham and put on show as the 'Eighth Wonder of the World', in front of a horde of giggling thrill-seekers. What greater humiliation for a creature formerly venerated?

Piled on top of this are further humiliations. Fay comes on to the stage with the poltroon who has stolen her from Kong – Jack Driscoll, the mate of the exploration ship. Driscoll flaunts his relationship with Fay in front of Kong. Then the final insult: Denham brings in the press, having primed them with the memorable exhortation 'Beauty and the Beast, boys, play up that angle!' The paparazzi charge on to the stage and unleash a fusillade of flashbulbs in the face of our hero.

Is it any wonder that he reacts like some simian Jonathan Aitken against this massed phalanx of intrusive sleazemongers? And then, a sensitive precursor of Stephen Fry, he takes the only course available to someone so hounded by the press – he ups and leaves the theatre altogether. From then on he is locked into the grim inevitability of tragedy.

However, it isn't just through the narrative of the movie that I seek to remove the tarnish from Kong's image. His demonisation is highly significant at the symbolic level. The distinctions that have been traditionally drawn between man and beast have always been arbitrary. When chimpanzees were first discovered by Europeans, and their bodies subjected to dissection, the similarities in anatomy between ape and human led theorists of the 'chain of being' to place them between Caucasians and Negroes.

Even with the advent of Darwinism, it can still be seen that the exclusion and demonisation of the great apes has always justified racism. To create an intra-species hierarchy, it is necessary to retain a rigid inter-species hierarchy. To label other races 'bestial', it is important to have beasts to which to compare them.

Apes, particularly chimpanzees, are our closest living relatives. In the case of the latter, some zoologists estimate that we have in common over 94 per cent of our genetic material. Yet both species are in the process of being irreversibly damaged, and will almost certainly become extinct. This will be a tragedy of unparalleled magnitude. The study of chimpanzees, who in evolutionary development split away from us only some five million years ago, provides us with our best chance of understanding our own development as humans: what makes us unique.

But, more emotively, the destruction of our closest relatives will in an important sense diminish what it is to be human – and possibly will even destroy it. For without their existence to shore up our differences, will we not perhaps collapse back into the slough of bestiality we have pulled ourselves out of?

In the 1933 film, one of the characters says early on that Kong is neither man nor beast. Really this could be applied to our highest aspirations for humanity, but in identifying what is essentially human as purely concerned with the mental, we are denying one of the most beautiful aspects of ourselves. For in the final analysis, Kong is all body. In a world of the anti-natural, the plangently cerebral, don't we need to celebrate a person who roars defiance at the regimenting of existence by tiny minds? Please, next time you see the film he stars in, cheer when King Kong routs the humans, and weep as he goes down fighting.

Independent, May 1995

47

Literary biography is writers' porn. For a professional writer to spend his time reading about the life and times of others has to be the ultimate act of uncreative onanism. For, while it can be asserted with some confidence that nothing is ever lost in the economy of ideas, and that a writer – being a compulsive generalist – may be allowed the luxury of believing that whatever field he reads within, some husks of ideas will be gleaned, there is absolutely no justification for reading about the lives of his fellows. I mean, even setting it out on paper like this raises the Borgesian conceit of a writer reading a biography of a writer who spent his life – when not writing – reading literary biography. Such a vision proposes navel-gazing as the central preoccupation of the author, with the actual literary works themselves as mere twists of lint.

Some years before the publication of his own memoir, Martin Amis said to me that there was nothing intrinsically interesting in a writer's life; after all, what exactly is it that we do, save for sit in a quiet room typing all day? Why should the biography of a writer be any more interesting – viewed as the recounting of the quotidian – than the life of a secretary? This, of course, misses the point on two counts: the lives of secretaries are often quite fascinating (the unrecorded life is inherently worth living, being perforce amazingly unresolved, unreduced to a mere stock of words); and the lives of writers present ample opportunity, away from the page, for the most plangent enactments of the experiential. No one, however dedicated, or psychically cork-lined, can spend that much of their time simply writing. Further, the literary life, with its flexible working hours, its intermittent rewards and its solitary cast, positively invites the writer to get up to all kinds of mischief. Sexual affairs, drug and alcohol problems, quixotic travel, naïve political engagements, amateur and professional dramatics – the writer's life is capaciously able to house these pursuits, and they make great copy.

No, I've no quarrel with the non-writer who reads literary biography, I understand the appeal only too well (it's the appeal of having my life), and while it's a statistic that I've never actually seen confirmed in print, it rings true when cultural commentators assert that sales of new literary biography now outstrip those of new fiction. This is often decried as the most telling evidence of the decadent character of contemporary letters, but I'm not sure that it's the case, for two reasons: I don't think people read literary biography because they're interested in writers *per se*; and also I genuinely believe that ours is a golden age for literary biography.

No, I think people read literary biography because of the character of the writer's life as set out above. The writer, in an age of mass standardisation, corporatism, stereotypy, and the remorseless eradication of any meaningful individuality (at the end of the nineteenth century sodomy was alarmingly transgressive; at the end of the twentieth it's only so if the sodomite isn't wearing a condom), represents the promise of an untrammelled life, a *modus vivendi* in which the individual lives by a product to which he alone has access, like a private mine for a unique mineral. All the jinks, high or low, that go along with this, are merely the gravy. The lay reader is interested in the writer's life, because it holds up the teasing possibility (although it is seldom truly the case) of a life that can be considered to be *sui generis*.

But for the writer, literary biography is wank fodder – plain and simple. It's notable that while almost all professional writers are exceedingly well informed about the goings-on of their predecessors, none of us will admit to consuming literary biography (or if we do, it's only in midnight, confessional, beery colloquy). The literary biographies are kept under the bed, or behind the cistern in the spare loo. There are few professional activities that should be considered less in the light of competition than literature, and yet writers, as a bunch, are some of the most point-scoring, fantasy-league-making, standing-on-each-other's-shoulders people you could ever care to meet, always erecting card-house hierarchies on the basis of sales, notoriety, reviews, or cachet, only for them to be toppled by the chill wind of posterity. Writers are all too human, neglecting the cardinal virtues of our calling for the ordinal ranking of tennis players, or bond traders, or piece-workers. Literary biography greatly aids us in this enterprise, enabling us to tee ourselves up against whomsoever we wish and come out the winner in whichever spurious category – sales, notoriety, reviews, or cachet – we light upon.

There's that, and there's also the delicious *schadenfreude* to be garnered from realising that while so-and-so may have scored exceedingly well in terms of writing an acknowledged classic before he was thirty, he was also hopeless in love, mired in addiction, or imprisoned by fascists. That in addition he may have failed to write anything else nearly as good – that oh-so-crucial 'second act' – only adds a *frisson* of pure, guilty joy to the whole hideous confection of gloating.

Anyway, besides the frankly disgusting voyeurism implicit in writers' reading literary biography (after all, why stimulate yourself through viewing someone else perform an act that's effectively intrinsic to your own being?), there's also the raw fact of repetition to make the whole business still more masturbatory: he writes his first novel – so do you; he divorces – you do likewise; he goes on the Grand Tour – you take a package one; and so on *ad taedium*. There's little to be gained from the revisiting of the minutiae of advances, proof-reading, lunches with agents, public appearances and plaudits, beyond a reacquaintance with the quotidian aspects of your own life – it's not going to help you toss off the next book any more easily than you did the last. And as for those biographies that offer textual analysis alongside the laundry lists, well, if as a writer you can't trust to your own judgement and interpretation of another's work, then, hell, you might as well become a critic!

Still, someone's got to get out there and fess up, break the conspiracy of silence and admit to being a writer who reads literary biography. Ours is an age of confessional writing, so why not confess to bad reading habits? I devour the stuff. I'm so addicted to beating the meat of the matter that I even read the biographies of writers whose works I haven't read! And how much worse can that be? I recently undertook to review Graham Robb's new biography of Rimbaud, even though I'd never absorbed so much as a word of the poet's work. Of course, I can attempt to justify myself (like the English literature academic who confesses to not having read *Hamlet*, in David Lodge's *Small World*) by claiming that Rimbaud is such an icon of the counter-culture that I've managed to absorb the impact of his *oeuvre* merely by swimming in the same waters; or that Robb's book itself offers much of the texts through a critical reading; or that I can – writer that I manifestly am – manage a critique of the biography without reference to anything – even its subject matter! – outside of it. But all this is flim-flam; the uncomfortable truth is that I'm a wanker – pure and simple.

I began self-abuse more or less at the same time as I began reading seriously, which I date to around the age of fourteen. Hot on the heels of a precocious tussle with the Russians came Henri Troyat's biography of Tolstoy. I've no idea whether it's considered to be a good biography, but for me it fulfilled all the requirements of the adolescent poseur. The Penguin edition was absurdly fat – a paperback engorged with its own portentousness – and featured a full-face portrait of the man himself, oozing beard and messianic charisma in equal parts. As for content, I can't remember a great deal about the Count's appropriations of Michelet and Stendhal, or his search for railway verisimilitude, but I do recall the epic swashbuckling of Troyat's Tolstoy. This was a writer who had it all – aristocracy, socialism, sin, morality – and who even got to die at a great age after running away from home; what could conceivably be more attractive to the adolescent mentality?

Well, Proust for one. I'd dabbled in *Remembrance of Things Past* (can one really say that? Surely it's a bit akin to fly-fishing for Moby-Dick), but the whole screaming, prancing, *épater*-ing, tittering, transgendering scope of the novel evaded me until I was marooned in the outback of Australia in my early twenties. None the less, I happily embarked on George Painter's ectomorphic biography of little Marcel, with nary a care for the fact that the two ways at Combray were as unknown to me as the Silk Road. Was this a mistake? Did the foreshadowing through autobiography of the grey area that lies between 'Marcel' and Marcel hamper or aid me when it came to breasting the turbid waters of those vast, paragraph-long sentences?

I rather think the latter, for Painter's Proust was so much the sniffling milquetoast that even the etiolated ephebe who narrates *Remembrance* became a veritable *fin-de-siècle* John Wayne by contrast. And anyway, I wasn't submerging myself in the detail of Proust's life for the sake of Proust alone: Painter's biography introduced me to the family tree of late-nineteenth-century French literature, so that I was able to appreciate that Robert, Comte de Montesquieu, was the real-life model not only for the Baron Charlus, but also for Huysmans's decadent aristo Des Esseintes in *Against Nature*. Via the method (i.e. far too much lying in bed reading), I was able to work my way into the mental recumbency of Proust. I'm not certain that I've ever been able to escape. Like the young Cocteau, I wanted to be able to rush across the backs of the seats in the Café de Paris, so that I could drape a fur coat around the narrow shoulders of the genius – but then relapse into an opiated stupor.

Opiated stupor was, of course, what attracted me to the work of

William Burroughs. Not that I'd experienced one at that point – it's just that from the perspective of drizzly, suburban London the idea of exile in Tangier with an international cast of ne'er-do-wells appealed enormously. I'm not saying that a youthful obsession with the life and times of the most notorious literary outlaw is a necessary precursor to heroin addiction, but if your kids are spending rather more time reading *The Naked Lunch* than they are eating their school dinners, I suggest you keep a sharp eye on them.

I'd always known a fair bit about Burroughs's life – it is, after all, more or less inseparable from the work – but when Ted Morgan's comprehensive biography (*Literary Outlaw: The Life and Times of William S. Burroughs*) came out in the early nineties I became an avid reader, then rereader, then multiple rereader. This is the episode of my literary-biographical self-abuse that I feel most uncomfortable about. In drug-addiction recovery circles it's a much remarked-upon phenomenon that the addict, when using, seeks to prop up the denial of his own condition by constantly comparing himself with other drug addicts he perceives as being far worse than himself. I'm not saying that there weren't plenty of people personally known to me with whom I performed this path-ological one-upmanship, but there were few to hand who, like me, were not only drug addicts, but publicly known to be so, and who had a reputation for writing books that, if not drug-fuelled in the execution (it's a shibboleth admirably refuted in Morgan's book that Burroughs actually wrote *The Naked Lunch* under the influence of heroin), were certainly entwined with the psychic tendrils of the author's own addictive personality.

Yes, I read Morgan's biography to make me feel better about my own drug addiction. 'Damn it,' I would reprove myself, aged thirty-two and collapsing under the weight of a massive cocaine habit, 'Burroughs hadn't even begun to use drugs at your age – you must still have some mileage left in you!' Or else I'd note that at least I didn't have the dual outsider's curse of being homosexual as well; or that I didn't have quite so many criminal convictions as Burroughs – and certainly not one for the man-slaughter of my wife.

It's tawdry stuff, and from the vantage point of drug-free sobriety, I not only find my own preoccupation with the demented fandango that Burroughs cut across the fringes of the counter-culture for sixty-odd years to be pathetic; I view the life of the man himself as irredeemably pathetic and lacking in spiritual value. My wife has, with exemplary intuition, come to convince me of murderous intent on Bill's part when he told Joan Volmer, his common-law wife, to put the shot glass on her head so 'we can do our William Tell trick'. There's nothing cool about witnessing the death from liver cancer of your only son, and Burroughs's later years, which he spent corralled in the Midwest, Dali-like putting his valuable signature to bogus works of replicated 'art', seem to be a kind of karmic fate. No wonder he ended up doing Gap commercials.

There was another literary biography of a drug addict that I read and reread, but in the case of Richard Holmes's *Coleridge: Early Visions* there's no way even a writer as arrogant as myself could be accused of seeking a comparison. Despite this, I was stunned when I reached the end of the book – in the very middle of the Pentland Firth! – to find that like me Coleridge was thirty-two; like me he was heading off into exile (in his case it was to Malta, in mine to Orkney); and like me he was in flight from both a failed marriage and a drug addiction. Anyway, there's no comparison between Holmes's book and Morgan's. The former is poetical, paradoxical and wildly inclusive. Like Coleridge himself, of whom it was said, 'He was the last man in England to have read everything,' Holmes's biography achieves a lyrical flight of erudition (as do all his other biographies); while Morgan's is executed from the standpoint of a clinical psychologist, sitting in the corner taking dry notes, while his experimental subject is tripping on LSD.

The sequel to *Early Visions* was eagerly awaited by me. What a bizarre idea, waiting for years to read the sequel to a literary biography. At times I even felt like going round to Holmes's house and standing behind his shoulder egging him on. When *Darker Proof* came out it was just as unputdownable – for me – as its precursor, I had to find out if Coleridge's fate might foreshadow my own; would I, like him, end up on maintenance prescription of opiates, a shadow of my former self, the seeds of my youthful plagiarism haunting my long twilight of decline? No such luck. With property and therapy prices as they are nowadays, there was absolutely no chance that I could ever afford to reside under a doctor's care in Highgate.

I could go on and on, turning this essay into a complete synecdoche of the condition I describe, but I won't. Suffice to say, this is but a fraction of the literary biography I've read over the years. On book tours in the USA I often make a point of rereading Ellmann's masterful biography of Wilde; not only is it the literary biography that, to my mind, brings you closest to what it must actually have been like to share a room with its subject, but Wilde himself was a formidable gigger, criss-crossing the States in a whirlwind tour of lectures on the 'House Beautiful'. Ellmann said of Wilde that he lived his life in two distinct parts, first as a scapegoat, then as a scapegrace. I've read the biography while myself being a scapegoat and then a scapegrace, and I can tell you that it holds up well from either viewpoint.

I like to think that at some point I will quit this essentially adolescent phase of onanism and progress into something that – to paraphrase the Freudians – could be described as 'full literary genitality', but in truth I can't even imagine what that might be like. In the meantime all I can say is that I've confessed in print, and like many other modern authors I feel shriven by this act alone. One last thing: if any writer ever attempts to tell you that they never read literary biography, please feel free to challenge them in the most rigorous way you can. If they don't then recant and admit their secret vice, tell them that I'm coming straight round to the house to rip the plain brown wrapper off all the volumes of their copy of Michael Holroyd's life of Bernard Shaw. That'll shut 'em up.

Books & Company, September 2000

48

Restaurant review: Elena's L'Étoile,
30 Charlotte Street, London W1

Apparently a group of politico-cultural luminaries have taken to eating at L'Étoile, in London's Charlotte Street, and discussing the prospects for the dawn of a new republican age. All power to them, I say. I yearn for the day when the Windsors are reduced to the same culinary circumstances as the rest of us.

Imagine it: Princess Diana sorting through a supermarket gondola for the appropriately lean cuisine; her errant husband *waiting* to be seated at a roadside Happy Eater; and the Queen herself (God bless her!) engaged in a spirited fight with the waiters at Wong Kei in Wardour Street over their non-acceptance of credit cards. (Even after becoming a commoner she still finds it hard to countenance carrying cash.)

In advance of this happy day, I decided to check out L'Étoile and see whether the establishment would gift me some hints as to what the new British polity might be like.

Arriving on a dark evening, we found the façade completely lit up and a cherry picker with a cameraman ensconced on it wavering about, filming. This, it transpired, was the fall-out from the 'outing' of L'Étoile as a hotbed of sedition. The previous week, when the republicans were meeting, a camera crew had burst into the restaurant. They didn't get the shots they wanted – so they burst in again. It was only as they were bursting in for the third time that the *maître d'* called a halt. Now they'd come back for the exteriors.

We sidestepped a man wearing a sleeveless anorak with thirty-five pockets who was doing something with a light meter, entered the establishment and encountered Elena, the presiding spirit of L'Étoile.

Elena is one of the original Soho characters. She ran Bianchi's for many years, then moved to a special niche at L'Escargot in the 1980s and has ended up at L'Étoile. She's a lively woman in her mid-seventies who, over the years, has broken bread for almost every theatrical and show-business figure of note. Elena is a genuine and unaffected lady who gains more honest pleasure from welcoming people in to eat than the Windsors have got from field sports in the past five generations. I think she was especially chuffed to see us because I had Dave in tow, and she remembered him from the 1970s when he would go into Bianchi's, eat up a storm and leave the tab to be picked up by his thespian father.

L'Étoile has a delightful, slightly distempered air of anachronism. There is a profusion of smoked glass and wooden partitions, painted a restrained yellow. The floorboards are varnished, the lighting points down. The tables are dressed sharply and crisply in the whitest of linen. All over the walls is an enormous collection of photographs of celebrities, everyone from Daniel Day Lewis to Melvyn Bragg (actually, that's not that far in terms of the cultural inscape!).

It's an instantly reassuring interior. This, one thinks as one advances to one's table, is what a restaurant should really be like. It's not difficult to imagine Cocteau climbing perilously along the top of the banquette, bringing Proust his cloak as the great writer waits by the door.

The menu at L'Étoile is a nice, chunky bit of board that covers the waterfront as far as intellectually uncomplicated, but aesthetically involved French cooking is concerned. Dave went for the duck salad. He said the bird was game, not fatty, and that the bed of watercress it arrived on was as cosy as a 42-tog duvet. I ruminated over the fish soup and munched my way through a surprisingly tasty set of crudités, the olives mulched up with shallots and herbs.

I'd begun by drinking Glenfiddich in an attempt to capture the spirit of the Union, but we now switched to the special wine on offer, a tasty and robust Châteauneuf-du-Pape, which had – as the oenophiles would put it – a fruity attack.

Feeling somewhat jaded and liverish I couldn't quite summon up the energy for a hefty main course and stuck with the ravioli, which came enmired in a happy goo of basil and tomatoes. Dave was on altogether sprightlier form and plunged on, ordering an ideologically unreconstructed calf's liver.

This poignant organ was borne to the table, residing on a high pallet of bubble and squeak – so high, in fact, that the dish was distinctly taller than it was wide. I have since learned that this was an example of so-called 'vertical food', a new kind of cuisine that has emerged from the teeming eateries of Manhattan. Suitable really, that most vertiginous of cities producing the most vertiginous of dishes. It makes you wonder what sort of food sculpture some of our domestic conurbations might come up with. Perhaps Birmingham will become well known for agglomerations of meat and vegetables that manage to bypass the plate altogether.

Together with my ravioli came a side salad, which I browsed on: nothing but the crispest of leaves, laid out in a gentle circlet. None of that hideous shredding and rending of lettuce which you get in so many restaurants. Elena had reappeared and was catching up on some twenty years of gossip with Dave. We ordered tarte Tatin, espresso and a couple of generous snifters of Marc de Bourgogne. The good food and republican atmosphere began to seep into me. I felt myself sliding into a vision of a happier, more democratic future . . .

Dateline: 2035. Charlotte Street. Elena, now a sprightly 115 years old, stands ready by the door of L'Étoile to welcome in a most important guest. After elections conducted under a new psephological system so complicated that it's forced Peter Kellner to retire, the first President of the Archipelago Republic (formerly Britain and Ireland) has been elected.

He's an unassuming man, the President, his pouched and lined face as weathered as the fells of his native Cumbria. Yes, you guessed it. The new President is Melvyn Bragg. Elena welcomes him with her characteristic warmth and guides him to his table while the rest of us stand, applaud and spontaneously break into a customised version of 'La Marseillaise'.

Later, Elena stops by our table for a gossip. President Bragg is deep in conversation with his minister of culture, Daniel Day Lewis. 'It's amazing really,' Elena whispers, 'but such is the respect accorded to our new President, that no one mentions the novels any more . . .'

Observer, April 1996

49

Restaurant review: Le Manoir aux Quat' Saisons,
Great Milton, Oxfordshire

Driving down the M40 on my way back from an international office-equipment trade fair at Birmingham NEC, I was considering stopping at the Three Pigeons near Junction 7 for a couple of pints of Old Speckled Hen and a meat pie, when I suddenly remembered that Raymond Blanc has a little place in this neck of the woods. I only had an hour or so for lunch, but figured that Le Manoir aux Quat' Saisons might be just the thing. I checked the glove compartment to see that I had some BiSoDol with me, and turned the Cavalier in the direction of Great Milton.

From the road it looked more like a sixteenth-century manor house than a restaurant, and I couldn't see a bill of fare anywhere. The least they could have done would have been to put one of those free-standing blackboards in the road with the day's specials chalked on it like they do at the Three Pigeons. Honestly, Raymond Blanc may be a master of the culinary arts, but in some things he's streets behind the average publican.

I parked up in a gravelled stable-block area, under a tree, and left my PA, Gruton, to deal with covering up our sample cases of Rolodexes and hole-punchers. Then I strode through a series of charming little courtyards, all bursting with blooming flowers, passed a pond where a bronze statue of a girl in a swimsuit reclined (marvellous attention to detail – the Speedo label clearly visible), and entered Le Manoir.

It's difficult to convey one's first impressions of this place. It's far, far more than just a restaurant. There's a small hotel as well; a garden where vegetables and herbs are grown for immediate consumption; an in-house florist; and in the grounds a superb Japanese garden (of which more later), as well as an orchard, a water garden, a swimming pool and a tennis court.

On consideration of all these facilities, and the ambience of sheer luxury which permeates the establishment, along with bevies of superbly trained, fawning staff, it occurred to me that come the revolution this would be an ideal concentration camp for the former heads of re-nationalised industries. We needn't expropriate them, just insist that they *live* at Le Manoir. Within a few months even Cedric Brown and the directors of Camelot would be cadging the price of their next bottle of Puligny Montrachet.

Gruton came puffing in, a vision in an off-the-peg chalk-striped suit from Littlewoods, and we were shown to our table by a *maître d'* whose consummate elegance and gentility made us both feel we really belonged. This is the truth about the very wealthy: they are spoiled so much by service of this kind that they become – spoilt.

We declined an aperitif and asked for the wine list. This was the size of a volume of the *Britannica* and listed literally thousands of superb wines. I asked Gruton what he fancied, and the reply came back, 'White.' Always good to have a connoisseur on board. I ordered a bottle of Meursault Sous la Velle, a snip at £65, about the same amount of money as a single mother with three children gets on Family Credit to survive for a week.

The dining room was distinctly on the chintzy side. Pseudo-grain had been painted on to the wood panelling, using shades of ochre and yellow. On shelves above our table were jars full of pickled things, and around the room were naïve paintings of French rural life. All in all, it was a Peter Mayle-style vision of luxury.

I won't trouble you with a description of the dishes offered on the main menu; suffice to say that some of them involved explication running to several lines. Just reading these gobbets made me feel like dialling James Hewitt on my mobile, to see if he knew the number of Princess Di's colonic-irrigation specialist.

Gruton and I turned our attention to the menu du jour. No problems here. There was a choice of two dishes to begin with: veg terrine or chicken liver mousse; and a choice of two dishes to follow: duck or mackerel. I forestalled Gruton's embarrassment at coming to a decision under the haughty gaze of the *maître d'* and simply ordered the lot.

Our Meursault arrived. Gruton thought it rather good, but as he's often to be found drinking a can of Two Dogs alcoholic lemonade in the stationery cupboard, I didn't set much store by his opinion. Then we were offered a tiny cup of gazpacho, some canapés and a selection of breads. The tiny cup of gazpacho is very much a part of contemporary *haute cuisine*; so much a part that different chefs rival one another to see just how tiny they can make it. I've heard tell that some of the more avant-garde are now offering gazpacho in 5ml hypodermic syringes – but I'm sure this is apocryphal.

Our first courses hove into view. The terrine of vegetables layered with roasted monkfish fell to my lot. It was laid out on the plate in a peculiarly deconstructed fashion, like a diagram for an Airfix model. Gruton's chicken liver mousse in vintage port sauce with tomatoes and bay leaves also looked like a blueprint for something else altogether. At the next table an odd trio were eating salads the size of hayricks.

I can describe what the food *looked* like, but I'm not sure I'm going to be able to adequately convey all the flavours. Raymond Blanc states, in a charming bit of blurb at the front of the menu, 'The table remains a powerful symbol of friendship and celebration of life,' but all too often in my experience the table is a powerful opportunity for terse, acrimonious arguments, followed by painful dyspepsia.

So it was on this occasion. Gruton got going on the contentious issue of why it is that while everyone else in the office has a Macintosh PowerBook, he is compelled to produce numerous documents and reports using a Junior Bulldog Printing Set. This little *embrouillement* kept us going right through the poached Cornish mackerel in a saffron-scented mussel soup, and the confit of duck legs with fennel. All I can remember about the mackerel was that the poaching had made it very un-oily and therefore rather un-mackerely.

We skipped pudding. I'd looked at my watch and realised that it had taken us nearly two hours to plug through two courses. We took coffee in the garden and considered going for a stroll in the Fugetsu-An no Roji. This apparently means 'Tea Garden of the Pavilion of a Deep Love of Nature'; but a more appropriate name might be 'Garden of Skiving Off Without Paying the Bill', because it's beautifully secluded from Le Manoir.

Of course the food was superb, but then at nearing £75 a head it bloody well ought to be. For that kind of money a lot of chefs I know will come round to your house, cook you dinner and shampoo your carpets into the bargain.

Observer, June 1996

50

To vote for any of the big four candidates for London's new mayoralty is to prop up a *status quo* on the very point of crumbling. The new city-wide authority is only a part of a devolutionary process that affects us all at a regional and a supra-national level. We need to register our vote for the sole candidate and the only party that understands this. The Greens reject wholesale the historic bipartisanship of London politics and in so doing are the only party fit to lead us into a pan-European future.

Although I am, and always have been, an unreconstructed left-winger I shan't be voting for Ken Livingstone. Why? Because he lied egregiously about his intentions. This big lie has retroacted on my view of Livingstone to expose him as the timeless London demagogue he really is. There's simply no point in wasting a democratic vote on a posturing demagogue – especially when the posture's been frozen for nigh on fourteen years. A vote for Ken Livingstone is an anti-Thatcher protest vote posted to the past.

As for Dobson, Kramer and Norris, all of them equivocate between appeasing the City of London and appeasing the Government. They're all political children playing with a two-piece card-house: will the City prop up the Government, or the Government prop up the City? Whether we can afford to maintain and expand the antediluvian public transport system using this public-private partnership or that privatisation package is neither here nor there, when set against these jokers' thraldom to this two-faced establishment.

The Greens are also the only party to reject the ethical nimbyism that dominates our thinking about community-based politics. I was born in this city and have lived here all my life, mired in its immemorial dolour. Despite being an enthusiastic car driver I'm fed up to the back teeth with pollution and congestion in London. My eldest son, when a baby, developed pollution-related asthma which has dogged all his young years. When will this idiocy stop? When will we cease to hearken to our foam-padded, petrol-powered arses and begin listening to our reason? And when will people remember that the fundamental basis of representative democracy is that it exists to restrain our worst impulses – not encourage our best?

The Greens are the only party contesting this election on a sound ethical footing, the only party unafraid to state that sacrifices must be made by the citizenry on an individual basis to safeguard our collective future. Should there be congestion charges in London? Of course there should – and now. Should green spaces be protected? Of course they should. Should there be more affordable housing in London? Absolutely.

Lastly, and by no means least importantly, a vote for Darren Johnson on 4 May is a vote for a politician wholly unsullied by the kind of moral equivocations – public and private – exhibited by the other candidates. The only openly gay candidate in the contest, he's also the straightest.

Evening Standard, April 2000

51

I'm standing in an art gallery, in central London. It's the first truly hot, clammy, oppressive, fume-tangy evening of winter – summer having been declared an out-and-out failure. The gallery is jam-packed with the sort of dudes you expect at this kind of event: middle-aged women wearing ethnically patterned dresses cut like bell-tents and porting asymmetrical, onyx earrings; young men precipitately shaven-headed, their eyes glassily intelligent behind thick, blue lenses; older, more obviously bibulous men, their chalk stripes, ties and trouser-legs just a tad on the wide side, their hair white through nicotine. And there's a BBC TV crew, and there are various snappers, *and* there are hacks with notebooks, and there's a fair assortment of other people whose stereotypes are too obvious to proclaim.

They're all swilling white wine from rented glasses, they're all talking, and realistically none of them could get a clear view of any of the daubs on the walls unless they were prepared to torch their way through the skulls of twenty of their fellow private-openeers with a flame-thrower.

I'm standing – as I say – letting this tide of cultured flotsam wash around me, idly taking notes and minding my own business. One of the advantages of being abnormally tall is that at a gig like this, where the fleshly press is so great that people can only tilt mouth to rim and back again in a tight arc, no one can lean far back enough to talk to you.

No one, that is, saving Rebecca Hossack, whose gallery this is. Hossack is a lanky, blonde, striking woman, with a nice line herself in camping dresses and light-fitment earrings. She's been running annual exhibitions of Australian Aboriginal artists' work at her Windmill Street gallery long enough for this year's to be entitled 'Songlines XVII'. An Antipodean herself, Hossack, a mutual acquaintance later informed me, once held the position of Australian cultural attaché – presumably having taken it over from Sir Les Patterson. Whether it's the result of her diplomatic or of her art-networking experience, Hossack has a near-photographic memory for names and faces. 'Will!' she exclaims, bearing down on me like a flightless bird that's adapted to a diet of canapés. 'Good t'seeya. You must come and meet the artists!' And without dropping a verbal stitch, she commences a surprisingly intimate patter, while parting the sea of aesthetes between us and a group of Aboriginals who are coming down the stairs.

I'm speechless – something that's happening to me increasingly nowadays. According to my neurologist Dr 'Big' McFee, I now have acute both nominal and facial agnosia – I can't put a name to a face, or vice versa. Such is the impact of Hossack's assumed intimacy with me that, as she propels me forward, I'm tormented by just how well she knows me – or vice versa. I rack my brain. Have I been to any of the Songlines I through XVI? I can't remember – although I know I've been in the gallery before. Are Hossack and I acquaintances? Or friends? Or even former lovers? Perhaps we're married? The possibilities shuffle in my addled forebrain like a bizarre game of consequences. Then we're by the stairs and Hossack (I know it is her – but don't ask me how) begins introducing me to the group of Aboriginal painters who've come all the way from Fitzroy Crossing in the Northern Territory of Australia.

There's nothing quite so powerfully other as Aboriginal people. Just to look at them is to make contact with a radically different world view. Their eyes are fixed on the horizon, their skin is a dusty matt black, and their hair lies in oily curls on their steeply canted brows. There are five or six of them here, all very short indeed. One is an elderly man, the rest women, who appear middle-aged. They're wearing mid-length denim skirts rather than *faux* muu-muus, and porting souvenir 'London' shopping bags instead of onyx earrings. Hossack introduces me to them all, but the only names I catch are Jimmy's and Daisy's – because I've already clocked their paintings downstairs – and their interpreter's, Joy.

Daisy Andrews has executed a marvellous panorama of her country entitled *Karu*. The explanatory tag underneath the painting informs us that 'after the rain the *karu* (small creeks) run through my country'. The trees are shaggy and feathery; verdant the way only savagely quick growth can be. Daisy has filled in the foreground with pointillist bushes and plants. In the distance are iron-red hills. The brushstrokes are fluent, but the colours and shapes are alien to a Western viewer, and the proscenium through which they're viewed is too wide-angle, too big-country.

Mind you, it's easier to see one of the posing private-openeers scoring for one of these than it is for one of the 'teaching' paintings. Although this genre of Aboriginal art is highly popular in the West, I can't quite imagine that its purchasers regard it as much more than interesting assemblages of colours and shapes; an elision between the ethnic and the abstract. Or do they invite people round to dinner, point at the vividly inscribed panel of concentric rectangles on the wall and intone, 'This is a teaching painting from Dreamtime. Two boys were out playing and they found some witchetty grubs. The women had left them there for the men who were out hunting for meat. The old women saw a big storm coming up and they went back to camp . . .' while their guests sip Chablis?

Who knows. I'm looking at Joy – she's looking at me. What can we discuss? How can we bridge the yawing gulf between outback and up front? Should I animadvert that I am no fan of Dr Germaine Greer who is due at the gallery shortly to give the opening address? Hossack has told me that Jimmy is a fantastic dancer. Should I get the old man to cut a few capers in his white Stetson? Eventually I say, 'It's hot in here.' And one of them replies, 'Too bloody right!' Next thing we're heading for the front door, out of the crush.

As I head towards Tottenham Court Road I wonder if this experience will become part of the rich mother lode of Australian metaphor. I can imagine them saying to one another in Fitzroy Crossing for years hence, 'I'll tellya how bloody hot it was – it was as hot as a gallery opening in W1!'

The Times, August 1998

52

The Lenders live behind the wainscotting of the house. They are small, human figures, perfectly proportioned. Both men and women wear serious business suits and glasses. They are quiet and purposive and have built a network of open-plan offices behind the wainscotting. Here they keep track of all the things they have lent to the people who live in the house.

The children of the house are up early watching Saturday morning television. Cartoons in fact. The smallest child has a toy rabbit she's particularly fond of. She goes to the kitchen to help herself to a glass of apple juice from the fridge. The Lenders appear from behind the fridge. One of them has a clipboard, and reading from it informs the child that they lent her the rabbit. They take it away from her and disappear with it into the wainscotting. Tragic and disturbing image of rabbit being pulled into mouse-hole.

The child, crying, goes to wake her parents, and tells them what has happened. The mother urges the father to get up and deal with it. He does so – with ill grace. He goes with the child back to the kitchen, and there, by the fridge, meets with the Lenders. They consult their clipboard again, then pull a small VDU out from the wainscotting. The father bends down so that he can read this. The Lenders inform him that the money he used to buy the toy rabbit was in fact lent by them. The father disputes this – although he is warned that the consequences of doing so may be disastrous. He puts the youngest child back on the sofa in front of the television, assuring her that he will get the rabbit back.

Cut to bank. The father is being shown in to see the duty manager. The father explains about the Lenders and demands proof from the manager that the money he used to buy the toy rabbit was lent to him by the bank. The manager is smooth and emollient, but confesses that although this was the case, the money the bank lent was actually lent to the bank by . . . the Lenders. Some Lenders appear on the manager's desk at this point, complete with direct computer link to the father's house. Once again the relevant figures are perused by all parties, and the origin of the loan is incontrovertibly proved.

Meanwhile, back at the house, the mother is having difficulty getting up and facing the day. She keeps pulling the duvet back over her head, despite the children who come into her bedroom and importune her to rise and make their breakfast. The Lenders appear, shinning up the side of the bed, and parley with her on the pillow. They explain that the resistance she feels is a result of her having drawn too heavily on her stock of motherhood. She has exceeded her motherhood overdraft.

How, the mother asks, can she repay this, so that she will be able to tend her own children? The Lenders suggest that she mother *them* a bit – this will help. The Lenders strip off so that she may suckle them. This she does, sitting upright in bed, opening her nightdress and placing one adult homunculus on each breast. Her own, neglected children wail and yammer.

Inside the wainscotting, the other Lenders have set the toy rabbit up in a bizarre temple, and are worshipping it as a deity of childhood. The rabbit smiles down on them benignly.

In another chamber in the interstices of the house, more Lenders are 'playing'. They have stripped naked and are swinging on a kind of Newton's cradle, their bodies taking the place of the ball-bearings. As they swing back and forth, banging into each other, they effect penetration in all the obvious combinations.

The father arrives home from the bank disconsolate, and goes to cuddle the frightened children on the sofa, in front of the still-gabbling cartoons. The children tell him about the mother. He races upstairs and finds in the bedroom a grotesque scene. The numbers of Lenders have swollen, and there is a press of them around the mother. Some are naked, others half-dressed, others still are clothed and pushing from the back of the seething, diminutive mob. The mother gives the father a piteous look.

The father rounds on the Lenders and demands to see their management. The management appear from the wainscotting. They are more heavily-built, more serious-looking and more purposive than the other Lenders. The Lenders who have been jostling to be suckled by the mother leave off and gather themselves together, begin dressing.

The father points out to the management the obvious: where did they obtain the money and the motherhood, the credit of which they extended to the family? There is a frozen moment – the Lenders' bluff has been called. Our POV goes back into the wainscotting. The wainscotting, of course, has its own more diminutive wainscotting, and from behind this come the Lenders' Lenders.

Our POV has the micro-bit between its teeth now, and we plunge on into the wainscotting of the Lenders' Lenders, and meet their Lenders.

We shrink down each successive stage until we get to the molecular structure of Lenders, the building-blocks of the Lender cosmos. These consist of many many particular men and women, dressed in sober suits, sitting at desks, and joined to one another in the manner of models of molecules by connective rods. Occasionally a free-ranging electron of a Lender will come barrelling out of the void and attack one of these molecular assemblages of Lenders, displacing one from his or her desk and forcing a reconfiguration of the molecular model. It is a harsh and pitiless scene.

We focus in on the desk of one of these molecular Lenders. They are doodling a sketch of the toy rabbit. We fade out on the smile of the sketch of the toy rabbit.

Video treatment for Massive Attack, 1995

53

Earth has not anything to show more fair:
Dull would he be of soul who could pass by
A sight so touching in its majesty:

Namely, a dirty great fan poised to blow all the filth out of the West End of London once and for all. At least, that's what I thought, standing on Westminster Bridge at around eleven o'clock on Sunday morning, straining to remain sufficiently still, and highly concentrated, so that I might actually be able to see the Millennium Eye Ferris wheel move, as it was cranked, infinitesimal increment by infinitesimal increment, into an upright position.

For those of us who've been keen Millennium Eye watchers for a good part of this year it was a heady moment – and we were out in force. When I got home my wife asked me what sort of people had gone down to take a look. 'It was astonishing,' I replied, 'but it turns out that this is the moiety I truly belong in. Both sides of the bridge were double-parked with crappy old green Citroën Dyanes, and there were at least eighty tall men with pockmarked faces, wearing leather jackets, smoking Toscanelli cheroots and squinting into the sky. Several of them approached me and asked whether I too felt that this sight – the giant, spoked wheel canted at forty-five degrees – was suggestive of a dirty great fan poised to blow all of the filth etc. etc. I mean, I knew London was a big city – but this was ridiculous!'

Anyway, what did it matter if I was a stereotypical, nerdy Ferris-wheel-raising watcher? I was enjoying myself. After two previous attempts had failed, there had been plenty of speculation in the media that the big wheel wouldn't even be up and running for New Year's Eve. From time to time I've found myself considering how David Marks and Julia Barfield, the architects behind the Eye, might've been feeling about the situation. But really, it didn't bear thinking about. I mean, all relationships (Marks and Barfield are personal as well as professional partners) tend to suffer from the awareness – on both sides – of things unsaid, subjects undiscussed.

At night, in bed, these 'things' tend to gather beneath the duvet, and form themselves into a hefty rampart, thrusting the partners further and further apart. But while the average couple may have to deal with piffling instances of neglect, betrayal and repetitive telling of anecdotes, Marks and Barfield must have been bedding down nightly for the last three months with 20,000 tonnes of steel crammed in between them. And no likelihood of getting it up before morning.

I like to think that with the wheel up their partnership will be on a roll again. Who knows, as I write they may already be planning another piece of astonishing architectural chutzpah. After all, I can't help feeling that the Eye – which Marks himself told me was intended as a feminine counterpoint to the phallic blocks of the City – won't be complete without its own, masculine partner.

It was reading about the 1939 World's Fair in New York that got me thinking along these lines. In a depression year, Lewis Mumford called the notion of the fair a 'completely tedious and unconvincing belief in the triumph of modern industry'. Ah, Mumford – my kind of a guy.

It was sited on Flushing Meadows, from where 6,700,000 cubic yards of garbage had to be moved and graded in under two hundred days. But these aren't the main parallels with our own millennial madness; and nor was the pre-pop-art National Cash Register building which busily counted in the customers. (Although that would've been a nice idea for the 'Money Zone'.) No, the landmark structures that dominated the 1939 fair were the Trylon and the Perisphere. These were respectively a 700ft-high tapered pillar ('the finite'), and a 200ft-in-diameter steel-frame globe ('the infinite').

Our problem is we've now got two of these 'infinite'-style structures for the millennium – the Eye and the Dome – and nothing that expresses the finite. We need, therefore, something thrusting, phallic, obdurate, and, given financial constraints, it has to be already *in situ*, on London's South Bank. Hmm, come to think of it I know the very thing. My near neighbour, Lord Jeffrey Archer, fulfils all the requirements. He lives on the Vauxhall Embankment, he's thrusting, obdurate, and beyond a scintilla of doubt the biggest dickhead in London. Let's all hope that he's finite.

Building Design, October 1999

54

It's at this time of the year, when the *Building Design*/British Steel Young Architect of the Year Award comes around, that my essential ignorance of the field begins to tell. In truth, it's not simply ignorance – it's a distinct repulsion. Like some personification of Gore-Tex, I begin to feel the need to keep the built environment from raining down upon me. To avoid the field – I'd happily crouch in a field.

I wonder if young architects ever feel this way? I'd like to think that at least some amongst you are far-sighted enough not to rush your edification. Take a break year, that's my advice. And go somewhere where there aren't any buildings to speak of, like the Empty Quarter of Arabia, or the forests of Borneo, or Frankfurt am Main. Get a good airy piece of emptiness around you and savour it, because before long you'll find yourself bricked up in the very foundations of professionalism, sunk deep within a shaft of endeavour.

You'll find yourself attending – as I did – gigs like the 'launch debate' for the Young Architect of the Year Award, an achingly serious affair which brought together professionals of all stripes and hues, to consider the weighty question: do young architects get the breaks they deserve?

Sod the breaks – do they get the canapés they deserve? is the question that needs to be asked at an event such as this. Held in the penthouse conference room of the RIBA, it was an opportunity for this journeyman hack to witness your profession in solemn colloquium, within its most hallowed of portals. (And I suppose you lot must hallow portals far more than anyone else.)

The first thing worthy of remarking on was the uniform. Architects have to be one of the most sartorially conservative bunch of professionals there is in modern Britain. Even politicians look as if they're dressing for the Rio carnival when set against you lot. Once and for all, constructors: simply because you don't wear a tie, it doesn't mean you aren't wearing a suit. Furthermore, simply because you're wearing slightly mismatched trousers (or skirts) and jackets, it doesn't mean you don't *appear* to be wearing suits when you're observed, *en masse*, sipping white wine, and back-lit by a row of rational windows. And another thing – while it may be true that grey is the old black, grey remains the old grey as well as being both the new black and, of course, the new grey. Also, giving a pair of black leather lace-ups a vaguely orthopaedic toe does absolutely nothing to detract from their essential character. Finally: shirts can be off-white.

Still, I suppose sartorial quibbles are the least of it. I'd never been in the RIBA before, and I suppose I anticipated it as keenly as a restaurant critic might look forward to dining in the staff canteen at Le Gavroche. Not. The impression the building gave me was one of being overwhelmingly *echt*. 'I hate it,' hissed a young architect to me as we milled during the pre-debate drinks; 'it represents everything I most loathe about the British architectural establishment.' I wanted to get more out of this fifth-columnist, this maverick, but in the split second it took me to lift a canapé to my lips, he'd faded into the mêlée and, given his grey jacket, black trousers and open-necked white shirt, was indistinguishable from his fellow nonconformists.

I'd anticipated the debate being a high-flown affair, a great, towering façade of reasoning upon which emblematic argumentation would be formed into a frieze. Instead it was a kind of informational swap-shop, during which young architects offered younger architects advice on whether to build practices, undertake collaborative ventures, or – if all else failed – seek out Spud-U-Like franchises. Nothing wrong with any of this, but it did seem to me that the general tenor of discussion assumed a perspective on the profession that demoted it from being – as it were – the fountain-head of human endeavour, to being more approximate to the drainage system.

On the way out I took the stairs, which wended down past the stares of previous presidents of the RIBA council. Their oily eyes scrutinised me with *echt*-seeking intensity. 'Hmm,' they seemed to be whispering in my ears, 'we see you have a black jacket, white shirt, black trousers. But those aren't lace-ups – they're boots! And they're brown! Exterminate! Exterminate!' I hit Portland Place running – and haven't stopped since.

Building Design, July 1999

55

Restaurant review: Bluebird, 350 King's Road, London SW3

I came to in a sort of foetal-cum-squat-thrust posture, all tensed up. I could feel the immaculately-cut trousers of my Jasper Conran suit cut immaculately into my testicular region. Idly, I considered the possibilities of marketing Jasper's suits with a free vasectomy offer. Then reality snuck back in. I was being carried inside some sort of giant ball or globe. Far from being rigid, or supportive, the container felt impossibly flimsy. I was aware first of thin bands of wire, and then of the paper stretched over it. Outside the globe there was an unconscionable babel of bourgeois braying and clattering of cutlery.

Eventually, the outsize, globular, white paper Habitat lampshade – for indeed, that was what it was – was set down on a stripped-pine table. My feet, braced on the lower strut of the lampshade, perfectly framed a segment of varnished whorls, as if it were some bizarre sampling ceremony for new kitchen furniture. There was a 'shuuk-shuuk' sound as a pair of outsize, chunky, steel cigar-clippers was efficiently employed to cut through the exterior of the lampshade. Familiar, rubicund yet tough features appeared in the tear. It was Sir Terence. His jaw-clamped stogie emitted minor thunderheads; his immaculately-cut Jasper Conran suit absorbed some of these exhalations, then released them in the form of airy threads, rising like ground mist from the nap.

The expression on Sir Terence's face was one of love rather than anger. Using his powerful, designer's forearms he tore open the lampshade and, like some surreal obstetrician, removed me, a quaking, embryonic style victim, from the wreckage of the iconic lighting accessory.

Cradling me in his arms, the Imperial Aesthete began, with clinical precision and yet infinite tenderness, to cut away at the fine, beige schmutter that encapsulated me. And as he did this, Sir Terence discoursed on the various unspeakable tortures that would be mine, the *echt* eviscerations that would be perpetrated on me for dissin' the Conrans.

'I've had a chicken brick specially made . . .' he purred, '. . . actually, not so much a chicken brick, more of a Will Self brick –' He broke off and turned to the gaggle of his conspecifics: 'Sebastian! Jasper! Tom!' he barked. 'Look lively and CRANK UP THAT AGA!'

I awoke screaming, in a pool of my own consommé. It had all been a horrific nightmare. Above my prone, wasted form, the paper world of Conran swung listlessly in the exhausted breeze from the open window. By my side, my wife, the beautiful, the poised Mrs Conran slept. Mrs Conran! I shot upright, the events of the previous evening thrown into sharp relief, like a serried rank of tough, durable, Le Creuset casserole dishes.

All right, I had always known it would be a thoroughly modern, consummately New Labour marriage, but still I was shocked when my bride-to-be vouchsafed that far from adopting my name after we were married, she would be styling herself 'Mrs W. W. Conran'. I railed at her, pleaded with her; we fought long into the night pelting each other with kitchen utensils that came in a variety of bright pastel colours. But in the end she managed to put me in an effective headlock with her close reasoning. Put simply, Mrs C's argument was that since Sir Terence had invented the whole concept of the aestheticised English middle class (before he came along, all there was were acres of Axminster and tea without end), we would feel better suited to our station in life if we just accepted the whole sordid gig and changed our name to Conran, read exclusively books by Shirley Conran, wore suits designed by Jasper Conran, took our children about in push-chairs designed by Sebastian Conran, drank solely at pubs owned by Tom Conran, ate in restaurants owned by Sir Terence, and at home ate solely food purchased at his delicatessens. Of course, in that very private, very personal dwelling every single utensil, every soft furnishing, every accessory, would be Conran coinage. We would – to all intents and purposes – be in a World of Conran.

The following evening we decided to push this conceit to the limit. I togged up in a marvellous little piece of suiting designed by young Jasper and, with Mrs Conran on one arm and an armful of Shirley Conran novels under the other, set off for Sir Terence's grand new noshery on the King's Road.

Some people think Chelsea is cool. But then they're the same kind of people who think that Alice bands and sleeveless anoraks are cool. Personally I've always hated Chelsea and desired to release anthrax outside the town hall and watch the appliquéd sheep on pullovers the length of the strand go belly up.

It's too late for that though, because Sir Terence's beano behemoth is now occupying these premises. There's a deli, there's a bar, and there's Bluebird itself, a vast atelier of artlessness in which the interior design contrives to make the conversation point for your evening the spectacle of eight fat, middle-aged men on expense accounts eating dinner.

Don't get me wrong, I'm not avowedly anti-Sir Terence. In a previous lifetime I even wrote a favourable review of one of his restaurants, the sub-Felliniesque Mezzo, but this time he's really gone too far. Bluebird isn't so much a restaurant – more a way of death. Mrs C and I staggered across the cobblestoned courtyard, swerving to avoid a kind of barbecue gondola with a gas flare burning on one end. Around the courtyard were studded various revolting Chelsea types; all Dolce & Gabbana sunglasses, *that* dress (i.e. the one they never should have dreamed of wearing) and immobile phones (the things are glued to their fucking ears). These were the kind of couples who are so ugly that we should be profoundly grateful that they're having sex with each other instead of inflicting their bodies on the rest of the world.

The exterior of Bluebird promises what the interior cannot deliver: the outside of the old Victorian wedding cake has been subject to slashes of post-modern refurbishment. Floodlights abound. The success of Sir T's other Pantagruelian pancake houses has, to no little extent, been predicated on their retro feel. Quaglino's with its cigarette girls in flaring red skirts and fish-net stockings is strongly reminiscent of the kind of joints where Bogie and Bacall stalked around each other like stylish pumas. Mezzo would be an entirely credible backdrop for Marcello Mastroianni and Anita Ekberg, and there's easily enough room for the Trevi Fountain in the stairwell.

But the interior of Bluebird is comprehensively marred by the exposed girders that support the roof. These are too industrial, too factory-floor to sustain the rest of the Conran appurtenances: the endless banquettes topped with smoked glass; the black slate floor; the space-pod waiting station and Mars module bar; the obligatory glassed-off kitchen area and sub-Beuys arrangement of olive-oil bottles.

The slate floor is really the meat of the matter. With a two-storey high room packed to the joists with the unspeakable speaking far too much, while busily ingurgitating the nearly inedible, the noise is phenomenal. Mrs C and I could barely hear each other's witty conversational sallies: 'You piece of shit; what can have been in your Psion Organiser-sized mind, drinking fucking Enigma lager all night in cardboard city . . .' Reluctantly we made a stab at reading Shirley's prose. It was OK. Really the opposite of purple – a kind of beige, or possibly even egg-shell magnolia writing style. But I'm afraid the content utterly escaped me.

Anyway, I was too distracted by the crotch of my trousers. I love Jasper Conran's clothes, and for many years I've worn a pair of his underpants that I stole from him. Jasper and I were staying at the Baron Bic's extravagant château in the Loire valley. While the potentate of plastic and the sylph-like bias cutter disported themselves on the ha-ha, road-testing some new prototypes of disposable razors, I sneaked off with the sensible, white M&S Y-fronts he had casually draped over a delightful little Ingres bronze. Like the pants, the suit I was wearing had been cut for someone with a slimmer, more delicate figure than my own. Someone like Jasper for example.

All around us, spirited conversations were being conducted, or rather people were shouting a load of inebriated cack at each other. Waiters in shirts of the ubiquitous cerulean blue were frantically mobile beneath a series of cerulean blue immobiles, which dangled from the girder zone. These poor bastards, I thought to myself, they're condemned to live in this World of Conran day in, day out, while I'm a mere carpetbagger, a neophyte. But they are existing in a hideous synecdoche, sentenced to be skivvies in the temple of the bourgeois.

I smoked with deep and sincere conviction, stubbing each fag out in the chunky metal ashtray designed by Sebastian, reflecting each time on the ironies attendant on the little relief of Malcolm Campbell's eponymous wheels on its rim. Nice to put your fags out in something adorned by the vehicle of a man whose son died in a ball of flame.

They didn't have the Meursault we wanted, nor the Pouilly Montra-chet, but they did have a reasonable Pinot Grigio. The food was all right, but by that stage of the evening the whole fucking ambience was beginning to curdle in my gut. All I wanted to do was tear the beautiful suit off, and the beautiful silk tie, and the beautiful cerulean blue shirt, abandon the beautiful Mrs Conran, and run screaming into the night.

So that's what I did. Dawn found me supping VP under Hungerford Bridge – and feeling right at home.

Eat Soup, July 1997

164

56

There is hardly anything in the British landscape that is more delusive than that landscape itself. At some peculiar, profoundly atavistic level we wish to believe that our countryside is a primordial place, a green Eden, steadily encroached upon by the concrete and stone lava of erupting urbanity. The country is held to be good and old – the city to be new and bad.

Yet how well I remember the sense of confusion that first descended on me when I travelled to those parts of the eastern United States where the farmland had fallen into disuse. How bizarre it was to witness secondary forest burgeoning in what were once wheatfields, to see collapsed barns and rusted equipment. How much stranger it was to realise that this land had been returning to the wild for more than a hundred years; that its farming lifetime had been but a brief workaday period, in between aeons of the arboreal.

Our British farmland is a profoundly unnatural construction, and it's fair to say that in many London streets you can witness scenes less changed over the past millennium than almost any rural vista. Even the moors of Scotland are a recent phenomenon, cleared in the eighteenth century. If you want to experience what the primary forestation of Britain might have been like, you'd do as well to thrust your head into a copse in rural Essex as wander any of the byways of Wiltshire or Somerset.

Now, as we plough our way into a new millennium, our countryside is on the verge of another human evolution. Put simply, in a world with global free trade in agricultural produce, our farmland will no longer pay for itself. The whole practice of farming in this country has become a marginal activity, a green fringe ready to be cropped off by a shift of a few per cent in world pricing. Yet to listen to the rhetoric of the 98 per cent of the population who live and work in the towns and cities, you'd never believe that we were anything but vitally integrated with our land; that while our heads are full of urbanity our feet aren't still firmly planted in the native soil.

What we need is a new kind of rural clearance – we need to clear away all the false and sentimental verbiage that hedges in our thinking about the countryside. We need to have – dare I say it – a common agricultural policy. The Government needs to stop dithering in this area and tacitly accepting that geopolitical considerations – like European integration and the economic viability of GM foods – are changing the whole character of the landscape without any input from or consent by any of us, urbanites or country-dwellers.

And we, the people, need to decide what it is we want our country for, because in a very important sense our land is an aspect of our polity. If we want it to remain economically viable, then we must resist European federalism with all our might and main – the two issues are inextricably bound up with each other. If we don't mind the encroachment of secondary forest, back after a couple of thousand years, then we should say so. In the country at least, we should know when to call a spade a spade.

Today, BBC Radio 4, May 2000

57

It's a well-known fact about Morrissey that his record contracts stipulate various wacky, star-like things. One of them is the presence of certain, very particular kinds of snack food in any interview context. So it is that the first thing that meets my eye when I enter the penthouse boardroom of RCA Records is a table, laid with plates of crisps (plain, or so I've read) and some KitKats; to one side are bottles of pop.

At the outset Morrissey is drinking a cup of coffee, and during our discussion he occasionally elides his way out of anything remotely resembling an impasse by alluding to these eatables. 'This is such great coffee,' he pronounces at one point, and when I ask him what's on his mind he replies, 'This KitKat.'

These are just the sort of tropes that Morrissey comes up with from minute to minute, turning phrases as he does, like rotating signs outside petrol stations. Morrissey is for many people irredeemably associated with the eighties – and even to say this brings that decade into sharper focus. In the eighties a particular kind of male adolescent angst and self-pity infused the *Zeitgeist*, and Morrissey was its avatar. He was the first male pop star to address a whole generation of boys who were growing up with feminism, a heavy underscoring to a period of natural inadequacy and uselessness.

His miserablism came from that archetypally grim, ravaged provincial city Manchester, where, cut off from a supporting popular culture with any remotely intellectual element, or political undercurrent, Morrissey forged the Smiths, the pop band who were to be the spokesmen for the Miserablists, and penned their anthem 'Heaven Knows I'm Miserable Now'.

Morrissey's hipness and artistry were always wedded to an exquisite taste for the most subtle kitsch of the recent English past, and slathered in Yank-worship. But mixed in with all this came his ambiguous campery, and a version of necrophile teen-death obsession that drew more from Cocteau's *Orphée* than from 'Leader of the Pack'. This veritable ragout of source material forged a strong and compulsively watchable performer, a paradoxical inversion of his just as alienated, but far less able, fans and imitators.

Suited darkly, booted sturdily, and wearing one of those jerseyesque shirts that almost define the retro-committed, Morrissey is very attractive in the flesh. The deeply-set blue eyes coruscate from beneath a high, intelligent brow, and given his self-professed celibacy one of the first things any conscientious interviewer does is to try and assess the quality of his physical presence, his essential heft.

Is this a man tortured by his own sexuality and that of others? Is this a man about whom there lingers a faint scent of fleshly revulsion? No, on both counts. His handshake is firm, warm even. His body language is far from craven. Indeed, there is something quite affectingly embodied about him. At one point in our conversation he commented on my face: 'You've actually got the face of a criminal who I've met . . . A very strong face. A very determined face.' Setting aside the content of this remark, it struck me that this was not the sort of thing that someone who is intent on denying corporeality would be likely to say.

And of course, while his well-publicised encouragement of the excess-ive – and physical – devotion of his fans has a double-edged quality about it – you can touch, but only in this contrived, aberrant way – in person he lampoons his own self-created shibboleths, again and again and again. When I suggest to him that stage invasions puncture the meniscus of stardom, and confront him with fans who are 98 per cent water, he replies, 'Let it be punctured, let it be punctured, that's my motto.'

The following week at Wembley Arena, the star goes so far towards puncturing the meniscus that he almost bodily hauls a would-be stage-invader through the arms of the bouncers, past the rank of monitors, and into his arms. He receives kisses on both cheeks as no more than his due. He also bends down into the thicket of arms waving towards him, and as much takes as gives out the benediction.

There's a submerged incongruity here, but one that works in his favour. Perhaps one of the central ironies about this most ironic of performers is that he clearly seeks adulation from those most indisposed to give it – the Dagenham Daves and Rusholme Ruffians who people his songscapes – and eschews the advances of those who regard his talent as essentially poetic. When I ask him if he's ever been attracted to the world of the intelligentsia, he is emphatic: 'Absolutely not. In fact, scorn is perhaps all I feel really. I feel quite sad for such people. I think that everything there is to be lived is hanging round the gutter somewhere. I've always believed that and still do.'

Which rather raises the question, exactly how much hanging round the gutter is involved in researching his marvellously deadpan little word pictures? He mentions 'certain pubs around north and east London. But I'm not the sort of person you're likely to spot, because I don't go about wanting to be noticed . . . I'm just slipping in and slipping out, and if you were looking for me you'd never find me.' A nice echo of the demonic wail contained in 'Speedway', the closing track of last year's *Vauxhall & I*: 'All of the rumours keeping me grounded/I never said that they were completely unfounded'.

Schiller made the distinction between the 'naïve' artist, who works through a cathartic and direct outpouring of creative imagination, and the 'sentimental' artist, who is compelled to intellectualise all he produces. I take it that Morrissey's preoccupation with 'loafing oafs in all-night chemists' is a willed attempt by his sentimental side to indulge his naïve capacities. For he is that most unusual of artists – both naïve and sentimental.

He tells me that performance for him represents 'exuberance', and when I tax him that this goes somewhat against his self-styled anti-fun posture, he grins and admits it. That being said, Morrissey's idea of post-gig kicks is not exactly what we expect from a pop star: 'Just pure silence. A quiet read. Just me. A locked door. Absolute silence.' I found this attitude refreshing, but it did act as a springboard for Morrissey to trot out some of his more *passé* attitudinising about life: 'Life's incredibly boring. I don't say that in an effort to seem vaguely amusing, but the secret of life is that there's no secret, it's just exceedingly boring.'

I got the feeling that these kinds of sallies are a form of bluff for Morrissey, and that he throws them out in much the way that aircraft in World War II dropped strips of metal to fool radar. If his interlocutors rise to such chaff – then they're not really worthy of consideration. But he's also an adept at sidestepping the conventional psychoanalytic thrusts of the interviewer. He manages this by a complex sleight of personality that is fascinating to observe.

When I mention the 'vexed question' of his sexuality, he replies, 'It doesn't vex me. I don't exactly think it vexes other people at all. People have their opinions and I don't mind what they are. I mean there's a limit to what people can actually assume about sexuality, and at least I'm relieved by that. I don't think people assume anything any more about me. I'm sort of classified in a non-sexual, asexual way, which is an air of dismissiveness which I quite like.'

The interesting thing about this speech is, of course, that the exact opposite is the truth: it *does* vex people, he *does* mind, there are *no* limits to what people can assume about sexuality (which is far from being a relief); and it is he himself who has struck the asexual attitude.

Perhaps it would be to trite to suggest that the plaintive refrain of 'The Teachers Are Afraid of the Pupils', the lead track on his latest album, *Southpaw Grammar*, is in some way an echo of this posture: 'To be finished would be a relief,' the singer proclaims, again and again and again.

The sting really comes when I say, 'Do you think you've pulled that one off?' And with another smile he replies, 'Yeah. Quite well. I think the skill has paid off quite well. I've managed to slip through the net – whatever the net is.' Then there's a neat little bit of wordplay, analogous in the Morrissey idiolect to a boxer's centre-ring shuffle. I interject, 'But –' and he overrides me: 'I know you're about to say "but", but so am I. It's not really an issue, there's nothing to say, and there's nothing to ask, more to the point.'

He's right. Unless I choose to be a boor and attempt to crash into his private existence, there really is nothing to ask. This is the 'skill' that Morrissey has perfected, and it's a skill that in anyone else would be described quite simply as maturity.

Yes, that's the only revelation I have to give you about Steven Patrick Morrissey: he is, against all odds, a grown-up. How exactly he has managed this growing up it's hard to tell. The potted biography gives the impression of a direct transferral from air guitar in front of a suburban Manchester mirror, to air guitar in front of hysterical crowds at the Hacienda, followed by thirteen years of – albeit anomalous – stardom.

Where exactly did he find those normal interactions, those normal relationships, necessary to effect maturation?

Of course, it's no secret in the business that his 'no touch' persona bears little relation to a man who closely guards his close friendships; and quite clearly something *is* going on here. It was once said of Edward Heath that if he did have sex at all, it was only in a locked vault in the Bank of England. I don't wish to speculate about whether or not Morrissey has sex, but if he does I think it's fairly safe to assume that the 'locked vault' is a function of two things: an unswerving dedication to maintaining a genuine private life; and a capability for generating immense personal loyalty – a loyalty vault, if you will.

When we discuss the notion of camp, which informs so much of his artistic sensibility, right down to the title of one of his solo albums, *Bona Drag* ('bona' meaning attractive or sexy in Polari, the secret gay argot), he veers off into *The Kenneth Williams Diaries*: 'It was quite gruesome, quite gruesome. I've read it a couple of times and each time it's been like a hammer on the head. An astonishingly depressing book. It's incredibly witty and well done, but the hollow ring it has throughout is murderous, absolutely murderous.'

I tax him that some people might view his life as being a bit like that, and he replies, 'It's not. It definitely isn't,' with a deeply-felt emphasis. So deep that I'm moved to put to him the possibility of the most extreme contrast to Williams's life of emotional and sexual barrenness: 'Have you ever considered having children?' 'Yeah,' he says, flatly, in his burring Mancunian voice.

When we tease out this issue, it becomes apparent that what bothers him about having kids is to do with his – quite legitimate – fear of overidentification with them: 'I wonder what they'd do. I mean, what do they do when they're eleven? What would they do when they were seventeen? . . . What happens when your child turns round and says, "Look, I don't like this world. Why did you bring me into it? I don't want to be a part of it. I'm not leaving home, I'm staying here, I refuse to grow up"?'

But if there are shades of his own (allegedly) willed infantility here, also discernible are the lineaments of grown-up Morrissey, Morrissey whose 'skill' has served him well. He seems to understand only too well the impact of the ambiguous images he has created, and the even more ambiguous images they have spawned.

Morrissey, it became apparent to me, is someone who finds his love for other people painful and overpowering. In this he is, of course, like all of us. He has given up on his favourite soap *Coronation Street*, but when discussing its replacement in his affections, *EastEnders*, he lets slip a yearning for a very populated, very unmiserable Arcadia: 'I think people wish that life really was like that, that we couldn't avoid seeing forty people every day who we spoke to, who knew everything about us, and that we couldn't avoid being caught up in these relationships all the time, and that there was somebody standing on the doorstep throughout the day. I think that's how we'd all secretly like to live. Within *EastEnders*, within *Coronation Street*, there are no age barriers. Senior citizens, young children, they all blend, and they all like one another and they all have a great deal to say, which isn't how life is.'

Perhaps here the complex mask of ritual, signs, signals and cultural references Morrissey has devised, to obliterate the very non-contrived human character beneath, slips a little, but I'd be wary of pushing it. To me he says, 'I wish somebody would get it right. I don't mind if they hate me as long as they get it right.' And yet 'getting it right' would be wholly destructive for the imago, if liberating for the man.

Throughout the solo career there has been a strenuous conflation of the notion of 'Englishness' with that of a camp, Ortonesque liking for 'rough lads'. Is Morrissey like William Burroughs, I wonder, possessed of an eternal faith in the 'goodness' of these rough lads? Is this atmosphere, so vividly captured in *Southpaw Grammar*, one he sees as an Arcadia, or merely one of nostalgia?

'It's pure nostalgia, really, and there's very little truth in it. I'm well aware of that. I know that it's all pure fantasy really, and 50 per cent drivel. Everybody has their problems and there is no way of being that is absolutely free and fun-loving and without horrific responsibilities. It just isn't true. And I think I've had the best of it personally. I don't think I'm missing anything because I'm not a roofer from Ilford.'

Did we really expect anything else? Every alleged 'Arcadian' image Morrissey produces is in reality shot through with irony. The eponymous hero of 'Boy Racer' is described thus: 'Stood at the urinal/He thinks he's got the whole world in his hands'. And as for poor Dagenham Dave: 'Head in a blouse/Everyone loves him/I see why'. Yes indeed! But then, by the same token: 'He'd love to touch, he's afraid he might self-combust/ I could say more, but you get the general idea'.

The implication being one of what? Chronically repressed homosexuality? Or merely the singer's own *taedium vitae* in the face of the exhausted husk of English working-class culture? The rubric here is one of subversion, subversion and more subversion. This is most graphically shown when Morrissey, thirty-six and rising, comes on stage at Wembley Arena, with his somewhat younger-looking fellow musicians. It's either *Happy Days* with Morrissey as the Fonz and the vaguely bat-eared guitarist as Richie, or else something altogether more sinister.

The backcloth is a giant projection of the cover of *Southpaw Grammar*, the face of an obscure boxer which Morrissey himself plucked from the anonymity of an old issue of *The Ring*. There's a wheeze and a creak from the massive bunches of speakers dangling overhead, and 'Jerusalem' starts up, being sung by some long-gone school choir. The effect, in tandem with the suited, cropped figures striding about the dark stage, is extremely unsettling. Is this the start of some weird Fascist rally?

Then the band crash into the opening chords of 'Reader Meets Author', and Morrissey begins to flail at the air with the cord of his microphone, pirouetting, hip-swivelling, for all the world like some camp version of Roy Rogers. He'd be run out of the British National Party in seconds if they caught him swishing about like this! Once again he has subverted the political in a peculiarly personal way.

Later on in the set, Morrissey and the band perform the dark and extremely depressing song 'The Operation'. Like many of his lyrics, this one is addressed to an unnamed person. Morrissey must be one of the few songwriters who uses the second person more than the first. 'You fight with your right hand,' he yodels, 'and caress with your left' – and as he joins up the couplet he wipes the arse of the air with a limp hand.

This is presumably what he means by 'Southpaw Grammar'; and the manifest and ongoing preoccupation with 'the other' in his work is so antithetical to his posture of bedsit isolation that I wonder again just how truly protean a person this is? To me he says, 'I don't feel trapped in your tape recorder and on those CDs. I don't at all. I can do whatever I like and I can become whatever I like, and if next week I want to have thirteen children and live in Barking, then I can and I will, and nobody will stop me.'

This is all very double-edged, very southpaw. On one reading it smacks of an arrested, adolescent will-to-omnipotentiality, but on another it's an indicator of great sanity, and of a refusal to believe wholly in the imago he has created. While in his first incarnation, as the taboo-busting frontman of the Smiths, Morrissey was prone to using his platform for issuing diktats on all manner of issues unrelated to popular music, his fame now appears to have been well worn in, like a favourite old overcoat.

He confirms this when I ask him how he manages to keep such tight control over the empire he has created: 'I only manage it by repeatedly saying "no". And then the obvious reputation gathers around you that you are a problem, because you are awkward, you are difficult, and you don't really want to be famous. But I just don't want to be famous in any way other than that which naturally suits me.'

I wonder what's going to happen to Morrissey. Among the trainspotters of the music press, his break with Johnny Marr, his songwriting partner in the Smiths, has been insistently viewed as a creative death for him. Yet some of the solo material he has recorded is just as strong as anything they ever did together – and by the same token, who outside the music press has heard much about Johnny Marr in the past five years?

My hunch is that he may well find pop iconic status becoming an increasing drag. He is a very funny man to be with, but he keeps his wit well reined in. Just one example of this comes when we dissect the 'vexed question' of my not having a television. 'Is that a political statement?' he asks, and when I say it is, he rejoins, 'Do all your neighbours know that you don't possess a television set?'

I think the wit is reined in because it's so destructive of the ironic edifice he has created. Stardom requires a certain kind of stupidity to sustain it, and Morrissey is far from being a stupid man. He is responsible for – among other things – encapsulating two hundred years of philosophical speculation in a single line: 'Does the mind rule the body, or the body rule the mind, I don't know.'

His ambitions as an artist clearly don't require him to feed the Moloch of celebrity with more creative babies. He once memorably sang, castigating yet another of his shadowy others for their sexual peccadilloes, 'On the day when your mentality/Catches up with your biology'. But I think the comparable day of reckoning for Morrissey will come when he allows his sense of humour to catch up with his irony.

Even at Wembley Arena it looked as if the band had invited their uncle to come along and do a turn with them. Morrissey has too acute a view of himself – one hopes – to become one of those grandads of pop, perambulating around the stage in support hose, permanently marooned in some hormonal stretch limo. He told me he could 'do anything'; I certainly hope he can. England needs him.

Observer, November 1995

58

Book review: The Annotated Alice: The Definitive Edition
*by Lewis Carroll, with Introduction and Notes by Martin Gardner
(Allen Lane/Penguin Press)*

There's something malodorous about this book – like the stinking petals of a rotting bloom. Gardner first published an annotated version of Carroll's 'Alice' books in 1960, and since then he has – with a pedantic avidity that makes trainspotters appear lazily dilettante – continued to amass more and more material concerning them. This attractively produced and painstakingly edited update contains a long-buried, excised episode from *Through the Looking Glass* (entitled 'The Wasp in the Wig' – although this also appeared in Gardner's intermediate *More Annotated Alice* [1990] in the USA); introductory essays for all three versions of his work; notes on 'Alice' on the screen, on Carroll societies, and on Tenniel's illustrations (many of which appear here, faithfully reproduced); and, of course, the vital annotations themselves.

But as I say, there's something not quite right about the work overall, something off-colour, off-key and distinctly iffy. Gardner himself – as the dates above would suggest – is a valetudinarian (born in 1914), who spent a short lifetime (1952–82) writing a monthly, recreational mathematics column for *Scientific American*. He's written numerous other works on mathematical puzzles and conundrums, and on the flyleaf bio of this work the philosopher Douglas Hofstadter hails him as 'one of the great intellects produced in this country in this century' – whatever that means. Like my old uncle, Robert Ross, Gardner lives in Hendersonville, North Carolina, and like Uncle Bob I imagine him to be one of those Americans who present an image of curiously antiquated gentility – Gramercy Park clubbable, Brooks Brothers tailored, *New York Times* erudite – as if, like certain hillbillies in the Appalachians, they have retained elements of an England long vanished over here.

I mention all of this because I can only hope that it's Gardner's recondite notions of *amour propre* that lead him into an analytic cul-de-sac of such tedious brevity that it almost entirely compromised my interest with and enjoyment of this work. For Gardner staunchly maintains that Carroll's obsession with prepubescent girls, his photographing and sketching them in the nude, his delight in kissing them, his revulsion from boys at a similar age, his apparent revulsion from adult sexuality of all forms – that none of this represents anything but 'complete sexual innocence' on Carroll's part. Gardner is a man uncomfortable with the psychoanalytic; of such interpretations of the 'Alice' books (which he disbars from his own annotations and sequestrates in the bibliography) he says, 'We do not have to be told what it means to tumble down a rabbit hole or curl up inside a tiny house with one foot up the chimney. The rub is that any work of nonsense abounds with so many inviting symbols that you can start with any assumption you please about the author and easily build up an impressive case about it.'

The problem is that Gardner's own analysis of Carroll proceeds via a false syllogism (a misapplication of logic that doubtless his subject – a pedantic and second-rate Oxford mathematics don – would have approved in his own defence, if not in his tutorials). For Gardner: (a) all paedophiles manifestly wish to have sex with their objects of desire; (b) there is no evidence that Carroll wished to have sex with Alice Liddell or his numerous other 'child loves'; therefore (c) Carroll was not a paedophile. Actually, this isn't even a false syllogism – it's just entirely false. Many paedophiles successfully hide the sexual nature of their interest in children behind other forms of engagement, but anyway, Carroll didn't – he photographed them naked. Gardner's uneasiness with the psychoanalytic – his inability even to engage with it – is part of his conflation of ignorance with innocence: we cannot see the erect penis in the 'devout Anglican' Charles Dodgson's trousers as he photographs naked little girls; therefore it doesn't exist!

Gardner even goes so far as to suggest that because there is no reference to Carroll in *Lolita*, Nabokov would have supported Gardner's own avowal of his 'innocence'. And yet he belies this by quoting from an interview with Nabokov (himself a translator of the 'Alice' books) where he spoke of Carroll's 'pathetic affinity' with Humbert Humbert, adding that 'some odd scruple prevented me from alluding in *Lolita* to his wretched perversion and to those ambiguous photographs he took in dim rooms'. I'm with Vladimir on this: Carroll was indisputably a paedophile – just not an active one.

All of this is important; we don't want to make 'any assumption' we please about Carroll's psyche, we wish to acknowledge one vital fact about his sexuality, and without that, any annotation of the Alice books becomes an exercise in wilful distortion. Gardner notes that Carroll practised the White Queen's advice to Alice in *Through the Looking Glass* to 'consider anything only don't cry'. In Carroll's introduction to his little work *Pillow Problems* (pretty suggestive in itself), he speaks of working at mathematical problems during sleepless nights to prevent his dwelling on 'unholy thoughts, which torture, with their hateful presence, the fancy that would fain be pure. Against all these some real mental work is a most helpful ally.' And the mental work he most conspicuously indulged in to keep these 'unholy thoughts' at bay was the children's books themselves, with their panoply of conundrums, devices, parodies and burlesques.

So, Gardner's annotations, with their obsessive dwelling upon the minutiae of factoids about the texts rather than their symbolism, are themselves a gloss upon a displacement activity. What, in my view, makes the 'Alice' books so enduringly central to the English literary canon is precisely their quality of heightened repression: the struggle by a tormented paedophile to keep the manifest object of his desire straitjacketed in a fallacious – yet socially condoned – dreamlike realm of sexual ignorance. It's this that made everything in the 'Alice' books – from the distortions in scale, to the surreal elisions, to the banjaxed language – such a mother lode of inference for those avatars of modernism Joyce, Eliot and Nabokov.

I cannot fault Gardner on his detailing of the proceedings of the Carrollians: it's all here, from the whimsical observation that Tenniel's depiction of the Mad Hatter was a prolepsis of Bertrand Russell's face, to the Caterpillar's inquisition ('Who are you?') as a retailing of a mid-Victorian mass catch-phrase (the 'at the end of the day' of its time). And there's much more, a lot of which – such as complete versions of all the poems and songs Carroll parodied, details of who was who in all the film versions of 'Alice', and explications of terms still familiar to the modern English reader but obscure to Americans – shouldn't be shoved down anybody's rabbit hole.

Gardner makes a strong case for the White Knight in *Through the Looking Glass* as a self-portrait of Carroll as a sad, wistful, chaste old man (he was forty when he wrote it), saying goodbye to his love who is doomed to hormones. Personally I wish Gardner had taken seriously the notion of Carroll as a dirty old man – then we'd have a truly animated 'Alice', rather than an annotated one.

New Statesman, December 2000

59

I flexed my generous muscles so that a visible bulge rippled across my shoulders, momentarily displacing the sleeves of my sailor-suit-style top. I uttered a hideous 'Errrrargh!' and, scissoring my blocky bare legs, threw myself at my opponent, a superannuated blond surfer boy wearing a ludicrous, Las Vegas-period-Elvis white trouser suit. In the background the stern, golden face of the Buddha looked down on us from the wall of a ruined temple. We were having a scrap in what appeared to be the ruins of Angkor Wat. My pointed shoe made contact with surfer boy's chin and he shot backwards, his body actually writhing in mid-air with the force of impact, before crumpling to the stone flags. 'KO!' the voice of Electronic God cried, and to bring this home to us mortals he wrote the letters in the sky above us.

I regained my feet and straightened my tartan miniskirt – which had temporarily ridden up in the heat of battle. I tossed my pigtailed head in a defiant sort of way and prepared to meet my next challenger. For I was Xioayu, a female fighter with a nice line in ditsy costumes; and my opponents, who had names like Yoshimitsu, Forest Law, Ogre and Eddy Gordo, were ugly martial-arts exponents who needed to feel the lash of my patent leather pumps. The arena we were fighting in was a solidly virtual one provided by a game called Tekken 3. I was, of course, in an amusement arcade.

'Oh! Give over!' cried my friend Nick, who was responsible for animating Ogre. 'You can't let yourself be beaten by a *girl*!' But Ogre could let himself, for I was no mere girl, I was Xioayu and I had discovered the ancient secret of how to win at Tekken 3: simply riffle all the buttons that direct your televised manikin to kick and punch as fast as you possibly can, while equally precipitately jerking the handle that makes it advance or retreat. Nick, in his role as Ogre, was still mucking around with tactics! Poor fool.

I'm not sure whether I believe that Tekken 3 will corrupt youth with either aggression or adrenalin. More likely is that it will corrupt them with poverty. Nick and I had a rather pedestrian hour in this inner-city amusement parlour and managed to get rid of twenty quid. For double that fee you could have walked around the corner and hired a *real* version of Xioayu to kick you in the face.

I'd started off poorly enough on a Lost World dinosaur-shooting game. This thing was encased in a kind of sled in which we sat and manipulated plastic pistols. Nick turned out to be surprisingly good at this, firing rapid fusillades of electronic pellets which demolished raptors, tyrannosauruses and pterodactyls with consummate ease. I, however, couldn't get over the idea that it was humans who were behind the whole fiasco, so as soon as one popped up on the screen I would let fly, earning myself a Voice of Doom crying, 'FAIL!' – and the inevitable writing in the sky, the amusement-arcade version of 'MENE, MENE, TEKEL, UPHARSIN'.

The thing I couldn't figure out was that even with close study and reasonable hand-eye co-ordination it would take you about a month of feeding the bloody thing with pound coins before you could get beyond stage one. You would have to *invest* in this Lost World. We soon grew disgruntled and turned our attention to the general-knowledge quiz machine next to it, which offered cash prizes.

Styling itself the 'IQ Computer', this gizmo offered you a series of questions for your pound, most of which demanded that you identify the stars of daytime soaps from indeterminate images constructed with pixels the size of sugar-cubes. If you made your way through the soap rounds you were offered a test where you were given about ten seconds to memorise the position and value of twenty playing cards. Manage this feat of near-mesmerism and you could be in line to get your quid back.

Actually, in fairness to the IQ Computer, not all the 'celebrities' you had to identify were soap stars: bizarrely there were questions featuring Tiny Rowland and Cap'n Bob Maxwell as well. I was hesitating in my identification between Tiny Rowland and Raymond Burr of *Ironside* fame, when a trench-coated middle-aged man who was peering over my shoulder snapped, 'It's Tiny Rowland!' I pushed the requisite button and the screen flashed up 'You're a Genius!' I turned to congratulate the man on his elevation to the ranks of Mozart and Einstein, but he'd faded.

If a workable definition of modern genius is being able to identify soap stars from indistinct images, then the working definition of joining the police *has* to include training. Disgruntled by our failure to master IQ, Nick and I signed up for the course. 'Police Trainer' was another 'shoot 'em fast' kind of game. Under the categories 'Speed', 'Timing', 'Judgement' and 'Acuity' we were called upon to blaze away at a gallery of green goblin-like figures. I was crap at it. I kept totalling suspects who were surrendering, while allowing the really bad mothers to escape. Nick was delighted: 'They ought to have a special feature for trainees like you —'

'Oh yeah,' I snarled.

'Yeah,' he guffawed, 'they could call it "Taking Bribes"!'

I sloped around the amusement arcade with a long, pimply face, waiting for Nick to finish wiggling around on an artificial Sega jet-ski game. I had become a bona fide denizen of the joint, my visage indistinguishable from those of the other adolescents playing truant. When he dismounted we strolled out into the sunlight. 'Well,' I asked him, 'did you have fun?'

'No,' he snarled back, 'I didn't. It was expensive and utterly unrewarding — how about you?'

'Oh, I loved it, but then I've always wanted to wear my hair in pigtails . . .'

The Times, February 1999

60

In Huysmans's famous novel of *fin-de-siècle* decadence, *Against Nature*, the aristocratic anti-hero Des Esseintes has a 'liqueur organ' built for himself. This bizarre contraption allows him to create different combinations of spirituous drinks without having to leave the embrace of his armchair.

I was reminded of this a couple of days ago as I stood in the still room of the Glenmorangie distillery, Tain, Ross-shire. For a start, I'm certain that Des Esseintes would appreciate the design of this cathedral of whisky. Glenmorangie has eight swan-necked stills, four of which are ranged along either side of the high, light room. The stills are seventeen feet high — the tallest in Scotland. Like all whisky stills they are copper; and the heat of the distillation process gifts them a peculiar distempering — like a temporary verdigris. The floor and ceiling of the still room are finished in blond wood; and through the low, broad windows there's a fantastic view of the Dornoch Firth and the mountains of Sutherland beyond. The overall effect is, quite simply, beautiful.

But the decadent best is to come. For, behind the incongruously high-tech control desk at one end of the still room, there is a bizarre glass and copper cabinet, which makes Des Esseintes's liqueur organ look about as exciting as a can of Top Deck shandy. Into this cabinet flows the entire yield of the eight stills. Not, I hasten to add, the first distillation – this is always ploughed back in; and even of the second distillation, only a third is retained for maturation. But eventually the precious, 70 per cent proof fluid is ready, and courses down a series of chutes into a glass bowl inside the cabinet.

From time to time the Glemorangie still man, Kenneth MacDonald, will open up the cabinet and give this torrent of hard liquor a judicious snort. He was kind enough to do this while I was there, and beckoned to me to share in the experience. 'He's got one of the finest noses in the business,' whispered my guide, Mrs Catherine Thomson, as the three of us submerged our faces in the intense fumes. 'What d'you think, Kenneth?'

The still man (who was young, tall, pink-cheeked, and generally about as far removed from the mental picture I had of a still man as was possible) stared off into the bright immensities of the Dornoch Firth for a while before answering, 'Citrus fruits – lots of citrus fruits today.' Well, quite so, but more to the point was this astonishing quantity of raw, honking booze! That, and the whole way the still room was organised so as to have a near-sacred atmosphere. Watching this spring of whisky, tumbling into its glass crucible, I could fully appreciate why the stuff should be called 'the water of life' in Gaelic.

I carefully ventured some remarks along these lines to Mrs Thomson, worried lest I offend some religious sensibility: 'Um, y'know it's almost like a kind of *cathedral* in here –'

'My words exactly!' she delightedly exclaimed. 'That's what I always say to the parties I take round.' Kenneth MacDonald looked suitably solemn – like the Prelate of Proof he so manifestly was.

The still room was the high point of my tour of the Glemorangie distillery, but really the whole trip was verging on the sublime. And if you do make the effort in winter, you can be assured of a warm welcome from Mrs Thomson. She'd had only twelve visitors in January thus far, and despite the fact that she'd already toured one sad-looking Volvo driver that morning, she happily took me around. The Glenmorangie distillery makes great play of the 'Sixteen Men of Tain' who make the holy brew, but as far as I was concerned it was the One Woman of Tain who deserved the plaudits.

'D'you want to see the mash room?' she trilled. Off we scampered up a series of iron stairways and into a cavernous space occupied by a number of enormous steel vats. 'These are the mash tuns,' said Mrs Thomson, vigorously unbolting a hatch. 'Into here goes nine and a half tons of the finest barley, and forty-eight thousand litres of water!' Add in the yeast and they had an astonishing eruption of colloidal gunge on their hands. The interior of the mash tun looked like the universe must have done a few milliseconds before the Big Bang. Wide metal sweeps rotated ceaselessly over the surface of this organic explosion, skimming it off and banking it down. The contrast between this intense inspissation and the pellucid stuff that makes it out the other end was remarkable.

But if the actual mechanics of the distillation process were exciting to watch, the overall atmospherics of the distillery were a cool balm. It was difficult to imagine, looking at this tidy little agglomeration of stone buildings and neat paths, that over three million litres of single-malt whisky were produced here last year. Three million litres! Enough to get the whole population of Norway utterly plastered – if they weren't plastered already.

Glenmorangie ten-year-old is the third bestselling single malt in the world, and after I'd sopped up all of the information on the water (from the Tarlogie spring, especially rich in trace elements), the barley (uniquely grown by the distillery themselves) and the barrels (aged with Kentucky bourbon, or port, or madeira, or sherry), it was easy to understand why. And that was before Mrs Thomson offered me a modest dram.

Her particular hangout was the shop, where you can buy all manner of whisky-style products, including a bizarre kind of picnic hamper, which seemingly holds little else besides three bottles of Glenmorangie. The shop occupies the old customs and excise warehouse, from the days when the distillery had to pay for an excise man to live on the premises, so that he could continually check to see that the spirits weren't being spirited away. Of course, before that distilling was illegal – it's estimated that there were anything up to fourteen thousand illegal stills in Scotland in 1826.

I wonder if the current anti-booze Government will move back in this direction at some point, or whether the whisky distillers will remain the sort of drug dealers they're only too happy to take donations from.

The Times, February 1998

61

When you've walked through the four large gallery spaces that house the work of the four short-listees for this year's Turner Prize, you enter a fifth. This fifth space is perhaps the most important for the exhibition as a whole, and the most representative of the condition of contemporary British art; for it's the education space, the exegetical space, the infospace (such a thing deserves its own coinage).

In the infospace there's a video monitor that shows four short films of the short-listees strutting their stuff – and explaining their work. There are also more wall-mounted screeds doing the same, for those who haven't troubled to read the wall-mounted screeds that are posted throughout the exhibition. There is also posted the useful information that should you feel that the artworks haven't quite been interpreted to your satisfaction, there's a website on the Internet (www.channel4.com) where you can obtain more enlightenment.

Furthermore, if it's the personal touch you're after – a machine can't, after all, convey all the nuances – then you'll be glad to hear that there's a panel discussion at the Tate involving such luminaries as Charles Esche of the Glasgow Tramway. Not only that, but you can come to the Tate any day before the judging, and there will be an art critic on hand to deliver a short lecture on the short list – Sarah Kent of *Time Out* and Tim Marlowe of *Kaleidoscope* are just two of these pedagogic aesthetes.

Lastly, should none of the above be tantamount to a true understanding of the works on show, you can always shell out sixty quid and attend a useful four-day course on this year's Turner Prize run by Anna Harding of Goldsmiths' College. After that you'll know more about the work of Messrs Hume, Patterson, Gordon and Horsfield than they do themselves.

It's difficult not to imagine that all of this educational push is a response – whether conscious or not – to the perennial moan of the non-initiate, that so much modern art is – to put it bluntly – toilet art. And by this I mean art that any old fool could conceive of when at stool, but which takes someone specially idiotic to get up, wipe themselves, repair to the studio and actually construct, or paint, or photograph.

There's that slur, and there's the other one. The one that recurs so often, and with such plangency, that it's possible – as I did – to stand in an exhibition such as this for a few minutes, safe in the knowledge that you will *definitely* overhear someone saying, 'It's all very well, but I'd like to see if he could draw something *realistically*, so that it looks like what it actually is.'

But these necessary rebuttals aside, I think there is another, more profound reason why the infospace is so important to the Turner Prize, and why other kinds of infospace are so crucial for modern art as a whole. Fifty years ago Levi-Strauss defined abstract painting as 'a school of painting in which the artist struggles to describe the kind of painting he would paint, were he to actually paint one'. I think this could be usefully updated to describe the current crop of Turner short-listees, for they belong to a school of art in which the artist struggles to impart the meaning of the kind of work of art he would create, were he by any chance to actually create one.

I don't mean by this to totally write off the claim of these artists to be producing art – there are moments of profundity to be gleaned from these offerings – but the most obvious meanings embodied in all four artists' efforts are meta-meanings, meanings that arrive somewhere between the contemplation of the object itself and the contemplation of the catalogue copy that grounds it in explanation.

William Empson memorably described art-exhibition catalogue copy as 'a steady, iron-hard jet of absolute nonsense'. I wouldn't go this far – the copy for the Turner Prize Exhibition has, at least, the virtue of being lucid – but it's difficult not to give a snort of joyful philistinism when you hear a Gary Hume apologist recast the old toilet-art canard, in the form 'I know people say why would anybody want to do that [i.e. produce such pieces], but in finding out why he wants to do it we become more aware and more intimate with the work of art.'

All of which explains not at all why the work of art in question is a load of crap – after all, the artist's motivation may be completely suspect.

By the same token, Hume's own videoed remark that he wants to 'empower and democratise the viewer' is both specious and megalomaniac. Hume's work – in contrast to the hard work he puts into accounting for its praxis – is the weakest on show, with the exception of one haunting painting. His use of materials – gloss paint on aluminium sheets, and even MFI – seems to be a conceptual joke in and of itself, but the actuality is distinctly unimpressive. If many people really find these works – as the artist himself does – 'unashamedly sensual', then there clearly is no need to ban David Cronenberg's *Crash*; for the metallic feel is already *de rigueur*.

For the most part, Hume's painting evoked for me memories of battered metal signs hanging from picket fences in the harsh sunlight of remote and dusty countries – but countries with a surprising appetite for naïve abstraction; for advertising devoid of a message. The one exception was a painting entitled *Kate*. Here, the use of gloss paint to represent the fabric covering the breasts of a near-Erte outline of a woman was cool: suggesting flesh and the fleshly. The fact that the female figure's face is suggested by a scratched, agitated area of bare aluminium conveys a sense of identity itself being both protean and diffuse – although, surprisingly, neither alienated nor incoherent.

By contrast *Innocence and Stupidity*, which is supposedly an image laboriously arrived at by deconstructing the formal properties of two rabbits, looked, to this jaded yet ignorant eye, like two big squashy tits – pure and simple. The fact of the work's praxis, Gary, is neither here nor there, when it's caught in such a trite act.

From the room of Humes, you move into a dark L of corridor. At one end there's a video monitor with a continuous film loop running, and if you advance towards it, you can turn the corner into another L of dark corridor with a second monitor. On the first screen, a hand grips a wrist and presses it against a rumpled sheet; on the second, the hands are reversed. One hand appears feminine and the other masculine, but in fact both belong to the artist, Douglas Gordon, who has shaved one of his forearms.

This piece, *Divided Self*, is the most affecting in the show. On first encountering the writhing hands, I found that my reaction was one of distress. The evocation of restraint is ambiguously poised, suggesting an encounter that may be either erotic, or psychically disturbed. I stayed some time in the darkened L of Gordon's piece, and felt the trip to the gallery worthwhile – at that point. But later that night, as I was watching a selection of *Fourmations* animated shorts on Channel 4, it occurred to me that there was more true artistry in a few frames of any of these films than there was in the Gordon installation. (Artistry in its complete sense: a mastery of form, colour and texture, as well as theme, narrative and *mise-en-scène*.) Once again the import of the work was shown up as being a meta-import, an inherently didactic experience, a function of what Timothy Leary termed – in relation to a very different poetics – 'set and setting'.

Gordon doesn't help matters in this respect by devoting the rest of his allotted and darkened space to an installation that comprises two massive screens displaying rear-projected images of Fredric March in the transformation scene of *Dr Jekyll and Mr Hyde*. Gordon has been much lauded for a piece not dissimilar to this entitled *24-Hour Psycho*, which, as its name suggests, is a slowed-down screening of *Psycho*.

The actual effect of this installation is peculiarly sacerdotal – a ritual for the old age of Winston Smith. The screens can be circumnavigated. On one, March's face is positive; on the other, negative. However, it isn't the images themselves that obtrude (a three- by four-inch catalogue shot, depicting a similar installation, but featuring a masked hysteric being forcibly restrained, imparts more emotional charge), but rather the materials: the giant screens showing their graticule of transmission, the dark corridor between them, the shadows of viewers passing behind.

The last piece of Gordon's work is the most unsatisfying, and the most void. Projected on to a corner at the far, oblique side of *The Confessions of a Justified Sinner* (the Jekyll and Hyde piece – a reference to James Hogg's Calvinist shock-horror novel of a similar name), is another infospace. This reads 'Hot is cold, day is night, lost is found, nature is synthetic . . .' all the way down to 'I am you and you are me . . .'; then all the reversals are reversed back up to 'cold is hot'. I think Gordon could reasonably have added, 'Words are images and images are words.' Said 'nuff.

I walked into Craigie Horsfield's bright space filled with large black-and-white photographs and thought, 'Ooh, a lot of photographs of Poland and Polish people.' In fact, they're photographs of Barcelona and Catalonian people, but I'd caught in one the essence of Horsfield's praxis. His aim is to chronicle the century and its passage with these vast and technically accomplished matt images. The only problem is that his technique seems to rub out the differences and create images that are peculiarly devoid of place, as well as time. Whether portraits, or cityscapes, or crowd shots, Horsfield's photographs capture an epochal impaction: the nineties as the thirties, the Pole as a Spaniard. One huge shot of a Barcelona apartment block is breathtaking in its composition and sweep – a static *La Dolce Vita* – but walking in from the Gordon space I was taken more by the sense of having quitted the innards of a television for the innards of a magazine.

The final space in the exhibition is devoted to the work of Simon Patterson. Patterson's *The Great Bear*, a detail of which graces the cover of the catalogue, was the conceptual work I found most irritating when scanning through: a version of the classic London tube map, the lines redone with stations named after philosophers, comedians and television journalists. This, on the face of it, was toilet art rampant, a veritable lick under the conceptual rim.

In fact, in the pasteboard, *The Great Bear* is revealed to be a cartoon, an enacted joke. You look at it and, if like me you are a native Londoner, burst into chuckles on noting that the station near to where you were born has been renamed – in my case – 'David Niven' (I missed being born at Groucho Marx by one stop), and the one where you now live 'Peter Arnett' (thankfully – a stop further would be Jon Snow). Once the tittering has guttered and died, you are left not with – as Patterson would have it – 'juxtaposing different paths of knowledge to form more than the sum of their parts', but merely with an old joke, as conceptually interesting as a Punch cartoon reread in a dentist's waiting room at the very end of time.

Patterson's work is both the most elegant of any of the short-listees', and that which most clearly conforms to the perverse schema of the infospace that I laid out above. His other two works are pretty enough: a wall-mounted diagram of a solar system made up of imaginary realms (Cockayne, Shangri La, El Dorado etc.); and three free-standing sails, each blazoned with the name and dates of a different writer; but neither says anything much beyond the raw visual joke – and the jokes aren't as good as *The Great Bear*.

No, Patterson's work really comes into its own when it's described, elucidated, interpreted and mused over by the artist himself. It is the most purely 'conceptual' of the *oeuvres* on view. And Patterson himself, a fresh-faced lad from Surrey, is that most peculiar of artistic phenomena: with his artworks looking like the visual aids for some particularly tedious corporate entity, he is more post-Thatcherite than post-modern.

You can go and see the Turner short-listed artists' work if you want – it's enjoyable enough stuff. It will certainly be a travesty if Douglas Gordon doesn't win, as his is the only substantive contribution. But remember, if you're feeling a bit tired you can always go straight through to the infospace – that's where it's all happening.

New Statesman, November 1996

62

Tony Blair has always been the air guitarist of political rhetoric, standing in front of the mirror of publicity while aping the convictions of others. He carried his Fender Stratocaster with him on the move from Islington to Number 10, but I doubt he's plugged it in that much. Nope, I suspect him of plink-plinking away on the dead strings, so as not to disturb Euan's homework, while great plangent Hendrix-style chords reverberate in his inner ear. It's exactly the same with his conference speechifying. There was Blair, up in front of the autocue, plink-plinking away, while in his mind's eye a new Jerusalem was being built in this brownfield site of an unpleasant land.

The word is that while this particular speech may have been drafted by Alastair Campbell, Blair himself spent days agonising over it, tearing it up and rewriting it. I have my doubts. Anyone who's ever attempted to get through a screed actually penned by the Prime Minister knows that he is, in fact, utterly incapable of parsing a proper English sentence. Nope, this one bears all the hallmarks of his master's tabloid voice: the slavish adherence to the law of threes – 'Under John Major [the Conservative Party] was weak, weak, weak. Under William Hague it's weird, weird, weird'; the tendentious historicism, which renders every political opponent responsible for the geopolitical crises of fifty or a hundred years ago; and the generous helpings of unverifiable statistics – £1.5 million of this improvement, £250,000 of that one.

The whipped cream of this – the sole variety of Campbell's tinned verbiage – was then generously aerated with the Prime Minister's own, inimitable delivery: his 'I say to you's and 'But let us not's, all the corny little catch-phrases and mock-sincere moues which betray more than anything else that Tony Blair cannot help patronising his audience. It's bad enough for those of us who are patronised *in absentia*, but how much worse it must've been for those who actually had to go to Bournemouth, had to sit through this bowdlerised blether, had to face up to belonging to a political party allegedly led by this man.

I don't envy them; and I especially don't envy all the working-class delegates who had to sit there in the Winter Gardens of discontent, listening to a cufflink-porting, designer-suit-wearing, public-school- and

Oxford-educated, six-figure-salaried, cut-glass-accented man, who's never done a day's manual work in his life, tell them that 'the class war is over'.

Oh yes, the class war is over all right. Over for one T. Blair. Over because it was a war won for him by his socially mountaineering father, dear old Tory-voting Leo, whose industriousness allowed our Tony to attend Fettes, to burnish his social standing by association, and to leap-frog from *petit-* to *haut-* while remaining distinctively bourgeois. When was the last time we heard a petit-bourgeois provincial who'd ascended the greasy pole to Number 10 tell us – like the torturer O'Brien in Orwell's *Nineteen Eighty-Four* – that black was white and that three fingers were being held up instead of two? Surely it was Mrs Thatcher (or 'Maggie', as Tony must perforce refer to her), when she informed us that 'Society no longer exists'?

It's in this conference speech more than any other of Tony's recent pronouncements that the hated Baroness comes back to haunt us. For the 'class war' our current Prime Minister is trumpeting on about is not the one in which battle is joined anew every day by those in our society who don't speak with the right accent, or wear the right clothes, or eat their meals at the right time. Oh no. This 'class war' is a bogus Trojan Horse of feigned conflict, inside which Tony Blair and his brothers and sisters in arms are allowing themselves to be pushed into the citadel of power.

Take fox-hunting for an example. Some still cling to the faint hope that this Government really does still have socialistic aspirations, and that their passive acceptance of the anti-blood-sports Jacquerie within their own party means that it's just that: a rising of peasants against masters. Not so. The sad truth is that the anti-hunt lobby – apart from its anarcho-traveller fringe – is largely made up of the kind of RSPCA activists who've always been conservative to the core. Conservative in this most important sense: they've always found it far easier to sympathise with some dear little fox, or bunny rabbit, or kitty, than with the disadvantaged, unfluffy humans who suffer under their noses every day of their lives. And suffer consciously.

Personally, I wonder how a public-school-educated prime minister, who sends his eldest son clear across London to a grant-maintained school, can possibly talk about equality of opportunity in education. Especially not the same prime minister who's presiding over the abolition of free tuition in higher education. How can he sustain such doublethink? I fear with the greatest of ease. For when the Prime Minister talks about an end to 'class war' and victory over the 'forces of conservatism', he's not talking about the conservative class as we all understand it. He's not talking about the vested interests of the wealthy and the powerful at all. Indeed, I don't believe he has any plans to make significant inroads into the culture of class in our society whatsoever.

No, the 'conservatives' he really wants to target are those idiotic workers who believed in – at the very least – true industrial democracy, and at the very most, the infamous ownership by themselves of the means of production. The 'conservatives' Tony wants to take out, like the die-hard warrior he is, are those propagators of 'libertarian nonsense masquerading as freedom', who had the temerity to view open government as the first viable sign of an administration committed to a genuinely democratic society. Presumably these are the same 'conservatives' who would oppose mandatory DNA samples being taken from every known criminal offender in the country, on the 'nonsense' grounds that such a policy would further make a mockery of any concept of rehabilitation.

And as for that 'class war', yes, I don't doubt you want to cut those blue-bloods down to size, Tony. I expect they looked down their noses at you when you and your guitar-strumming, God-bothering pals used to trip across the quad of St John's, on your way to an Ugly Rumours rehearsal. But isn't it ironic that you've ended up so completely aping their styles and modes in order to make yourself electable? Not really, because there's nothing commonly understood in the notion of 'class' that you object to at all.

You believe in income differentials to reward achievement. You believe in the right to private ownership of the means of production. You believe in a society in which the least well-off have just as much social responsibility as the rich. Your sop to all those of your impoverished citizens who have – in real terms – seen their living standards decline, and decline and decline over the past twenty years, is to tell them that society is about providing an equality of opportunity. You call it a 'third way', but it sounds like good old-fashioned one-nation conservatism to me, a philosophy always well-adapted to the *arriviste*.

Keep on with the air guitar, Tony, we all love to hear you strum 'Stairway to Heaven'.

Independent on Sunday, October 1999

63

Restaurant review: Granita, 127 Upper Street, London N1

The trouble starts from the off. I call Granita, the trendy, minimalist Islington restaurant, notorious as a haunt of Tony Blair, and, because of some kind of psychic legerdemain, commit the dreadful solecism of making a reservation in my own name.

'As in Will Self,' snaps the woman on the other end of the phone.

'I've nothing to do with the bloke,' I reply through gritted teeth.

'Oh,' says the woman, 'I'm so sorry – you must get that all the time. It's just that we've heard he's going to be reviewing us.'

'Really.'

'Yes, and to be frank we don't like reviewers that much.'

'Why's that, then?'

'Well, they're always banging on about Tony Blair and the fact that he eats here – it really annoys us.'

Having allowed this individual to vent a bit of her spleen, I complete the arrangements and hang up. How the hell do the people who run Granita know that I'm going to be reviewing them before I even know it myself? Have they got some hotline to my cerebellum? Perhaps that's what that coaxial cable draped over my shoulder and running from a jack plug implanted in my forehead is all about.

And what about the New Labour angle? Does Blair dislike me as much as I dislike him? Does Granita hate both of us more than we hate each other? It's like an awful, prisoner's-dilemma-style logic problem. There can only be one way to solve it. I call Granita back and make a second reservation for the same day and time, but in the name 'Blair-Self'.

When we turned up, the woman who met us asked for the name of the reservation.

'Blair-Self,' I said, with an insouciance I simply didn't feel.

'Oh.' She looked a tad fazed. 'That's all right, Mr Blair-Self. It's just we thought that you might be Will Self.'

'No, no, *Blair*-Self,' I replied with heavy emphasis. She led us to our table and I ordered a large Scotch on the rocks for myself and a gin and tonic for Ken Hoxha, my companion.

I'd brought Ken along because besides being a celebrated interior decorator – and thus capable of judging the design of Granita far better than I could – he's also the youngest son of Enver Hoxha, the former dictator of Albania. If anyone could cope with Islington society, it had to be Ken.

The drinks came with commendable speed and were served by a waitress charmingly dressed in a silky, black round-necked tunic and black trousers. With kit like that on, she could always get a job doing re-education sessions for the Khmer Rouge if the waitressing wasn't steady.

My whisky was Johnnie Walker Black Label. I like a Black Label; for a blend it's an honest, muscular Scotch. Frankly, I'd give a good review to any restaurant serving Black Label – or even a pub for that matter.

Granita is a stark sort of a place. It's long and thin, running back from a plate-glass window at the Upper Street end. The side walls are a burnt lemon colour, the back wall a Mondrian square of cerulean blue. The floors are wooden and heavily shined; the tables are metallic, with swirly, prismatic, zinc tops. The chairs are austere, wooden, and mysteriously kinked in the leg, so as to resemble a person squatting.

Half-way down the room there was a bar station, which, like everything unpainted in Granita, looked as if it was made out of Ancient Sumerian breeze blocks. I found the décor peculiarly calming and restful, but for some reason Ken was agitated. 'I don't mind minimalism,' he averred. 'It's incredibly easy on the eye, but it does make an awful backdrop for people – they stand out so.'

He was right. All around us, Islingtonians were cropping on mounds of salad, and petting their moneyed neuroses. They all had rather strong features and wore trouser suits made out of brightly-patterned Peruvian peasant blankets. They looked pretty awful – like characters in a Fellini film cast by Susie Orbach.

The cadre reappeared and took our order. Ken had the spinach, goat's cheese and marjoram tart (at £4.95 only marginally more expensive than Labour Party membership) to start, and the pan-roasted cod with lentils, coriander and sugar-snap peas to follow. I risked the salad of oak leaves, rocket, chicory, grated Gruyère cheese, mushroom and fennel for an entrée, and another long list of ingredients – headed by the word 'lamb' – for my main course. Really, I couldn't miss out on the oak leaves – it's not every day you get to eat the National Trust symbol.

I also ordered a bottle of Coldstream Hills Cabernet Merlot 1992. I'm not wild about Australian wine – except in Australia – but almost everything on the Granita wine list was New World. Most of the selections seemed to come from those God-squad-ridden places where Brer

Blair goes to talk divinity with knock-kneed old Anglicans: 'Lower taxes for the rich, Tony? Mandatory balloting for strike actions? Best pals with Rupert Murdoch? Jolly good! Jolly good! *Of course* you can still call yourself a socialist – we're a very broad Church.'

A vast bale of herbage arrived on the table and I pitchforked my way in. It was dead colourful and the grated Gruyère was a nice touch (apparently, Norma Major grates up cruddy old bits of Cheddar and keeps them in the freezer. I wonder if Granita have picked up on this toppermost tip), but there was a problem: both my salad and the salad garnish with Ken's tart were absolutely suffused with balsamic vinegar. This wasn't a dressing – it was an inundation. The only way, I reasoned, that the chef could have got so much balsamic vinegar on to these leaves was by pouring several bottles of the stuff into a washing-up bowl and dunking the whole messery in the solution.

'Oh dear,' said Ken, blinking back tears, 'you don't think they've rumbled us, do you?'

'We'll know when the main courses arrive,' I replied. 'If your sugar-snap peas are arranged on the plate so as to form the slogan "Fuck off Tony", I think you can safely assume that they have.'

In fact, the sugar-snap peas were so carelessly strewn that even a paranoiac researcher at Smith Square would have had difficulty reading anything into them. The cod was firm, the lentils nicely crunchy. My lamb with a long list of other things wasn't bad either. The lamb was *al dente* and little-girlishly pink; the other things were . . . well, other things.

I sighed and took a hefty pull on the Coldstream Hills. It was looking good – just a crème brûlée and coffee to finish with and we'd be home free. But Ken was agitated again. He kept staring over his shoulder to where a rather swarthy, heavy-set fellow wearing a striped apron was leaning against the bar station.

'Psst!' he hissed. 'Why's that man staring at us? He looks really pissed off.'

'Ken,' I said in my best, party-political-broadcast voice, 'there are only three possibilities. Either he thinks you're me – in which case he hates your guts. Or, he thinks you're Tony Blair – in which case he hates your guts. Or, he thinks I'm Tony Blair – and just can't believe that a talented, career woman such as yourself, Cherie, would want to lie down under me.'

'Oh Tony,' said Ken, 'you know I'll do *anything* that's necessary to get you erected.'

Observer, September 1996

64

Restaurant review: Emma's, Royal College Street, London NW1

'In Camden Town . . .' Suggs warbles, 'I'll meet you by the underground . . .' But the truth of the matter is that *all* of Camden Town looks like an underground. The long, cavernous streets that plunge through stark-fronted terraces seem to me always to be psychically tiled. The darkness at noon and the permanent rumble of the traffic crank up this sense of tunnelling beneath the metropolis. Limp chip-wrappers furl in the wake of gritty gusts; the pavements are studded with discarded take-away fodder, pancake rolls jettisoned alongside prawn birianis, alongside 'southern' fried chicken, to fashion a mondial snack for dossers with myxomatous faces.

This grimiest, and in many ways grimmest of north London inner suburbs (what could possibly be grimmer than marauding phalanxes of Balkan au pair girls and Benelux exchange students, buying black things at exorbitant mark-ups from superannuated hippies) now, at last, boasts an eatery that can relieve its urban dolour. Somewhere Jonathan Miller, Alan Bennett and the rest of the *bien pensants* of Camden can gather to discuss their favourite television series. Who knows, maybe Brer Blair will consent to pilot the Side Impact Protection System (Tough on Physics, Tough on the Causes of Physics) over from Islington and join us.

I never thought I'd be recommending a Swedish restaurant on Royal College Street. The last time I sojourned on this maculate esplanade it was to go to gigs at the Falcon, where we'd neck sulphate wrapped up in Rizla papers. In those days a relationship was something that lasted for hours, and Volvos were objects of utter derision. Now I find myself sitting in Volvos for hours, discussing relationships that have endured for years. Bergman has come home to roost.

The other night, the only thing that could get me out of the 760 turbo, where Dr Klangenfarben and I were anatomising my unsuccessful psychoanalysis (after five years on the couch I was still under the impression that Dr K was a chiropodist, and kept asking him to get out the clippers), was the artful little board outside Emma's proclaiming, 'Swedish Cuisine!' 'Come on, Klaggy,' I cried; 'this'll buck you up.' Not a bad idea, really, since even on a good day Dr Klangenfarben closely resembles the character of Death in *The Seventh Seal*.

We were met at the door by a charming, willowy, Nordic maiden – perhaps Emma herself? At any rate, she was tall and her restaurant is – how can I put it? – dinky beyond belief. It has a minuscule, walnut-and-marble bar station; tiny little white-clothed tables with sensible, bentwood chairs; weathered floorboards; strips of gingham tacked up to waist height; and above that bilious rag-swirls of gloss. In the adjacent vault dwarf halogen lights twinkled merrily. The first time I went to Emma's I dined in the back part of the restaurant, a sort of glassed-in pygmy conservatory, but this time we squatted in the main body of the place.

A personable hornhead brought us glasses of schnapps. This stuff – called Herringjar, or possibly Jarherring – came chilled, and sank down my oesophagus trailing fruity vapours. I immediately felt a peculiar ambivalence steal into me with the liquor. On the one hand I felt like laughing, skipping, stripping naked and beating myself – and Dr Klangenfarben – with birch switches; but at one and the same time, I seriously considered moving to a dead-flat island, north of the Arctic Circle, where I could spend the rest of the winter in silence, mutilating sheep with a chainsaw.

The menu at Emma's is a three-part affair. First come the all-important *forratter*, or starters; next the main courses, or *huvudratter*; and lastly the afters, or *efterratter*. Cool language, Swedish, dead easy to pick up.

I had the smoked reindeer with a pesto of beetroot and horseradish to start while Dr K – pining as ever for his rustic, Tyrolean childhood – had the farmhouse pâté with lingon sauce. There is no established etiquette in Sweden as to how you should order reindeer. Some gastronomes have been known to carry a small bridle of bells which they jingle ever so subtly; others mutter 'Rudolph?' under their breath. I, with typical English panache, simply placed my hands either side of my head and wiggled my fingers to simulate antlers. Dr K frowned and took some notes.

Smoked reindeer is delicious. Light, delicate strips of very pink meat, that are gamey but toothsome, really it's like a much, much better pastrami – what you are always looking for in pastrami, but pastrami doesn't deliver. The strips came attractively draped over a mound of appropriate garnish, while the pesto of beetroot and horseradish was sweet rather than tart. Dr K also effected the transference of some of his farmhouse pâté to me, and this was coarse, rich and altogether yummy.

There's a passable little wine list at Emma's, but we stuck on schnapps, and then had a beer brewed in Lapland that was called something like Lapherring. This was surprisingly full-bodied, with a barley finish. It slid down well, and I began to imagine myself spending the rest of the winter in a yurt, wearing a nappy made from sphagnum moss (this lives off your natural waste products, obviating the need to quit the yurt for the call of the wild), holding hands with a Lapp, while rocking back and forth and reciting endless sagas. Dr K kept on with the notes.

For our main courses, I chose the braised loin of lamb with a potato cake and green peppercorn sauce, while the author of *The Psychopathology of All-Day Breakfasts* went for the Swedish meatballs in a creamed sauce with mashed potatoes. My lamb was a tad school-dinnerish, in that the slices swam in the sauce alongside the potato cake, teasing you with their ambiguity. But that's a minor gripe – it tasted great. As for the Swedish meatballs – which I had on my first visit – they are something the Swedes should be justifiably proud of. Other cultures may have invented gunpowder, or reached the moon, but the Swedes must have been visited by the World Spirit when they nailed down this: the definitive meatball. Small, delicate, full of herbs, and succulent, they are such that Dr K didn't even look up from his plate when I suggested there was something distinctly bizarre about watching a practitioner of the talking cure shove a lot of balls in his mouth.

Neither of us felt like *efterratter*, although a selection of cheeses should never be rejected lightly. Instead we headed back to Dr K's, for a screening of the new CinemaScope, director's cut of *The Silence*. The bill came to £35, including service. Emma's is a thoroughly nice, unpretentious restaurant, serving good food at sensible prices. Please get down there as soon as possible – they desperately need custom. Indeed, looking at the place the other night I was reminded of the despairing sign I once saw in a café window: 'Come in and eat – before we both starve!'

Observer, March 1997

65

Having purchased a Mobylette moped while travelling in central Anatolia – despite the considerable derision of John, my companion – I looked forward to driving it into central London. But after puttering happily over Waterloo Bridge and beginning the descent into the Kingsway underpass, I encountered a hold-up. The gates were closed at the entrance to the tunnel and the traffic was backed up for fifty metres. So I propped the Mobylette on its stand, clambered up on to the roadway and began looking for someone to blame for this impasse. I only saw a few obviously innocent passers-by, but on returning to where my moped had been parked I found it gone! 'What the hell's going on!' I bellowed, as quick as any Londoner to embrace road rage. How could it have been stolen when it was blocked in fore and aft? Had a weightlifting thief managed to manhandle it out of the underpass?

I leapt back on to the roadway above and moved purposively towards the passers-by I'd seen before. Obviously they weren't innocent after all – they were massively culpable. I'd give them what for . . . ! But then, just as I was closing in on the knot of putative motorised-bicycle thieves, something bizarre happened. No, bizarre is a grotesque understatement – something marvellously, triumphantly, unimpeachably transcendent, something the like of which I never thought I could experience. I realised – in one delirious surge of giggling, intoxicated, sympathetic glory – that I had become . . . ENLIGHTENED; that I had shucked off my tedious old ego as easily as if it were a raincoat, and left it lying in the road; that I felt no anger towards the people who might have stolen my moped, because it didn't matter AT ALL. Nothing mattered, except this sense of hilarious, total identification with all things sentient, with the godly hydra-head that is all creatures. If I looked into the eyes of the urban foot sloggers all around me, I was instantly at one with all their dreams and hopes and longings, but not in a painful, burdensome way – this was a dynamic, beautiful and extremely funny form of sympathy.

Giggling like a small boy, I strolled away from the underpass. Obviously, I couldn't really be enlightened – that would be absurd. It took years, I knew, of disciplined meditation and prayer, under the firm tutelage of a spiritual master – whether Sufi sheikh, eastern guru, or

Christian divine – to achieve such a state. No, I must be suffering from one of those delusory states that come upon mystical initiates. What I needed was a sharp blow on the head from the person who knew the condition of my soul better than any other: my wife.

Without being aware of getting there I found myself standing at home, in the entrance hall of my house. The front door swung open and in came Deborah. She looked at me strangely and said, 'What's got into you?' I knew what she was thinking, that I was drunk, or in a still more unsavoury state. I could conceal the truth no longer. 'It's very funny,' I tittered, 'but I've become enlightened!' She stared deep into what had once been my eyes, and in a matter-of-fact way said, 'Oh, so you have . . .' And the 'have' lengthened and deepened, oscillating up and down the scale, until it became an amplified ululation . . . until it became the muezzin, howling out over the public address system of the mosque adjoining the Mevlana Müzesi across the road. I was jerked awake. It was a late-December dawn in Konya, central Turkey, and so far was I from really being enlightened that my first thoughts on coming to consciousness were of how narrow and hard my bed was, and just how overheated Room 217 of the Hotel Balikcilar remained, despite the window having been wide open all night.

I retail this peculiar dream at such length purely because it really did happen, complete with its distinct levels of lucidity. After all, it's one thing to dream that you've been enlightened, quite another to be aware within the dream itself that this may be false. It's one thing to go looking for a vicarious religious experience – but it's altogether stranger to have one thrust upon you unbidden. I suppose I'm as cynical about spiritual tourism as I am about any travel that makes you a voyeur, extracting trivial pleasures from the profundities of other cultures. When Westerners are young we tend to do this in a material dimension, taking our cheap holidays in other peoples' misery. But when we grow old enough and rich enough we might think we're behaving more laudably by taking expensive ones in other peoples' piety.

On the face of it I was as bad as any other in this respect. My friend John had suggested the trip to the Mevlevi Festival, where the dervishes famously whirl. Until then I knew no more of this Sufi sect than that raw fact: they whirl. In English parlance, to act like a 'whirling dervish' is to behave with an uncontrolled frenzy. As for the Sufis and Sufism in general, I had no more acquaintance with these than a back-of-the-cereal-packet fact file. I knew they represented the mystic, heterodox wing of Islam; and once or twice in Morocco, I'd ended up chatting late at night, in pidgin French, to young men who were members of Sufi brotherhoods. But was it the smallness of the hour, the inadequacy of my French, or the potency of their hashish, that led me to cod-mystical appreciation of their wisdom, when they uttered such sentiments as 'God is breath'?

My vision of modern Turkey was similarly warped and occluded. Edward Said has propounded the thesis that the West's view of the Orient has always been a distorted projection of its own negative cultural capabilities, and certainly I had absorbed plenty on Turkey's downside. This vast oblong of territory between the Black Sea and the Mediterranean, the Middle East and the Aegean, styled itself as a democratic, modernising bulwark against Islamic fundamentalism. But was Turkey not also the implacable pursuer of territorial claims in Cyprus and Kurdistan, which meant that the former had remained for three decades with its sovereignty in escrow, and the latter was an unmentionable word, a non-designation? Shortly before I arrived in December 2000, the case of Abdullah Ocalan, the Kurdish rebel leader captured by the Turks and sentenced to death, was referred to the European Court of Human Rights. The Turkish Government had agreed to abide by the Court's decision, and in a sense this was the very pivot around which Turkish membership of the European Community – for so long a matter of debate – revolved.

Then there was a $10 billion emergency loan from the IMF to bail out the Turkish economy; and the ongoing hunger strikes by Marxist rebels in Turkish prisons (which culminated, the week after I left, in an armed assault by the security forces leaving fifteen prisoners dead – they'd set themselves on fire). With the cosmically vexed question of the Armenian holocaust of 1915–17 – a fact the assertion of which remains a criminal offence in Turkey to this day – it was difficult not to think of the nation as, if not the proverbially 'sick man' of Europe, at any rate a fervid-to-overheated kind of a place, physically proximate, but linguistically and culturally isolated. And, of course, there were also those dervishes.

On the BA flight out from Heathrow to Istanbul I began my crash programme of instruction in Sufism and the cult of the Mevlana or 'teacher'. Known as 'Rumi' (literally 'from Roman Anatolia'), but called 'Jelaluddin Balkhi' by the Persians and Afghans, the poet was born in Balkh, Afghanistan, in 1207. Sometime between 1215 and 1220 he and his family fled the threat of invading Mongols and emigrated to Konya in Turkey. Rumi's father, Bahaeddin Veled, was a theologian and mystic, and after his death Rumi took over the role of sheikh in the dervish community in Konya. The word 'dervish' derives from the Persian *darwish* meaning 'poor man' (this expresses the poverty of man in relation to the richness of God rather than literal poverty), but up until 1244 when he encountered the wandering dervish Shams of Tabriz, Rumi's life was that of a relatively orthodox religious scholar. Shams changed all of that with a single question about the primacy of Muhammad's teaching, and the two then embarked on a *sohbet*, or mystical conversation, which was only interrupted by Shams's disappearance to Damascus when he sensed the jealousy of Rumi's disciples. On Shams's return the *sohbet* was resumed, only to be finally interrupted when the mendicant was murdered, possibly by Rumi's own son.

It's difficult to express the intensity of the friendship between the two men in any conventional framework – this was a total melding of minds. It's said that when Rumi and Shams were in convocation they had no need of sleep or food for weeks on end. It was his relationship with Shams that made Rumi into a mystical poet, and after his disappearance Rumi reached the conclusion that he had wholly absorbed Shams's identity; indeed, that Shams was now writing through him. He called his huge collection of odes and quatrains 'The Works of Shams of Tabriz'; and during the last years of his life he composed and dictated the vast, six-volume masterpiece called simply *Mathnawi*, or *Spiritual Couplets*.

Just as it's impossible to place one definition of Sufism itself, which is in reality a vast, multi-stranded skein of Islamic practice, commentary, interpretation and belief, so Rumi's poetry, some sixty-five thousand verses in Persian, defies any reduction to this, or that. Rumi has been compared to Shakespeare in the range of his impact and his cultural centrality to his own, emerging world. Like Shakespeare's writing, his poetry can seem, even on slight acquaintance, to be a vast palimpsest, a working-up out of diverse sources – mythic, folkloric, lyrical, ecstatic – of an entire metaphoric realm. Some of Rumi's verses are couplets with all the paradoxical confusion of Zen Buddhist koans – 'I am the kebab, God is the spit' – while others have the pithy air of tough, homespun advice, and still others the feel of love poetry, only in Rumi's case the beloved is God himself.

Suffice to say, even in four hours I'd read enough to feel enthusiastic about my trip to Konya for the *sema* or Mevlevi Festival. Each year, in the week preceding the anniversary of Rumi's death – 17 December 1273 – the whirling ceremony is held twice daily. My guidebook was disparaging about the modern version, saying that it was inauthentic: it took place in a basketball court, the tickets were 'pricey', and the whirlers themselves were not even professing Mevlevis. It painted a picture of

Konya as a conservative, unlovely, close-faced metropolis of half a million, beset by the sub-zero temperatures of the Anatolian plateau, and where hotels and restaurants doubled up their prices for the pilgrims, while the shops were full of kitschy whirling-dervish memorabilia.

How wrong the guide was. Authentic is not a synonym for 'picturesque', and our experience of off-season Turkey felt profoundly real. From the moment I rendezvoused with John – who for the purposes of my narrative occupies a Shams of Tabriz-type role – at Pandeli's, a famous restaurant in the Egyptian Bazaar of Istanbul, we were plunged into a conversation which, if not evidence of a profound mystical union, was at any rate tantamount to a philosophic discourse, while entering a milieu shorn of tourists and occupied by Turks who consistently displayed towards us a manner of weary acceptance, verging on the bullying intimacy of an older brother: 'Don't cross the road there!' they shouted to us as we barrelled across the cobbles. 'There is a tram coming.'

We ate lamb at Pandeli's and talked of religion and science ('I am the kebab, God is the spit'); we ate lamb in Konya. When we got to Cappadocia we ate lamb there too. There was traditional, limp salad, and occasionally some chickpeas. We didn't object – we were visiting slap-bang in the middle of Ramadan, and while it wasn't impossible to get things to eat and drink during daylight hours, there was a persistent atmosphere of strained tolerance when we asked for food. In Konya no one smoked in the street, and when dusk fell the restaurants and cafés were filled, then evacuated, by the populace within the space of an hour, as if the city itself were some voracious bivalve.

John, who'd visited Istanbul before, gave me three hours of edited highlights. At the Aya Sofya – 'the Church of the Divine Wisdom' – which was for a millennium the largest enclosed space in the world, I marvelled at the louring interior of the giant dome, complete with its stalagmite of scaffolding, so dense and complex that in the gloom it appeared like charcoal shading. We admired the porphyry columns, the ecstatic mosaics, the ramp-like staircases Byzantine noblewomen had ridden their horses up. Then on to Yerebatan Saray, 'the Underground Palace', a fourth-century cistern – again on such an enormous scale, with its four-storey columns sunk in a pellucid pool, that whole legions could have tenanted it. And finally to the Blue Mosque, where we made our obeisance under the calligraphic literalism of another vast dome.

Outside it was dusk. In the precincts of the mosque people were beginning to throng. You could feel the tension of the fast on the verge of being broken. Around a small fair, urchins were running, shouting and playing. Young women sat at the outside tables of cafés, smoking hookahs and chatting. Men strolled arm in arm. We sat and drank several of the ubiquitous glasses of strong tea that fuel Turkey, and continued the philosophic debate that had been driving us forward all afternoon. John, an avid reader of those modern Tao-of-physics-style books, inclines to a sense of awe at the intellectual comprehensibility of creation; while I, already slightly tipsy with culture shock, and the sips I had taken of Rumi's poetry (which frequently employs drunkenness as a metaphor for abandonment to God), was already cruising for a mystical experience.

At the airport, a mere twenty minutes' cab ride from the mosque (a further disorientation in this ancient city of confusion), we had two more hours of circular debate before we boarded our flight for Konya. By the time the Turkish Airlines flight was aloft, we were so dizzy with speculation that neither of us nervous flyers remembered to be anxious. Edward Said's thesis was entirely forgotten as John flipped through *Sky Life*, the Turkish Airlines equivalent of the magazine you're now holding, and after a hour tunnelling through the sky we landed in the darkness of central Anatolia.

The next morning, in Konya, the sunlight had a milky quality that suggested it was only the sub-zero temperature that was keeping the dust of the steppes at bay. The city is situated in the middle of a region styled 'the bread-basket of Turkey'; but in midwinter, in the bustle of headscarfed women pilgrims, lottery-ticket sellers and shoeshine operatives, with the omnipresent hoot of traffic, we felt suffused with urbanity. Our hotel, the Balikcilar, boasted peculiar murals in the dining room depicting the famous troglodyte dwellings of Cappadocia. The lobby too was encrusted with knobbly stonework. The night had not been a comfortable one. There was the heat of the rooms, the narrowness of the beds, and in next door to John the mounting hysteria of a woman having a full-scale nervous breakdown. While we were consulting in the corridor as to what to do, a huge Nordic character had emerged from a room further along, and after gaining admission succeeded in either comforting or eliminating her. On the television I watched the *sema* on the local station, eighteen dervishes fluidly revolving on the floor of a basketball court, their white skirts flaring out. Even in black and white their smooth synchrony seemed the antithesis of religious frenzy.

We had one of those days that only happen in remote places where you don't speak the language, hardly anyone speaks yours and you're otherwise ill prepared. We visited the Mevlana shrine itself and saw the tombs of Rumi, his father and his acolytes, all caparisoned with iridescent drapery. Chandeliers hung on long wires from the high ceilings. The tombs were canted at an angle, their curiously phallic, turbaned tops like the pommels of saddles. They looked like suspended-animation chambers carrying their occupants to some distant planet. The literalism of Islam was on every available surface, and as we were carried forward in the press of pilgrims – the headscarfed, keening women holding their hands open beseechingly in front of their faces – eerie, ululating singing played from hidden speakers. We examined some hairs from the Prophet's beard in the adjoining chamber, together with brilliantly illuminated manuscripts of the poet's works. And everywhere, despite the press of worshippers, there was the same air of grudging yet total tolerance of our presence, and the handful of other Westerners in attendance.

Outside the shrine we met Arum, a young man intent on improving his English. And improve it he needed to. We spent two hours in his company, trekking on foot down the dusty boulevards to the Atatürk Sports Stadium, to this office, to that office, to an ethnographic museum, to a third office, hunting for where we thought they might have our reserved tickets for that evening's *sema*, while revelling in the full weight of each other's incomprehension. About the only point of true communication was summed up by the words 'Britney Spears', and that's a very low denominator indeed. Eventually, in a side-street, we found a crowded office where an envelope was discovered bearing John's name, phonetically transcribed. We were given free posters depicting a whirling dervish and the legend that this was the 727th Mevlevi Festival.

That evening, as we sat on part of an island of leatherette sofas in the lobby of the Balikcilar, I felt a strange, liquid undulating beneath me. For a full twenty seconds I thought it was the motions of the distinctly heavyweight people in the seat behind, but then I noticed the staff had left off serving tea and were bolting for the door. It was over within a minute, and we were all outside, standing across the road on a traffic island oddly decorated with a bed of cabbages. It wasn't until the following evening, when we were having a telly supper three hundred kilometres away in Cappadocia, that we learned via *BBC World Report* that the earthquake had toppled a minaret in Konya, killing six.

The tremor was a fitting preamble to our visit to the *sema* itself, introducing a further note of disorientation to our experience of the Orient. Back at the Atatürk Sports Stadium there were headscarves in abundance. At an urn in the dusty lobby a man performed a tea ceremonial of high-speed riskiness, whipping four glasses at a time under the stream of boiling water, as if attempting to manicure his outstretched hands with third-degree burns. Inside the auditorium about two thousand people were settling themselves on plastic chairs. Photographers and camera crews were roving around the edge of the court. There was even a camera positioned on the gantry holding the basketball net. Banners inscribed with the verses of Rumi were hung up around the walls, together with many others bearing the single word 'ARCELIK'. Later, by a deductive process involving scrutinising advertising hoardings, I worked out that this was the name of a Turkish washing-machine manufacturer. Washing machines? Whiter-than-white robes? Whirling dervishes? Could this be some form of commercial sponsorship? On the one hand, it would seem a desecration of the religious character of the *sema*; on the other – it made perfect sense.

For, as the lights went down, and the musicians in their long robes filed in to take up their positions, it occurred to me that while the whirling-dervish order remained to some extent clandestine, this officially sanctioned exhibition was the public, popular face of contemporary Sufism in Turkey. Atatürk banned the Sufi sects (which had enormous political influence under the Ottoman Empire) outright in the 1920s, and although the ban never really took, there is still a sense in which such practices are frowned on. Not that you would have realised it from the speech of an official from the Ministry of Culture at the lectern, who, in between the musical and the dancing parts of the programme, told us that the Mevlana had anticipated the theory of relativity, genetic engineering and the moon landing; as well as exhorting us not to use mobile phones or take flash photographs during the *sema*.

For an hour and a half we listened to hypnotic *ayin*. These complex compositions are played by a small orchestra including the *ney* (an end-blown reed flute), the kettledrum, the *rebab* (a pear-shaped fiddle played with a bow) and the *kanun* (a large zither), among other instruments. Vocal pieces preceded and followed the *ayin*: *ilahi*, hymns comprising words from Rumi; and *zikr*, trance-like repetitions of some of the ninety-nine names of God by a soloist with an electrifying ability to shift his tone.

When the dervishes entered – from beneath the opposition's basket – they looked imposing, in their floor-length black cloaks, which symbol-ise the tomb itself, and their high, conical, camel-hair hats, which symbolise the tombstone. Filing down the tramlines of the court they took their places in several colloquies of cushions and proceeded to enact in dumb show various aspects of the dervish lifestyle, such as discoursing over religious texts and welcoming a new initiate, who poignantly – if a little fetishistically – was called upon by the *seyh* (the current head of the sect – or the man *playing* the current head of the sect) to kiss his hat.

Eventually the *seyh* marshalled them together again, and they dropped their black robes to denote that they had escaped the tomb and all other worldly ties – a piece of symbolism perhaps a tad undercut by the fact that the white skirts they wear underneath are intended to resemble the funeral shroud. But no matter how morbid these accoutrements, or how hammy the performance of the *seyh* (who paced about looking distinctly self-important and performing his obeisance with all the gravity of a small-town mayor), when the dervishes began to whirl all was explained, all was clarified, and all the background camera flashes and rumblings of the audience faded into the darkness of the auditorium.

The dervishes whirl steadily and metrically. Their motion is intended to represent the heavenly bodies, and there is something other-worldly about these men as they revolve, their skirts flaring out, canted at an angle. They hold one arm extended up, receiving grace from God, and one down, distributing it to humanity. Their feet, moving one about the other in a tight three-step, seem wholly disconnected from their static torsos. They are released by the *seyh*, one after the other, and float up one side of the court, then down the other, then into the middle, until the whole area is carpeted with their white blooms, yet at no point – despite the fact that their eyes are half closed – is there any possibility of collision. While they whirl, the musicians sing of the desire for mystic union.

The whirling was over in an hour or so, and after it had finished we rushed for the cab rank in the darkness as if we'd been at any other kind of gig – Britney Spears perhaps. The next day we hired a car (expensive, but not catastrophically so) and drove two hundred kilometres over empty roads, through a landscape of blue hills that seemed in their very contours to be remembering the tramp of the myriad civilisations that have passed through them.

In Cappadocia we saw the wind-eroded rock valley of Göreme, and the fairy chimneys of Ürgüp. We climbed into the tiny churches hewn out of the volcanic tuff, and at night, in a deserted hammam a masseur lathered us and cracked our vertebrae. We returned to Konya the follow-ing afternoon and attended the *sema* again. For some reason the faces of the dervishes appeared to be those of old friends: the young one with the swan's neck; the middle-aged guy with the notably black beard; the small old one with the face of a British comedian. However, whether it was the daylight streaming into the hall, or our familiarity with the ritual, this second helping felt like one too many. It was the first that stayed with me.

As I walked back to the hotel, exhausted by four of the most incident-filled days I can remember ever having, a cavalcade of sinister black Mercedes with tinted windows screeched to a halt outside the Mevlana Müzesi. Behind them came uniformed police who sealed off this busy section of road. From the darkened cars a politician, complete with his entourage, emerged in double-quick time – the apparatchiks all in sharp suits, the security men fanning out about them, ostentatiously patting their armpits to check their firearms were still concealed. The largest and most threatening of the minders walked straight towards where I was standing, by the outdoor fountain of the mosque. For a few seconds I thought he was going to accost me, but then he veered off, went over to one of the taps, took off his jacket – exposing his shoulder holster – and draped it over the stone balustrade, then sat down and removed his shoes and socks so that he might wash his feet.

Modern Turkey – ancient Turkey. Who would've thought so much could be absorbed in so little time? But then, that night, there came the dream.

High Life, May 2001

66

Television review

God I hate *Friends* (Channel 4). No, I don't simply hate it – I loathe it; I'd like the earth to open up and its creators – the pin-headed Bright, Kauffman and Crane – to disappear down into Hades. I like to think there's a special circle of the inferno reserved for the creators of shows like *Friends*, in which they're obliged to go through the action of just one of the mindless skits they've spawned, inhabiting the minds of the cardboard cut-outs they've created, over and over and over again, while being incapable of altering the action one jot. It would be like *Groundhog Day* without free will, and after a year's worth of this (17,520 episodes, for anyone who's counting), they'd come to rue the day they ever conceived of a song called 'Smelly Cat', or imagined that 'Central Perk' was a witty name for a coffee shop.

But why do I need to wish this fresh hell on Bright, Kauffman and Crane when they're there already? They've done another twenty-six-episode series of *Friends* – their sixth to date – and now it's we who must suffer for their comedy. Yes, I hate *Friends*, and frankly I'm not in the least bit surprised to learn that the actor who plays Chandler has recently been in treatment for his addiction to prescription pain-killers. I'm screaming out for the things every time that credit sequence rolls, and we're propelled into this saccharine little cubicle of a cosmos, where the inner children of its creators have been confined for too long, pissing on the lino.

Have you ever noticed how nobody in *Friends* really belongs to an ethnic group? Sure, it's obvious that Ross is Jewish and I suppose Joey must be Italian, but no one ever makes a big deal about it. Has it struck you at all that the Manhattan backdrop to *Friends* is as implausible as Oz? Not just that the dirty, scummy city of Gotham has been transmogrified into a vapid lot in Hollywood, but that the dirty, scummy mores of its inhabitants have all been air-brushed into ditsiness?

Occasionally, over the six years the show's been running, I've found myself slumped down with friends of my own and we've begun watching it. As I moan and groan they reassure me that while this particular episode may not be that good, the show used to be better in the past; that once upon a time there were some absolutely vintage gags, and if I'm not enjoying it now I certainly would've then. No wonder people take this sentimental line with *Friends*, because what it's all about is an evocation of young adulthood – seen through the eyes of children. The characters in *Friends* act as prepubescent kids like to imagine that young adults behave: living a near-carefree existence, where their only troubles are the gratification of small desires, and the bruising of the aorta rather than the breaking of a heart.

The world evoked by *Friends* is one in which everyone is on a lifelong sleep-over, playing at sex and relationships, watching TV and eating Ben & Jerry's. No one smokes and they get drunk solely for the comic effect; their bodies only seem to metabolise coffee. Have you ever clocked that the characters in *Friends* not only act like big kids, they also talk like them and even walk and skip like eight-year-olds? But what's bizarre and hateful about adults' liking *Friends* is that it's an indulgence in an imagined past that not only never has, but never could have, existed. Liking *Friends* is the Holocaust denial of television appreciation – and if I were in control I'd pass a law against it.

Another thing: it's so sedative watching *Friends* that if you allow yourself to settle in front of it for more than a few minutes, you're in serious danger of remaining there until your brain turns to cream cheese. I can just about bear my kids watching *Friends*, but only if I stay with them the whole time, whispering in their ears, like a slave poised on a chariot behind a Roman general at his triumph; 'It's a load of cack. Adolescence is awful. You will experience a lot of pain and disillusionment in your twenties. New York is not Never-Never Land, it's full of venal, money-grubbing perverts.' I suppose the one good thing to be said about the show running for this long is that the actors are getting damn long in the tooth. It won't be long before Joey makes his entrances behind a Zimmer frame, and Rachel falls down and breaks her hip every five minutes because of osteoporosis. I'll no longer have to do my whispering act and my kids will be grown-up themselves and deriding some other piece of dumb-ass dreck.

The only good actor in *Friends* is Lisa Kudrow, and significantly she's also the only one who's got together a decent alternative film career. Why do you do it, Lisa? Have they kidnapped your family? I can't imagine you enjoy the motivational hugging that the whole cast apparently indulges in before each episode is shot. I had the great misfortune to watch a documentary about the making of *Friends* before the launch of the new series, and from this I learned that what I'd assumed to be canned laughter is in fact a 'live' audience. Granted, their laughter is filtered and remixed and digitally enhanced until it sounds robotic, but the initial expirations are from living, breathing humans. Spooky.

More bizarre still is another piece of childishness on Channel 4, this time the home-grown *Big Brother*. This is an inner-city version of *Castaway*, in which ten 'adults' are marooned in a custom-built house. There they interact with one another under the eyes of myriad cameras, while talking gobshite into radio microphones shackled to their hips. At the end of each week of their sojourn in the *Big Brother* house, the audience votes on who should be evicted, and thus miss out on further exposure of their toilet habits (yes, there are cameras everywhere), and the chance of winning seventy grand in prize money.

I watched the first episode of *Big Brother* in a lather of indifference. The psychologists have done a better job than the lot employed by *Castaway*, but then all they had to come up with were ten people who were reasonably good-looking, unpleasantly extrovert, and tediously meretricious. The pressure of continual exposure drives this lot to get their kit off and lark about within the first three days; by the end of a couple of weeks they'll probably be forming a conga line of buggery.

But what amazes me most about *Big Brother*, which was trailed for weeks before it appeared on screen by a series of billboards featuring giant staring eyes, is that it's the second show to be broadcast in Britain that takes its name from a George Orwell novel. We've already got the celebrity pet-hates romp *Room 101* – what can possibly be coming next? A holiday show called 'The Road to Wigan Pier'? A cookery slot entitled 'Homage to Catalonia'? Or maybe a little late-night soft porn on Channel 5, where they know what use to make of a clergyman's daughter.

Independent on Sunday, July 2000

67

What on earth would Poor Old Oscar (as his intimates shall unto eternity refer to him) make of the peculiar 'psycho-object' the sculptor Maggi Hambling has made of his image? The sculpture – which constitutes a century-late public acknowledgement of Wilde, his genius, and his enduring impact – takes the form of a rigid, slightly-bigger-than-life-size, granite sarcophagus. Carved at the foot of it is Wilde's own epigram 'We are all in the gutter, but some of us are looking at the stars.'

At the business end there is a writhing froth – if bronze can achieve this effect! – of Wildean furbelows: curls of hair, lianas of features, the exploded foliage of a buttonhole – the infamous green carnation, greener now in ageless bronze. And poking from the whole Medusan caboodle is the inevitable opiated cigarette, clamped between his hosepipe lips; it's clear Poor Old Oscar is chaining his way to Utopia.

Apparently Hambling's idea is that the body of the sarcophagus should provide a place for people to perch and converse with the Great Dead White Gay Male, presumably using the epigram above as an inspiration. How much more suitable would've been 'When critics disagree, the artist is in accord with himself.' Wilde was, above all, a supremely self-reflexive artist, almost the critic-as-artist – and also had no difficulty in accepting (indeed some might say it was another original invention of his own) that the true mantle of the modern satirist is a willingness to be woefully misunderstood.

Anyway, I feel ambivalent towards Hambling's memorial. I do think Poor Old Oscar should've got both a more salient site (he's tucked away in a pedestrian zone behind St Martin-in-the-Fields, within tottering distance of Trafalgar Square but invisible from any road), and a less supine conception – why does he have to lie down for eternity? Is it because of the sexual nature of his notoriety? On the other hand, Hambling's memorial is daring in this way: it closely mimics the way a chieftain's corpse would've been laid out amongst peoples at the very dawn of history – the propping up of the head is particularly distinctive.

Take this from Julian Jaynes's *The Origin of Consciousness in the Breakdown of the Bicameral Mind*, where he is writing of the Eynan people who were a settled people in early Palestine: 'I am suggesting that the dead king, thus propped up on his pillow of stones, was in the hallucinations of his people still giving forth his commands . . .' Now Jaynes means this in a very literal way – he thinks prehistoric people were largely unconscious, the voices of gods taking the place of our modern, internal 'I'. But is it fanciful to observe of Wilde, whose *An Ideal Husband* is currently playing within metres of his new effigy, and whose epigrams, tropes, witticisms and apophthegms are still retold every minute throughout the great metropolis, that in a way we still do hallucinate him, imagine his orotund tones in our mind's ear?

Considering the brouhaha that danced attendance on the unveiling of the work, it's nice to think that Poor Old Oscar's psyche may be with us – but if he is I'm sure he'll be mightily displeased, not just with the ridiculous persiflage its unveiling blew up about the Cabinet's homosexuality, but with the shrine itself. After all, this was Oscar! – a lifelong dandy, a man who took to designing his own fuller fig, at a time when all respectable men dressed to be utterly alike. Look through the graphic material massed to illustrate Richard Ellmann's superlative biography of Poor Old Oscar (the confraternity read and reread this tome much in the way other fanatics see *Cats* 273,000 times), and you find Oscar kitted out as a cavalier for a college ball; as skirted Greek partisan on a Peloponnesian tour. Then comes the celebrated 'cello coat' he designed for the opening of the new Grosvenor Gallery in 1877, which, as its name suggests, was a tail-coat fashioned like the musical instrument.

When Wilde went on his American tour in 1882 – to lecture on, among other things, dress and interior design – he was photographed by

Napoleon Sarony, in New York, in a most fetching ensemble of vast foulard tie, soft collar, silk breeches and stockings, and a fur coat of his own devising. Wilde's dandyism was of a piece with his championing of the Aesthetic movement, and it's no accident that both were epitomised – and then apotheosised – within his own career.

And remember, this was the man who could recite vast tracts of the classics from memory, who was, indeed, a first-rate classicist, whose own poetry represented – until the bitter, Reading end – an over-impaction of near-baroque formalism. Surely this Oscar belongs on a plinth, high above Theatreland, and triumphantly staring out the 'nation of hypocrites' – as he so memorably described the English. He should be in full Aesthetic regalia, and sculpted so as to accord with the bodily aesthetics of the great Italian masters whom he so adored. In other words, *massively idealised*.

Instead, I think Hambling's Oscar is really Sebastian Melmoth, the shambling, moribund, destroyed man who was released from Reading Gaol to spend the short years left to him before death wandering the Continent, addled with absinthe and raddled by life. Perhaps it is this man she would have us contemplate, lying down like any other homeless person, speaking of the gutter, endlessly admonishing us – quite rightly – for the bigotry and persecution and lack of generosity we wreak on our fellows?

As I say – I'm deeply ambivalent.

The Times, December 1998

68

My name is Bond, James Bond. No it isn't. I never fantasise any more about driving along the Grande Corniche in my supercharged Bentley, one of my triple-gold-ringed Morland Specials clamped between my fingers, and my Walther PPK automatic in its customised holster underneath my immaculate white tuxedo. No, the whole charade is now a load of sad cobblers as far as I'm concerned. I can think of few other fictional characters whose stock has fallen as low – in my estimation – as Bond's; except possibly Simenon's Inspector Maigret (fatuous old bore, always pulling on his pipe while he 'intuits', and treating Madame Maigret like a skivvy).

Interestingly, both characters originally appealed to me as much because of their sumptuary and sensual proclivities as because of their drive to apprehend the enemy – whether forensically or fantastically. I loved James Bond for his food and his fags and his Martinis. I loved the locations, and, thankfully, I was too young to understand the current of relentless – and really very disturbing – sadism running beneath all of Fleming's writing about sex.

I'm talking, of course, about the literary character; the filmic Bond has never been quite as disturbing – or as well drawn. Which is why, I suppose, it's been possible to have him serially portrayed over the years. This point is underscored by the fact that an otherwise splendidly po-faced and hagiographic exhibition of James Bond film memorabilia (entitled portentously the Official James Bond Exhibition) contains an admission on one of its information boards: 'In Fleming's novels torture is often linked to sadomasochistic motifs – this was heavily criticised . . .' – and naturally largely omitted from the films.

Sure, they're as sexist as a seraglio of misogynists, but the women are there to be sexually exploited – not have the crap beaten out of them with the dried tails of manta rays (cf. *Octopussy*). And what women they were! At the Official Exhibition there was a continuous video loop showing various Bonds taking off various women's dresses in various ingenious ways (magnets, pulleys, retractable arms). And these were proper women, with big breasts and thighs and discernible rolls of avoir-dupois above their hips – not the etiolated waifs who pass muster for feminine sexuality nowadays. And as for old Sean Connery, this was a man who would have had (and presumably now has still more) serious problems deciding at which point – on the way down – he should stop shaving. It's a grave shame that this marvellous Esau of a man should be denied a knighthood by the Government, simply because he supports a political programme that implies the redundancy of such honours.

Anyway, enough Sean. But it has to be said that once he'd quit the Bond films they collapsed into achingly awful self-parody. I mean, who could ever have seriously taken on board the idea of Roger Moore in bell-bottoms as a defender of the free world? If it had been left to Cubby Broccoli (crazy name, crazy vegetable!) the West would have lost the cold war.

It's this phase of the Bond films that comes most plangently to mind as you stroll around the exhibition. The ridiculous Lotus Esprit which transforms into a mini-submarine in *The Man with the Golden Gun* is given much prominence, as are other bits of adolescent tat like the towing sleds from *Thunderball*. I was rather more taken by the original posters: the one for *From Russia with Love* has the slug line 'His New Incredible Enemies!'; and the one for *Dr No* reminds you in a timely way that Bond 'has the licence to kill when he chooses, where he chooses, and whom he chooses'. Sounds horribly like the Yorkshire Ripper to me.

There's an anecdote about Joseph Conrad that came to mind as I strolled around the display cases full of ex-props. Apparently, towards the end of Conrad's life he was visited, for an interview, by a young American woman journalist. Everything seemed to be going swimmingly for a while as the two of them sat in the Great Man's study and discussed his *oeuvre*. However, as time passed Conrad began to get more and more agitated, until eventually he shouted out, 'For heaven's sake! Aren't you going to ask to sit in the chair where I wrote *Heart of Darkness*?'

I wonder if the committee of the Ian Fleming Foundation – a US-based operation that has assembled this ludicrous collection of old cobblers – feels as intense a passion about, for example, the handle of ski-pole-cum-rifle which George Lazenby (the actor who had the good sense to play Bond only once) used to dispatch a couple of S.M.E.R.S.H. goons in *On Her Majesty's Secret Service*. I can imagine the committee – looking something like the committee of S.M.E.R.S.H. itself – sitting around a table in various states of choler, their chairman screaming at me, 'Don't you want to hold the handle of *that* ski-pole?!' Then pulling a lever which deposits my chair in a tank full of sharks concealed in the basement.

I told my brother-in-law that I'd been to the Official James Bond Exhibition. 'Did they have Rosa Kleb's shoe?' he asked without batting an eyelid. 'No,' I replied mournfully, 'only a replica.' Of course they did have M's real office door – but that was just a door. Far more interesting was the concept of an exhibition of movie memorabilia that faded out into an exhibition of film merchandising spin-offs (a timely reminder that what goes around comes around – usually costing more) that in turn faded out into an exhibition of real merchandise. Never has capitalism seemed so triumphant.

I saw the Official James Bond Exhibition in Glasgow. But don't think for a minute that you'll be able to avoid it by staying put – it's touring the entire country. If only I'd kept the bloody thing secret.

The Times, March 1998

69

I'd have hated to be a using heroin addict in London over the past week. In fact, I'd hate to be a using heroin addict at all and anywhere. But this past week in London I would have been subjected to a continual taunt from hoardings advertising the listings magazine *Time Out* and, by extension, the film *Trainspotting*. The taunt is a line from the film extolling the virtues of the hit of heroin: 'Take the best orgasm you've ever had, multiply it by a thousand and you'll still be nowhere close.'

Imagine being a sick junky, your bones aching, your bowels loosening, desperate for a hit but without the wherewithal to get one, and seeing that! Worse still, imagine being an intravenous drug user with HIV or Aids, contracted by sharing needles, and seeing it. Being taunted by it.

It was kind of inevitable that the film of Irvine Welsh's masterful depiction of Edinburgh junky lowlife would pump up – yet again – the thick vein of debate on drunk iconography. The book itself is not so much unremittingly bleak as sophisticatedly nihilistic. The protagonist, Mark Renton, is an intellectual *manqué*, who is not above describing his ability to get his own way in a job interview (appear to be willing to work so his dole isn't cut, but fail to get the job) as a '*coup de maître*'.

The book, by interleaving different voices, and therefore different angles on the whole subject of drug addiction, manages never to sensationalise or traduce the experiences of the people on whom it's based: sink-housing, working-class youths in an Edinburgh a native I know once described as 'a desert wi' windies'.

The smack problem in Scotland has been compounded in the past decade and turned into a public-health (and therefore human) disaster of quite staggering proportions. The criminal failure, initially, of the Government to provide needle exchanges, and a proper prescription policy for heroin addicts, meant that the practice of sharing needles continued long after this was known to be a sure-fire way of spreading the virus. The result has been rates of HIV infection in Edinburgh, Glasgow, and most especially Dundee, that are far higher than the national average.

The book never dodges the emotional, economic and psychological realities of this – but the film adapted from it manages to do all three. I very much doubt that anyone who comes out of *Trainspotting* will spend the next few hours earnestly debating the whys and wherefores of the human tragedy it profits from. The punters drawn in by the poster I described above are far more likely to have the reaction of a group of sophisticated people I know in their early twenties, who saw a preview of the film and told me that they came out of it feeling 'uplifted'.

When I pressed them on this, it emerged that this was because the actual depiction of drug use in the film wasn't what had impressed them. Rather, they had seen it as evocative of a more generalised nihilism that infests twentysomethings at the moment, irrespective of their toxic portfolio.

I think that this reaction to the film is a function of two related, but disparate, phenomena that are bound up in any depiction of drug use. The first of these involves me in risking a peculiar piece of potential libel. I don't believe, on the basis of having read his book, and having watched the film adapted from it (with his own imprimatur – to the extent of his appearing himself as a dealer), that Irvine Welsh has ever had an injecting drug habit. If he had, I don't see how he could have countenanced the making of a film in which a human tragedy is turned into a source of rich belly-laughs.

While it is possible for a drug voyeur – which is what I believe Welsh to be – to write convincingly about the travails of drug addiction, once that writing is translated into filmic imagery the disparity between the felt and the observed becomes glaringly and unsettlingly obvious.

The great virtue of *Trainspotting*, the book, is that it avoids the acts of closure involved in linear narrative. The 'story', such as it is, is rather a torch of awareness, passed from one character's internal monologue to the next. But the film is utterly linear: bloke is on smack, has horrible time, gets off, goes to London, his mates catch up with him, they go back to Scotland, do a smack deal, go back to London, fall out over the proceeds, and the hero heads off with the swag into the wild blue yonder.

Events that in the book have no effective encapsulation – the hero's grapple round the U-bend of a toilet for some opium suppositories he's shat out in the effluvium of withdrawal – are in the film given tee-hee punchlines: he swims down through the liquid shit into a blue lagoon. Indeed, these punchlines begin to come with such monotonous and predictable regularity that I began to wonder if it oughtn't to have been called 'Gagspotting'.

Any artist who had really experienced the tragic monotony and deadly bathos of hard-drug addiction could not possibly have allowed this 'Carry

On Up the Hypodermic'. Why, in the film even the death of one of the principal characters from Aids has to be given a comic pay-off, whereas in the book there is no such thing.

When drug voyeurism is allied to a nifty soundtrack and freaky imagery it becomes a form of pornography. The connection between the orgasm and the hit of heroin is no mere accident in this context. The punters who get a kick out of watching the hit are directly exploiting someone's pain for their pleasure. Not, of course, because there is anything intrinsically wrong, or even necessarily destructive, about taking heroin, just because there is *in this case.*

As Lou Reed crooned 'Perfect Day', and Mark Renton subsided through the floor on an opiated magic carpet, I began to feel as if I was watching an extended pop video rather than a work of filmic art.

Other great examples of recent drug pornography, concocted by those who haven't been there, include Quentin Tarantino's lamentable drugsploitation film *Pulp Fiction*, in which the hypo full of adrenalin plunged between Uma Thurman's tits was in reality the cock of every hetero man in the audience. This was a film for people who want to tempt and taunt themselves with the 'naughty but nice' image of hard-drug use, in exactly the same way that they might with any other form of fetishism.

But another problem with drug iconography in film is also evidenced by *Trainspotting*. Heroin is not a hallucinogenic drug; it provokes no visions either with its high or with its low. *Trainspotting* is honest in this regard to the extent of depicting the shooting-up of the drug in a resolutely graphic way. The inside of the syringe being flushed with blood is shown in such tight close-up that you can see every bit of unfiltered crud that is entering the poor bastard's vein. But the scenes of surreal bliss and surrealer withdrawal, to the accompaniment of a pretty young girl lip-synching New Order are not heroin as I – or I believe anyone else – know it. Psychedelic drugs have always been much easier to deal with in this regard. You can go back to a film made almost thirty years ago and watch *Easy Rider* if you want to see an accurate and wholly believable depiction of an acid trip. The same can be said for the tripping sequence in *Midnight Cowboy*. On the other hand, even a film as perspicacious as Gus Van Sant's *Drugstore Cowboy*, which covers much the same territory as *Trainspotting*, comes a cropper when it attempts to envision a heroin high as a species of Magritte-inspired wallpaper.

Cocaine isn't up to much in the visual department either, but none the less, the cocaine paranoia sequence in Scorsese's *Goodfellas* captures perfectly the state of mind it wishes to portray. This is either because

Scorsese is himself One Who Knows, or because he's made the correct estimation of what cocaine experience is like: hyperreal, rather than surreal.

I once conducted an experimental screening of Cronenberg's *Naked Lunch* to a group of using heroin addicts. They sat through the film in complete silence, and when the lights came up at the end, one of them remarked, rather regretfully, 'I've been taking smack for twenty years – but I've never seen a typewriter turn into a giant cockroach.' And indeed, *Naked Lunch* seemed hardly to be about heroin at all, directly, rather it was about the interface between Burroughs's art and his life, refracted through Cronenberg's lens.

Really, if you want to get a dead accurate portrayal of heroin use, you need to go to films such as *Christiane F* or *Sid and Nancy*, where all imagistic frills are rejected by their directors in favour of harsh, public-toilet-style lighting, black blood and white gear. Of course, this is a portrayal of drug use as pathological behaviour, cooking up – as it were – the shot in the kitchen sink. How much more difficult it would be to show unproblematic heroin use.

The depiction of intoxication in art is as old as art itself, and I have no axe to grind with this. Nor do I believe that filmmakers or writers should shy away from it, or try to pretend that what can be an ecstatic experience is necessarily hedged around by degradation or death.

But for all that, I do think there is a moral imperative involved in depicting a form of intoxication – such as injecting heroin – that is both dangerous in the first place (ask any doctor: when you break the blood-air barrier you are doing something physiologically far more problematic than if you swallow a pill or take a toke) and rendered still more dangerous by the collective, social attitude towards it. It's a fraught area, because, of course, social attitudes change quite rapidly. Last century's panpathogen (universally evil substance) is this century's favourite tipple. Two decades ago's marital-therapy aid (ecstasy) is this decade's child-murderer. But I believe that those artists who stick to what they know, and stick to accurately portraying the effect of a drug on an individual – rather than a stereotype – can still mine this particular shaft for all it's worth.

Which brings us back to that line from the film, comparing the hit of heroin to an orgasm. This is accurate solely in this respect: many junkies do make such a comparison. But then, is it any wonder? Because one of the first things that prolonged heroin use kicks into touch is the ability to have an orgasm. It isn't so much that the hit of heroin is directly comparable to an orgasm, it's that it has *become a substitute* for that orgasm. The potential punter is thus being encouraged to share a perception that is as dodgy as a used set of works.

Irvine Welsh has in interview sidestepped the whole question of whether or not he has taken heroin to any great extent – or indeed any other drug. I think this is wise of him. Once you've fessed up to it, it can become a millstone round your neck, forcing you on to soapbox after soapbox (like this one). But I can't help feeling that now the film of his book has hit the streets, and is the coolest, most hyped product on the block, his equivocations in this area look a little shabby. After all, if he admitted that he hadn't, he could be open to the charge of benefiting from the low ground of others' suffering.

Remember, we're not talking about Happy Valley sybarites sniffing Morningside speed here, we're talking about the chronically disadvantaged being resolutely shat on. In such a context I can't help wondering if the closing sequence of the film, in which Mark Renton – free of junk – heads for the open road with a flight bag full of cash, having ripped off his mates, isn't in some way an ironic reflection of Irvine Welsh, breaking for the border with his profits from this meretricious adaptation of an important book.

Observer, February 1996

70

When a new set of ornamental gates for Hyde Park was unveiled a couple of years ago, I thought to myself: now, at last, the pusillanimous British public will take a long hard look at this monarchy of ours – and get rid of them once and for all. For the gates, which were erected in honour of the Queen Mother, looked, with their rampant unicorns and lions, and their petrified convolvulus of silvery fretwork, as if they'd come straight out of a fairy tale. Fairy-tale gates = fairy-tale monarchy. But, as ever, I was underestimating the great capacity of the British public to suspend disbelief in this expensive string of clothes-horses.

Damn it all, if we can withstand tape transcripts of the faithless heir (motto: *Semper non-fidelis*) working his way, via the method, into the mind-set of a tampon, and we can tolerate the beatification of his mind-bendingly gauche, Sloaney wife too, then I daresay we can cope with anything else they have to fling at us. Prince Wills a junky? No worries – his great-uncle was one too – just make sure the royal hypodermic has been sterilised. Prince Harry a homosexual? Fine – we've had a fair few of them, but be careful with that poker, flunkey!

No, I fear the only thing that could conceivably reduce the House of Windsor to its proper status as a badly decorated Barratt home would be a generous dollop of dirt being divulged concerning its *real* – rather than titular – head: the good old Queen Mum. (The sad mad Bowes-Lyon relatives discovered hidden in the attic were, I'm afraid, merely par for the course.) Ah! Bless her! Did you see her at Clarence House the other day, welcoming the crowds who'd come to wish her a happy ninety-ninth birthday? Now that's true nobility – and real royalty. Given the recent deaths of those striplings the King of Jordan and the King of Morocco, surely we must all be worrying that the Queen Mum's imminent demise will have the same effect on our populace? That the streets will be crowded with headless-chicken citizenry, wondering how the nation will survive now she's gone?

In the case of the two dead, dusky monarchs, BBC commentators were quick to observe (and re-observe *ad nauseam*) that many of their subjects had never known a time without them, indeed could not conceive of a future without them – and these two were mere youngsters when compared with the Queen Mum. I mean to say, no one under sixty has *ever* known a time when Elizabeth Bowes-Lyon was not either the power by the throne, or the power behind it.

Of course, for those significantly over sixty, there can be little difficulty in understanding why this should be so. If the Queen Mum's first love – that terminal epigone the Duke of Windsor – had retained the throne, there wouldn't even be a Britain left to rule over. The British *anschluss* would've probably occurred in the same year as the Austrian one, ensuring our participation in – rather than opposition to – the Thousand Year Reich. Instead we got the stammering younger brother, and his by-then wife, the fantastically conscientious Elizabeth, who is widely credited with 'saving' the British monarchy.

How exactly did this daughter of a Scottish aristocrat, who had never opened a pair of curtains for herself, or cooked a meal, or balanced a cheque book or probably even tied her own shoelaces, manage to pull off such an astonishing *coup*? Especially in the early thirties, when much of the citizenry didn't have curtains, meals, cheque books or shoes. I think the answer lies, in part, in her legendary charm. Charm, as Cocteau so wisely observed, 'is that quality which solicits the answer "yes" before the question has even been posed'. In other words – it's a manipulative bluff. The British people have been saying 'yes' to the Queen Mother's confidence trick for decades now, without even understanding what it is.

On the face of it, the material she had to work with wasn't inspiring; and indeed the Windsor blood-line, despite her own infusion of new genes, has conspicuously degenerated over the last two generations. (Incidentally, if you ever wonder why it is that horse-racing is the sport of kings – it's because like royalty, racehorses are subject to highly selective breeding. And like royalty, the results of this are often sports and monsters quite as much as champions.) None the less, Elizabeth was able to coach the stammerer into presenting a wartime portrait of doughty courage; if you will – the monarch as Supreme Clerk. Yes, together they toured the East End and withstood the Blitz, and – if you'll believe this you'll believe anything – lived on their ration books. It would be churlish to point out that they had so many holes to bolt into that such 'courage' was purely notional when compared with that of their subjects. But then I am a churl.

No, she had a good war, and she had a good peace as well. She managed to convince the British people that the Royal Family were a kind of super-middle-class creation; Mr and Mrs Khan and their corgi Genghis. The reason the biscuit tin and the mug became the favoured items of memorabilia is that Elizabeth sought to insinuate her family into the nation's teatime, as a vicarish presence. When George VI – displaying a flair for timing that was utterly absent in his lifetime – upped and died, the way was clear for her to inhabit her logical position as the *éminence cerise*, the bolster behind the throne. And like a very slightly animated sofa – Norman Hartnell really should've been in soft furnishings – that's where she's stayed ever since. Notoriously the Queen defers to her, and the Tampon Apparent too. Doubtless the little Lil-lets are in complete awe.

It's currently being touted that the Queen Mother is on the verge of acceding to a meeting with Camilla Parker Bowles, the Royal Mistress, despite the fact that she is legendarily opposed to divorce. Opposed to divorce, but not – it is rumoured – to dumping the troublesome Diana. No, I daresay, because what the Queen Mother really stands for is that odious informal motto of the Windsors: 'Never complain, never explain.'

That's why she couldn't stand Diana – she was rocking the Firm's boat, putting the spondulicks at risk. Because what's the reality of all this? The Queen Mother is a woman of dyed-in-the-silk, wholly unreconstructed bigotry. She's a spendthrift who's been known to run up overdrafts of four million quid, and a glutton for luxury who maintains a fleet of limos and a flock of flunkeys. She's a *savante idiotique*, who couldn't recognise T. S. Eliot when he was actually in the room reading *The Waste Land* to her. Behind that mumsy exterior is a tough old bird, who despite being born with the silver spoon rammed right down her gullet, has never for a second relaxed her avaricious jaws. Yet the real reason we continue to not simply tolerate her, but in many misguided instances *worship* her, is because of atavistic attitudes of our own, which we find it hard to abandon.

In truth, we know what the Windsors themselves understand only too well. That in a nation that has aristocratic houses whose land holdings date back to before the Norman Conquest, they are mere parvenus. When we seek genuine *noblesse oblige* we look to our own nobs, rather than Low German interlopers. After all – we only invited their ancestor to govern us because we couldn't depend on the home-growns to defend our established Church. The whole status of the monarchy in this country has been *entirely* provisional since the so-called Glorious Revolution. No, Elizabeth Bowes-Lyon is one of us: bigoted in the way we are, snobbish in the way we are, profligate in the way we are. The historian Felipe Fernandez-Armesto has characterised Britain in the twentieth century as a nation that has 'willed itself into decline'; and our apparent veneration for this ancient aristo has to be considered a large part of such collective autosuggestion.

And now she's the beneficiary of a truly bizarre piece of serendipity – she's the same age as the century. In a culture in which attention spans tend to be measured in seconds, it's easy to understand why contemplating this antediluvian chunk of avoirdupois should make some people go misty-eyed. 'She's been with us all along,' they'll say, 'she's weathered the years, seen the cavalcade of history. She's a living embodiment of the nation.' Indeed she is; the focus of a bizarre living-ancestor cult, especially since she never makes a public statement of any kind of significance whatsoever. And no, she hasn't been 'with us', she's been in the Royal Enclosure at Ascot.

Yes, we've subjected ourselves to a rule of charm, a praesidium of politeness. She never even had to pose the question to us: 'Do you think I'm authentic?' – because we'd already answered 'yes'. 'Yes' because we don't want to think for ourselves; 'yes' because we don't want to govern ourselves; 'yes' because we still choose to believe that democracy is only demagoguery waiting to happen. But really she's as important to us as the mummy of Lenin was to the Soviet Union; and, frankly, as in need of disposal.

Independent on Sunday, August 1999

71

To construct, to build, to fabricate, is, in a word, to *make*; or even – if we're being a little bit more high-flown – to *create*. Architects, civil engineers and builders of all stripes have the unalloyed certainty that at least what they do is creative in the purest sense: out of materials will come structures. It's as deterministic a relationship as that between carbonated drinks and burps.

Furthermore, there's the scale in which most of you work. It's big. Even the largest sculptural works of a Henry Moore, or an Anthony Caro, would be dwarfed by the average municipal sports centre. And as for the pictorial and decorative arts, at times you must have difficulty in not seeing these as mere impedimenta, props for your stages, flats for your Bayreuth productions. Thinking about how the architect of a vast building might conceive of such artefacts reminds me of the time I visited my publisher's and found the sales director piling up a teetering ziggurat of hardbacks. 'What're those?' I asked him. 'Don't tell any of the writers,' he hissed, 'but I've got a deal with the manager of — [a world-famous department store]; he buys these remaindered hardbacks off us to put in the bookcases they're flogging.'

Just think of it, labouring for years to produce a decoction of your own experience, or to perfectly realise an imagined (or vanished) world, only to find the result sold by the yard to garnish flatpack pseudo-Hepplewhite. It would have to seem like the most hideous traduction of all that it is to be a creative person.

But at least that's a relatively private matter (or at least it was until now). It must be that much worse in every respect for the originators and fabricators of the built environment who find out that their work is to be destroyed, knocked down, levelled; in a word, subject to *demolition*.

Demolition has intrigued me for many years. Indeed, it's worthwhile reminding you professionals that the blowing up of Ronan Point made just as much – if not more – impression on the general public as the erection of a thousand blocks of flats untroubled by design faults. It was Bakunin, the anarchist revolutionary, who said that 'the urge to destruction is always creative'. I wonder if he moonlighted as a demolition contractor. Indeed, I have been wondering for some time whether or not those who pull down the built environment feel as impassioned about what they do as those who construct it. As children, did these people feel as great a surge of satisfaction when they kicked down a sandcastle as others of us felt when we built one?

Perplexed, I called an old schoolfriend of mine who I'd learned had become a demolition contractor. Actually, Maurice was the boy least likely to raze. A gentle, almost fey character, he always kept his exercise books neatly covered with plastic and labelled with Dymotape. We used to take the piss out of him mercilessly. Now he owns one of the biggest knocking-down shops in the country.

'Maurice,' I asked him, 'you were always so quiet and well behaved – were you always nurturing a secret passion to level every building you clapped eyes on?'

'Not *every* building,' he replied in carefully measured tones, 'but certainly a fair few of them. And yes, I did secretly nurture a desire to demolish from an early age. I would buy plastic models of famous buildings, make them, and then torch them with lighter fuel, or pound them with a hammer, or simply kick them to bits –'

'What sort of buildings?'

'Well, put it this way, by the time I was fifteen I'd worked my way through most of the Gothic revival.'

I was prepared to accept that Maurice had a genuine vocation, and certainly when he spoke of the elegance and economy implied in placing explosive charges within a structure so carefully, so *artfully*, that split seconds after it's subsided it's as if it was never there, I was impressed. It seemed that Maurice genuinely believed he was benefiting the built environment; that like some dentist of the carious city he was determined to drill out decay. But what, I wondered, did he feel like, when having eliminated one monstrosity, another was simply built in its place? Didn't this entirely vitiate the value of what he was doing? Wouldn't a truly creative demolition contractor have to be *proactive*, have to go round to architects' offices and rip up blueprints, destroy CADCAM files and generally ensure that the space he'd created remained just that?

Maurice looked pensive for a while, then said, 'I think that's an absolutely fantastic idea . . .'

Building Design, February 1998

72

I know I promised you last week that this week would see me out in a greenfield site, knees deep in slurry and swapping badinage with a quantity surveyor, but somehow probity has a way of eluding me. And anyway, before I got on to contemplating just how it is Costain, Bovis, Wimpey et al. intend shading in the rest of this brown and unpleasant land, I needed to take a more sedentary, more historical and more personal view of the home.

As I've had cause to remark in the past, I grew up in that Platonic ideal of a suburb, the Hampstead Garden Suburb in north London. Begun in 1907, at the instigation of the philanthropist Mrs (later Dame) Henrietta Barnett, the suburb was intended to be a social test tube, within which the social classes could safely react with one another. The plans for the suburb were the responsibility of Raymond Unwin and Barry Parker, who had designed Letchworth Garden City in 1903. Lutyens was responsible for some of the better buildings, including the brick-heavy churches (Free and Anglican) which dominate the sensibly-named Central Square. But while good, vernacular building was done in the core of the suburb, the fringes – where we lived – were full of less impressive, post-World War I semis.

We lived next to Mrs Ruben, who was a widow. I never knew anything about her save for that. Incredible. She had a highly polished three-litre Rover, which a heavy-set man (son, lover, lawyer?) came round to drive her out in from time to time. Her gardens – front and back – were immaculate, almost sterile. The kind of gardens that need dusting rather than weeding. I have only distant memories of the interior of her house. I must have gone in a couple of times as a very small child. All that remains are impressions of curved banquettes, glass-topped furniture, billowing nets and the onslaught of furniture polish. It's not much, considering that the first seventeen years of my life abutted seventeen of the last years of hers. It's not much, considering that during this span we micturated, masticated, mused and – in my case – ejaculated within inches of each other.

But then the semi was always an odd hybrid, combining the proximate living of the lower-class terrace with the splendid isolation of the bucolic villa. The first semis to appear in the world were on the Eyre estate in St John's Wood in the 1790s. It seems particularly apt that they should have been proposed by an anonymous author, because, given the right mix of psychic and cultural factors, these dwellings can reinforce alienation just as much as they encourage neighbourliness.

We knew the Weins, who lived on the other side (and whose property was divided from ours by a garage, three feet of privet and two paths), somewhat better. Lewis and Mary Wein owned a wholesale dry-goods business in Kentish Town called LewMar. They were a fussy Jewish couple of indeterminate age who had an adopted daughter. You could tell she was adopted because she looked nothing at all like the Weins. She was twice as big as them for a start. Their household was Rubenesque compared with our own – nets, glass tops, furniture polish and all – but in one respect we were highly compatible: both families were resolutely dysfunctional and subject to loud rowing. The climax of the bellowing *chez* Self was normally accompanied by my mother's hissed imprecation to 'Be quiet – the Weins will hear us!'

To this day, I cannot raise my voice without the profound anxiety that I am being eavesdropped on by a middle-aged Jewish dry-goods wholesaler.

'The front elevation asserts its individuality by picturesque variations in details, though the house is in fact exactly the same in height and plan as all its neighbours.' So wrote Michael Robbins of the semi. This was true of the houses on our road, except for the 'picturesque variations in details' – for there were none. Or rather, just the one. Each of the houses had sets of *faux* slatted shutters, either side of the top windows. They didn't make the houses look as if they were in Provence (which is presumably what was intended), but they did provide an opportunity for the householder to paint them a different colour to those of the adjoining properties. Ours were blue, the Weins' were green, Mrs Ruben's were black.

I took my children back there the other day to see where I grew up. I hated suburbia and got out as quickly as I could, but as I drove out there from the inner city, what struck me first is what strikes everybody else: the space, the lack of on-road parking, the greenery . . . I feel an acute reversion to type coming over me.

Building Design, September 1998

73

Restaurant review: Sir Charles Napier, Sprigg's Alley, near Chinnor, Oxfordshire

My friend Dave and I decided to get Christmas over and done with well in advance. Neither of us can quite cope with the emotions (the sense of anomie and purposelessness, coupled with surfeit and woozy excess), and added to that it had been made abundantly clear to me that I wouldn't be getting that much-coveted Pink Power Ranger suit.

In previous years I've dealt with the problems associated with Christmas by starting drinking in early December and pushing on through to New Year with barely an interruption. But last year I ended up cradling a bottle of Night Train under Hungerford Bridge in the early hours of Boxing Day, my just-gifted Green Power Ranger suit an unseemly mess of stains and burns, and resolved that I would make changes.

'Why not get out of town a few weeks in advance?' I reasoned. Go to some pleasant country inn, eat well, drink lightly, take a good, woodland walk, have an exchange of tokens and call the whole thing a wrap.

We opted for the Sir Charles Napier in Oxfordshire for obvious reasons. As any fool knows, Napier was the man who, after relieving the siege of Sind, sent Queen Victoria a telegram reading simply 'Peccavi', or 'I have sinned'. I confidently expected that this teasing, admonitory moniker would draw in a commensurately guilty clientele: a few members of the Nigerian Government, perhaps, or the copywriter responsible for the new Playboy satellite channel advertising.

But no, on a dappled day of leaf-fall and sunshine, there was nobody there besides us. The Napier stands on Bledlow Ridge, the last heave that the Chiltern Hills make before collapsing into the green, rolling sea of

Oxfordshire. This is pheasant country and indeed, on walks in the Chilterns I have often found myself surrounded on all three sides by posses of mortgage brokers banging away at their whirring prey.

A relatively undistinguished ramble of buildings faces the road, but you realise there's something up when you park your car by a giant concrete snail. Inside the rooms are low-ceilinged, beamed, irregular and snug. An open fire gutters in the grate. A cosy bar beckons. This is the sort of parlour a faintly eccentric uncle might have. An uncle with a taste for figurative sculptures of uncertain provenance (a kind of mock-Eric Gill torso of a young woman rests on a table, apparently smoothly carved out of a breeze block).

There are sculptures all around the Napier: mostly animals and women, but also odd agglomerations of objects that have a constructivist feel. The sense of being inside some ongoing artwork was underscored by the loud hammering that was coming from upstairs. Was this a new sculpture in the making? A fruit bat made out of MFI and chipboard, perhaps?

The dining room itself is an elongated shoebox of a room. There are animal bronzes here, one to each table. We got the rhino table and, although it was a cuddly enough creature, all through lunch I wished we could be with the adjacent gorilla.

The cooking at the Napier is precise, light English *nouvelle*. The menu is heavy on the fish, but while crab cakes and sea bass beckoned, we were feeling Michaelmas-meaty. We both kicked off with the carrot and parsnip soup. This was a delight, with an interestingly chunky consistency, each nodule of vegetable clearly distinguishable. We also tackled a plate of scallops, which came on a bed of sorrel, rocket and bacon and were cooked to exactly the right warm, disintegratory point.

We stuck to beer throughout. The wine list is comprehensive, with some good-looking highlights, but I'd been tipped off that the Wadworth's at the Napier was particularly fine and I wasn't disappointed. This was a perfect heart-of-England pint with plenty of wood in it, watery and full at the same time: a stereoscopic treat for the palate.

For the main course I plumped for pigeon. I was in a game mood and pigeon well cooked is to my mind one of the best game birds of all – rich and full, but without that insistently cloacal overtone that pheasant and grouse can have. The pigeon was in strips, tousled up with nicely acerbic leaves of rocket, slivers of mushroom and bedded down on an absorptive pad of bread. I wolfed it down. Dave tackled a chunk of sirloin that was also beautifully cooked: braised on the outside but internally succulent. This came with some potato rösti which was good to look at, but strangely bland in flavour, and some Dürer-quality cabbage – all delicate curlicues and adumbration.

For dessert Dave took on the date and walnut pudding. To call this rich would be to miss the mark. This was a John Paul Getty of a pudding; just taking a bite of it increased my Standard & Poor rating to triple A. I summoned up the cheese board.

The Napier is known for its English and Irish cheeses and they have a fantastic selection – strong on the goat, but good Cashel Blue, Swaledale and domestic Brie as well. I also had a rather idiosyncratic cheese 'covered with ash'. Exactly what sort of ash our waiter was unsure, but it definitely wasn't cigarette ash, because that's what I normally eat *chez* Self.

We braced ourselves with a couple of stiff espressos, settled a thoroughly reasonable bill of £65 and set out for a walk in the adjacent woodland. Here we tottered around in the leaves and mud discussing the more painful portions of our lives, for all the world like two characters in a John Schlesinger film. But then, what's the point in being English and middle-class if you can't totter around in a wood discussing your emotional life?

We had at least managed to dodge Christmas and I can think of few nicer places to dodge it than the Napier. They gave me a copy of the Christmas menu before we left and it looked fantastic: Norfolk turkey with chestnut and sage stuffing. Mmm! They were full, but not completely confirmed. They said I could come if they had a cancellation. They'll even let me wear their daughter's Pink Power Ranger costume in the dining room. (As long as I don't mind being interviewed by social services.)

Observer, November 1995

74

*Restaurant review: The Red Pepper Restaurant,
8 Formosa Street, London W9*

'I was at this time sitting directly opposite him; and at last he frankly told me, but with the kindest and most apologetic air, that he was really under the necessity of begging that I would sit out of his sight; for that having sat alone at the breakfast table for considerably more than half a century, he could not abruptly adapt his mind to a change in this respect, and he found his thoughts very sensibly distracted. I did as he desired; the servant retired into an anteroom; and Kant recovered his wonted composure' – Thomas De Quincey, *The Last Days of Immanuel Kant*.

Let's get this straight – I'm not as bad as Kant in this respect, or at any rate the somewhat apocryphal portrait of the great philosopher concocted above. But that being said, I don't think that the business of public eating should necessarily involve elbows, breath, spectacle frames, or any other portions of alien bodies impinging upon the trajectory of fork to mouth.

I was moved to recall Kant's extreme aversion to eating in company by an episode that took place last Sunday. Family Self (described memorably by a friend of mine as 'the dysfunctional Brady Bunch') had decided to go for one of our infrequent lunches *en famille*. Alastair Little, a chef for whom I have no small admiration, had recommended the Red Pepper Restaurant to my wife.

She booked a table for four, for one o'clock. At the last minute Dave (you remember him, he was last seen floundering around a muddy field in Oxfordshire wearing a Power Ranger suit) decided to come, too. We thought this would be fine – one of the children could sit on an adult lap.

We set off in two cars, and I arrived first at the restaurant. To tell the truth, this segment of London, between Little Venice and Maida Vale, has never really appealed to me. The buildings – large, imposing terraced houses and mansion blocks of flats – are just that bit too big and that bit too white. They don't really have the right scale for human habitation. It's rather as if they were intended for some Swiftian creatures. Perhaps Houyhnhnms with bad dress sense and charge accounts at Harvey Nichols.

I also once went out with an intensely neurotic woman who lived in this neck of the woods. Her flat was like unto a wind tunnel, and I spent many an hour struggling in the wan glow of a single electric bar, matching her frigidity to my own.

The Red Pepper Restaurant (great name, that, also shared by various musical combos and a left-wing periodical) was set behind a conventional store-front of plate glass. Inside all was delightfully *echt*: plain wooden tables, plain wooden floors, plain off-white walls, plain-looking counter at the back. 'Wow!' I thought, making my way across this plain of plains. 'How plain can you get?'

But there was something else about the place that immediately impinged. In an area no bigger than the average sitting room, about eight tables were set. I felt like I'd blundered into some distortion of scale.

Was this place frequented by people, or Munchkins? Even if you could have managed to back a Houyhnhnm inside, he'd barely have had room to deal with a nosebag. Granted, I am on the large side (even my three-year-old daughter is the same height as a Filipino cabinet minister), but any restaurant should be capable of seating customers of more than six foot.

A woman wearing trousers that could have been either leather or vinyl confirmed our reservation and remonstrated with me for being late. I apologised. It was now 1.30 and only two of the doll's-house tables were actually tenanted. I found it hard to believe that Red Pepper was about to suffer a stampeding influx. The vinyl/leather woman offered me a choice of two tables, both of which were immediately abutting the two tables already taken up. And these two tables were respectively in a kind of niche and right by the front door. If I had sat at the former I would have had to share the sensible Marks & Spencer cable-knit woolly of one paterfamilias, and if I'd sat at the latter I could have shared a kidney with the other paterfamilias.

Cognisant of the fact that we had an unannounced supernumerary, I asked if we might sit at another table, one that looked as if it would comfortably house at least five Barbies. 'Oh no,' vinyl/leather admonished me. 'That's for seven.'

Suitably chastened, I sat at the door table, ordered a beer and waited for the rest to arrive. When they did, vinyl/leather emerged. Gesturing to the offending Dave, she said, 'You have another person!' We replied that one of the kids could sit on an adult lap. 'You should have told us how many you were, and then we could have accommodated you,' she snapped at us. Her tone was beginning to rankle. Dave then said – and later he told me that he said it purely in a jocular spirit – 'If it's any trouble to you, we'll happily leave.'

Instead of demurring in any way at all, vinyl/leather made doubtful noises under her breath. Then eventually she grudgingly said it might be OK. It was too late. The idea of having to in some way *plead* to spend money in this place was getting ridiculous. If there had been a reasonable ratio of floor space to diner, it wouldn't have mattered, but we were in the absurd position of begging to be uncomfortable.

'No,' I said, 'we'll leave. How much was the beer, and do you want any compensation for not taking up the table?' To vinyl/leather's credit, she didn't ask for compensation. Even so, the whole attitude displayed was petty, unfriendly and annoying. It makes no difference whether Red Pepper was booked to the hilt or not. If restaurateurs choose to behave

229

in this fashion they are contributing to a divisive, New York–style culture, where the yuppie obsession with getting into the eatery of the moment has become frankly absurd.

Observer, January 1996

75

Towards the end of his 1991 *Relentless* video, recorded live at the Montreal Comedy Festival, the late, great comedian Bill Hicks utters these immortal words: 'Let me tell you something right now, and you can print this in stone and don't you ever forget it: any, any performer that ever sells a product on TV is now and for ever removed from the artistic world. I don't care if you shit *Mona Lisa*s out of your ass on cue – you've made your fucking choice.'

It's an uncompromising statement – and one that jarred me to the bone. I was sitting up late, capturing the Hicks act for the first time in my life; and already he'd kicked his way through some of the more sensitive tripwires in my psyche, releasing the booby-traps of conscience. This loud-mouthed, dead American comedian was manipulating me from beyond the grave – how could this be so?

The answer is twofold. First and foremost, Hicks just *was* a brilliant stand-up, one of the best ever. For years friends had been trying to turn me on to his work, but he was one of those acts that managed to squeeze by me. Then he was dead anyway, dead of lung cancer in his early thirties. And who would want to listen to that – it just ain't funny. Even if the circumstances of his death didn't topple over into an estimation of his work, there was the indisputable fact that most stand-up routines, no matter how good, are as ephemeral as a pimple on an adolescent's cheek.

We've all had that experience of slamming in the old tape of our comedy favourites, and adjuring our new-found friends to sit quiet, because this is really going to make them unhinge their jaws. Only to find after fifty seconds, or five minutes, that this stuff really *isn't* funny any more. Worse, it's impossible to imagine that it ever was remotely funny, except to an educationally subnormal Norman Wisdom fan.

But with Hicks this didn't obtain. My wife said he was a great comedian – and so it transpired. His mien – a face capable of contortion from aggressive psychopath, to simpering *ingénu*, to corrupt politico and back again within nanoseconds; his movements – lubricious, dangerous, worryingly slack-kneed; and, most importantly, his words – dramatic, subversive, and delivered with the effortless timing that's like psychic prestidigitation. The fact that this set had been recorded seven years previously hardly bothered me, even when he got into lengthy raps about the Gulf War – this was material that might well prove eternally valid.

Of course, the ultimate reason for the survival of Hicks's routines, while so many others have become corpsing corpses, is that Hicks himself was obviously a profoundly serious man. This much was self-evident when he got on to the contentious issue of smoking (contentious anyway, but in view of his own death not long after this was filmed, well-nigh disturbing). 'If my smoking bothers you,' quipped the moribund Hicks, 'then I suggest you take a long, hard look around you at the world, and then mind your own fucking business!'

This, surely, is the very core of libertarian arguments about sumptuary freedom, or, as Hicks puts it elsewhere, with an admonition that becomes his catch-phrase, 'I'm not trying to tell you how to run your life . . .' Maybe not, Bill, but as I watched you pirouette around the darkened stage, debunking, goading, trouncing, I wondered what you would've made of my dilemma concerning Natural American Spirit, the cigarettes that are *almost* good for you.

A couple of months ago I supped with the devil in the form of Robin Sommers, the healthy runner who manufactures said cigarettes in Santa Fe, New Mexico. Robin put the bite on me: I'd already agreed that Natural Spirit were better than average cigarettes, the aftertaste more wholesome, undoubtedly a function of their being made solely with organically-grown tobacco, and free from any nasty additives whatsoever. But Robin wanted my soul – he suggested I shift entirely to Natural Spirit, on the grounds that my smoking *would actually decline*.

Oh Bill! up there in heaven, puffing away – what should I do? Ever since I undertook the challenge, cartons of Natural Spirit have been arriving from Santa Fe with such regularity that when the bell goes at seven in the morning my wife simply rolls over and grunts, 'Fed-Ex.' I have switched entirely to Natural Spirit and my smoking *has* declined. Before, I was smoking around twenty-five untipped Camels a day, and now I'm level-pegging at under ten long, smooth, delicious, well-packed Natural Spirits.

It's a confusing moral problem. By endorsing any cigarette, am I in fact providing no endorsement at all, since my image is such as hardly to lend any credibility to doing anything at all? I bet if I were to front a campaign for breathing, people would suffocate rather than join. And anyway, even if I am, *de facto*, endorsing a product, surely this is entirely vitiated by the fact that I'm saying Natural American Spirits are great because I smoke fewer of them than I do of other brands, thus neatly putting nice Robin Sommers right out of business before Congress can?

It's so confusing, and not helped by the fact that ever since I watched the Hicks video, an awful image of him doing his smoking rap has stayed right with me: Bill applying his still-burning fag to his throat, as if he were a cancer patient puffing through a tracheotomy hole, and saying, 'If you're smoking out of a hole in your neck – then I'd consider quitting.'

But you didn't, Bill, you didn't . . . And why is it that whenever I spark up a Natural American Spirit, I hear that rasping drawl in my ear: 'You've made your fucking choice.'

The Times, June 1998

76

In Peter Carey's short story 'The Fat Man in History', the eponymous heroes are deposed capitalists who plot to subvert the revolution by eating the statue of its leader. I'm not sure that my response to the World's Biggest Single Event doesn't have something of the Fat Men's tactics about it. For, faced with the prospect of two weeks of baying, screeching, ululating football obsession dominating the media, the streets, the conversation of all and sundry, the only response I could come up with was visiting an exhibition of football paintings.

You see, football and I have never really got along that well. Sure, I had my phase of absolute conviction (I would captain the 1970 Arsenal side which did the 'double'), along with every other ten-year-old possessor of a shrunken scrotum, but in my case – figuratively speaking – the balls never really dropped. By the time I was eleven I was wandering around the place combing my blond tresses and reciting Keats; no wonder I was always last to be chosen for playground kickarounds.

Traditionally, not being *sportif* hasn't been a crushing problem. Up until a few years ago when Ian Hamilton, Nick Hornby et al. embarked on a campaign to make football intellectually respectable – or, at any rate, worthy of discussion at middle-class dinner parties – it was possible to neatly sidestep the turgid ball, or even do a dummy: 'Yes, yes, it's amazing how Peter Shilton's stayed the distance . . . But one wonders whether Camus – you know, of course, that he played in goal for Algeria – would have fared had he not died so precipitately. By the way, have you read *The Myth of Sisyphus* . . . ?'

You catch my drift. But over the past ten years the footie fans have upped the tempo of their obsession and infiltrated it into almost every corner of our lives: Eat Football, Digest Football – Excrete Footballs. Painful. A recent compilation of essays on the great game was preposterously entitled *Soccerati*, summoning up a Pythonesque vision of Noam Chomsky and George Steiner clashing hard in the penalty area.

Of course, I've always maintained that rather than dragging the game up to the level of Games Theory, the impact of the middle-class footie fans has been to drag the collective level of intellectual discourse down to that of a commentary: 'And he's manifesting the failure of post-feminist men to accommodate their changing socio-sexual roles . . . Yes, yes, he's manifesting it! My God! We haven't seen a manifestation like this in a long time . . . And he's begun beating up on his wife! Phew – what a scorcher!' This is what happens when we allow ourselves to become too Hornby-sized.

But I knew that my arguments would be to no avail. There was absolutely no possibility that the myriad supporters would suddenly throw up their arms and cry, 'No! We don't want to watch the World Cup! We'd rather see a good performance of *L'Après-midi d'un faune*!' So, resigned to having a least some football within my purview, I set off for Flowers East Gallery in Hackney to witness an exhibition of paintings by Peter Howson.

Now, I'm not suggesting that Howson's motives in doing these daubs are in any sense meretricious, but there does seem to be a nice coincidence in producing depictions of thirty-two national sides when an enormous international tournament is about to kick off involving . . . just these thirty-two national sides. Mind you, I think Howson's titles (*Nigeria 1998*, *Chile 1998*) are admirably spare when set against the likes of Damien Hirst's *Beautiful Snail Crunching under the Boot Painting*.

233

And the paintings themselves aren't at all bad. Largely compact and dense with pigment, Howson's brushstrokes render these footballers as stakhanovite workers, all bulging biceps and monumental thighs, arms pumping as they shovel the ball into the net as if it were a heap of coal. In keeping with this propagandist feel, some of the paintings have the air of hortatory Maoist wall posters; while others dissolve into the fluid, watery lines of a poster advertising Vittel mineral water.

Howson has constructed some nice pieces of impossibilism, like Scotland scoring against England with a thirty-five-metre drive, but on the whole the paintings are faithful Fauvism – if that isn't a contradiction in terms. I particularly liked *England 1998*, which depicted three beefy players in mid-air, as if they were some strange Gordian knot of flesh. And at a mere £3,000 plus VAT, it's certainly cheaper than buying scalped Final tickets. I toyed with the idea of purchasing a Howson – preferably one showing a goalmouth incident – and sitting in front of it for the next couple of weeks, with a gross-pack of lager, chanting, 'Expressionism's coming home! It's coming home!'

My little reverie was broken in on by Matthew Flowers, scion of the gallery and a man who looks as if he single-handedly put the 'gone' into epigone. It was infinitely reassuring to have him there, as the two of us offered as great a contrast with Howson's beefcake as it's possible to imagine. Like two Giacometti sculptures in a field full of Teletubbies.

We floated around the place for a while before coming to rest in front of *Germany 1998*. This canvas had already been shot with a little red dot. 'Bit naughty, that,' said Matthew, his long pale hands wafting about. 'At the opening I saw someone eyeing it up who I knew was a Tottenham fan, so I cruised up and said the blond chap in the painting was definitely Klinsmann. In truth, I haven't a clue whether it's Klinsmann or not – what d'you think?'

I goggled at him, appalled. 'I tell you what I think, Matthew –'

'What?'

'You know far, far too much about football to be a contemporary art dealer.'

The Times, June 1998

77

Good morning. How I hate a catch-phrase, how I loathe what an oft-repeated nonce slogan can do to your thinking. A few years ago, morphic resonance was all the rage. This was the theory that if a cohort of Japanese schoolchildren learn by heart a poem, in Japanese, on the other side of the world, then another cohort of people over here will find the same poem, in English, that much easier to memorise. This counterintuitive example of seeming causation helped to explain why it was that certain habits of thought, and ways of doing things, so effortlessly transcended the various human cultures.

I don't know whether there's any truth to morphic resonance, but I do know that 'morphic resonance' itself became an annoying catch-phrase for a while. Personally, I find this a more felicitous explanation for the wildfire spread of annoying catch-phrases than the alternative vision, which comes to me during late-night insomniac duvet-gnawing sessions. Namely, that somewhere deep under the South East of England there's a bunker resembling a World War II RAF ops room. Instead of pushing symbolic fighters across the table-top map of the country, the sinister cabal who stand round it are plotting the dissemination of these verbal viruses, shoving squadrons of 'at the end of the day's hither and thither.

'At the end of the day' – isn't it vile? Doesn't it madden you with its cod eschatology? At the end of what day precisely? Do you mean in summation, in conclusion, or resulting from? And if it's any of these three, why the hell can't you just say it? I say 'you' – but I mean me as well. For despite my best efforts, I too have experienced the terror of being a sentient ventriloquist's dummy, and felt the hated words splurge forth involuntarily. Of course, ten years ago the madness of the crowd was expressed with that touch-feely catch-phrase of the me-generation psychobabblers: 'D'you know what I mean?' In a decade that had seen the progressive erosion of social empathy, was it any wonder that everyone should find themselves spasmodically requesting it from their fellows?

It's the same with 'At the end of the day'; although ostensibly a carry-over from the football field, this catch-phrase became our mantric match report on the late-twentieth century. I believe that every time someone regurgitates 'At the end of the day', they are in fact giving voice to a profound sense of unease about the non-appearance of the apocalypse, and calling attention to our culture's superstitious conflation of imminence and immanence. God may be dead, but like a thousand thousand little Pascals, at the end of the day we fear He's going to pop up again and, before meting out the punishment for our massacres of one another and our destruction of the planet, He'll tell us that He was hiding under the bed all along.

Anyway, whether you agree or not, at the end of this year I'd like you to join me in a solemn pledge not to retail this catch-phrase during 2001. I'd say it was past its sell-by date, but that would be a *reductio ad nauseam* – d'you know what I mean?

Today, BBC Radio 4, December 2000

78

Scab

The scabs on my arms are my sorejeant's stripes. God, what an execrable pun – and yet it's by no means the worst one I have in me, the lowest I could squeeze out. Anyway, within this vector of facile semantic exercise there is, none the less, an important truth: that I, like so many self-mutilators, see my perversion as a long, bitterly-fought campaign, executed in mountainous country, by an overextended conventional ground army, which is being consistently harassed by savage guerrilla bands, who strike at its flanks, slash at its withers, before fading once more into the formlessness of their own, immemorial hinterland.

Seen in this way, the ovoid, vaginal, open weeping sores on my thighs have a more ambiguous message. Unlike the scabs on my arms they are no mere designators of rank – they're more like the squashed semaphore of modern campaign ribbons, wound round my thighs, tightened up into tourniquets.

Anyway, I'm rehearsing these distinctions – while adopting the peculiarly sphinx-like posture required of me, if I'm not to undo the good work the nursing staff do, spreading my stripes and ribbons with antiseptic, antibiotic, intensively caring cream – when Doc-tor Shamannamundy comes by. I always think that this is a good way to differentiate psychiatrists from the rest of the profession: Doc-tor, that's how their title should be pronounced – and written – so as to rhyme with 'sore'. Shamannamundy is a queer enough thing. Half Tamil, half Irish, he wears three-piece suits cut from three separate weaves of sharkskin, and gunmetal-grey, pointed shoes, with matching, clocked socks. Can you imagine that? A psychiatrist who wears matching socks and shoes – how terrifying can that be?

Shamannamundy bids me, 'Good morning,' very much the sore-side specialist. Shamannamundy also whispers, 'God bless,' when he departs, as if this were the only natural valedictory book-end to his consultations. Why does he whisper? Is his deity omniscient yet marginally deaf? I have vowed to beard him on this matter, as soon as my treatment has sufficiently advanced.

Anyway, he bids me unholster my side-arm, take off my bandoleer, remove my Sam Browne, drop my combat kecks – until I stand, gloriously stippled with sores, maculate with pus, in my true and puckered uniform. Sorejeant de Chirico – ready and waiting. Shamannamundy ignores my badinage; his manner is such as to imprison my rampaging, agonised bull in many many filaments of soft concern, a gauze of seeming-kindness. 'Look,' he says, gesturing at the stripes, the ribbons, 'look what you've done to yourself. Let me see your nails.' And when they've been exhibited, 'See,' he points out the crescent moons of dried blood, 'why d'jew do it? Why?'

Why indeed. Why – indeed. Perversion is a question to which the only answer is a dialectic: pick, open sore, scab. (Where pick is the thesis, open sore the antithesis, and scab the synthesis.) And anyway, precious Shamannamundy, what can you know of the beautiful integrity of my rank? What can you understand of that moment when one's own flesh ceases to be flesh at all and becomes instead an altogether more mortal, more malleable clay?

At night the nursing staff here patrol on the half-hour, for which they receive time and a half. They deploy torches, as if they were Nazi guards, and yet this is an exclusive, private clinic in the very humming heart of London. The wavering beams finger my fucked-up form, where it lies on the grainy mattress; they stroke my face with lucent disregard. In between the patrols I work on the tunnels I am boring through myself – the vermiculation of my very soul. I have arranged pads of antiseptic gauze over the points of ingress in order to fool the medical staff. But once these have been removed, the way is open for my brave fingers to pinch and gouge and distress the flesh. To feel its gritty, bloody, purulent shapeliness. To load it cleverly under my nails. To transport it to the sheet, to the pillowcase, to my stinking T-shirt. Then I replace the bindings, cover up the campaign, and wait for Aurora to ride ahead of me, inaccessible, inviolate in the microwavable bag of her perfect dermis.

Morning finds me in pain, in the basement canteen. Moneyed neurotics toy with sausages that are little more than skin tubes stuffed with greasy breadcrumbs, such is the comprehensive nature of the fiddle the Filipino catering manager is engaged in. I sit, triumphant, over a smallish dish of acerbic grapefruit segments. My arms, my thighs, various junctures of my body – all flare with unbearable pain.

Shamannamundy diffidently approaches across the up-market carpet tiles. 'You did it again last night?'

And will again tonight.

It will be a long campaign, but in the end victory is certain.

Sebastian Horsley exhibition catalogue, February 1999

79

Book review: On Holiday: A History of Vacationing
by Orvar Lofgren (University of California Press)

I was going to begin my review of this book with a snide crack about the price, something like 'At £35, this represents a fair slice of the cost of a brief vacation, so perhaps you should avoid the theory and move straight on to the practice.' But the truth is that you only have to shell out £18.50 to read – and own – Lofgren's lengthy *tour d'horizon* of the history of tourism. Not bad for a handsomely produced, chunky tome from an academic press, which comes complete with a selection of black-and-white illustrations, some drawn from the author's own postcard collection.

If only my poor old mum had been a professor of ethnology, for she had a postcard collection second to no one's, as well as a view of mass holidaying so dyspeptic that she should've vacationed regularly in the BiSoDol factory. After she died and we went through her chattels we found the awesome assemblage: shoebox after shoebox of the laminated three-by-fives, covering a lifetime of excursions from Yasnaya Polyana to Portmeirion and back again. Personally, I found these hoarded mementoes the saddest aspect of her bequest. I mean – why the hell did she bother? Did she look forward to an afterlife of feverish p.c.-based correspondence? Postcards not so much from the edge, as from the beyond? Who can say.

Still, Lofgren's book does at least put Mum's obsession in a decent historical context. He informs us that the postcard craze in Sweden in 1904 reached such a fever pitch that the population of only five million were responsible for sending no fewer than forty-eight million of the things. And further, that the Swedish word for a postcard – *vykort* – means 'a card with a view'. Of course, in Mum's case the views were mostly back-to-front with more of the same.

One might be forgiven for thinking that the west coast of the USA/ west coast of Sweden axis, along which most of Lofgren's *vykorts* on the history of vacationing are displayed, might give this study a parochial, or at any rate distorted feel. Not so. It transpires that Sweden has been a social laboratory for vacationing just as much as it has been for Side Impact Protection Systems, varnished wooden toys and state-sponsored sterilisation of the mentally handicapped.

So Lofgren gives us an account of the 'English' landscaped gardens at Forsmark, where late-eighteenth-century travellers were encouraged to encounter the most farouche of scenes via their artificial transliteration. He samples the journals of Linnerhielman, a prototypical tourist much impressed by Forsmark, and in particular its grotto, where he finds 'in its shadows a hermit, sitting with a book in his hand. He is dressed in a deep purple cloak, and has a gentle but serious expression.' With typical, Swedish irony, Lofgren goes on to inform us that 'the figure was made of wax and later eaten by rats'.

But in essence the Swedish experience of the creation of the picturesque was remarkably similar to our own, a psychic colonisation of the wild by the imposed architectonics of civilisation. It's these opening sections of the book that, in keeping with the growth of holidaying itself, make the reader feel as if she is on a craven mission into a brave new world, spreading her towel by an isolated brook and indulging in some scary skinny-dipping in the sinuous rills of Lofgren's not inelegant prose.

Unfortunately, once the tourism becomes mass we find ourselves venturing on well-trodden paths – literally as much as metaphorically. I had the good fortune to read *On Holiday* while I was actually travelling around northern Europe (from England to Finland, to Germany and back again, albeit not on holiday at all), and although I was in transit, both of the books I'd decided to take with me (Lofgren's, and Paul Theroux's *The Pillars of Hercules*) made use of the same fixed point of reference, a quote from Evelyn Waugh's *Labels: A Mediterranean Journal*.

No doubt you're familiar with it too: Waugh, having recapitulated the typical, starry-eyed traveller's account of Mount Etna at sunset – 'the mountain almost invisible in a blur of pastel grey, glowing on top and then repeating its shape, as though reflected, in a wisp of grey smoke . . .' – then concludes with the oh-so-funny snob put-down 'Nothing I have ever seen in Art or Nature was quite so revolting.' Oh Evelyn – what a card you were! Still, the effect on me of this near-instantaneous quote recurrence was as unsettling as being dry-humped by a straw donkey in a Majorcan bodega.

Which is not to say that all of *On Holiday* consists of such *déjà revu*. Lofgren works hard to develop parallel and intersecting concepts of the occidental tourist as either Robinson Crusoe or Phileas Fogg. And unlike Evelyn, Lofgren will have no truck with snide élitism, whether inspired by money, or by taste. He deals sympathetically with the needs of the working class for relaxation as well as their desires for diversion. Readers of *Condé Nast World Traveller* need not apply to this volume. Still, while much of *On Holiday* is diverting, engaging and even entrancing, this is still primarily an academic exercise, and hence quite hard work.

New Statesman, November 1999

80

Some people have a little difficulty in accepting that they may be a bit eccentric – I'm not one of them. If I see a crowd hurrying in one direction I feel an almost uncontrollable urge to rush off the other way, which is perhaps why I wasn't too fazed to find myself, in December, in a nearly snowbound Stockholm Airport, waiting for a delayed night flight to the

Arctic Circle. True, I wasn't feeling exactly rubicund, nor the essence of jolly. In fact, I was moodily sipping beers that required a small mortgage to purchase, and watching the snowploughs – strange robotic things called 'Elephants' – attempt to keep the runways open.

I tried imagining I was a man with a mission – perhaps on my way to interview Santa himself: 'Mr Claus, this is your first interview with a British newspaper – can you explain why you've chosen to speak now?'

'I have bad news – there will be no presents delivered for any of you this year.'

'Any particular reason for this?'

'First there were no elves, then there were no presents. Now the reindeer are off sick – you British should understand these things.'

It was no good. Santa Claus remained a curiously indistinct figure in my mind's eye. Would he live in some kind of igloo, or a more orthodox house? Which ethnic group would he belong to? Would his red suit be made out of Gore-Tex, or some more traditional fabric? Actually, my real mission – to visit the ICEHotel in Jukkas Jarvi – was almost as strange an idea as the Santa exclusive. Despite having seen numerous photographs of this bizarre exercise in tourist accommodation and read the exhaustive blurb produced by its PR people, I was still no nearer to imagining what it could possibly be like.

I think it's because I suffer from the same kind of 'leaves on the line' problem with my imagination as the rest of the British – we just can't quite wrap our heads around the idea of extreme cold. In London, at gathering after gathering in the preceding weeks, when I'd ventured that I would be visiting the ICEHotel, sophisticate after sophisticate would say, 'Oh, I've heard about that; it's that hotel in northern Sweden made completely out of ice. I wonder if it's cold in the rooms?'

Cold in the rooms?! Of course it's *cold* – the thing's made out of ICE! But ever willing to challenge the laws of physics, people would still insist that there must be heating; or failing that they would dredge up from somewhere the idea that Eskimo igloos are really rather toasty on the inside. They are, compared with the ambient temperature, which can be down to -40°C, but they're still made out of ice! And that's where I was headed – me, who even drinks his vodkatinis resolutely straight up; why oh why oh why?

On the flight north I found myself wedged in next to a young woman. I was porting full British Arctic gear, namely fifteen woollies, scarves and mittens. She was in combat trousers and a light mac. It turned out she was going to the far north of Norway; her husband would be picking her up at 1.00 a.m. in Kiruna – where we were bound – and then driving the five hundred kilometres home.

I was incredulous. 'But this is the Arctic – you can't tell me he's doing a round trip of a thousand kilometres over night?'

'Oh yes, it's no problem. Anyway, where we live on the coast it isn't cold like Kiruna. It only gets down to ten below.'

Only? I munched moodily on the coldest slice of pizza I've ever had in my life, and sipped a glass of gelid Rioja. Below, the country was opening out into great swathes of snow and forest; even in the plane the sense of desert emptiness was palpable, and this was only enhanced when the lights of Kiruna came in view and we circled to land. Kiruna is a big mining centre, and it looks it – all vast derricks festooned with lights, clouds of smoke and louring slag heaps. And all of it covered with ice and snow and frost.

We kissed down on to the rink of a runway and coasted to a halt. I needn't have worried about the Swedes having 'leaves on the line' – these are people who really know how to run infrastructure under adverse conditions. Damn it all! Their mobile-phone industry is the best in Europe – perhaps the world. This is a culture that takes side-impact protection seriously. My fellow passengers were out of the plane, through the terminal and on to the taxi rank in seconds.

By the time I got there, the last cab was just about to wheel out. 'To the ICEHotel?' I implored the driver.

'Sorry, I can't – I'll order a cab for you, it will only take fifteen minutes.' And there I was, left staring balefully at a stuffed reindeer in the terminal, standing at an Arctic taxi rank.

The ride was twenty minutes along well-gritted roads. At the Reception to the ICEHotel, tacked to the door there was an envelope addressed to me. Inside was the key to Hut 16. It was nearly 1.30 a.m. and the moon was up. I could see something gleaming beyond the row of chalet-style huts as I crunched towards my quarters – the ICEHotel – and beyond it a vast sweep of frozen river, and beyond that a forested mountain. I crunched on down and stood feeling the spiracles of chill invading my creaking lungs. It was beautiful, with the moonlight infusing the mounded bulk of the hotel. All I needed now was a serious outbreak of the aurora borealis and my long day would be made.

No such luck. I entered Hut 16 – a functional, three-roomed, well-insulated structure, the interior of which was predictably sauna-like – supped yet another beer and stared moodily at a poster showing an enormous vodka bottle lighting up the Arctic sky, with the caption 'Absolut Borealis'. Quite so.

In the late morning the sun eventually pushed above the horizon – and it was a clear, beautiful day. I'd heard a lot of activity outside while it was still crepuscular, but when I eventually emerged, the environs of the hotel were buzzing with snow scooters, tractor sleds and even JCBs. Some Japanese women were pulling blocks of ice around on little sleds, and in amongst the huts the maids were doing their rounds, their cleaning gear atop still smaller sleds. It reminded me of nothing so much as a *Dr No*-style installation – the Arctic lair of a sinister character bent on world domination.

Up at Reception I found a shop selling trinkets, tat and clothing made out of every conceivable part of the reindeer, and rendezvoused with my 'ice guide', the charming Asta Vormeier. She looked sceptically at me: 'Is your clothing warm enough for the tour?' And of course, despite being resolutely bundled up, I could only manage about thirty minutes outside – it was fifteen below. On the other hand I was proud – like Robert Falcon Scott – of my ill-preparedness. You can certainly tell national groups by their extreme-weather sartorial tendencies. Inevitably it transpired that the hotel was currently full of French, Belgian and Italian men – in small, outwardly-bound conference groups – who were all dressed identically in jump suits (the French), Gore-Tex pantaloons (the Italians), or nylon protective suits (the Belgians).

The hotel, which is made of some 30,000 tonnes of ice and 'snice' (compacted half-and-half ice and snow), is rebuilt every year, beginning in the autumn. While I was there they were aiming hard for completion, which is on 30 December, so it was heads-down no-nonsense work. Everywhere Asta and I crunched there were people chiselling and chipping, stacking and smoothing. The hotel comprises a series of interconnecting, high-arched, chapel-like halls. These are formed by moulding snice around an aluminium arch and then removing it. The vaults are supported with circular columns of pure ice blocks. At the ends there are high 'windows', again of astonishing translucent ice, quarried from the frozen river. It is really quite amazingly beautiful.

And yes, everyone, bloody cold! We checked out the bedrooms. These are caverns of snice, flickeringly lit with candles and each individually decorated with weird, Modernist ice furniture and ice sculpture. The place feels like Superman's polar lair, or Narnia under the reign of the Witch. Asta cheerfully encouraged me check out an ice bed. Yup – they're ice: blocks of ice with a wooden board on top of them, then a conventional mattress, then the ubiquitous reindeer hide. 'Really very good for insulation,' as Asta explained.

I exchanged a few hurried words with Arne Berg, one of the architects who started the project, but he like everyone else was racing against the deadline – not simply the grand opening, but the all-important launch of the Absolut Ice Bar, which was scheduled for the next weekend. In this cavern of the hotel, an enormous icy S-shaped bar furnishes drinkers with eponymous shots in glasses made from – you guessed it – ice. 'But,' I asked Asta, 'isn't it true that drinking too much in sub-zero temperatures is extremely bad for you?'

'Ah yes,' she replied with Scandinavian rectitude, 'we do try and limit intake a little.'

The ICEHotel is very much conceived of as a gestalt – an involved work of art. While I was there they were putting the finishing touches to an igloo gallery which will mount an exhibition of the Arctic photos of Michio Hoshino; the Japanese women were a delegation of ice sculptors from the northernmost island, where apparently they are 'very advanced' at such things. There were Finnish lighting-effects specialists and even an Italian glass-blower who had a little hut of his own abutting the hotel. All very impressive – and undeniably aesthetic, although I suppose a cynic might remark that an exaggerated concern with such impermanent architectural forms does smack of a certain decadence.

But then the ICEHotel is really for romantics, as the entirely jolly and rubicund proprietor of the hotel restaurant informed me that evening: 'It's the Japanese, you know. They come here for their honeymoons – lots of couples. And they believe that the Northern Lights give great good – how you say – karma. Yes, they believe a child conceived under the aurora is very lucky. So, I think maybe there's a lot of action down there –!' He collapsed into resolute ho-hoing.

Unfortunately Mrs Self had been indisposed, and the idea of me – a chronic insomniac who can't go to sleep alone unless he is simultaneously reading, smoking, drinking and listening to the radio – spending a long dark night of the soul inside a block of flickeringly-lit ice was right out of the frame. I wimped out and went for Hut 16 again. But in fairness, the hotel isn't in any way conceived of as a permanent residence. The visitors all have a hut as well, to which they can retreat for toenail-cutting, minimal satellite TV and ablutions. The starkness of the frigid rooms is reserved for the wee wee hours, when guests lie entombed in sleeping-bags, presumably musing on how they might copulate without losing their extremities for ever.

Not that the ICEHotel doesn't have other things on offer besides this extreme sleep experience. There's a lot of sled-based action and other such manly pursuits, as well as cultural excursions to grok the Sami people (the Lapland natives) and their ubiquitous reindeer. None the less, I can't help feeling that the main constituency for this sort of venture are very randy couples with a high disposable income, and the kind of hearty fellows who like to snowboard down Everest. Indeed, were there to be a 'Volcano Hotel' I'm sure it would be full of the same types as flock to its chilly counterpart. And they'd be sitting there in the 'Magma Bar' discussing the best kind of flame-retardant clothing.

It's probably just sour grapes, the loneliness of the solo Arctic traveller. As I sat in the restaurant that night, I consoled myself with a few Absoluts (drunk resolutely at room temperature), a chat with the proprietor, and a buffet of gargantuan proportions. This was truly the *ultima Thule* of buffets – the buffet at the end of the world. There were about twenty different kinds of pickled herring alone! There was a cupboard gushing sweets and gingerbread! It made *Babette's Feast* look like a take-away. Those Swedes – they may not be the world's most natural hoteliers, but they sure as hell can do a buffet.

Oh, and mobile phones as well. They're dead good at them.

The Times, December 1998

81

This year in Britain art has become the new art. Truth to tell, this has been a cultural eruption that's been a long time rumbling. Those of us with sensitive aesthetic seismographs could've foretold something was happening as long ago as the early nineties. But certainly by two years ago, when the Royal Academy of Art put on a show called 'Sensation', featuring the works of such subversives as Damien Hirst (stuffed shark in formaldehyde), the Chapman Brothers (child manikins with grotesquely enlarged genitalia) and Marc Quinn (cast of his own head filled with congealed blood), it was clear that the phenomenon of 'High Art Lite' – as the new British conceptualism has been dubbed – was cheerily insinuating itself into the back passage of the establishment.

With the opening of Tate Modern, a vast new modern art gallery in the very centre of London, the volcano of self-affirmation (and self-congratulation) has finally spewed forth. The magma of publicity has rained down, while the lava of acclamation petrifies any doubting critics to mere pumice. After all, why shouldn't art be the new art? Look at how feeble the pretensions of other media have been. Pop music lost its cachet when Brian Eno gave up recording anything remotely commercial and took to producing – gulp! – art. Fashion only ever verges on art when it's at its most artificial, and despite the vaunting of London as the new fashion capital of the world, our top, arty designers – such as Alexander McQueen – are still taking the Parisian shilling. As for my own discipline, literature, no one's ever been daffy enough to think of it as art at all, although a few years ago it was styled 'the new rock 'n' roll', presumably while rock 'n' roll was taking a sabbatical trying out for the art position.

No, everyone's agreed now – art is the new art. The Queen's agreed – she went to open the new Tate Modern in May. The Prime Minister agreed, as he wandered the arty throng during the first-night beanfeast grinning inanely at all and sundry. What a guy! I love the way he always wears thick, orange, TV-studio-strength pancake make-up – it makes him look like . . . a work of art. Mick Jagger agreed – he pitched up and tottered around some, although he cried off when asked for a comment on the gallery's innovative curatorial policy (the works have been arranged schematically rather than chronologically), saying that he left all that kind of stuff to his old mate David Bowie.

And, natch, Media – like the jaded old floozie that she is – agreed too. I don't imagine a new art gallery has ever received the bonanza of coverage that Tate Modern did. There were programmes on all stations, live television coverage of both the opening ceremony and the party that evening. The press was full of it: at last we Brits were back on top of the aesthetic world, with its biggest modern art museum. Sod off Musée d'Orsay! Come on Bilbao if you think you're hard enough! And as for Manhattan's MoMA – a mere outbuilding, m'dear, a veritable annexe! You want Rothkos? We've got bags of them – Warhols and Pollocks ditto. We've got Dalis and Duchamps aplenty. We've got so much stuff we can afford to juxtapose a Richard Long circle of found stone with Monet's *Waterlilies*. The old Tate could only ever show around 15 per cent of its modern collection, but now there's so much space they've been able to drag all of it out of the closet.

The party had been billed as the event that would define 'who's who in twenty-first-century Britain'. Given that we're only a few months in, this might be deemed – as we Cockneys say – a little 'previous', but who cares, the public bought it. Two days before the doors opened, invitations were trading on the black market for a grand a pop. Just imagine it! A thousand pounds to go to an art opening! When we turned up, the paparazzi were six deep behind police barriers. 'Come on, Will!' they screamed. 'Show us yer tits!' It was then that I realised my *décolletage* might be a little deep for an early-evening event.

Tate Modern's own, vast embonpoint was really the star of the show. The gallery hasn't been purpose-built, but rather slotted into the hulk of a long-disused sixties power station. Bankside Power Station was designed by Sir Gilbert Scott, who also built the famous London landmark Battersea Power Station (remember the cover of Pink Floyd's album *Animals* – that's the one). With its single looming, 300ft-high stack, its 200m frontage, facing St Paul's and the City's Square Mile (to which it's soon to be connected by a Richard Rogers footbridge), and its curiously pointillist façade – comprising as it does some 4.2 million bricks – the building has always struck me as a happening-in-waiting.

Architects Herzog and de Meuron have kept the building's structural integrity and carved slices of light into its baked casing. From the café on the fifth level there are now the finest views of the London skyline ever to be had – unless, that is, you're a pigeon on ketamine. They've also glassed over the massive, 85ft-high turbine hall, and put a vast ramp in at the west end, down which the art-lovers can process into this modern ziggurat – albeit looking distinctly naked without a ton of stone to drag behind them on rollers. The idea is that the huge hall will act as a kind of agora for this portion of London when the footbridge across the Thames is finished, but it poses the question of what to fill it with art-wise.

Even enlarged Epsteins, or the most massive Moores, or colossal Caros would look like mere netsukes scattered around on its 3,300 square metres of floor. The solution hit upon by Sir Nicholas Serota, the overall boss of the Tate, and the man behind Tate Modern, was to specially commission a series of pieces by the veteran Franco-American sculptor Louise Bourgeoise. These comprise three free-standing, 70ft-high spiral staircases, and a bloody great spider. One of the staircases has what appears to be an assemblage of enormous dental mirrors positioned around its top. The artist herself has come up with the usual art-crit nonsense, speaking of the way these staircases allow the people who schlep up them to 'experience intimate space', but really the main thing about them is that they're big.

That, and the great opportunity they afforded me to crack wise at the opening party. 'Where's so-and-so?' someone would ask me, attempting to crane their neck above the four thousand Significant Brits – it was damn hard to work a room of that size. 'Oh,' I'd airily retort, 'I think she's gone to climb up the Bourgeoise.'

But climbing up the bourgeoisie isn't all that Tate Modern is about. I'm as doubting as Descartes when it comes to just about anything, but there's no gainsaying the impact of the building, the appurtenances (fab cafés, toothsome restaurants, and non-patronising information points) and the works themselves. But the people! My dear! A hundred and twenty thousand went through its portals in the first four days of opening; there were punters standing eight deep around a Joseph Beuys as if it were Sharon Stone and Madonna locked in a nude, mud-wrestling clinch. Yes, art may be the new art in Britain, but I'm inclined to think that this makes the whole notion of art itself more than a little bit suspect.

Of course, I don't object to the vast numbers at Tate Modern on principle – I've no axe of élitism to hone on the dull whetstone of the masses. It's just that with its cathedral-sized central hall, its thronged, cloistral galleries, and its very appellation, Tate Modern seems to suggest that the 'modern' is now an accomplished, if not transcended, epoch. That from now on the modern belongs inescapably to the past – and this means that never before has the future seemed so dated.

US GQ, June 2000

82

I loved shooting when I was a kid. When I was little I'd do anything I could to lay my hands on projectile-weapon toys. One of the sixties' wackier cold-war spin-off toys was the Secret Sam Briefcase, a shameless steal from 007, comprising an attaché case stashed with collapsible sniper's rifle, automatic pistol and in-built camera – which really took pictures. The guns also fired 'real' plastic bullets with their spring mechanisms, and although I can't remember what the velocity of these was, I daresay anything as sinister as this assassin's portmanteau would certainly be banned in these days of actual safety and imaginary extreme violence.

I think almost all male children fantasise about warfare and violence, albeit in a highly abstracted way. Indeed, without the proximity to World War II of my childhood, it's difficult to see how any contemporary war gamers can find much to fantasise about when it comes to pretend combat. What do they say to each other? 'Come on, you be the Yugoslavian Federal Army and dig into the sandpit, and I'll be NATO and throw water bombs at you. Emily can be the Kosovan refugees and carry that laundry basket to the end of the garden.'

In my own mind I closely link enthusiasm for imaginary warfare and an excessive love for contact team sports. By the time I'd lost interest in thrusting my head between the arses of two of my peers and trying to kick the shit out of some other boy's ankles, the blood lust had departed as well. Granted, there was a late flowering of violent irresponsibility when I got my own air pistol at the age of twelve, but it was mostly confined to shooting pellets into the sandwiches of unsuspecting office workers who took their lunch break on the bench outside our house. A bizarre form of harming at a distance.

Anyway, now, with eclipse-like predictability, I have to deal with my own eldest son's propensity for imagining himself in possession of an armoury that makes Rambo look like Bambi. Lex – aged nine – is subject to porting an elaborate arsenal of reproduction plastic weapons, usually including an M-16, an antiquated Bren gun, a Kalashnikov and a couple of mean little Glocks. I'm reasonably confident that this phase will pass, especially as he's also always spent vast amounts of time in front of the mirror styling his hair. But all the same, with high-school kids spraying one another with bullets in the States, a rash of Yardie gang murders in London, and the content of films and television programmes becoming ever more graphically violent, I, like many another parent, would rather my son's desire to shoot were worked off in a harmless way.

The skeet shooting game looked good from this angle. Skeet shooting is itself a bloodless cousin of game shooting, so a skeet shooting game is even more removed from reality. Indeed, this game is fine from that point of view. It does have one game that allows you to destroy myriad alien invaders, but unless we discover sentient life in other galaxies this isn't such a bad way to get target practice.

No, Lex's and my problems with the game began with the fact that it was hard – even in our quite large house – to find a room that could be adequately blacked out enough to make the visuals (which are projected stereoscopically on to the wall) come to life. There was that, and there was also the fact that the aliens were far too easy to shoot down. Lex only had to wave his mock ray gun in approximately the right direction for sound effects to sound and pellets of light to disintegrate. We played it a few times, and then he began getting at me to go to a certain park a little way away.

'Why do you want to go there?' I asked – it isn't a very prepossessing place.

' 'Cos it's next to that shop.'

'What, the paper shop?'

'Yeah.'

'What do you wan –' I began, but then it dawned on me: 'One of those plastic guns they sell?'

'Yeah.'

So much for the fantasy short-circuiting of violent tendencies.

Stuff, August 1999

83

Restaurant review: China China,
3 Gerrard Street, London W1

There are the restaurants you merely go to, and there are those you actually eat in. Ever since, aged sixteen, I discovered the delights of Poon's Wind-Dried Duck Co., I have been a devotee of Soho's tumultuous, egregious, Chinese restaurants.

In my teens and twenties, strapped for cash, I would frequent the teetering, vertiginous and fantastically cheap establishments on Lisle Street. In Poon's you would pile up a narrow, twisting staircase, past pocket dining room after pocket dining room, until you gained your seat, more often than not crammed between two sets of tourists from the opposite ends of the earth.

While English waiting staff often make a poor show of deference, only the Cantonese really refresh you with the candour of their contempt. The Cantonese – arguably one of the most scrutable peoples on earth –

feel no need to hedge round the business of serving with false deference. At one of the Lisle Street restaurants – called Man Lee Hong, although I always referred to it as Manly Hung – the tough waitress would meet you at the door and, pointing to some handkerchief-sized surface, screech, 'You sit there!' There could be no question of demurral; the one time I tried it she told me to fuck off.

I also used to eat at another establishment a few doors down. This place, like most of the Soho Chinese restaurants, accepted cash only. Apparently – and there are good, self-protective reasons for believing this anecdote apocryphal – one American tourist who began to make a stink about being unable to pay his bill by credit card was summarily relieved of the need ever again to scrawl on a counterfoil. For one of the chefs, catching wind of the dispute, came belting out from the kitchen and chopped the tourist's arm off with a cleaver. Neat, huh?

If the small joints began to tire me, I would switch my custom to the vast and labyrinthine Wong Kei, not so much a restaurant, more an entire parallel world. My mate Scraggy, an appalling junky, once had the bright idea of going into Wong Kei and asking one of the waiters to recommend a good acupuncturist, with a view to alleviating his withdrawal symptoms. The communication between Scraggy and the waiter didn't go too well – Scraggy's Cantonese not being up to speed – so he ended up miming the action of various needles being inserted into his body. The waiter seemed to have got – literally – the point. He led Scraggy out of the restaurant and into some dingy spieler down the road. Here an elderly man offered Scraggy an ounce of smack for sale – at a surprisingly reasonable price.

The Lisle Street Chineses had the benefit of being dirt-cheap and open at all hours. You could – and still can – have the deliciously topsy-turvy sensation of eating at three in the morning while reading the first editions of the papers, which were hawked around the tables. But with age have come fixed bedtimes and achingly responsible behaviour. The only clubbing I do nowadays is the occasional all-comers' seal cull in the Faeroes. Horlicks has replaced hot licks. So, in line with this maturity, I've switched my regular custom round the corner from Lisle to Gerrard Street.

Gerrard Street is the core of Soho, a pedestrian precinct with ornate, wrought-iron arches at either end, complete with dragons and horny bits. There are pagoda-style phone booths and all manner of Chinese businesses besides the restaurants. I once had my hair cut in the Chinese barber's, and was amazed how a straight fringe introduced a certain oriental cast to my features. I ate for a long while in the Lido, but jacked it in after the refurbishment, which makes the gaff look like a set from a Bruce Lee movie. I also have a liking for Lee Ho Fook, down at the Wardour Street end, but less for the food than for the fact that it appears in Warren Zevon's song 'Werewolves of London': 'I saw a werewolf in Lee Ho Fook's/He was eating some beef chow mein . . . Aaaaoooh! Werewolves of London' etc. etc.

I met Zevon in Los Angeles a couple of years ago and told him how much I liked songs that name-checked Chinese restaurants – he seemed strangely unmoved.

Which brings me, at last, to the joint where I actually do eat, China China. This great restaurant dominates the east end of Gerrard Street, and is glass-fronted on both sides of the right angle. One view affords an excellent prospect of effulgently glacé, mutantly spatchcocked ducks, hanging on mini-gibbets, behind which labouring chefs pull great hanks of noodles, or bales of dark greens, out of steaming cauldrons. The other view is of a large circular table set right in the window; this is where you should sit.

To do so you ought to go alone, or with only one other. The window is so big, and so clean, that as you trough you really feel part of the street scene outside – a must for lovers of the urbane. As for food, I estimate that I have eaten by now somewhere in the region of a hundred won ton noodle soups in China China. This is one of the world's great soups: globular dumplings, skeins of noodles, Chinese cabbage and a distinctively wholesome broth. Looking into a bowl of won ton noodle is like peering into the primordial soup; left for long enough I'm convinced it could generate new life forms. Mind you, if you really want something utterly viscid – try the congee.

You can go for a traditional Peking duck with pancakes, plum sauce and the trimmings, but I usually give myself a masticatory work-out by opting for duck and roast pork with rice. The duck jointed in that way invariably provides interesting gnawing, and the rice is so glutinous that even the most cack-handed can shovel it up with the sticks. If you're in a more adventurous mood, the mixed meats with rice comes with odd little nodules and curlicues of unidentifiable animal protein that tease with their incognito.

I always have tea, and frequently sake, which has the advantage of tasting like hot sweat and going well with Chinese food. Even with booze, I'd be candidly amazed if you managed to get the bill up above thirty-five quid for two – inclusive of tip.

I've been eating at China China for so long now that one of the waiters *almost* recognises me. At least, I've seen his eyebrow move upwards, fractionally, on a couple of my entrances. But please, if you recognise me eating at the round table in the window, don't commit the awful solecism of introducing yourself. I'll only screech at you, 'You sit there!' And if you persist, tell you to fuck off.

Observer, January 1997

84

*Restaurant review: The Old Fire Engine House,
25 St Mary's Street, Ely, Cambridgeshire*

One of the greatest problems presented by writing a column such as this is how to deal with representing one's dining companion. Should you be coy about him/her, giving them some sort of nickname or chintzy ascription? Or should you come right out and admit that your helpmeet, the Sancho Panza to your Don Quixote, is in fact a trichologically-challenged mortgage broker from Grays Thurrock?

I've tended to opt for naming those of my companions such as Dave the Power Ranger and Dave the Garagiste, who appear only intermittently; and retaining the naff neologism 'Significant Other' for she-who-shares-the-32-tog-duvet, the portion of spare ribs whom I've taken away on a more or less permanent basis.

Truth to tell, these columns would be considerably duller without the input of the SO. She can be guaranteed to come up with some succulent statement or astringent *aperçu* when the critical going gets tough and there just doesn't seem any other way to describe pan-fried river trout without recourse to obscenity, or the thesaurus, or both.

Another compelling aspect of the SO is the bizarre fact that, while she has a biological age in the three-decade region, psychically she was brought up in the inter-war period. Hers was a childhood of nursery teas, coats with velvet collars and bicycling curates clad in gaiters. Her ignorance of almost all popular cultural events since the late thirties is, I find, a salutary corrective to a world characterised increasingly by an orgy of ephemerality.

In the space inhabited by the SO, the clock always stands at ten-to-three and there's always time for tea – usually with a fresh honeycomb, de-crusted cucumber sandwiches and Earl Grey in willow-patterned cups.

The above being noted, even I was shocked by the SO's response to the death of Timothy Leary. We were at breakfast, tucking into kedgeree. I was reading a freshly ironed copy of the *Telegraph*, the SO was perusing the *Lady*. I dropped the leading edge of my paper and said, 'I see Timothy Leary has died on the Internet.'

'Who,' queried the SO in Lady Bracknellish tones, 'is Timothy Leary? And why did he see fit to expire on the railway?'

To the SO's credit, once I'd filled her in on the career of the maverick Harvard psychologist, and his trip from West Point via the League of Psychic Discovery to the status of international fugitive, she became intrigued. 'I would not mind,' she said with some deliberation, 'tuning on, dropping in and turning out.' Which is how we came to find ourselves eating at the Old Fire Engine House in Ely, with the SO doing what in psychedelic parlance is termed 'peaking'.

I like to think of myself as something of a natural philosopher, and while lysergic acid diethylamide may have been thoroughly discredited as a short cut to spiritual enlightenment, or a cure for alcoholism, I don't think its potential as a restaurant-reviewing aid has been properly explored. In what follows I have transcribed the SO's random synaesthetic jottings verbatim, and provided below my own, rather more lucid exegesis.

'Hot, hot, hot. Weddings on both sides of the sideboard. Tall boy inside – short boy outside. Cool green tomato brain.'

From the outside, the Old Fire Engine House seems to be an unassuming, eighteenth-century brick-built town house. On a hot Saturday afternoon, weddings were taking place in the church across the square and in the cathedral, at the end of the parched close. Once I had manoeuvred the SO inside, we were seated in a cool, stone-flagged room next to a tall boy (he later departed, leaving a mingy 5 per cent tip). I ordered iced tomato soup for both of us and a bottle of Volnay Premier Cru Les Caillerets 1983. Both were the equivalent of a cold compress applied to a hydrophobic dog.

Two ladies with prognathous jaws – who looked like twins although separated in age by some twenty years – were tucking into generous portions of sherry trifle. The SO became fixated by them and noted, 'Southern belles not. Bell-shaped women. Yes. Summoned by bells the school-dinner women come, bringing school-dinner smell, school meat and veg. But comfort wine.'

I think the first part of this free-associating screed was inspired by the chronoclastic twins' cloche hats. The SO then refers to the rather bustly, yet cadaverous, middle-aged waitress who presented us with lamb and boiled potatoes (for me) and a whole roasted pigeon with boiled potatoes (for the SO). There was also not just a truckle of vegetables, but a whole truck, which evinced, in its bean buttresses and corbelled courgettes, all three architectural periods that the construction of Ely Cathedral spanned: Romanesque, Perpendicular and Gothic.

The SO's choice had to have been a mistake, because it called forth from her the following note: 'Pigeon skull like woman who served us.' I could see her point; there was something rather sinister and skull-like about the pigeon – and the lamb, although well-cooked and beautifully presented, did have a stringy, school-dinnerish texture. The SO's discomfiture was to my advantage. While she retreated to the bathroom, I tucked into both dishes with abandon and ordered another bottle of the Volnay.

I was beginning to wonder what she was getting up to upstairs – the Old Fire Engine House has a small gallery exhibiting water-colours, but the state the SO was in, Jasper Johns or Mark Rothko would have been more up her alley (not that she's ever heard of either of them) – when she returned bearing a sanitary disposal bag with a single, absurdist remark scrawled on it: 'No conversation in this bathroom.'

It was time to beat a retreat. I asked if we could take coffee in the delightful walled garden, refulgent with flowers, herbs and shrubs. In the far corner a small girl was oscillating vigorously on a swing dangling from the bough of a spreading chestnut tree. It was a peaceful, immemorial, quintessentially English scene, marred only by the presence of the SO, who had adopted a foetal position beneath the bench I was sitting on and was mewling in a rather pitiful fashion.

'Buck up old thing,' I urged her; 'the bill is only seventy-five quid despite the two bottles of Volnay. Take a look at the beautiful garden.' But instead of emerging she only tittered in a knowing fashion.

I sipped the excellent coffee, which had come in a cafetière with accompanying chocolates. Never had coffee seemed so coffeeish, so black-beany, so reeking of Costa. The girl on the swing was going higher and higher, until at the limit of her arc she disappeared into the foliage –

and didn't re-emerge! I stood up. Rainbow beams of light coruscated from the SO's brown eyes. She giggled inanely, displaying teeth the size of tombstones. 'You little bitch!' I cried. 'You've spiked me!'

Observer, August 1996

85

Book review: High Fidelity *by Nick Hornby (Gollancz)*

If I were Nick Hornby I'd be shitting my whack. Not just shitting myself, mark me, but actually dumping my load, dropping my ballast, in the very demotic eye of north London. Because that's Hornby – as we all know. He's the man standing on the North Bank at Highbury, with a plastic beaker of Bovril in one hand and a Wagon Wheel in the other; he's the anal retentive who can remember – like Borges's Pierre Menard – every nuance of his life, once it is trawled to the surface by his obsessive recall of the 'worlds' of pop music and football; he's the New Man, who's never made the mistake of merely coming, and whose horror of fisticuffs is just about matched by his glee in voyeurism; and last – but by no means least – he's a literary critic who's undertaken to write what on the face of it appears to be a novel-length work of fiction.

No! Not that same Hornby who wrote just a mere three years ago that 'the influence of post-modernism is such that although everyone knows the orthodox novel is dead, nobody is sure what they should be producing in its place'? Not the Hornby who so plangently opined in the same piece, 'It used to be the case that you could not be a proper writer until you had mythologised your adolescence, satirised your friends, deified an ex-girlfriend or excoriated your parents in a novel'? Yep, the very same. I have the piece in front of me as I write.

Hornby penned it as a riposte to the Granta list of 'Best Young British Novelists' that had recently been announced. The piece (for the *Sunday Times*) was subheaded 'Nick Hornby analyses the literary under-achievement of the thirtysomethings'; and in column four we have the delicious pull-quote 'Thirtysomething literary fiction is like a doughnut, with a hole in the middle where an overpaid group of coddled literary superstars should be smirking.'

This was a big mistake. Because, even now (three years may be a long time in football, honey, but it ain't in books), he has to confront the fact that he has written a *novel* that: mythologises his adolescence, satirises his friends, deifies an ex-girlfriend and excoriates his parents.

As for the 'overpaid group of coddled [and smirking] literary superstars', I don't believe Hornby thinks they exist any more than I do. But he would have to admit that his footballing memoir *Fever Pitch* sold inordinately well. So well, in fact, that once when I got into a cab, the cabbie, without prompting from me, launched into a disquisition on what a good book it was! The cabbie! I ask you. Yer average Julian Sensitive would tear his own penis off to get a cabbie to so much as glance at a copy of his book, let alone read it.

As I recall, *Fever Pitch* was on the bestseller list for some time; and while I wouldn't go so far as to say that Hornby is smirking on the cover of the proof of *High Fidelity*, he doesn't exactly look consumed by existential angst, or even more quotidian miseries. Like a cash-flow problem, for example.

So, as I say, Nick Hornby must be shitting his whack. Because on top of these lit-crit-type problems – and what are they but mere persiflage – we also know that he has more personal problems with taking criticism. In *Fever Pitch* he mused on the congruences between his profession as a literary critic and his support of Arsenal, a club universally disliked, saving by its fans.

'Like the club,' Hornby wrote, 'I am not equipped with a particularly thick skin; my oversensitivity to criticism means that I am more likely to pull up the drawbridge and bitterly bemoan my lot than I am to offer a quick handshake and get on with the game.' Oh dear, oh dear, oh dear, how is he going to cope with criticism of his first novel then? An experience that may be ranked as the most profoundly, psychically intrusive probing by potentially hostile strangers that you are ever likely to encounter.

Hornby also admitted in *Fever Pitch* that some of his attitudinising as a literary critic derived from the terraces. The tendency to roar in disbelief at the efforts and awards of other writers was so summarised: 'Perhaps it was these desperate, bitter men in the West Stand at Arsenal who taught me how to get angry in this way; and perhaps it is why I earn some of my living as a critic – maybe it's those voices I can hear when I write. "You're a WANKER, X." "The Booker Prize? THE BOOKER PRIZE? They should give that to me for having to read you."'

I resisted reading *Fever Pitch* for a long time. People kept telling me it was a book about much more than football, but I couldn't really believe them. My failure to get to grips with this central shibboleth of male bonding has always made me feel an outsider; and in time my ignorance of all things *sportif* has become something of a badge of pride. As Montaigne so wisely remarked, 'Mistrust a man who takes games too seriously; it means he doesn't take life seriously enough.'

I only read it because I had to for this review. But I'm glad I did. There's something about being charmed by a book you thought you would hate that is truly captivating. I knew within a page or so that it was exceptionally well written. The prose has that implied mutuality of lucidity (you, the reader, understand perfectly what I, the writer, am saying to you) that is the hallmark of good memoir. But on the second page I also laughed aloud, and on the third or fourth my eyes were pricked by tears. In a year that also produced *And When Did You Last See Your Father?* by Blake Morrison, it was remarkable to read another such poignant evocation of a modern boyhood.

I read the book in one sitting, and called up a footie-loving friend to tell him how much I had enjoyed it. Then I turned my attention to its successor, *High Fidelity*, fervently praying that it would be as good.

Unfortunately it isn't. For a start it has a dreadful title. As Rob Fleming, the protagonist of the novel, might say, 'List your top five favourite novels with titles culled from Elvis Costello songs.' To which one would have to reply, '(1) *Less Than Zero*; (2) Err . . .'

But there is a point to it. The title heralds what has to be the novel most replete with ephemeral cultural references you're likely to find outside an airport bookstall dump-bin this year. (Next year it will probably be there itself.) Hornby's characters work in a record shop, so I suppose that does mean that the endless lists of records and musicians lend some verisimilitude, but do we really want to read any text with the following even mentioned in it: Dr Ruth, Danny Baker, Susan Dey from *LA Law*, Gerry and Sylvia Anderson, Paul McCartney, Whoopi Goldberg, John Cleese, Woody from *Cheers* – that isn't the *Radio Times*?

Maybe this is where 'the novel' (rather than the novel) is going to? As the conceit around which *High Fidelity* revolves is the increasingly serial quality of all aspects of life, from entertainment to emotional commitment, it must be the ideal candidate for transferral to CD-ROM. With this nice convergence of medium and message, the life of Rob Fleming could be pushed still further into the future at the reader's behest. We'll get myriad new editions of *High Fidelity* in which there will be a place for not just Peter Frampton, but also Mr Blobby; not only Nirvana but also Massive Attack; Hugh Grant in addition to Keanu Reeves. People could sponsor each other to appear in *High Fidelity* . . . No, I'm getting carried away.

And anyway, as the main psychological theme of the novel is that thirtysomethings (there's that coinage again! It doesn't just come up in his journalism, it makes several appearances in the novel as well – three in direct reference to the television show, the rest, as it were, as spin-offs) are all leading dull little lives in which their personalities are defined by a stale pot-pourri bowl of cultural artefacts, it could be argued that they are there to express a deep sense of collective malaise.

On this reading, *High Fidelity* is a sort of *American Psycho* for trainspotters: a friendly, heart-warming sort of attempt to make you appreciate the crass materialism and record-collecting greed that define your life. This defence might work if Rob Fleming were a reasonably hateful character, but he isn't. He's a nice, cuddly sort of bloke aware of the difficulties of making emotional commitments and obsessed by pop music. Not unlike our own dear . . . Nick Hornby!

In most instances, unmasking the autobiographical character of a fictional work is either crass, or otiose, or both. But remember those quotes from the *Sunday Times* article. Hornby cannot, I must say, have his cake and eat it. There are far too many congruences between Rob Fleming and the authorial persona of *Fever Pitch* for them to be coincidental. All right, Fleming is from Watford and Hornby hails from the Maidenhead locale; Fleming runs a record shop, and every day Hornby writes the book; but beyond this the similarities are legion: physical, psychological, biographical and, dare I say it, tonal. The voices of the two are recognisably one and the same, although Fleming's is neither as authoritative nor as funny.

The action of the book – boy loses girl, girl's father dies, boy experiences various epiphanies and regains girl with renewed commitment – is simple enough. The problem is that the 'girls' and 'boys' in question are in their mid-thirties. Hornby may be speaking for a considerable social trend when he characterises these people, lost in the wildernesses of a grossly elongated adolescence, a stretch limo of the hormones, but he doesn't speak to this reader. It's the same with the record conceit, and all the references to TV and radio. It's as if he wanted to write a book that somehow exemplified all his theories on the redundancies of fiction.

In *Fever Pitch*, even though my grasp of football doesn't even extend to knowing the shape of the ball, I was pulled into the game – and actually felt some nascent interest in it – by the way Hornby renders his obsession universal. In *High Fidelity* I found the protagonist's obsession with pop alienating, and his attempt to use it to provide a motif around which to interpret his life – at the beginning of the book he lists his 'Top Five Rejections' – merely irritating.

The art of using an ephemeral cultural reference in fiction – even when it is for a satirical purpose – is understatement. If overstatement is to be employed, there must be no expectation of sympathy with the character who is immersed in such trivia (cf. Bateman). Irony, by the same token, is a form of humour that assumes a small, privileged group of people 'in the know'. But Hornby's attempts at irony, such as the trope 'Bonkus Mirabilis', fall flat because everyone in the country knows what 'bonk' and '*annus mirabilis*' mean. A 'universal' irony is an oxymoron.

And Rob Fleming is just a moron. Hornby wants us to sympathise with Fleming, by laughing at his foibles and feckless forays into the world of romance, but we don't. Or at any rate I didn't, I just rather wanted him to leave.

Eventually he did – taking with him the charismatic supporting cast of Barry and Dick (they work in the record shop and are keen on lists – we never really learn the physical appearance of either), Laura (the girlfriend, who has spiky hair and works as a lawyer), and the exotica, a real, live Texan singer called Marie, who bears a distinct resemblance to Susan Dey in *LA Law*.

Nick Hornby has written a novel that can rank as a reasonable piece of juvenilia. There are passages in it that are affecting and describe emotions that are recognisably those of thinking, breathing adults. Some scenes, notably the post-coital ones, and the girlfriend's father's funeral (deaths small and large), are well-paced and believable.

His turns of phrase can be diverting – although even just an hour after putting the book down I'm buggered if I can remember any of the diverting ones, although I can remember verbatim such honeys as: 'We're like Tom Hanks in *Big*. Little boys and girls trapped in adult bodies and forced to get on with it'; 'People who know dead people, as Barbra Streisand might have sung, but didn't, are the luckiest people in the world'; 'People who are doing OK but have still not found their soul-mate should look, I don't know, well but anxious, like Billy Crystal in *When Harry Met Sally*'; and the absolute corker 'Have you ever looked at a picture of yourself when you were a kid? Or pictures of famous people when they were kids? It seems to me that they can either make you happy or sad.'

It is not by such acute tropes as 'I felt like a new man, but not like a New Man' that Nick Hornby will be making his living. But I'm not worried for him. In the *Sunday Times* piece he characterised his generation as one of late developers (thanks, Nick, speak for yourself). He's now written an autobiographical novel that mythologises his adolescence etc. etc. – obviously because he feels the need to be a 'proper' writer, of novels. With that off his chest at the age of thirty-eight, I suppose we can confidently look forward to his mid-period flowering by the time he reaches sixty. And who knows, perhaps a Mary Wesleyan comeback sometime towards the mid-twenty-first century.

Modern Review, May 1995

86

In Patrick Marnham's fine book about the French Resistance hero Jean Moulin (*The Death of Jean Moulin: Biography of a Ghost*) he uses the Panthéon in Paris, where his subject's remains were eventually interred, as a means of disentangling the complex web of mythologising that has come to enshroud Moulin.

To paraphrase Marnham, the story of the Panthéon is itself the narrative of France's inability to come to terms with its religious schisms. Originally conceived of by Louis XV as a *Deo gratias* church for his recovery from a serious illness, it wasn't completed until after his death. Dedicated in 1789, it was then desecrated and closed in the inundation of the revolution. In 1791, inspired by the death of Mirabeau, the Revolutionary Assembly decided that the Panthéon should be transformed into a 'Temple of Fame', a final resting-place for the great men who had fought for liberty: 'The church's bell towers were razed to the ground, its tall side-windows were filled in, the cross above the dome was removed, and in gilt letters over the west doors the motto "To its Great Men, their Country's Gratitude" was fixed. Mirabeau's remains were placed inside, followed by those of Voltaire, Marat and Rousseau.'

Of course, with the restoration of the monarchy the building was finally consecrated as a church and the freethinkers' remains voided.

Then, with the institution of a notionally constitutional monarchy in 1830, the cross was removed and the building became a national necropolis. And so on – with each successive regime the building was remodelled, crosses came and went, mottoes were edited and replaced. It wasn't until 1885 and the Third Republic that the current compromise was achieved. The church was deconsecrated – but the cross remained. The motto went back up on the pediment, and the revolutionaries were reinterred.

This tale, of how a supposed national symbol becomes instead a cracked actor on the French political stage, contrasts mightily with the nature of the symbolism in our own built environment – and by extension the regimes of which it speaks. Ours is a state in which the only substantial changes have proceeded with profound gradualism. The Protectorate was simply not long enough to institute its own constructional permanence. The changes wrought upon our nationalist symbols have been by time, fire and property speculation. Ours is a capital remodelled not by a Napoleon, with the aim of producing nodal points from which artillery could subjugate the revolting citizenry, but by a species of powerful estate agents, intent not on creating a reified architectonic, but on maximising the value of freeholds, leaseholds and even rents.

It wouldn't be going too far to say that ours is a regime of gentrification, and that our long history of toshing things up – whether public buildings or private homes – is a vital analogue of the thick (yet curiously insubstantial) morass which is our political life. The two millennia of bricolage explain why our property values remain so ludicrously high in the capital; after all, no one's going to flog off cheap a gaff that represents so much added value. The demented patchwork of London's development goes a long way towards explaining the demented nimbyism that characterises our foreign policy – for, with such ancient and hazy demarcations, it's exceedingly difficult to know what *is* your back yard.

It's against this palimpsest of building that the aims of any given government to write itself into history with the ink of mortar must be assessed. It's one thing to come along and remodel existing structures with a view to transforming their symbolic lode – it's quite another to just take over an existing structure and then hope that its mere completion (on time and within budget) will somehow add lustre to the greater glory of the regime. I'm not for a minute suggesting that we'd have a better society now if we'd been subjected to the changes of regime that the French have – national destinies are more convoluted than any possible linear narrative – but by their response to the symbolic demands of national buildings shall we know the true character of those who govern us.

On this analysis the current incumbents can only be exposed for the fourth-rate hucksters they so clearly are. All the national symbols to have matured over the millennium have been the work of architects and developers working with either lottery or private money, or both. It's undoubtedly churlish to criticise the merits of buildings *ex post facto* on the basis of their funding – but I am a churl. Blair and his cronies are carpetbagging on the buzz produced by buildings financed by a tax on stupidity engineered by their predecessors. *Vive la patrie!*

Building Design, June 2000

87

Last Friday morning I indulged in a little reverse commuting. That's right – reverse commuting. You see, I left my home in central London, and went to work in suburban Watford, right in the heart of the commuter belt. Not only that, but my work that morning consisted in touring a Barratt home, the archetypal commuter dwelling. It was the purest piece of reverse commuting I've ever managed; and as I wheeled the Cavalier north on to the A41, my spirits were swinging in time with the double-breasted jacket dangling from the hook behind my head. 'Agadoo' was playing on Radio 2 and I was in heaven.

It took me back to my heyday in the eighties, when I ran a small corporate publishing company. One of my clients was Rentokil, the exterminator. Except that they weren't too keen on the tag. Indeed, Mr Bateman, the publicity director (I kid you not), once told me that the bane of Rentokil's corporate life was that they couldn't ditch their name, because it had such high instant recognition with the public; but that it no longer adequately reflected the great wealth and humming diversity of their current undertakings. Such as supplying yuccas planted in cat litter for atria, and bilious yellow sharps-disposal bins for hospitals.

Mr Bateman and his assistant Kate Furr (it's true! It's all true!) were highly serious about this Rentokil image problem; although their zeal was rather undercut by the presence in the former's office of a large pantomime rat's head.

But what triggered my torrent of recall on this particular morning wasn't the pantomime rat's head – I haven't worn one in weeks – but the knotty conundrum of corporate image. The Barratt spokesman had been fairly difficult to pin down when I'd requested a visit to a new Barratt home built on a greenfield site: 'You want to take the piss, don't you?' he'd said, but I demurred, 'No, no, I want to get across to our readers how the stereotype they have of Barratt homes is unjustified.' Eventually I won him over – although he requested anonymity in this piece. I couldn't ascertain what it was he was worried about; I mean, you haven't exactly heard of PR people being hounded from their houses by vengeful mobs, like convicted child-abusers. Not yet, anyway.

Actually, he was a most personable PR man – attractive, erudite and well armed with a plethora of information on Barratt all designed to correct my petty snobberies. (Of course, I'm just the kind of suburban boy who is riven with anti-suburban prejudice.) Did I know that Barratt was responsible for a revolutionary new apartment development called the Pierhead? It's opposite the Millennium Dome and is built in a sinuous question mark. And what about the large amounts of social housing and shared-ownership developments that Barratt is responsible for? Did I know that Barratt was refurbishing large amounts of local-authority housing stock? Did I know that Barratt rebuilt on the Ronan Point site? Did I know that Barratt offered assistance packages for home-buyers, including part-exchange facilities?

And so on it went. I began to feel distinctly queasy about ever having denigrated this visionary outfit, this Peter the Great among house-builders. From now on in, I resolved, whenever I thought of a Barratt home I would visualise the Pantheon or Versailles. The one thing that counted in my favour and against the Spokesman's – the pantomime rat's head, as it were – was that we were actually standing in a small, archetypal Barratt development of some nineteen houses. Some were semis, some detached; some had mock-Tudor façades, some didn't. There were barge-boards aplenty, also quoins, porches, bay windows, carved stone lintels, and numerous other timeless suburban accoutrements. Not only that, but the Spokesman had told me, 'A dentist lives over there, and next to him there's some guy who works in computing.'

Earlier we'd toured the interior of a five-bedroom house, designed – I think I'm right about this – according to the 'Salisbury' pattern. Barratt have a portfolio of seventy different standardised house designs, which are continually updated. The Salisbury was a reasonable enough gaff. The Spokesman pointed out that the fitted kitchen came as standard, although the profusion of pelmets, swags, ruches, gold-painted fake fruit, occasional tables made from giant fake editions of La Fontaine's fables, and sconces were presumably extra.

I quite liked the Salisbury, although I'm certain its 'kerb appeal', as the Spokesman termed it, wasn't aimed at me. Nor, I have to say, were the rooms (too low), or the beds (too short), but then I am like unto a baobab tree, salient on the savannah. Height-wise, that is. The Salisbury weighed in at a cool £420K RRP. But if that sounds steep, the Spokesman was quick to point out that this reflected the 'footprint' (initial value) of the land, which was high, although the ground itself hadn't required 'remediating' (cleaning up). And anyway, this was a home for the kind of people who liked to move right in, unpack, and get on with life. Not fanny about for months transforming the nice Barratt interior into a trendy minimalist loft space.

For a spokesman, the Spokesman was surprisingly full of recondite terms. He told me his favourite was 'flaunching'. Apparently this refers to the practice whereby chimney pots are embedded in stacks using a collar of mortar. I was so taken by this coinage that I took my leave and headed for home and the *OED*, as fast as the Cavalier would carry me.

Needless to say I couldn't find 'flaunching', but then I've only got the 'Shorter' edition. Still, I was so impressed by the Spokesman and his deconstruction of the Barratt-home myth that I've decided to take him at his word. If he ever catches me denigrating Barratt again, either in thought or in deed, he's welcome to flaunch me sideways.

The Times, October 1998

88

'The very terminology invites – and gets – criticism.' So states the authoritative *Oxford Dictionary of the Mind* in its short yet judicious entry on the psychiatric condition termed depression. Actually, it's not really *that* judicious an entry – if it were truly definitive it would confine itself to this statement alone, for the torturous nullity of feeling low is by no

265

means a semantic conundrum; it's a place of darkness and despair where the psychic lint gathers in dense tumbleweeds.

Years ago a psychiatrist friend – not altogether an oxymoron – admitted to me that the profession really knew alarmingly little about this condition, and that rather than classifying depressions as 'endogenous' (caused by internal stimuli, genetic, metabolic etc.), or 'reactive' (caused by all your friends laughing at your dancing), the profession should concede that depressions can only be defined retroactively, by appealing to what it is that's alleviated them. Given this view of depression it would be easy to spot Got Meaningful, Satisfying and Remunerative Job depression from its easily confused sister aetiology Feel Enormous Self-Esteem and Have Left Abusive Partner depression.

However, psychiatrists don't have such gross nostrums as these at their disposal: they cannot erect factories, detumesce bullies, or implant insight. Instead they rely on tried and tested cures for depressions. For the really serious ones, the ones with the fateful snicker-snack of psychosis about them, they advocate modern, rational treatments, such as eating metal, or having an electric current put through your brain; but for the lighter-weight moods, the mere 'neurotic' miseries which in the good old days would've been beaten out of the sufferer while he received the bizarre imprecation to 'pull yourself together', the shrinkocracy have a bur-geoning palette of neuropharmacological aids with which to palliate melancholy. Drugs, to you and me.

In the old days these were crude knock-out drops and sedatives. My late mother, who was as miserable as a stuck pig for most of her life (marvellous metaphor, but what can it possibly mean? Stuck in a door? Stuck to something? Or run through with a short lance by a member of the British officer class? In her case it's definitely the latter), often had recourse to the laudanum of her day, Valium and Librium pills courtesy of Roche Pharmaceuticals. Yup, up in her bedroom she'd lie, on a pink fluffy cloud of inert sedation; then after a few days she'd come down, come down and resume being stuck.

When my own adolescent depressions kicked in in the early eighties it was the boon years for a new kind of go-go candy, the so-called 'tricyclics'. These were allegedly more tightly targeted on the miserable portions of the skull goo, and involved the user in bizarre abstinence from Chianti and soft cheese. (It's a useful index of how dodgy a drug may be: the more specific the foodstuff, the more useless the chemical.) I threw these things down for years with absolutely no noticeable effect whatsoever, saving a pronounced fondness for the writing of Mario Puzo.

In the early nineties I turned my warped imaginings on to the idea of an invented antidepressant called 'Inclusion', the effects of which would be to make it possible for the sufferer to include anything he heretofore had disdained into his arid life. The problem with the drug was that its effect was too promiscuous; say you were watching curling on television – you'd become well nigh obsessed with it, and anything else on which your attention alighted.

It's a cardinal error to try to predict the future if you write fictions – because all too often they roll right into a rampaging reality. A year or so later, the modern commercial phenomenon that is the SSRI (Selective Serotonin Re-uptake Inhibitor to you, sucker) burst upon the neuropharmacological scene. And in the fullness of time it has come to occupy a select position in the commercial firmament, along with other drugs such as Viagra and Tagamet, which makes it one of the mobile phones of the neuronic, inner universe.

Now, I'm not one to lay out terminology like law, but doesn't someone notice something fishy about the umpteen millions of these pills that are being doled out every year? I wouldn't deny for a second that there are some people with depressive conditions who respond extraordinarily well to these drugs; I know several personally and intimately. It isn't the sheer fact that physicians are prepared to dole out such vast quantities of these pills that leaves me knock-kneed with anxiety.

In the wake of a particularly stuck period in the middle of last year I ended up being prescribed Seroxat (an SSRI) by a Harley Street shrink with co-ordinated foot- and sockwear (bad move, I hear you scream – but remember I was depressed). It was fine. I felt chipper. The trains of negativity would stand chuffing at the platforms of my consciousness, but find themselves unable to depart into the hinterlands of my being. Granted I couldn't sleep, and became increasingly manic – but what's that set against the hysterical misery of depression?

No, it was what the two-tone shrink did when I went back and told him the Prozac-alike was making me too speedy that profoundly shocked me. In place of my Seroxat he prescribed me a hip new antidepressant from the States called Dutonin, and in case that didn't keep me on the mental level he chucked in some stuff called Carbamazepine, which is normally prescribed for epileptics but which levels cyclothymic types (like me – allegedly) right out as well. Oh, and just in case I still wasn't sleeping he chucked in a few boxes of a hypnotic with the heroic name Zoplicone. Mother's bloody little helper? I needed one to carry the stuff back from the pharmacy.

End result – I've jacked it all in. I know it's a commonplace to worry about the depredations of the tight commercial alliance between the doctor's writing arm, a much-trumpeted new illness and huge profits for multinationals. But you have to admit – it is depressing.

The Times, February 1999

89

I was in the kitchen listening to the radio with my wife. I wouldn't't've said I was loaded, but I have to admit to being a player in a strange, dramatic irony: my toxicological profile was probably not that dissimilar to that of the occupants of the Death Car when I heard the news. All of them put together, that is.

There are, of course, the conspiracy theories – we're going to have a plethora of them for the next hundred years – but one thing I already know, with some certainty, is that the Devil's dandruff was making the rounds on that fateful night. Will it tarnish the Princess's posthumous reputation when they realise she was a snow bird? I doubt it; things have gone too far already. This is a woman who – everyone would have us believe – shat chocolate ice cream. I'm not convinced.

Like I say, we were listening to the radio and rapping when the newsflash came on; and that was it for the rest of the night. Lacking cable – we've just moved – we had to rely on the terrestrial channels for the next four or five hours. It was fascinating to watch. The initial footage was all grainy and direct – shots of the Death Car in the underpass, interspersed with footage of Diana in the days when she wore blouses with collars that looked like pie crust. But eventually they began to get their act together, and the shocked profundity of this earlier material gave way to the oppressive glibness of professional broadcasting.

My wife is a magazine editor, and despite her being nine months pregnant, we were hooked for the duration. The initial disbelief lasted all of five seconds, and then we knew in a deep, swelling sort of way that this was going to get bigger, and bigger and bigger. It was like the sensation you get when your surfboard is finally grabbed by a wave.

Both of us are republicans; neither of us has any time for the principle of heredity as applied to temporal power. But in the days, and now weeks, since the event, people have begun to talk all sorts of utter nonsense about what Diana Spencer's death 'represents'; most of this represen-tation has been little more than the hysterical projections of a lot of people who are willing to abnegate responsibility in every way, shape and form.

If Diana stood for anything it was a miserable Oprah Winfreyisation of public culture, in which egregious tit-beating came to be synonymous with honour and probity. The opposite – the famed, and illusory, English 'stiff upper lip' – is no more honourable or true, but there's still ultimately no need for anyone to be taken in by the bogus syllogisms upon which authority is always predicated. Sure, she did charity work – but so what? Remember, when you give money to one charity, you take it away from another. It's always those who have most to lose by a genuine levelling of the economic playing field who take the keenest interest in persuading other people to give away their money.

But to persevere a bit with the logical analysis: just take away any one of the factors that have made Diana Spencer's death such an astonishing *cause célèbre*, and you have nothing. If she'd died choking on a chicken bone we wouldn't be having any of this; ditto if she'd looked rather more like Mother Teresa than like Sharon Stone; and the same applies – of course – if she had never been addressed in her lifetime as 'Your Royal Highness'.

People's willingness to abase themselves before wholly unworthy auth-ority figures never ceases to astonish me. People's willingness to accept that Tony Blair was so moved by the news that he completely abandoned the habits of twenty years in politics, and gave an unscripted speech. Yeah, yeah. Then we had the most appalling week of hypocritical drivel in the press; and dreadful traffic on London's roads. You Americans come over here and think all of this ceremonial is quaint and affecting, but I can tell you it's a righteous pain in the ass to have to live with it all the time. The Sex Pistols memorably sang about 'a cheap holiday in someone else's misery', but you come for a cheap holiday in someone else's – alleged – majesty.

On the first Sunday evening we went up to Kensington Palace, to see the crowds, to see history – to paraphrase Marx – being made not by the 'mass of individuals', but simply by the mass. And what could have been more mass – and indeed more massy – that the great banks of cut flowers that began to line the railings of Kensington Palace, Harrods, Buckingham and St James's palaces? This was a nation behaving like someone guiltily visiting a moribund relation in a nursing home. This was cut flowers as a substitute for genuine social utility.

Yes, cut flowers; and pot plants, and cards, and placards, and stuffed animals and even bottles of champagne. These ramparts of mourning tat that built up around the royal palaces – especially Kensington – were almost awesomely naff. What did this trashy monumentalism represent? Was it some bizarre counterfactual: a kind of People's Conceptual Art, to stand against the new 'Sensation' show opening – to much furore – at the Royal Academy in the middle of September?

It could be. The kind of people who created this landfill-in-waiting are just the same types who howl in anguish at the thought of Damien Hirst's cut-up cows being humped through the hallowed portals of the Academy. They were the people who keened and sobbed as the television cameras and radio mikes probed the painful zones of their grief. Because, of course, unacknowledged in their minds was the true horror of Diana's death, which had a ghastly parallel to Hirst's analogues of discorporation. She lay in the car for a long time. She may have been conscious. Her body was shattered, torn apart.

All that week conversations would slide in and out of 'the news'. The effect of such intense ubiquity is to somehow warp the normal laws of mortality. On at least two mornings I woke to the dreamy thought: I wonder if she's still . . . In truth, she's now more alive than she ever was when breathing; the magnificent elision of techno-death and world celebrity has imprisoned her reality, encapsulated it for ever.

Then we had the funeral. For days beforehand, students of extraordinary popular delusions and the madness of crowds were scanning the ether. Would London – as was initially posited – play host to a million mourners, two million, or the eight that were anticipated in the middle of the week? People battened down their hatches. At my local hypermarket the manager told me sales were up 30 per cent on the Friday. I was unable to buy a bottle of Stolichnaya vodka – now that's suffering. We cancelled all travel plans and hunkered down with the kids. My son (Lex, aged seven) had the most phlegmatic view of the whole shebang: 'She had to die – because she was called Di.'

But in the event it was estimated that only a mere million turned out. Instead of the hundred-deep groaning phalanxes anticipated, all along the route, there were just the kind of travelling posses, darting through the trees of Hyde Park, that you expect to see at race meets, or lining the route of the Tour de France. I could see, watching the funeral cortège, how people could succumb to a desire for oceanic sadness and orgiastic melancholy. I've had my losses too. Because that was what was happening. If you squinted your emotions a little, it was your mother/father/child/partner in that box, not the corpse of a thirty-six-year-old woman who you really didn't know personally.

They dragged the corpse of this young woman right around the centre of town on a cart. And in so doing they reinforced the fundamental idea that underpins our 'constitutional' monarchy (really a profound oxymoron as there is no, written, British constitution). And this is the pantomime of authority; the monarchy exists to show the people – or 'commoners', to be more accurate – the manner in which they would choose to exercise power, were they by any chance to actually have any. It is the therapy of authoritarianism.

They dragged the death cart from Kensington, and as it came to St James's Palace the line of princes, plus the Duke of Edinburgh and Earl Spencer, swung in behind. 'It's the Men in Black,' I remarked to my wife, 'protecting the world from the scum of the universe.' She peered at the television. 'Oh no – I'd say it's pure *Reservoir Dogs*. You know, "Let's go to work."' She was right. Mr Charles, Mr William, Mr Harry and the others were working hard to mark out the formal relations of power in the British polity.

All the alleged breaches in immemorial protocol – which is in fact, in most places, a system of royal rote only in place since the beginning of the twentieth century – were as nothing compared with this enormous underscoring of *realpolitik*. And that's why I think it will change nothing, at either the personal or the political level. Tony Blair and Peter Mandelson had a superb week, a week in which they managed to reinforce their role as the true Men in Black; I have little doubt that they'll be able to make the Windsors do precisely what they want. And that is – continue to rule us.

The proxy MiB walked first in the direction of the City – rightly, for this is the traditional current of power in Britain: between Money and the Crown. But rather than enter Trafalgar Square, with its associations of riot and affray, they wheeled right into Horse Guards Parade, passing Churchill's wartime bunker. Finally the death cart arrived at its destination, Parliament Square, where temporal authority – the House of Commons – and the ludicrous established Church – Westminster Abbey – contended to decide who should finally rive the body of this most riven of young women. It was a nice – in the Shakespearian sense – irony. The 'girl without a past', selected to provide an heir for a moribund monarchy, was being received into death by a bogus institution, created by a despotic monarch in order to provide ideological justification for a divorce, which was necessitated by his need to find an heir.

It was a hell of a show then – and it remains so now. But it can't go on.

Commissioned for George, September 1997

90

Television review

I've been teasing my editor on the Culture section for a couple of weeks now about my forthcoming review of Simon Schama's *History of Britain* (BBC2). I told him that Schama and I had been lovers for a while, and that the eminent historian had a taste for sadomasochism of a particular bent: he liked to tie me up so that I resembled a *tableau vivant* of the past – Joan atop the faggots, or Marat stabbed in the bath. Needless to say the editor fell for my little joke, so much so that when I spoke to him a couple of days ago he alluded to it once more. 'We're really looking forward to your piece,' he said; 'Janet [the newspaper's editor] is very excited about it.'

Oh my! If only everyone were as gullible as the senior staff of the national broadsheets, what an exciting world we'd be living in. I haven't ever had sex with Simon Schama (although the late A. J. P. Taylor often used me as a loofah), and judging from the first two episodes of his much-trumpeted *History* it's difficult to imagine him pitching up on the wilder shores of love, for this is a veritable missionary position of a series, with Schama on top, firmly hammering away with the facts, grunting his way through the battles, and ejaculating the names of the kings.

Schama is a talented historian who first made a mark with his *Embarrassment of Riches*, a study of the golden age of the Netherlands. Since then in works such as *Dead Certainties*, *Landscape and Memory* and *Rembrandt's Eye* he's displayed a talent for uniting the telling detail with reconstructive imagination and broad theory, to produce a form of history-as-*mélange* that is more familiar to us from the works of the great French structuralist historians – such as Braudel and Aries – than from the drier narrative peregrinations of the Brits. Which is why it's a surprise to see him fronting up such a pedestrian exercise in educational television as this. The strength of his written history is the quantity of allusion stirred into it – although this is also its weakness, in that it becomes clotted and unreadably rich. All that we get of this viscous stock in *Britain* is a thin, metaphoric *jus*, drizzled across a meat-and-two-veg account of our island story, which must be familiar to anyone who has snoozed their way through GCSE lessons, let alone remained alert.

None of this is to say that *Britain* is bad – it has some excellent touches, and Schama, if not comely enough to get me into bed, is none the less an attractive expositor. In his dark shirts buttoned to the collar, and his slick, hip-length mac, he discourses like a thinking person's Loyd Grossman (the result of decades across the pond), bringing a jaunty air to his well-worn tramp through the past. And the camerawork, while relying far too much on aerial shots of the sea (yes, we know we're surrounded by it) and gusts of dry ice (yes, we know it gets foggy round here), is mostly sumptuous and atmospheric. I say mostly, but whenever anyone is being kidnapped, or running into battle, or fleeing from battle, or battling, the camera goes all wobbly and hand-held. Tussocks of grass and thrashing legs loom up as if the Anglo-Saxon house-carls entered the fray toting a double-headed axe in one hand and a camcorder in the other. There's that, and there's also rather too much in the way of John Harle's incidental music, ranging from meaningless Celtic plaints to plangent booms and fanfares.

I suppose my quarrel is with the 'reconstructions' of historical events in general. The first half of the first programme didn't have any of these and was all the better for it. It was only once we got to Boadicea razing Colchester (and don't you sometimes wish she'd do it again?) that the woad-smeared extras began to tramp across our screens. By the time we got to 1066 we were watching a bizarre action movie, in which the camera cut from the Bayeux tapestry to the extras, to Schama wandering around the battlefield scaring sheep, back to the luvvie cavalry again. The trouble was not only that this left us little room for our own imagination (if you take the tapestry to have any level of verisimilitude, King Harold closely resembled a Beanie Baby), but also that some of what Schama said – 'The Normans were the scary half-skinheads of the early feudal world' – was then directly contradicted by actors playing Norman knights with perfectly healthy barnets.

How much more evocative were those little touches, such as Schama handling King Harold's ring, or reading the Vindolanda tablets, fragmented letters of the Roman legionnaires, or deciphering the runic graffiti of the Vikings who raided the Orcadian tomb of Maes Howe, details that conveyed the essential intimacy of the past – how we occupy the same places that these former Britons did, touching the same things, feeling the same breezes. One of Schama's favourite catch-phrases is to say such-and-such 'must be imagined', and I rather wish he'd let us do just that. One of the most fascinating facts he imparted during the second programme was that when William the Conqueror finally died, his courtiers deserted him, his corpse was looted by his servants, and his body was left to rot for three days. Creepily disturbing stuff – but how much less disturbing when you then actually see a guy playing dead William?

There was a drogue on my suspension of disbelief, and there was also Schama's tendency to air-brush over any problems of historiography. We were told that the chronicler who wrote of William's deathbed confession (Sorry I nicked your country) had no reason to falsify it, given that he himself was of Norman lineage, but we were also told that he was writing some 150 years after the events he described – could there not have been some diffraction of his rear view as a result?

Not according to Simes – for this was television history as certainty. So sure did he sound about things that when he described Harald Hardrada as 'built like a Norwegian cliff-face', I expected to see two pictures pop up, one of the King, the other of a cliff-face, so that we could observe they were one and the same. Of course, people will say that this series isn't really aimed at the likes of me (which rather makes one wonder why it goes out prime-time), that it's intended for young people who're coming to British history afresh. But I suspect that the BBC sees this series as an opportunity to reassert its control over the hearts and minds of its subject viewers. The writing of British history, ever since Macaulay and Carlyle, has been the very core of the citadel of our national identity and imperial mission. In the twenty-first century it's only right and proper that a televised history of Britain should be perceived as a touchstone of our contemporary sense of ourselves. And what does Schama add to Britishness thus far? Not much. For him the Roman occupation was on the whole a Good Thing – while the Norman invasion was a Bad One. But personally, when he solemnly pronounced that half the indigenous nobility perished at the Battle of Hastings, I couldn't help thinking that this was a disappointingly low body count.

Independent on Sunday, October 2000

91

At what precise point when poor old movie star Hugh Grant picked up poor old prostitute Divine Brown on Sunset Boulevard last month did he embark on an episode of what might be termed a secret life? Was it when he clocked her, along with the other brasses, one leg on, one leg off the kerb, as they wiggled and jiggled, a garnish of unsafe sex on top of the poisoned dish that is Hollywood? Or was it as the car oozed to a stop in the side-street and she – we assume – undid his flies?

Given that the minute the LAPD knew who it was they had in their clutches, their press office unleashed a fusillade of faxes to the British press, can we somehow chart – as it were – the negative incrementation of Hugh's stab at secrecy? If we imagine effects to be exactly contemporaneous with causes in this instance a strange kind of scenario develops: with each quarter-inch that Divine's lips travel *en route* to the Grant penis, a further five hundred column inches of glib, crapulent newspaper copy is generated; a further ten thousand futile conversations are launched on 'should she forgive him?' lines; and another ten thousand relationships are placed under strain as the interlocutors wonder if *their* secret lives are somehow going to be dredged up in the ensuing brouhaha.

Celebrity may present an extreme example of the search for a secret life. After all, because of their constant exposure celebrities must become somewhat like children who imagine that because they cannot see, they cannot be seen. But who's to say that famous people are in any way exceptional when it comes to embracing the dramatic irony of betrayal?

Statistically speaking it must be the case that a good number of the people reading this piece are currently engaged in some kind of secret life, and are now blushing internally and perhaps looking across the table at the unsuspecting face of the person it's being kept secret from.

The fact that the 'secrecy' here is infidelity, a form of sex disapproved of, viewed as aberrant, seems to me neither here nor there. Sex is a particularly gaping hole through which to access the secret. It is by its very nature – in our culture – a 'secret', or at any rate private, undertaking. People do not copulate freely in our streets and parks; they remain buttoned up against the prying eyes of the herd.

Many people who commit adultery say that the sex itself isn't nearly as important as the sense of danger, the sense – I would hazard – of self-realisation that comes from stepping outside your socially defined role. What could be more telling evidence of this than the fact that many, many people are apparently opting for forms of 'virtual' secret life on the Internet. They set up home pages on the system, complete with details of themselves, their aspirations, their likes and dislikes, their pastimes, and then solicit relationships with others which may be highly intimate (within the confines of pixilated imagery). However, it all takes place at the level of secrecy, of dissimulation.

This may appear faintly ludicrous (after all, what would you most want to convince a virtual lover of on the Internet? Probably that you aren't the sort of computer nerd who goes searching for their jollies in electronic space), but for all that is completely understandable. Because, I would argue, having a life of your own *is* having a secret life; and not to have some elements of your being that are undiscoverable by others is to be a citizen of Oceania, with every innermost thought constantly available for examination by the Big Brother of the media, or gossip, or opinion.

The potential for virtual infidelity does, however, point up the fact that the really interesting secret lives, the ones that intrigue me as the extreme forms of this perfectly normal drive, are those that confound us with their normality. After Andy Warhol died and the 'full truth' came out about his life, the most intriguing secret of an existence that was compartmentalised in the extreme was that Warhol had remained a devout Catholic throughout it all. Every day he went straight from the Factory, with its writhing bodies fuelled by Methedrine, to the church, with its genuflecting bodies fuelled by the mass.

Or take one of the most famously and brilliantly documented tales of a secret life, J. R. Ackerley's memoir *My Father and Myself*. Ackerley senior was a solid, prosperous paterfamilias, who ran a fruit-importing business in the City and kept a substantial upper-middle-class establishment in Richmond. On his death, his son learned that he had in fact maintained another family less than a mile away for over twenty years. But there was nothing particularly weird about this secret life; the three daughters Ackerley senior had around the corner were as unaware of his other children's existence as his apparently legitimate progeny were of theirs.

This to me is a truly secret life, and it teases out another aspect of what it is that pruriently fascinates us about such scenarios: the fact that for a secret life to be of real interest it needs to cut against the grain of expectation. If Hugh Grant can get oral relief – as we assume he can unless he's in a strangely sexually circumscribed relationship – legitimately, then why does he seek it in such potentially dangerous circumstances? If Ackerley senior already had one conventional establishment, why on earth did he want another?

The answer surely is that it's not the acts performed in secret that are important – it's the secrecy itself. And, more importantly, the crucial opportunity to be someone you aren't. In one way, the case of Grant is extreme – it's difficult to imagine the peccadilloes of the rest of us being given such lick-by-lick attention. But in another, it exemplifies the extent to which all of us are now bound into an increasingly tight sphere of existence by mass electronic society. The lot of the bigamist is not nearly as easy today as it would have been before the advent of computers and the regimentation of our lives that they bring. This, I would argue, is one of the barriers to effective secrecy. Another – and this won't make me popular – is the egalitarianism of contemporary relationships.

In the past, most men led lives outside the home that were, in effect, secret lives. The personation required in being a man in civil society was profoundly different from that entered into in the home. Men were allowed to be ruthless and uncompromising in their dealings in the public arena, backed up by the moral fillip they obtained in the home. By the same token, their home life was often secreted from the eyes of those they encountered in the public arena.

This division has now been blurred. And in some respects it's analogous to the way that men and women have changed in their relationships with one another. The importance of male and female sodalities as a counterbalance to heterosexual relationships has been undermined. You are now expected to be both best friend and lover at one and the same time – two separate personations that leave little room for a part of yourself to be kept secret.

Don't get me wrong, I'm not arguing that men need to be sucked off by prostitutes in order to realise our essential being. But I suppose I am saying that there needs to be some arena in which we can personate ourselves separate from our loved ones. And I believe the same is true for women.

Arguments based on a kind of evolutionary reductionism are not often convincing, or popular. But I don't believe that humans are meant to be entirely transparent to one another, and I believe the cult of celebrity we worship at has elevated this spuriously. Celebrities are engaged in trying to promote an image of themselves that is profoundly unreal. They are required to be highly sexual at the same time as being effectively disembodied. The same goes for politicians of all hues (with the notable exception of Ron Brown), who are among the front-runners when it comes to living secret lives.

It is difficult to imagine either of the current party leaders lost in the throes of ecstasy, so carefully have they air-brushed their lives to make themselves electable illustrations of *Janet and John* banality. And while some might argue that the idea is both nauseating and inapposite (we don't want a cocksman for a premier, but a helmsman), how much more revolting is the image of a sexuality so covered up and annulled as to amount to a form of psychic celibacy – which, as far as I am concerned, and to paraphrase Oscar Wilde, is the only known sexual perversion.

So, we have an elected but not an erected chamber; and poor Stephen Milligan dies on his kitchen table with a plastic bag over his head, a victim of a collective as well as an individual psychopathology.

Men often want to get laid without the emotional frills. Indeed, that is one of the main attractions of consorting with prostitutes. Women, driven mad by the idea that they should be physically perfect, often end up treating their own bodies in perverse and cruel ways, simply in order to gain a kind of control over themselves that they see being destroyed on all sides. What could be more solitary, more secret, than the clutched rim of the toilet bowl, the lost world of voided food?

In our regimented lives we have so little opportunity to be free from the obligation of who we are. Everything has become rather extreme. We move from one locus of intensely personal bonds – the home – to another – the workplace. Perhaps only in the interval, in the heaving anonymity of the crowd, do we find any space in which to be free of others' expectations of us.

Because, of course, there is a secret life available to us all that doesn't involve betrayal of trust, or dangerous subterfuge. Indeed it's a secret life that doesn't require that we personate anyone but our true selves. This is the secret life that we find in solitude. I may be out on a limb, but I'd hazard a guess that when Hugh Grant, or Alan Green, or any of those prominent men crawled the kerb, they were feeling perilously alone, feeling their solitude not as a positive presence, but as a gaping absence.

Amyr Klink, the Brazilian poet, made a journey to the South Pole where he remained for seven months completely alone. Of this secret life he wrote, 'Not to be able to share special moments might have been a problem, but at sea, there are certain situations not to be shared. Some so beautiful and unique that they should continue with the person who experienced them and only then be transmitted: entire.'

Not all of us have the opportunity to create such secret lives, but perhaps we need to consider whether the dramatic irony of our infidelities, our gossipy lies, and all our covert activities, hasn't worn a bit thin. And whether by communing with a religion of psychobabble that portrays all secrecy as pathological, an attempt to evade the sordid truth, we haven't stifled the part of ourselves that can imagine – in secret – what it might be like to be free.

Elle, July 1995

92

Book review: Storms of Silence *by Joe Simpson (Jonathan Cape)*

I like reading books about mountaineering. I like reading books about mountaineering while I'm lying down. I like reading books about mountaineering while I'm lying down in low-lying countryside. Suffolk, where I spent last summer, was ideal from this angle – of repose, a landscape of ingress, like a tired body reclining on a broken-backed sofa.

The more vertiginous and alarming the position of the mountain climber, the better pleased I am. Ideally, I'd like a mountaineering book entirely set on a near-vertical ice face, told (in real time) from the point of view of a climber in imminent danger of falling some thousands of metres to certain death. Juxtaposing this with my own prone, utterly earthbound condition would give me a thrill of the most profound *schadenfreude.*

From this almost subterranean perspective, the first book I read by Joe Simpson, *Touching the Void,* was a *tour de force,* a minor classic of the genre. In it, Simpson told the tale of his rapid, two-man ascent of the west face of Siula Grande, a particularly nasty little six-thousand-metre peak in the Peruvian Andes. Following the ascent – which, described tautly by Simpson, was dangerous in the extreme – came the descent. Unfortunately for Simpson this was no less rapid, since he fell something like three hundred feet of it in two separate accidents. In the first he badly broke his leg. His climbing partner, Simon Yates, then heroically lowered him down 2,500 feet of sheer ice face, before running out of rope and having to cut the injured Simpson loose, or face certain death himself.

Simpson fell into a deep crevasse, but survived. It took him six hellish days to get out and crawl back down the mountain to their base camp. He was only just in time to catch his companions before they departed.

The book maintained the tensility, and narrative glissade, of a frozen rope throughout. Judging by the slack feel of *Storms of Silence*, its successor, this must have been in part because Simpson confined himself to the technicalities of getting up mountains – and the brutalities of falling off them. He described the nature of his own horrific injuries and physical depredations, and his response to them, with Jamesian clarity.

It was no surprise to me to find out, through the pages of the new book, that having been given no chance of recovering well enough to climb again, he in fact fought his way back upright, and then back up. Certain kinds of physical courage must be predicated on a determined lack of imagination.

Of course, in the year after Alison Hargreaves's fall to her death from K2, it is evident that the question of the will-to-risk embodied in mountaineering still exerts a compelling hold on the popular unconscious. Simpson's natural take on all of this is to supply the antithesis, the dark side. What he's really good at isn't climbing mountains – it's falling off them.

Storms of Silence is bound to disappoint on this score, consisting as it does largely of attempts by Simpson to get up high enough for a really spectacular fall, being frustrated by the nagging of his old injuries, failure to acclimatise to high altitudes, and other, more numinous, impediments. As Simpson gave up on peak after peak, the little angel on my right shoulder applauded, while the little devil on my left cursed, cheated again of that delicious thrill – which I knew would only come to me when he was well and truly a dangling man.

But there are other, interleaved disappointments. The narrative is spread over a longer period, covering a trip to the Himalayas, one back to the Peruvian Andes, and a fair amount of anecdotal and factual digression in between. Simpson also wants to tell us something important in this book, or rather, several important things. First, and most unfortunate, of these is that his conscience over the Chinese-implemented genocide in Tibet makes it hard for him to climb Cho Oyo, a tricky little peak of over six thousand metres which straddles the Nepal-Tibet border.

This stated, Simpson then embarks on a description of Tibet's recent history that takes us well off the mountain. He's borrowed heavily from source texts – albeit with acknowledgement – to tell us what is admittedly a shocking and woefully little-known story; but this not only hamstrings our sense of the physicality of his narrative, it also cheats us of any *schadenfreude* whatsoever. It's difficult to feel cosily supine while reading of Tibetan monks being hung up by their arms and tortured with electric truncheons. Not the dangling men we had in mind.

Simpson is sincere, but his grapplings with his conscience undercut the whole business of his climbing mountains at all – he begins to worry about 'credit-card adventurers' – and our enjoyment of it. He seems on the one hand to want to link the will-to-risk of mountaineering to some general theory of human aggression, and on the other to tell us about some of the freakier 'coincidences', quasi-mystical and otherwise, that have affected him in his career.

The trouble is that on the first count he is too woolly and vague to conjoin such disparate events as a potential ruck in a Sheffield pub, a mudslide-cum-avalanche disaster in Peru, a childhood trip round Belsen, and Tibetan genocide, into a Unified Field Theory. And on the second, his mysticism, somewhat perversely, fails to get off the ground, consisting as it does mostly of aural hallucinations, synchronicity and vague supposition.

It's a shame, because the ingredients are here: odd encounters with Tibetan refugees who may be sheltering an infant lama; acute descriptions of both physical geography and physical extremity. Simpson quotes in the text from the unjustly neglected *Mount Analogue*, by the French mystic and mountain climber René Daumal. It's unfortunate he doesn't follow this line (one also swarmed up by Aleister Crowley, another maverick *ascenseur*) in the direction of Gurdjieff and higher things. Instead he gets bogged down in fatal lowlands of prosaic moral exposition, cast usually in the form of uninspiring dialogues with climbing mates.

One other quibble, which may, I concede, reflect only snobbery on myself, concerns the book's title. In a book called *Storms of Silence*, one might have hoped for some. Simpson keeps reminding us throughout that he climbs while mainlining through a Walkman. That's pretty gauche for those of us armchair mountaineers who want our impressions of the sea of clouds minus a soundtrack. But when I finally learned what sort of noise he's been listening to – 'White Wedding' by Billy Idol – my patience snapped.

Simpson is staggering foolhardily – as he admits – across a treacherous mudslide in a Nepalese valley, while he listens to this mindless, ersatz AOR. Sibelius I could have borne. Much as I admire him, I think Simpson should stick to what he does best – falling.

Observer, October 1995

93

In countless satirical narratives by writers about their experiences in Tinseltown, the point where they realise they're about to be shafted by the studio is the ride back to the airport. The ride there has been in a stretch limo, chauffeured by Adonis; the ride back is in a battered Fiat, autopiloted by a thyroid case with a drink problem. While on the way into town the writer was daydreaming castles of greenbacks; on the way back out he finds himself being shaken down on the roadside for his last few bills.

At least I didn't endure such treatment the other day, when I was flown to Nice by a Very Important Movie Producer, then driven into Cannes to have lunch with him. Lizzy from my literary agency wanted us to take the proffered helicopter flight, but I pointed out to her that when the rotors stop moving in mid-air – the thing *falls*. So we stuck to ground transport.

Actually, on the Côte d'Azur a lot of the driving is quite like falling anyway. We had an archetypal, wiry, balding Piquet *manqué*, who managed never less than 100 k.p.h. on the corniche, and better than 140 k.p.h. when we hit the *péage*. He tailgated mercilessly, seeming to respond not so much to the indicators of other vehicles as to an anticipation of them. How else to explain his dramatic stripping of the steel willow?

Lizzy sat, immune to this deathly two-step, making calls on her mobile. She was trying to net in one of the film subagents we deal with, who had engineered the meeting with the VIMP. But he said he couldn't rendezvous because he was babysitting Bruce Willis. This conjured up a ludicrous vision of Bruce Willis wearing a giant Babygro and being led around on some reins. When we got to Cannes the vision became a reality.

I had forgotten just how gauche the French can get when exposed to the sartorial pitfalls of beachwear. They become a nation of the naff, with an alarming preponderance of gold belts and leopard-skin Lycra on show over caramelised flesh tones. Add into this heady brew a vast procession of photographers, hacks, and every single bimbo on continental Europe, and you have an explosive cocktail. Wandering along the promenade at Cannes I wouldn't have been in the least surprised to see Willis in a Babygro; Lizzy thought *every* male in Cannes looked like Willis: balding, intense, and a putative 'roid rager.

Hollywood may descend on Cannes because it resembles southern California, but somehow the movie people manage to turn it into Weston-super-Mare. They were everywhere: standing in front of bill-boards advertising yet-to-be-made films; strongarming deals; and brandishing mobile phones as if they were *Star Trek* phasers. The whole of this tiny littoral — a couple of streets, the esplanade, the beach — was choked with this horde, who, like brown rats, seemed to communicate by mood transmission. Every few minutes the arrival of a limo, or the doffing of a swimsuit, would cause a boiling in the tumult; from nowhere, squeaking packs of teenage French girls would coalesce in order to crane and stare.

We wandered up and down for a while. On the steps of the British pavilion a T-shirted young man was lecturing a group of journalists, photographers and cameramen about lottery funding: 'We've got to have the fucking money instead of it going to dodgy causes. This is a real film and it might do people some good to back it.' I wished Chris Smith MP could have been there to witness this fine pluck. We wandered on, past the chic Italian pavilion and the uncompromisingly empty Arab Radio and Television pavilion. Everywhere there were Bruce Willis lookalikes porting video cameras; and everywhere there were awful mime artists, and dreadful 'art' for sale.

At lunch with the VIMP (in a hotel of such uncompromising stuffiness it could only be called Le Gray d'Albion), I ventured that it was ironic, in the landscape of Cézanne, to find such plangently awful art on sale in the street. '*Cézanne!*' the VIMP exclaimed, brushing crumbs of *langouste* from the frames of his shades. 'Goddamn *Chagall* was born only a few miles from here! It's a disgrace!' A few bottles of Badoit later he said — apropos of a brilliant new film by a highly respected British director — 'I guess I could buy it, but I can't get the distribution. So I'd be buying it to stick on my mantelpiece.'

Later on, after I'd gift-wrapped my soul for the VIMP, I went down to the beach for a paddle. I sat in the Hotel Majestic enclosure, watching two uniformed guards who were patrolling a compound further along the beach with some frisky Dobermanns. I half hoped a posse of bimbos might try and run the gauntlet. Out to sea, giant yachts closely resembling buoyant seventies housing estates bobbed on the waves. For a few minutes I was in Arcadia – then there was an attack by fifty-foot bimbos. Three of them arrived – standard issue: one blonde, one dark, one steatopygous – together with an entourage of film crew, snappers and teenage French girls. A huge, dark-suited security man with a walrus moustache began pushing people around, while the bimbos took their kit off. And all of this within a few feet of where I was sitting with my trousers rolled.

Lizzy turned up. 'That's Cannes, really,' she said. 'All tits.'

'And Bruce Willis,' I reminded her.

An hour later we were falling back to Nice.

The Times, May 1998

94

It was the Saturday after Christmas and I stood by the side of a cool dusty road in Jordan. I was some thousand metres above the entrance to the narrow gorge that contains the famous ruins of Petra, the Nabataean necropolis so famously used by a famous Jew – Steven Spielberg – as a backdrop for Indiana Jones, his swashbuckling gentile *alter ego*.

On the long coach drive from the Israeli border at Aqaba – and during the still longer wait at that border, occasioned by the mutual antagonism of all officials concerned – I had noticed the pensive, sensitive mien of a bespectacled man of around my own age, who I guessed was an English Jew. We now stood in a loose dyad, watching a young Jordanian lad attempting to persuade some of our fellow tourists to have their names described in coloured sands and encapsulated in glass vials. Improbably large raindrops began plashing from the leaden sky. He turned to me and asked, 'Is this your first visit to an Arab country?' I muttered something negative and returned the query. 'Yes,' he replied, 'and from what I've seen so far it looks . . . interesting . . .'

'Indeed,' – I drew closer to him and, ever the compulsive stirrer, returned the conversational lob with a drop-shot – 'and our Jordanian guide's obvious pride in his country is a welcome contrast to the chauvinism of the Israeli guide who brought us from Eilat, wouldn't you say? Even as a Jew I found all that stuff about how the Jordanians would fleece us changing money, rip us off for horse rides down to Petra and subject us to insanitary toilet facilities a bit much to take.' The pensive man looked at me with reinforced thoughtfulness before replying, 'Well, I'm a Jew too and I can't help agreeing with you.'

It had happened, the moment I had been waiting for ever since arriving at Ben Gurion International Airport three days earlier – I had finally bonded with one of my coreligionists. What a delicious and consummate irony that I'd had to quit Zion to apprehend any of my own Jewishness.

The Austrian Jewish writer Walter Abish once wrote a story entitled 'In the English Garden', about a German Jew going back to a small German town that has suffered a convenient, collective amnesia about its role in the Holocaust. On arrival the protagonist finds himself transfixed, looking at the map of the town, experiencing a shocking epiphany. Everything here, he realises, right down to the very rivets that secure the metal map-frame, is German. Teutonism is shot through the material world like words through a stick of rock; it is monadological, this Germanness, every atom of the German world containing within itself an infinity of German aspects and all of them implying the greater, encompassing Germany.

Abish's story is about identity and essentialism, about defining oneself by what one irreducibly is. My problem has always been to know whether what I am is an essential property, or only something arrived at in contrariety; whether my Jewishness is an absolute or a relative construct. Of course, for most of my life I've attempted to avoid the issue, a task made beautifully facile by the aggressive secularism of contemporary English society. The only tangible form my willed ignorance has taken – besides my avoiding any overt ceremonial – has been a determination not to visit either Germany or Israel. Either destination might, I felt, break down the partitions within me and expose poorly insulated psychic cavities.

The German trip eventually came about three years ago, when I went to the Frankfurt Book Fair for a couple of days. Even before the Lufthansa jet had lifted off from Heathrow I was getting the Abish sensation; I was surrounded by German people, German metal, German plastic – even German seat covers; and I was Jewish at last, truly, deeply Jewish. So

Jewish that like some Woody Allenesque character I could feel skull locks sprouting from above my ears, and the leather bands of phylacteries wrapping themselves around my temples. A few seconds more and I was convinced I would start rocking back and forth like some Hasid at the Wailing Wall.

This sensation of Jewishness stayed with me throughout my brief sojourn in Germany. Everywhere I went I saw lumpen figures stuffing themselves with bloody sausage; every face I looked into that was over sixty-five I scrutinised for traces of culpability – overt or covert. But even at the time I realised that this was a negative Jewishness, a Jewishness arrived at out of fear of exclusion – not desire to be included.

In a way there's no mystery about this. When it comes to being Jewish I am not so much deracinated as never racinated to begin with. My mother, who was a second-generation American Jew, quickly slipped the slack cultural bonds of her upbringing, heading off on an exogamous trajectory that led her first into marriage to a WASP American academic, and then into marriage to an Anglican English academic – my father.

When I was growing up in the Hampstead Garden Suburb in the sixties my mother would oscillate, sometimes quite wildly, between protestations of Jewishness – 'We just *are* funnier than other people' – and Jewish superiority – 'You have to ask yourself why it is that Marx, Freud and Einstein were all Jews . . .' – and, conversely, really quite craven denials: 'You aren't *really* Jewish; and people here don't know that I'm Jewish. I mean, I don't look Jewish, and anyway of course there's no such thing as a Jewish look – Chinese Jews look Chinese, you know . . .'

This was the identity she retailed me, one made up in equal parts of Semophilia and that most corrosive of anti-Semitisms: Jewish anti-Semitism. In the last analysis I was a Jew not because I had been circumcised or read my portion of the Torah – neither had happened, rather I'd been christened – nor because I identified myself as being Jewish, but because if the Nazis came back *they* would haul me and my mother off before my father. They would know me for a Jew. There was that, and there was also the fact that Jews claimed – and still do claim – me for their own. Thus I have always been in the peculiar position of being freighted with an identity by two, violently opposed groups; groups that have been internalised within my own psyche.

But if this sounds too dramatic, there is always the limiting constraint of Englishness. Time and again English gentiles would reassure me that I really didn't have to 'go on' about being Jewish, that it really wasn't an issue. But on plenty of occasions when I would take this bait, I'd find that it was poisoned, that the invitation to deny my own Jewishness would be a prelude to induction into cosy, clubbable, mild anti-Semitism – that distinctively English anti-Semitism which pivots eternally on the turncoat phrase 'Some of my best friends . . .' etc. etc.

At school in Finchley my demi-Semitism wasn't that remarkable, but with three gangs naturally formed – the Yocks, the Yids and the Pakis – I found myself teetering unpleasantly on the margins. If I went to synagogue with Jewish friends on Yom Kippur I had to wear a paper skull-cap, which felt so insubstantial atop my seventies bouffant that one hand had to constantly hover over it, lest my pate be exposed to the gaze of a deity I wasn't even sure existed.

As a bloodthirsty twelve-year-old I had followed the progress of the October War on my trannie, in between hits by Bowie and T-Rex, and secretly exulted in the idea that Jews could be tough guys. Those Arabs – I would chortle – don't know what's hit them. Then came politicisation. Along with the unpleasant realisation that Jews could not only be tough guys, but also be aggressive, chauvinistic thugs, came the acknowledge-ment that the Palestinians had a point. More and more wedges were being hammered into a log already split. My Jewishness was now so fractured, my loyalties so broadcast, that apart from drunken sallies into atavism and a conviction that my wiseacre absurdism had a distinctively Semitic cast, my Jewishness came to mean little more than an indicator of disjunction from the oppressive, sheltering sky of England.

The last thing I wanted to do was go to Israel. This, I felt, would, whatever my ambivalences and ambiguities, act like a ferret down either leg of my sembled identity. Would I find myself ululating with the best of them as I shoved prayers into the wall? Or would I become transfixed by the kind of anti-Semitism that I often saw afflicting my mother when we went for late-night hot salt-beef sandwich blow-outs in Golders Green? A visceral anti-Semitism, a rejection of the host body by an organ that felt itself to have been crudely transplanted.

Love conspired to get me to Israel on Christmas night. I didn't object to the two-hour grilling the El Al security staff gave me at Heathrow – they were only doing a job. And anyway, nobody apart from for-hire literary critics has shown that much interest in my work for years: 'Tell me, Mr Self, what kind of satire is it that you write exactly?' Nor could I reasonably object when they confiscated my miniature camera and the face-off for my car stereo – it was stupid of me to bring them in the first place.

The same kind of understanding of the excruciating position in which the Israelis find themselves stayed with me throughout my short trip, and cushioned me through repeated interrogations by officials of one sort or another, who suspected the extempore nature of my decision to visit a land notionally holy to me on two counts. The Israelis feel themselves surrounded by enemies and percolated by them as well. The borders of the Jewish homeland are more like the holes in a colander than any straightforward zoning. As I arrived, the whole dog of state was about to get a serious wagging from the tail-end, four hundred and fifty Jewish 'settlers' who have elected to sabotage a possible Israeli-Palestinian deal over the disputed township of Hebron: a state within a state within a state; a peculiarly vertiginous sovereignty.

There was that understanding, but there was no epiphany for me, no antidote to the Frankfurt experience, no acknowledgement of belonging to a people, a faith, or even some nebulous 'look'. I stood in front of the Wailing Wall and stared at it with emphatically secular eyes, impressed but not awed. The Dome of the Rock affected me more – for here was an achieved building of indisputable aesthetic quality, rather than a buttress of a building demolished two millennia ago that cannot be rebuilt for reasons of Messianism. Indeed, overall, the impression the inhabitants of Jerusalem give, in all their polyglot diversity – Muslims, Jews, Christians, of all nations and peoples – is of understudies to an overwhelming history, constantly attempting to make the right gesture, the proper entrance, as they revolve around a tiny enclave where nothing is *not* sacred.

In Jerusalem we stayed in the Christian Quarter, but once we headed south to Eilat I began to experience the peculiar quality of Israeli boorishness. These may sound like tiny, insignificant gripes, but somehow they did add up to more than the sum of their parts. On buses people constantly pushed and shoved with no demurral; adolescent boys shouted and bayed as if to deliberately annoy everyone around them; the women friends I travelled with were crudely propositioned both sexually and fiscally. (One friend who refused to pay an exorbitant sum for a cab to a tourist site was told she was 'a lazy girl' and should work harder so as to be able to spend more money in Israel.) In Eilat itself, Christmas had been marked with a defiant embrace of racial stereotyping: all the charges in the hotel had been put up by 10 per cent!

The sense of arrogant offhandedness that so many Israelis – and in particular the younger ones – seemed hell-bent on projecting inevitably made me wonder about what had put the Swiftian 'yahu' into Benjamin Netanyahu's name. Why, I asked myself, did Israeli parents not teach their kids to at least be polite to those European and American tourists who might reasonably be expected to have some sympathy for their situation? Surely this pervasive rudeness wasn't simply a reflection of kibbutz egalitarianism? Spartan, no-frills social living? For it grated so terribly within the context of obvious affluence. (The Israeli teenagers with whom I shared a row of seats on the return flight, and who were going to London on a group trip, had armed themselves with one thousand cigarettes a head for their London sojourn.)

No, the more I was chivvied and bullied – in Tel Aviv the cabbie didn't want to take me to the Yemenite Quarter: 'I know somewhere better! You will go there!' – the more I saw the Israeli mentality as being that of the laager. It's no wonder ties have been traditionally strong with white South Africa, because like the Boers, certain sections of the Israeli population have decided to define themselves in racial contrast to their – Arab – neighbours. This – as my mother could have told them – is a spurious homogeneity. Israel is teeming with Jews of all shapes and sizes, from the dark, Ethiopian Falashas to blond kiddies who wouldn't look out of place in the choir of King's College, Cambridge. By attempting to make Jews more than a loose amalgamation of peoples, some Israelis have been party to a most bogus and insidious nationalism.

The ironies that danced attendance on me for five days reached a giddy climax as, exhausted, I waited in the departure lounge for my flight out. Looking around me at all the people rushing, clamouring, pushing and yammering, I was visited with my belated epiphany – but not the one I wanted. They all look the same, I thought to myself. They all have the same peculiarly repugnant, definably *Jewish* faces. It had happened – I'd experienced a pure hit of true anti-Semitism. Of course, it wasn't really anti-Semitism – it was anti-Israeli-ism. The trouble is for a lot of the time neither they – nor we – can tell the difference.

Observer, January 1997

95

Restaurant review: Blooms, 90 Whitechapel High Street, London E1

So it's Sunday evening and you're feeling – how can I put it – just a little depressed, a little shut in. The clocks have gone back and you're imprisoned in an annexe of childhood. It feels as if there's nothing to look forward to but homework tonight and then school tomorrow. The sensation is so acute you half imagine that downstairs your parents have started to anatomise their relationship, without troubling to anaesthetise it first. Christ! How you long to be grown-up. How you long to escape all this.

Well, if you really want to crank this galvanic generator of recollection up to full pitch, you could do worse than a Sunday evening trip to Blooms kosher restaurant. There's the more famous one, within crawling distance of Aldgate tube station, and a subsidiary, no more than twenty Mercedes-lengths from Golders Green tube station.

When I was a child, my mother, a woman whose Semitic anti-Semitism (the most virulent kind) took the form of her frequently admonishing her children that 'No one knows I'm Jewish', would sometimes crack – usually on a Sunday evening – and take us for hot salt-beef sandwiches at Blooms in Golders Green. The thick, white rye bread; the slabs of stringy unginess; the aroma at once meaty and wholesome; all contrived to make me believe that there must be some special kind of Jewish cow that produced salt beef. A bovine wearing bifocals and cracking wise.

On this particular school night we opted for Whitechapel, on the grounds that if you want East End authenticity you need to be within chanting distance of Cable Street.

The frontage of Blooms is redolent of the 1950s – glass, stainless steel and neon. Inside, the large, lozenge-shaped room was empty save for rank upon rank of snowily clothed tables. One side of the restaurant is dominated by a huge photo-mural of Petticoat Lane, shot from the air. The other side is entirely mirrored. So despite the lack of clientele, we still felt as if we were in a lively street scene.

Light oozed from overhead, its source tucked away underneath some ceiling coping. The cutlery coruscated, and on each side plate was inscribed the slogan 'Buy Blooms Best Beef'. A waiter bustled over, white-jacketed, hair brilliantined, and deposited a yard of rye bread on our table. (You can imagine a sort of Jewish pub jollification: 'Who Can Eat the Yard of Rye Fastest?') Chopped liver followed hard on its heels, looking so brown and smooth that it might have been removed directly from the chicken using an ice-cream scoop.

East European Jewish cuisine is, as even the most ignorant yock knows, heavily dependent on chicken stock. So dependent, indeed, that it is rumoured that beneath the Knesset there is a secret reservoir of some four million cubic metres of chicken stock, in case of emergencies. Our party opted for the full stock of stock options. I had the kreplach, little ravioliesque nodules floating in chicken broth. One of my companions had the *heimishe* barley soup, a marvellously glutinous and glaucous bowl of macerated vegetables (in chicken broth), which reminded me of the famous 'creamed corn' scene in David Lynch's *Twin Peaks*.

Another of our number had the knedelach, or matzo balls. These also – what a surprise – came in a chicken broth. In fact, they dwarfed the chicken broth, standing out of it like doughy planetoids that had fallen leadenly to Earth.

By now, my girlfriend, known throughout north-west London as 'the shiksas' shiksa', was beginning to respond to the ambience. 'Do you think the Jews invented school dinners?' she said with effortless ingenuousness. Of course, *heimishe* really means 'home cooking', but I suppose you could string together an argument of the form: we are the people of the Book, the exegetists supreme, so is it any wonder that our home cooking tastes like school dinners?

She began to make heavy weather of her meatballs. So heavy that one of the waiters came barrelling over to our table to ask if anything was wrong. 'If you don't like them,' he said, 'I'll take them away and you can have anything else you want from the menu.' Not exactly the sort of treatment any of us used to get at school – or at home for that matter. Others of our number had locked antlers with turkey schnitzels of prodigious size. So big, in fact, that they had the appearance of whole turkeys that had been entombed alive after some volcano had erupted breadcrumbs.

I, wisely, stuck with the speciality of the house and had salt beef. This came in pastrami-thin slices, together with a potato latke of uncompromising rigidity. The salt beef was more delicate than I remembered, but then conceivably I've become more robust. For veg we had a sweet mush of butter beans, carrots and fruit known as *tzimmes*. This is better than it sounds and goes with the salt beef much as a condiment rather than a conventional bit of greenery. We also had a great platter of pickled cucumbers, or 'wallies' as they are known in the East End. (Arguably, I am also known as a wally in the East End, so a nicer confirmation of the fact that you are what you eat it is difficult to imagine.)

We were all feeling a bit puffed up by now, clasped within the suety bosom of Semitic cuisine, but none the less we pressed on and had halva, apple strudel and lokshen pudding to finish. The lokshen pudding was particularly worthy of note. Some of our number claimed that it tasted of Jif, but I thought the lemony acerbity nicely complemented the wedgy, noodly look of the dessert. (Lokshen are egg pasta noodles, used in soups as well as puddings.)

The halva came in its box – what better way to ensure freshness and quality, as well as advertise the exact size of the mark-up (the price tag was still on it). The apple strudel was dense and leaden, but for all that rather tasty. It fell down into my stomach accelerating at 32ft per second per second. So heavy was this strudel that I feared looking down, in case I saw a corner of it visibly poking through my stomach wall. It reminded me of the chocolate cake my grandmother's cook Doris used to bake. This was of such uncompromising weightiness that it was a family myth that a slice was responsible for holing the *Titanic*.

Blooms helpfully indicates on the menu the ABV of the insipid lager and the robust Israeli wine it serves. We had a little of both and finished off with milkless coffee. Blooms is supervised by the Beth Din, which means that rabbis watch you eating from behind one-way mirrors.

The service was not just *heimishe*, but redolent of a long-established family business (the restaurant has been open since the 1920s). The bill for four came to £110 including service, and while I wouldn't exactly say my palate was titivated, it was certainly sedated and I was able to go back to tackle my homework with great gusto.

Observer, November 1995

96

Restaurant review: Virgin Flight VS1 Newark to London

Some years ago, I suggested in a magazine article that I would be prepared to perform a highly unorthodox sexual act on Richard Branson, if he would see to it that in future I was always upgraded on his airline.

It would be churlish of me to complain that he hasn't fulfilled his side of an unasked-for bargain, but I still can't help feeling aggrieved. The thing is that it's not simply Upper Class on Virgin Atlantic that I covet – I want to be a part of the whole Virgin concept, the Virgin ethos, the Virgin *thing*. I see myself making inspirational corporate videos, wearing a woolly and sporting a trowel-shaped beard exactly like Our Leader's. I think I'm just the kind of person the organisation needs: I'm youthful, go-getting, entrepreneurial yet caring, and, most important of all – I'm a virgin.

I mean it – I really am. Apart from the aforementioned promise to Richard, I haven't plighted my penetrative troth. I'm saving myself. If it doesn't sound grandiose, I cherish a vision of being enshrined as a kind of corporate mascot: 'the Virgin virgin'. I would be called upon to open new megastores and bless the fuselages of new 757s. My innocent features would be incorporated into a snappy logo. I would be entirely surrounded by Virgin products, enshrined – as it were – in virginity.

Obviously, this peculiar marriage between the state religion of Ancient Rome and modern marketing couldn't continue indefinitely. I'm thirty-five now; at best I could ask for only five years as flagship Vestal. So the day would come when my splendidly caparisoned red-and-white barge would gently cruise up the canal to Little Venice, and there he would be, grinning as broadly as ever, a dear little hot-air balloon appliquéd on the front of his woolly. He would hand me from my barge to his, then introduce me finally – and beautifully – to the estate of manhood.

All these thoughts and visions ran through my head as I queued at the check-in for Virgin Atlantic's red-eye flight from New York to London last Sunday night. Has Richard been paying attention to the little billets-doux I have been addressing to him through the press? He'd been good enough to stump up an economy return with a *potential* upgrade – but would it materialise? 'Any fear of an upgrade?' I asked the charming, dapper, smiling Virgin employee who was tapping the keyboard. 'Sorry, sir, the flight's full.'

For some seconds I was stunned with the rejection, but then I summoned myself. I would still be inside something of Richard's – and that's what matters. And beyond that, the truth is that Virgin Atlantic is really an extremely good airline. You get on the plane, they start up the engines, they fly you through the air. At the other end they put the plane down on the tarmac, and that's pretty much the end of it. I don't know about you, but that's all I really want out of an airline.

I mean, you wouldn't seriously want an airline that made its planes like restaurants – people talking nineteen to the dozen, being pretentious over the wine list, arguing over the bill, the waiters snotty, the food inedible – now would you? On the other hand, you seldom have to sit in a restaurant for six hours all facing in the same direction and watching widescreen films that have been 'digitally reformatted' for a video screen the size of a fag packet.

People always grouse about airline food – and with good reason. It's pretty much crap. But then look at the logistics of serving a choice of three items to some six hundred people, to whom you have access only down narrow, jolting walkways. I think that on the whole, the broad mass of air travellers have enormous sympathy for the hard work that cabin crew do; it's the only possible explanation for our not bursting into loud, sarcastic laughter when we witness their hairstyles. (As my companion on the New York jaunt put it *sotto voce*, 'Man, that's really *bad* bun action.')

We may have been barred from Upper Class, but we were allowed into the Virgin Clubhouse at Newark, and what an excellent clubhouse it was. There were newspapers, there was a free local-call facility, there were comfy seats and charming *faux* virgins. Most importantly, there was a free bar. My companion had difficulty levering me out of the place. I had several hits of Virgin vodka (it's great – like other vodkas, but purer!), two of which were needed to gulp down Marvin's Mix.

Marvin, a New Yorker friend, had been primed by me to assemble some sort of mixture of medicaments to sort out a little difficulty I'm currently having with flying – it terrifies me. This is only intermittent, but I'd had a bit of a turn on the flight out and didn't want anything to spoil the Virgin organisation's perception of me on the return leg. Obviously, my status as the Virgin virgin would be tricky if it were to become known.

Marvin gave me a handful of things he described as 'a galaxy of gland-scrambling go-go comfits – but all legal and all guaranteed to do the job'. Remind me never again to trust a man who has an omega symbol shaved into the hair at the nape of his neck.

Take-off was as smooth as could be wished for, and as the lights of Long Island slid away beneath us, I leafed through the in-flight magazine, sipped another Virgin vodka and basked in the consummately virginal ambience (if that's not a contradiction in terms). Then it hit me – Marvin's Mix. Suddenly I felt like an ancient Norse warrior clicking mead horns with the gods in Valhalla; I felt like an entire Busby Berkeley chorus line, high-kicking its way down a giant brass staircase; I felt like a wildebeest shot by a high-powered rifle bullet on the veldt; I felt like calling my therapist.

What I did instead was eat. I ate *all* of my dinner, even the hideous wedge of cheese and the dessert bloblet with aerated cream. I ate the roll, I munched the crackers, I devoured the salad and I positively romped through something allegedly curried. Then, as my companion had yielded to the intensity of this situation by falling asleep, I ate all of her dinner as well. It could have been a beef and ale pie served with a dumpling, creamed potato, cabbage and carrots – or it could have been something else altogether. It didn't matter; the important thing was that it was warm and comforting.

And as I ate, I found the plane around me transformed. I was wrong: it isn't that you wouldn't want a plane that was like a restaurant – a plane really *is* a kind of restaurant. And so much better than the terrestrial ones. You don't have to look at your fellow diners, the waiting staff are as keen to keep things quick as you are, there's no bewildering menu choice and there are no hidden service charges. All right, the décor is a little bleak, but as everyone can watch their fag packets it hardly matters. And as for this business of all diners facing the same way, it helps to reduce conversation, something devoutly to be desired.

Apparently there was fairly bad turbulence on the flight and a lot of people freaked out, but I was oblivious – I'd done it, I'd eaten two airline meals at one sitting, perhaps the only person ever to have done so. Surely Richard would grin even more broadly? Sod the upgrade, probably the next time I go to New York he'll fly me himself. I wonder what kind of meals they serve on the balloon?

Observer, November 1996

97

In Ray Bradbury's prescient science-fiction novel of 1953, *Fahrenheit 451*, the firemen of the future don't put out fires – they start them in order to burn books. In this painfully delineated utilitarian dystopia, trivial information is good, while knowledge and ideas are bad. The fire Captain, Beatty, explains it this way: 'Give the people contests they win by remembering the words to more popular songs . . . Don't give them any slippery stuff like philosophy or sociology to tie things up with. That way lies melancholy.'

The novel's protagonist, Guy Montag, is a book-burning fireman undergoing a crisis of faith. His wife spends all day with her television 'family', imploring Montag to work harder so that they can afford a fourth wall-sized television monitor. Each morning a script of a kind of real-time soap opera is delivered to the Montags' house, with lines already written in for Mrs Montag. She sits in front of three walls of television images all day, and from time to time one of the actors in the 'family' turns to her and says, 'So, what do you think . . . ?' And she interpolates her own lines.

Even from this brief synopsis, I think you'll have no difficulty in agreeing with me that *Fahrenheit 451* presents a far more accurate view of the society implied by Channel 4's hit game show *Big Brother* than the George Orwell novel *Nineteen Eighty-Four* from which it takes its name. *Big Brother* comes to an end this evening, after a nine-week run. The final three contestants – Craig, the pawky scouser; Anna, the lesbian, skateboarding former Catholic noviciate; and 'Big Daddy' Darren, the black father-of-three with a nice line in narcissism – will find out who the viewers have voted the 'winner'. One of them will then pick up the £70,000 prize money, while the other two will have to amortise whatever notoriety the show brought them into cash.

Within a couple of weeks of *Big Brother* beginning, the show eased its way into the popular consciousness of the nation. Although only five million or so viewers actually tuned in, the whole implicit concept of death-by-voyeurism seized the imagination not only of couch potatoes, but also of armchair pundits such as myself. While Tracy, my three-year-old's nanny, was happy, downstairs in the playroom, to discuss the character and motivation of the participants – who was to be nominated that week by the contestants from their own number, and who, therefore, would be 'evicted' come Friday – I've been sat upstairs in my office, evoking the name 'Big Brother' as a synecdoche of the British polity, or as an enactment of McLuhanite prophecies, or as a terminal symptom of the death of British television.

Even when the 'Nasty Nick' revelations were transpiring, Channel 4's ratings didn't climb much above seven million, and yet the *Big Brother* phenomenon achieved a huge degree of resonance, like a coaxial cable lashed between high and low culture, and vigorously bowed by contemporaneity. In the *Independent on Sunday* last week, my colleague David Aaronovitch wrote an inspired critique of the current state of British television, to which, as the paper's miserable television critic, I could only nod my head in weary assent. He pointed out that with the Balkanisation of the networks, not only were programmers facing a ratings war, driving them to worse and worse excesses of cheap titillation masquerading as entertainment, but with the very stage upon which high-quality drama might be enacted progressively shrinking, it was questionable whether such productions would even continue to be made.

It's an irony worth noting that the Reithian broadcasting culture, the heyday of which Aaronovitch so eloquently mourned, itself matured in the wartime culture of propaganda that inspired Orwell's *Nineteen Eighty-Four*. For 'the Ministry of Truth' read 'Broadcasting House'. And anyway, the old three-channel television duopoly in Britain had become a state corporatist anomaly in a nation intent on gorging itself on the Big Mac of global capitalism. But during the last few years, it hasn't only been the market that's driven television standards – with some exceptions – into a downward spiral; we've also entered a new era of virtuality, where the interpenetration of a plethora of communications media, from CCTV and mobile phones to webcams and cable channels, has created an environment in which never before have so many watched so many others, doing so very little.

In media-studies faculties at the moment, the debate rages as to whether Marshall McLuhan was right, and these new media are themselves the message – the message being 'buy more media, and everything that they advertise' – or whether, rather, his pabulum should be idealistically reversed to read 'the message is the medium', implying that the global reach and accessibility of the new media will mean a new golden age of participatory democracy. Frankly, I think that the latter view, given streets full of people chatting purposelessly on mobiles, our own Government financing social services through phone franchises, and the stock exchange booming off the anticipation of on-line retailing, is sheer California dreaming.

No, we're living through a period when the face-to-face bonds that personalised even mass societies and made them bearable are being transmogrified into the anonymous encounters of virtual space. *Big Brother* stands as the acme of this culture of depersonalised anonymity – which explains the painful resonance of its banal triviality. I've watched a fair bit of the show over the summer, and not only for professional reasons. I've absolutely no doubt that the way the contestants were selected for *Big Brother*, together with the editing of the 24x7 footage from umpteen concealed video cameras, has provided us with a perfect biopsy of the cancer that as I write is hypostasising throughout our culture.

It's a culture of equality all right, for the contestants are equally unquestioning, equally sheep-like, equally directionless, equally lacking in anything that passes for a social conscience or a spiritual value. Self-selecting for narcissism, exhibitionism and a sorrowful dependency on the good opinion of others, the *Big Brother* contestants are the first cohort among other equals, in a wholly statistical nation.

It's no accident that the 'tasks' the contestants are asked to perform are so redolent of other television shows. Whether doing a turn from *The Krypton Factor*, *The Generation Game* or *Countdown*, these poor saps are only pirouetting in a hall of video monitors. This is our 'family', and like the twenty-to-thirtysomething clans depicted in other popular shows such as *Friends* and *Ally McBeal*, it's made up of 'kidults', those adult children of juvenescence, the scurf on the collapsing wave of the baby boom, who are intent on stretching the elastic of their promiscuous, intoxicated adolescence, until senility snaps it back in their faces.

Watching *Big Brother* is best done by mixed groups of parents and prepubescent children. All can revel in this enactment of a seventy-day sleep-over, where no one bothers to get out of their pyjamas except to sunbathe or dress up. Oh yes, it is heartening to see that in the brave new world of Blair, a black contestant and a gay contestant have made it into the last three, but what this suggests to me is that tolerance in our society has only been won at the cost of diversity. The extent to which the viewers haven't been prejudiced against these minorities is exactly the same as the extent to which they no longer offer any alternative lifestyle choice. With everyone middle-class, childless and a restful shade of beige, we're living not so much in a melting-pot as in a Cup a Soup. Or so we wish to believe.

It's no surprise to me that *Big Brother* was originated in the Netherlands, that claustrophobic cockpit of social innovation, where an ancient culture of cheese-making supports an ephemeral one of utter cheesiness. Nor is it any wonder that the format for this show has replicated throughout the globe, like some awful media virus. It offers us the spectacle of pure voyeurism, and its interactivity leads the way to new forms of narration that will no longer require any suspension of disbelief.

In traditional story-telling, whether on page, stage or screen, the audience is invited to emotionally identify themselves with a protagonist whose fate is determined by a *deus ex machina*. But in television shows utilising ordinary people, the action of which is propelled by collective decision-making, there is no need for viewers to exercise that feat of creative empathy, whereby they can 'become' a Prince of Denmark suffering a proto-existential crisis, or a nineteenth-century aristocratic Russian woman tormented by sexual desire – let alone surrender themselves to dictates of chance, or fate. Like mere servomechanisms, extensions of the wilfulness of their contemplators, the pawn-participants in these projects will be required to enact increasingly grotesque playlets to satisfy the jaded palates of their manipulators.

Make no mistake, in terms of what the genre has to offer, *Big Brother* is a mere lukewarm entrée. Novelty, combined with the vestiges of our national rectitude, prevented anything from getting too steamy or nasty in the *Big Brother* house, but in the future, opportunities to interact with sexual and violent experiences will become a *sine qua non* of such shows, as the next tumbrel of entertainment to trundle on to our screens – Channel 5's *Prisoner* – will amply demonstrate.

Yes, we should be worried. The atrophy of the empathetic muscles necessary for the appreciation of traditional narrative is happening in step with the development of entertainment media – the Internet chat room, the interactive television show – that substitute anonymous equivalence for personalised identification. Why bother labouring to translate your being across space, time, gender, ethnicity or religion, when you can watch some bimbo exactly like the one next door plucking her bikini line on live television? Or better still, on a little postcard-sized vignette, in the corner of your PC's screen, while you employ the Intel inside to multitask your way through the next spreadsheet or corporate report.

For me *Big Brother* was over two weeks ago anyway, with Claire, the breast-enhanced flirt interest, sent packing. There was no doubting that poor Mel, the least psychically secure contestant, and the subject of a hate campaign by the herd without, would be the next to go. There was a hideous moment when, as Mel was sprung from behind the razor wire (and how disgusting the setting for this bathos has been, a kind of Ikea Belsen, marooned in Bromley-by-Bow), she heard the lowing of the bovine punters bellowing 'Whore!' and 'Slut!' It took her a split second to adjust to the correct posture of puppetry, and then she leapt up and down like a teenager afflicted with mass hysteria at a pop concert, and began screaming the triumphant affirmation of the eradication of her soul.

Now that it's down to the final triumvirate of trivia, the popular vote will go with the man who best understands and exemplifies populism, Craig, while the dissenting vote will go with Anna. And *Big Brother* being the kind of television show that it is – veritably powered by populism – I hardly think it likely that dissent will carry the day. A few nights ago, chatting to my ten-year-old boy about *Big Brother*, I asked him why it was that the contestants hadn't banded together ages ago and smashed all the cameras in the house save for one. Then they could've taken over the means of the production of the show and broadcast their own demands to the nation. 'They couldn't do that,' he said; 'the people who make it would've switched it off.' 'Ah,' I replied, 'they couldn't afford to do that – it would've lost them hundreds of thousands of pounds in revenue – and anyway, it'd make great television.' He looked at me with the pitying expression of someone who's being parented by an anarchistic dinosaur, while I looked back at him with revulsion at the media dupe I'd spawned.

Marshall McLuhan said that we advance into the future imposing our historic archetypes of communication upon the new media that we invent; thus we steer the car using the rear-view mirror. I think he had a point, but what I can see in the rear-view mirror is Bradbury's *Fahrenheit 451*, and another episode featuring the 'family' is about to be screened.

Independent, September 2000

98

When we drive around Hyde Park Corner, the kids and I, our attention never fails to be grabbed by the triumphal banner that now surmounts the netting covering Constitution Arch. (And isn't the netting around building works a pleasant addition to the face of the city, resembling as it does a veil hiding the crumbling maquillage of some old slapper?) This banner reads 'English Heritage – Nobody Looks After English Heritage Better', or some such tautologous bullshit. I've pointed out to Alexis (aged ten), that if English Heritage cannot be banked upon to look after English heritage, then who the hell can? And this insight into the follies of former grandeur has grabbed his imagination to such a degree that now, when we swoop up on to Park Lane, it is invariably to the accompaniment of his chortles.

I confess, I may not have hothoused my kids in any other branch of learning, but when it comes to irony they're true prodigies. I daresay in a few years' time Lex will go on the run with a mime troupe, and release a press statement saying, 'I had to get away from the relentless need to recognise bathos, the tyranny of the knowing aside, and the eternal quest for deflation . . . I needed to find myself with people who wear leotards without shame while impersonating daisies . . .' Good luck to him. It could have been worse: I could have drawn his attention to the fact that the arch derives its moniker from Constitution Hill, which in turn is named not for the codification of the governing principle (since we have none), but – probably apocryphally – for Charles II's habit of strolling there.

Only a completely headless monarch would want to stroll around Hyde Park Corner nowadays, while the juxtaposition of EH's banner and Decimus Burton's overgrown trilithon puts me in mind of another part of their demesne that they're in the process of screwing up.

What are we to make of the protracted cock-up at Stonehenge? Last week's *Building Design* described it as a 'long saga', following the announcement that EH is 'starting from scratch' on the procurement of the new visitor centre. The considerable amounts of money and time spent by two partnerships, both of which had been given the impression by EH that they'd won, are now effectively traduced by the announcement of a new competition. The wonk at EH says that neither partnership came up with a scheme that 'satisfies all of [the] . . . criteria for a world-class heritage visitor centre'; while Lord St John of Fawsley proclaims, 'It's such an important site that I think the Prime Minister himself should intervene and take charge of it.'

Me too. Given the content of TB's leaked memo, I can't see why he wouldn't want to take charge. After all, he feels the need for the public to see him in the vanguard of every 'defence' initiative and drug bust; why the hell shouldn't he tote a few breeze blocks and barrowloads of sharp sand, just so as we know he cares as much about the most important archaeological site in Britain as we do?

Or perhaps we should all be a little bit more philosophic about Stonehenge? While the most recent radiocarbon-dating techniques suggest that the monument itself was built over at least fifteen hundred years, who are we to quibble about a mere quarter of a century being taken on the visitor centre? Anyway, the prospect of an interminable wait while the mighty sarsen stones of bureaucracy are dragged upright, and the blue stones of finance are knapped until they're significantly reduced, teases us with the notion that, in several millennia to come, archaeologists may find themselves locked in dispute over what precisely went on here.

The report of one of their digs might read as follows: 'We excavated a narrow trench, leading from the faint remains of a bitumen-surfaced cart-track, across the collapsed tunnel which connects the concrete bunker we have already disinterred with the far older remains of the megalithic circle. Certainly, there does seem to be a relationship between the two sites, despite radiocarbon dating that places the construction of the bunker over three thousand years later than the megalithic circle. Could the remains we found close to the midden of discarded, flattened metal vessels supply the explanation? The position the bones were found in indicates that this man, aged around fifty, died while seated, his fingers clutched around a residue of wood-pulp fibre. It's invidious to draw too many conclusions from this until English Heritage grant further excavation permissions – permissions that should be forthcoming by the year 4563.'

Building Design, July 2000

99

So, whatever scepticism remained in our dear leader's sainted brow concerning the Millennium Dome has now evaporated, like some dew of uncertainty burnt off by the hot sun of reason. As Lewis Carroll wrote, 'O frabjous day! Callooh! Callay!'

I wonder – purely in passing – whether Our Leader's attitude towards other monumental British buildings has undergone a similar conversion experience. I like to imagine him waking up at dawn, in Number 11, and taking a Wordsworthian stroll across Westminster Bridge. Instead of him allowing his keen, metaphoric mind to focus and flirt with the ruckled, glaucous surface of the Thames, I like to picture him transfixed by the beauty of St Thomas's Hospital.

Yes – Tone would think – this isn't a building that should stand for only a few years, it should endure into the next millennium, a potent symbol of . . . what exactly? In a very important sense, in our culture, the hospital is the primal structure, the architectural alpha and omega. It is both our womb and our grave, a giant ziggurat full of life-sustaining technology (and increasingly life-destructive superviruses. Indeed, it could be not so much a nice as a cosmic irony if, in some far distant future, a Sir Edward Carstairs-type archaeologist were to succumb to the mummy's curse when excavating a long-buried maternity hospital.)

I myself was born in the old Charing Cross Hospital, which now no longer exists – or rather it's been relocated right across London to the Fulham Palace Road, where its sub-Bauhausian irrationality appears subject to more than the usual depredations of under-funding.

That's the thing about hospitals; in the absence of an ecclesiastical architecture that either operates from the top down, imposing an arcane architectonic on the people from above, or expresses the core spirituality of the people in vernacular terms (one thinks of the superb, carved-angel ceiling at Blythburgh Church in Suffolk), it is left to the hospitals to express the relationship between eschatology and the built environment.

And what a messy business it is. The architects of modern hospitals may set out, with the best will in the world, to reconcile form and function, only to find that their work is consistently suborned, altered and undermined – even as it's undertaken. Provision must be made for extra wards here, a new kind of laboratory needs to be built over there, and in the meantime the funds necessary to sustain this particular clinic have quite simply evaporated.

No wonder that the experience of walking around most large, modern hospitals is so profoundly disconcerting. Yes, there may well be electric doors triggered by photocells – but they're defunct, so that the doors are wedged open with orange plastic milk crates. Indeed, the atrium is a fine idea, introducing as it does a well of space and light into what might otherwise be a diseased termite heap. On the other hand, it's no help at all that the atrium is overgrown with weeds, and features a Brancusi-style bronze which some imitator knocked off while at stool.

The ranks of escalators suggest a speedy, efficient rise to the different departments of this health store, yet inevitably they're out of order. And when you gain the upper storeys you find yourself wandering through abandoned wards with stripped bedsteads, and then barely functioning wards where the patients are tethered by life-supporting shackles. Naturally, there is no one to blame for any of this. Hospitals must always be built in a spirit of optimism; there's little point in setting out purposely to build a necropolis – unless you're a Parsee, that is.

None the less, what strikes me most when I visit hospitals – and I do it no more nor less than anyone else – is the way the ebb and flow of funding, and the restructuring of fiscal administration, have queerly synergised with their monumentalism. The solution to the closure of this department and the establishment of that lab is to enhance the sense of the structure as a mucilage of little units. Nowadays almost every major hospital is surrounded by its own *favela*, or shantytown of Portakabins.

Listen, I'm not going to make a great stink about this; I understand all too well the pressures everyone concerned is under: the determination of the tax-paying public to have complete and free palliation of everything that ails them. But still, I can't help feeling that a truly attractive, integrated hospital might well go some way to inspiring the patient with confidence.

In the meanwhile, with their John Menzies franchises, and cash points, and coffee shops, the big hospitals increasingly resemble air terminals for the dying.

Building Design, June 1998

100

Flying into Los Angeles International Airport (known colloquially, and rather queasily, as LAX) can be a daunting experience. On a clear day, it almost certainly won't be clear. The plane will make a lazy circuit as it descends, turning far out over the Pacific and then running in over Santa Monica Bay. From twenty thousand feet the city will be as oceanic as . . . the ocean – and you won't be too bothered about its complexion. But once the descent has begun in earnest, the effects of the massive smog bank that blankets the Los Angeles area become all too obvious. From ten thousand feet the city appears to have been subjected to a hideous gas attack, rendering the streets, the houses, the freeways, all leprous and distempered. Bright lights have aureoles around them – and it's difficult to imagine that anything not equipped with an aqualung is breathing down there.

As the plane hunkers down into this miasma – it gets worse. By the time you're about five thousand feet from touchdown you're seriously worrying whether or not it's worth landing, or if the captain is going to come on the PA saying, 'We'll be rerouting this flight today to somewhere you'll be able to *breathe* . . .' – but then suddenly you're through the smog bank; or rather – you're *in* the smog bank, and so can no longer appreciate quite how bilious it really is.

One of the great ironies of Los Angeles – for me – is that this aerial view, occluded by pollution, more or less corresponds to a pictorial map that I was given by my publisher's escort on my first tour of Los Angeles. This woman has the thankless task of ferrying visiting writers from interview, to reading, to bar, and then – usually in a fireman's lift – to bed. The map she gave me was entitled 'Literary Los Angeles', and showed an idealised, anachronistic gathering of writers who have been resident in the sprawl; all the way from Thomas Mann to Joan Didion, taking in Aldous Huxley and William Faulkner along the way. The writers were depicted in evening dress, gathered round an enormous map of the city, with their residences indicated by bursts of light on the murky grid.

The trouble is, by the time I've got to Los Angeles on an America-wide literary tour, the only writer I'm really capable of identifying with is the deranged eponymous hero of the Coen brothers' film *Barton Fink*. This poor playwright, transplanted from New York to wartime LA, becomes increasingly loopy as he stalks the garishly wallpapered hallways and corridors of a monolithic hotel. His meetings with the studio boss who's flown him out there are abusive bordering on violent; and a psychopath in the next room is intent on landing him with a gift-wrapped severed head.

In the past the only way I've found of 'taking control' in LA is to hire a car as soon as I hit the ground. At the wheel of a big, sloppy Thunderbird, or Corvette, bucketing along Sepulveda Boulevard, the Hollywood Hills banking up ahead, I feel the city looks as it should, the car's windscreen supplying the framing normally provided by the cinema screen. And that's really the only way to treat the place – as a movie. It's no wonder that

Christopher Isherwood, the original proponent of the 'I Am a Camera' approach to literature, should have ended up living here for decades.

But this time there was no car rental for me. This was to do with the fact that on my previous trip, having pulled out of a petrol station on Santa Monica Boulevard, I found myself mysteriously heading the wrong way into four lanes of oncoming traffic. Desperate to rectify my dense, Britisher mistake, I endeavoured to persevere by heading over the central reservation. Sparks flew as transmission scraped over concrete. As I hit the other carriageway there was the joyful 'whoo-whoop!' of a siren. Images of Rodney King-style beatings flitted across my inner eye. I feverishly estimated my alcohol intake for that evening, and prepared to meet my LAPD nemesis. 'ID?' was all he said, while I, as to the manor born, went into English upper-class-twit mode without dropping a beat. Offering him a credit card, I stuttered, 'I'm awfully sorry, officer – this is all I appear to have on me.'

The helmeted motorcycle cop – all leather and leathery attitude – examined my Visa card for some time, before handing it back to me with the ultimate condemnation: 'This isn't ID – it's a piece of shit.' Then he turned on his heel and departed.

Since then I've felt more comfortable in cabs. Cabs that bucket you along the illimitable freeways, from bizarre interview to awkward confrontation. On one trip I was interviewed sitting on a tiny dais, set up on a vast sound stage, in a hangar-sized studio in the San Fernando Valley, by a large woman called Connie Francis. She was heavily made up, and swathed in what might have been chiffon. She was also brilliantly informed, highly literate, and gave me one of the best interviews I've ever had in my career.

The same went for the utterly peculiar duo who interviewed me for a public broadcasting service radio station next to Universal City in Hollywood. She was almost obese; he was absolutely diminutive. While the – live – interview was in progress, this mismatched pair commenced stroking and fondling each other with great deliberation. You couldn't have seen anything odder on Venice beach; and the weirdest thing was, that despite the on-air petting they never missed a cue.

But on this trip all I had to do was make it to my hotel, the Château Marmont, rest up, and then head out to do a reading at Skylight Books, one of the oldest – and most beautiful – bookstores in LA.

The Château Marmont is a balm to the touring writer afflicted with Barton Fink syndrome. There is no garish wallpaper, there are no peculiar staff, and if there are psychopaths in adjoining rooms they keep themselves to themselves. This is the kind of hotel where in addition to a copiously stocked minibar, there is a wicker basket in your room with a selection of half-bottles of gin, vodka and whisky. I haven't felt so relaxed since I checked into a hotel in São Paulo, Brazil, and found that the minibar was called the Self Bar. Full justification – if ever any were needed.

The classic Hollywood tale for the visiting writer goes something like this. You arrive at LAX to be met by a stretch limo which will convey you to your meeting with the Enormously Powerful Studio Head at the Beverly Wilshire. But, somewhere between the airport and the hotel, the EPSH has read three pages of your novel and realised he doesn't want to film it. On arriving at the Beverly Wilshire you are unceremoniously extracted from the limo, inserted into a two-door Fiat driven by a hebrephrenic, and directed back to the airport.

I've had my version of this stop-action decline and fall. When I first came to LA I had a gung-ho agent at Writers and Artists, one of the best agencies in Hollywood. She talked up a storm, met me after my reading, and took me out to dinner with her boss. We ate at a barn-sized restaurant that appeared to have been furnished after a trip to a garage sale given by the Medicis. The talk was all incredibly upbeat. Vistas of multimillion-dollar movie productions of my books stretched into the future; a shimmering, magic carpet, woven from starlets and Krug.

Now, four years down the line, and not a single option sold, I entertain my agent for lunch at the hotel and we talk – amicably enough – about our marriages. The words 'option', 'treatment' and 'script' do not figure anywhere in our discourse.

That evening I headed off to Skylight Books, a mere twenty blocks away. The bookstore is beautiful, featuring an enormous, curved, wooden ceiling dating from the thirties (and that's *old* in this town). The turn-out is good. People are surprised by this – that LA is a place where there are actual readers. But I don't find it surprising: confronted with the relentless alienation of this nation-sized urban sprawl, I'd be tempted to stay at home and curl up with a book. There's that, and there's also the fact that some of the most dedicated book-collectors in the world are to be found in LA. They will collect anything: any edition no matter how obscure or insignificant. I've had people come up to me in the line-out after readings in LA and ask me to sign copies of magazines I contributed to when I was at university nearly twenty years ago, the battered covers of this student tat lovingly plastic-encapsulated.

After the reading, the screenwriter Bruce Wagner, with whom I've corresponded for some years, took me for a tour of his LA in his giant

Lincoln Towncar. If anybody knows LA it's Wagner, who's a native Angeleno, and an exhaustive chronicler of the follies of Hollywood. We ended up crawling Sunset Strip until the small hours, when I poured myself back into the Marmont and to bed.

The following day my publisher, Morgan Entrekin, turned up from New York, and we headed up to the San Fernando Valley for a Booksellers Association dinner at a museum of uncompromising modernity. It was an excruciating affair – one of those gigs where the writers' names are announced and you have to stand up and introduce yourself to the gathering. Naturally, when I stood up no one applauded, because no one had ever heard of me. I kept moaning and bridling, and Morgan kept assuring me that this was 'good for business'. There was that, and there was also the fact that I would be getting my reward later that night in the form of an A-list Hollywood celebrity party. I bit my lip and tried to maintain.

When our – hired – Lincoln Towncar pulled on to the apron of tarmac outside the venue for the party (the house of a Very Famous Actress), we were immediately surrounded by *Reservoir Dogs*-style security men, equipped with ear-pieces that would have made Lieutenant Uhura green with envy. Once we'd made with the invitations we were admitted to the Elysian Fields of celebrity. It was only a *bijou* little gathering – about five hundred people. I wouldn't have said the bar was 'wet' – it was more of a waterfall. Everywhere there were bustling waiters doling out food and booze – and everywhere there were the mega-famous.

It's a most peculiar sensation, finding yourself in a queue for chicken gumbo with Rod Stewart, Sean Connery, Geena Davis and Jack Nicholson. It makes you feel as if you've strayed out of some ordinary reality and into one of those films where live-action characters interact with the screen gods and goddesses of the past. That was the trouble with my night of a hundred stars: I may have chatted with Jack (he doesn't get out much nowadays), and flirted with Geena (she really is very beautiful), but by golly the whole thing was so . . . great LA word, this . . . *unreal* that it was almost as if it had never happened.

At least the hangover was real. Morgan and I staggered out of the house of a Very Famous Screenwriter – where we'd gone on to – at about eight o'clock the following morning. The southern California sunshine was doing its best to turn my publisher into a pile of dust. 'It's too bright! Too bright!' he moaned, staggering about in the driveway like a vampire suited by Brooks Brothers.

'Morgan,' I said to him, 'my flight out of LAX for New York leaves at midday. You must accompany me to the airport.'

'No!' he howled. 'That's too much to ask!'

I let him off – merely insisting that he sit with me while I pack. Then I high-tailed it to the airport, resolving that if I managed to make it out alive this time, I might not be back for quite a while. I checked in, I made the departure gate. I had fifteen minutes to kill. I decided to persecute Morgan. I called his room at the Château Marmont.

'Wha' wha'? Who's thiss?' he slurred delightfully, surfacing from fathoms of alcoholic sopor.

'Morgan,' I trilled – and then lilted, 'I just called to say, I lo-ove you!'

'No-o! You bastard!' he screamed and banged the phone down. I slumped down on a handy banquette, chortling delightedly. Then I fell sound asleep.

I awoke an hour later. My flight was gone. I had the hangover from hell. It wasn't going to be easy to get another flight out that day. I should never have toyed with such hubris, such arrogance, in this town. I felt like the dead guy in the swimming pool at the start of *Sunset Boulevard*. Poor fool; I seemed to recall that he was a writer too . . .

High Life, December 1997

IOI

I didn't give up smoking on National No Smoking Day, any more than I gave up drinking on National No Drinking Day, or breathing carbon monoxide on National No Pollution-Related Asthma Day. I did, how-ever, hear the hortatory remarks of the Prime Minister in the Commons when, once again, he called our attention to the massive drain on the NHS's resources inflicted by smoking-related ailments. The Prime Minister feels comfortable chiding us, being himself a former puff daddy. But surely, Mr Blair, we smokers should be congratulated on our feat of hypothecation, given that we contribute far more to the Revenue via taxation on our vice than we can ever subtract from the virtuous Health Service?

The veteran anti-psychiatrist Thomas Szasz described modern govern-ments that seek to regulate not simply the ethics of the citizenry, but our psyches too, as 'therapeutic states'; and in the therapeutic state that is New Labour Britain, Tony Blair is the chief consultant. When the Prime Minister delivers such admonitions he's affecting a bedside manner. Britain lies hacking on the couch, and Our Leader tells us, 'Now really, you can't expect me to go on treating you for chronic bronchitis when you still insist on lighting up.'

The fact is, though, that what goes around comes around, and as long as there have been governments there have been politicians who think they know what's best for us better than we do ourselves. It's worth noting that in the America of the 1870s, public smoking was banned in no fewer than seventeen states. Of course, smoking was banned in the White House during the 1990s, but then the President was going somewhere more intimate to enjoy his cigars. I have no real objection to the idea that governments wish to intervene in our sumptuary habits; it's the hypocrisy I can't stand.

The truth is that there does seem to be a correlation between certain forms of legal impediment and our rather more harmful proclivities. As the licensing laws were progressively freed up throughout the last century, so all the indices of alcohol abuse rose. But the counterexample to this is that between the 1880s and the 1920s, the opium use that had been endemic in Britain in the nineteenth century disappeared with nary a whimper from the people. It wasn't government intervention that was responsible for this – the Defence of the Realm Act which restricted the legal sale of opiates was passed only in 1916 – it was the invention of aspirin as an alternative analgesic.

What this all serves to demonstrate is that there are two components in any state intervention over smoking: the therapeutic and the moralistic. It's quite all right for the Government to say that smoking is inherently evil and ban it on those grounds, and it's similarly OK for them to say it's bad for our health and ban it on those; the hypocrisy arises when the two are elided. The double amputee who sparks up despite having lost his limbs through smoking-related arterial sclerosis is exactly the same kind of addict as the alcoholic who drinks himself into dementia, and both require the same therapeutic solution, while neither of them bears any relation to the vicar enjoying a glass of sherry and a panatella after evensong. Until Mr Blair recognises the distinction, he'll stay sucking on his rhetorical humbug – unless, that is, he's forced to give them up for National No Dental Caries Day.

Today, BBC Radio 4, March 2000

102

I love Kristin Scott Thomas – it's as simple as that. But she has nothing to fear from me; I'm no psycho stalker, no agonised fan. No, I'm just an adorer from a distance. A real distance – I have absolutely no intention of getting anywhere near her. In fact, she phoned me last week, and the conversation went something like this:

Self (*slurring*): Yeah?

Scott Thomas (*engagingly warm and breezy*): Hi, Will?

Self (*still slurring*): Yeah?

Scott Thomas (*still making with the banter*): It's Kristin Scott Thomas here –

Self (*summoning up a semblance of coherence*): Oh yeah . . . right, yeah . . . Kristin whosie . . . yeah. Sorry . . . yeah . . .

Scott Thomas (*concerned*): It isn't a good time to talk?

Self: When is, that's what I ask myself . . . when is . . .

She actually forced her phone number on me, but I've managed to mislay it beneath the heaving pile of torn-up cheque books, writs, unpaid bills and letters from credit controllers that constitutes my working environment. I've made a couple of feeble attempts to get in touch with her since then, but quite rightly she's dismissed me as a waste of DNA. It was the same with my mate Nick. He loves Kristin and went to interview her in New York a couple of years ago. Like me, Nick couldn't remember any of her movies, or even her name for much of the hour-long encounter. Ms Scott Thomas was suitably glacial, and – a particularly engaging little detail – vertically furrowed her fine brow. Nick said she was the sort of rather bony, nunnish figure you might have a platonic crush on if you were eleven. Naturally he became intensely besotted with her and now ejaculates her name whenever he ejaculates. (Fortunately he's married to someone called Kristin, so no worries there.)

I don't have any such thoughts about Kristin, such vicious, impure thoughts. I've another mate, Mark, who's in love with Kristin solely on the basis of the sight of her bathing nipples making ripples in *The English Patient*. Mark is a bit of an English impatient as far as I see it – he doesn't realise that for your true Kristin-lover, sex doesn't enter the equation.

No, Kristin is the dame dangling out of a conical-roofed tower, wearing a conical hat, when you're out on a twenty-two-castle lute-strumming tour. It's courtly loving that she requires. The gig would be to wear her garter on your sleeve while some horse-riding dude punched a hole through you with a giant fondue fork. Then – but only then – she might let those perfect lips graze your dying brow. But sex with Kristin? No way.

Of course, I've read some of those profiles, and she comes across as a conventional enough sort of woman. Apparently she likes looking at people in public and making up stories about them. Lucky, that – because that's what we do to actors, make up stories about them when we see them in public.

In the last analysis, that's why I really love Kristin – the two of us are made for each other. It'll be like Arthur Miller and Marilyn Monroe all over again. And the mental communion we could achieve would be fantastic, because I'd script her for life.

US *Esquire*, June 1997

103

Terry Gilliam has mounted a truly exceptional exhibition in Croydon. I think I may have waited my entire career in journalism simply to pen that one line. For a lad such as myself, reared in the suburban fastness of East Finchley (home, you will recall, of *The Goon Show*'s Bluebottle), the outer London 'burbs have always had an enigmatic awfulness about them: all of human bondage is here, an eternity of Pooters shuffling to the overground. But it was a high, bright day when I alighted at East Croydon Station, home – a vast placard informed me – of Nestlé (never in the course of history has so much powder been manufactured etc. etc.), and the people thronging the concourse were contributing just as much revenue to Vodacom as any similar cohort in the centre of town.

The Clocktower Centre occupies the old Croydon Corporation offices, and underneath an impressively solid, brick pseudo-campanile, serried banners proclaim unlikely services such as 'Tourist Information'. You can imagine the scene in São Paulo, or Tokyo: 'Oh, where can we take our holiday this year? The possibilities of this vast world seem exhausted –'

'Had you considered Croydon, my sweet?'

But enough of this suburban badinage, because the fact of the matter is that Gilliam's exceptional exhibition will be touring the entire nation until well into the next millennium, replicating with its jerky progress the actions of some of the bizarre automata that feature in it, so there's absolutely no need for anybody at all to go to Croydon unless they happen to be there already. Although, that said, I enjoyed my trip to Croydon so much that I'm planning to go there again as soon as possible, *and* I'm going to take my wife and children as well.

Gilliam was asked to choose eighteen objects that he believed best represented the twentieth century. He then presented them to eighteen artist–constructors, who have fashioned mechanical models which further reify. He did well, choosing the technical imperatives: the telephone, the skyscraper, the television, genetic engineering; and the cultural pervaders: the psychoanalyst's couch, Mickey Mouse, the linked flags of the USA and the USSR. The Clocktower Gallery is a neat, two-roomed affair, and the automata that have resulted from this peculiar invitation throng it with cranky animation.

The first thing I saw on entering absolutely captivated me: Tim Lewis's *Telephone*, a tiny, rotating circlet of plastic manikins, which, when activated by your presence, revolve in the flicker of a strobe light. The piece resembles the famous, pioneering stop-action photography of Muybridge which so powerfully influenced Francis Bacon – among many others. Gawping at the hideous, jiggling rondo I was persuaded that all of physicality was captured here, in a perspex box the size of a large ashtray.

James Chedburn's evocation of the nuclear holocaust, a nuclear family of bronze wire manikins, infested by continually scraping cockroaches, is sad and admonitory, especially as I write at a time when tough boys are rattling tough toys. Joe Holman's *Road to Nowhere*, when activated by a switch, turns into a miniature tower of Babel which actually *contains* the M25. I kid you not, this automaton is a greater contribution to road safety than Sir Robert Mark's entire DNA, *and* it closely resembles the sort of cake-stand last seen on Tennyson's tea table.

Beside it was a screen-shaped slot through which you could view people and animals constructed from fluorescent wire who appeared to be watching you. Turn a crank and they would flop and spasm. Darcy Turner's *Television* comes with the instruction to 'wind cranks slowly', which, if you think about it, is what television largely does. As George Trow so knowingly remarked, 'Nothing good can ever come of it.'

There were many other equally entertaining pieces. Indeed, I was so carried away in reveries of childhood – the old penny-activated *tableau vivant* on Brighton's West Pier depicting the beheading of Mary Queen of Scots; the models of Nile cultivation in the basement of the Science Museum in London; ah! *Où sont les neiges d'antan?* – that I found myself being sucked into Ralph Steadman's orrery before I knew it. (Incidentally, I know this will drive you all right out of your minds, but it happens that 'orrery' turns out to be one of the few obscure words that my computer's spellchecker *does* recognise, a nice conceit when you consider that the orrery itself is a form of computer. The term derives from the fourth Earl of Orrery, who purchased a clockwork model demonstrating the movements of the planets of the solar system from John Rowley in 1712.)

Steadman's orrery was entered via a curving passageway, on the wall of which the inimitable bard of Oddbins had inscribed, 'The Newstead-manation Universe – before the storm clouds of doom and dismay, decadence, despair and dissolution . . .' The heavily determined Steadman universe was about six feet high, founded on paper-winged rocs, embossed with slinky-trunked, metal Ganeshes, and surmounted by free-floating human organs and a grotesquely gregarious profile of a man. The whole thing whirred, clicked and burbled while stars fell with the sound of dentists' drills. I was so entranced I sat down cross-legged like the East Finchley schoolboy I remain and contemplated it for some minutes.

The nice young man who was running the exhibition came in and found me. 'I suppose,' I said, 'you must have a lot of difficulties with these, I mean with kids banging the buttons.'

'Well,' he replied, 'we had two school parties in yesterday and they gave the automata a fair work-out – but we've got maintenance men permanently on hand to deal with that.'

Like automata, I thought. But really, it is a fantastic exhibition. Another school party was coming in as I left – if you haven't any kids to take, go, and become one. There are a heap more models that I haven't mentioned which are equally good, including a violently rotating act of catharsis, a shrine to Jimi Hendrix, and a half-melted birdcage.

As I bowled back to the station I saw another placard informing me that on every street in Croydon there are two vacant properties. Who knows . . . I mused to myself, who knows . . . ?

The Times, February 1998

104

Book review: High Art Lite *by Julian Stallabrass (Verso)*

On many, many an inebriated occasion, I have entered the snooker room of Soho's Groucho Club (which, with its dormer windows, outsize television screen replaying sport and its overgrown, overstoned adolescents, is like some teenager's Elysium), only to find myself confronted by a plastic version of a blue, English Heritage plaque, the kind found on buildings where the famous have either lived or worked. This pseudo-plaque reads 'Borough of Kensington/Gavin Turk/Sculptor/Worked Here/1989–1991'. The original was Turk's sole submission for his Royal College degree show (the degree was not awarded) and subsequently, when Turk was signed by a private gallery, became available in a limited edition.

Whether through inebriation, ire or innate criticality, I've always found myself compelled to open the nearest window and throw the thing out. Not, you understand, that I've anything against Turk himself – indeed, I once lent him a woolly. In Julian Stallabrass's fine, critical *tour d'horizon* of the British art scene in the 1990s, Turk is one of the nihilistic, personality-obsessed, conceptual sculptors who gets the lightest of drubbings. Stallabrass finds Turk's waxworks of himself in various guises (as Sid Vicious, as a homeless man), and his negligible artefacts posing as useless commodities, to have at least the virtue of being honestly silly – unlike the more portentous works of his peers, such as Marc Quinn and the acknowledged avatar of the scene, the pop singer and restaurateur Damien Hirst.

Really, Stallabrass's coinage 'High Art Lite' says all you might need to know about the artistic tendency that has, at various times, been labelled 'Young British Artists', 'the new conceptualism' or, put more simply – and economically – 'the Saatchi Collection'. It captures perfectly the marriage between opportunism, commercialism and nihilism, which made it possible for Hirst, the curator of the 1989 exhibition 'Freeze' (regarded by all as the seminal moment, the *locus classicus* of the wannabe movement), to move in eight short years from living in a council flat in Brixton, while staging an alternative degree show in a derelict East End factory, to being the seigneur of a Devon estate and the co-owner of a Notting Hill hangout for tarnished trustafarians.

Not that I've anything against Hirst personally, you understand. Indeed, at the launch of his book *I Want to Spend the Rest of My Life Everywhere, with Everyone, One to One, Always, Forever, Now* (which Stallabrass characterises as 'extravagantly banal'), I found myself driven – could it have been inebriation, ire, or innate criticality? – to pick the chunky conceptualist up in my arms and stroll around the gathering, while cooing to him, 'You're so-o tiny, Damien, and so-o cuddly . . .' Needless to say, Hirst is not the kind of artist who'll accept the loan of a woolly.

Yup, I've had Sarah Lucas and Angus Fairhurst gouch out on my sofa; I've traded lagers and insults with Tracey Emin; I've linked arms with the Chapmans; and on more than one occasion I've returned to Angela Bullock's fifth-floor loft in Shoreditch, to jig away the night with the whole giddy rondo of the lite-art crowd. Wouldn't you? Artists, being untrammelled by the solipsism, fantasising and outright envy of the literary world, make far more entertaining companions than writers, many of whom seem to have leather elbow patches sewn on to their very cerebella. The group shows, the common background in the art schools, the very spaciousness of the atelier, and the very laxness of the working practices – so much easier to get up in the morning with a savage hangover and drip Dulux on a board, or put a kebab on a table, than parse a proper sentence – all made for camaraderie + *bonhomie* = scene.

And there was never a crowd for partying like this lot – they had it all: the cachet of anti-Thatcher anger; the decadence of the *fin de siècle*; the wit of a surrealistic lager advertisement; all shaken up and spurted over the British public in a froth of fuck-you philistinism.

But now the real friends have drunk their champagne, what real pain remains for sham friends? What did it all add up to? (And 'did' is the operative word here; as Stallabrass, good Marxist that he is, acknowledges, only a savage recession can save most of these artists now from real, rather than feigned, *taedium vitae*.) What was it all *for*? In dry, measured prose, mercifully devoid of the pseudo-theoretical cant that has in the past constituted so much serious art criticism, Stallabrass carefully unlimbers the pop-gun of high art lite from the carriage of history and investigates whether it can fire anything other than a small flag with 'bang' blazoned on it.

Stallabrass is no mere annihilator of high art lite's nihilism; he – like me – thinks there are individual pieces that should be saved from the scrapheap. He favours the painting of Fiona Rae and the video installations

316

of Gillian Wearing – I incline more to Hirst's vitrine-enclosed animals, and Quinn's extruded forms of the artist's own body. But I cannot help but endorse his analysis of the high art lite tendency (and 'tendency' it was, rather than movement, the work of individual artists as diverse as Chris Ofili and Sam Taylor-Wood being an imbrication rather than a palimpsest) as almost wholly eaten up by its abject willingness to be fucked up by the nineties cult of celebrity; fucked over by the nineties boom in consumerism; fucked sideways by its adoption of the styles and modes of popular culture; and fucked to buggery by its co-option by Chris Smith and the New Labourite idiot-ology.

In getting the drop on this most ironic of art tendencies, it's richly ironic that it should be the observations of the mini-maverick, quondam rightist George Walden that, as quoted by Stallabrass, ring down the curtain most effectively on this fag-end era: 'Some of [high art lite] is capable of affording entertainment or distraction, but if those are the criteria, in terms of wit, intelligence, originality, social commentary or philosophical undertones, it rarely rises to the level of the most accomplished American television shows, such as *The Simpsons*.'

Walden makes explicit what I had always – as I rubbed the rotten rheum from my eyes after another night on the tiles with the artists themselves – suspected about much of this work: that at its best it raised the cartoon to the level of high art, and at its worst did the reverse; that its finest practitioners were really great cartoonists – at least as good as John Glashan, or Matt Groenig. Stallabrass, in a pertinent, diacritical chapter of this work, surveys the paucity of art criticism in turn-of-the-century Britain, and adumbrates the observation made by George Walden. This put me in mind of a lengthy, self-debunking gag told by the cartoonist Jules Feiffer in a television documentary, when asked about the difference between a great artist and a great cartoonist.

Feiffer describes at great length the life of the great artist, minutely detailing his daily routine; the ministering of his dutiful wife; the caressing of his pliant mistress; his avid acolytes; his travailing dealers; his compliant critics. At the end of this ten-minute paean to the life of the great artist, Feiffer fixes the viewer with a wearily witty eye and says, 'That's not what the life of a great cartoonist is like.'

So, the high art lite tendency may not have acquired a great, high-cultural critic in the shape of Stallabrass; but peculiarly, in him, with his fusty, stolid, Marxian analyses, his unfussy prose and his measured discursiveness, they've got the critic they deserve – as cartoonists. This, taken together with a handsomely produced, beautifully stitched, and resplendently illustrated (save for where a couple of tetchy cartoonists have denied permission for the replication of their works) book, makes *High Art Lite* a must for anyone who danced to this decadent drum of techno trivialising. And I did – Lord knows – I did.

New Statesman, January 2000

105

Concert review: Oasis at Earls Court, London, 27 September 1997

It was an emotional night for me – as it was for so many others. The minute that Liam Gallagher reached the centre of the enormous, cod-surrealist set at Earls Court, I knew that we were in a situation of life-meld. He was dressed entirely in white, stretchy clothing, which made him look as if he were wearing a colossal Babygro. Then he took up his posture at the microphone – arms clenched behind the small of his back, legs akimbo – and began to push, and push, and pu-ush! Wrenchingly giving birth to the words: 'All my people right here right now – d'jewknowhatImean . . .'

Approximately twenty-four hours before – and time is, of course, of the essence in a discussion of all this – I had been assisting my wife to adopt exactly the same posture as Liam: the upper body tilted forward, the arse end pushed back. But she wasn't holding a tambourine, and she was giving birth not to pop history, but to Ivan Self (eight and a half pounds).

I wonder what Liam will do when his first child is born. You can imagine him dealing with the midwives: 'Is that great big thing gonna come out of her fuckin' fanny? That's top, our kid . . .' Arguably all of Liam's singing career has been an anticipation of this moment. I certainly felt this as I watched him bend in the spotlight; that he was in some way pushing out all of his tormented childhood, externalising it, voiding it. The fact that he was dressed in a Babygro only served to underline it, as did the two enormous, ovoid monitors that flanked the stage. These beamed pictures of Liam and Noel contorting their monobrows, as if they were in the process of being squeezed out of some giant uterus.

All right, I know where I was when they were getting high – getting completely fucking wasted myself. Pint after pint after pint of frothy Carlsberg disappeared down my neck as the band belted on. It's probably the best means of producing piss in the world. Carlsberg had the concession closest to the VIP section at Earls Court, and I may be long in the tooth but I've never seen this before: two ranks of bar staff, one lot pouring the pints and setting them up, the other lot handing them to the punters. It was the famous Wall of Lager, which is presumably Oasis's version of Phil Spector.

In truth the mix must have been calibrated for the mixing desk itself, which at Earls Court is some hundred metres from the stage. Where I was – about a hundred feet from the stage – the noise was so loud, so throbbing, that my trousers actually vibrated against my legs. The Dali-inspired set itself, with its tilted objects – phone booth, clock, padded bar – was coped with lights that curved up and round to form yet another shape suggestive of intimate feminine anatomy. I've got to hand it to them – it was awesome. Whatever one's overall doubts about the status of Oasis's work to date, on Saturday night at Earls Court, even a cynic such as myself could believe that he was in at the birth of rock history.

Certainly the fans felt that way. As we came up Warwick Avenue to the venue, the atmosphere among the throngs of casually dressed people was comparable only to that of election night in May. They were elated and chattering and moaning. I found it beautifully ironic that these quintessential working-class heroes were doing a stadium gig, the organis- ation of which was severely predicated on divisiveness: we, the elect, were allowed the front half of the auditorium, while the masses, the great unwashed, were relegated to the back. Well done, boys. This is what you worked for all this time: to create a situation where the privileged are yet more privileged, and the paying punters are herded like cattle.

The gig began with some geezer in the costume of a doorman at the Ritz – shades of Di-Dodi death there – running about the stage like the White Rabbit, frenziedly reacting to the ticking of the outsize clock. When the hour struck and the band emerged, the entire audience went mental. And they stayed that way for the next couple of hours, while Liam knelt, strained, strolled, struck attitudes, and Bonehead remained utterly and incontrovertibly static.

They played a set that neatly interleaved the new album with the great, anthemic hits. Oasis aren't just a band who adapt well to stadium venues, they are a band whose music is purpose-built for stadiums, coming as it does from the chorus-line tradition of ''Ere we go, 'ere we go, 'ere we go . . .' I'm not saying the boys weren't good or anything – they manifestly were: no prima donna-ish antics from the Brothers Grim, only appeals to the 'fans' to stop letting off flashguns in their eyes, and exhortations to give generously to the striking Liverpool dockers who were collecting outside – but my attention was focused mostly on the crowd.

This was the real story: the forest of arms, the glazed eyes, the thousands of mouths synching in perfect time, ' 'Cos after all . . . you're my wonderwa-all . . .' Critics may carp, posterity may condemn, but for two hours I watched rock fervency at its zenith. It's Oasis's great virtue that they bestow the common touch to the commonality. Fuck it – anybody could be Bonehead, multitudes of Mancunians can belt it out like Liam, and Noel isn't that dab a hand with an axe. Really Oasis are the Spice Girls of rock: five guys making the very best of the modest attributes that have been bestowed on them. And this is certainly what the audience at Earls Court were responding to on Saturday night. It may not have been the greatest rock 'n' roll gig ever, but damn it all – it came close. And they are ours. God love 'em, I say.

New Musical Express, October 1997

106

Up aloft on the smoothly revolving London Eye I felt more vertigo than I could possibly have dreamt of. There was something about the slowness of its movement – not unlike being poised on the hand of an enormous clock – and the almost tangible sense of the 20,000-tonne bulk of the edifice, that curdled my guts like an ill-digested bowl of glutinous fettuccine. I wanted to heave. I wasn't helped in this by my two-year-old, Ivan, who insisted on climbing up on the first of the rails that bound the pod, so his chunky little body was suspended in the void, the only thing between him and the big drop a couple of inches of – allegedly – bullet-proof glass.

Still, this trip had been a long time in the offing and I did my best to enjoy it. A friend had assured me that there was a peculiarly revelatory content to the experience, because, since the Eye pushes your own viewpoint upwards in a forty-five-degree arc, the disposition of London's buildings is revealed to you as if they were massive paper sculptures, emerging from some pop-up book of urbanity. He was right about this: there was a marked difference in the sense of perspective afforded by the Eye as against the fixed vertical prospect granted by the ascent of a building; or the horizontal, traversing view you get from an aircraft.

The Eye also gives you a much clearer sense of the disposition of London's parts. From the Eye, the total irrationality of London's centre, its mashing together of districts, became an enacted fact. The buildings and open spaces appeared as arbitrarily conjoined as I felt the several parts of my intestines to be linked. I'm sure that my queasiness also had a lot to do with this being my home town. In my experience there's nothing more unsettling than staying the night in a hotel in the city where you actually live; the juxtaposition of arbitrary transience and real permanence gives you a perspective on your entire life that's like looking into one of those model ants' nests, pinioned between two sheets of glass.

It was the same with the Eye: as the streets and parks and buildings where I have spent most of my life expanded from elevation into three dimensions, then retreated to plan, I was visited with an overpowering sense of my entire life's rodentine passage in this expanded warren. Thank God for the commentary of our self-styled pod 'captain'. This guy had a quip for every building we could see, every vista we encompassed. According to him, the pods' glass is bullet-proof because the Queen – who objects to the way the Eye looms over her back garden – likes to take potshots at it from time to time, the way any other householder might wield a pair of garden shears at a neighbour's *leylandii* hedge.

It was all good flip stuff – and it helped to stop me flipping over the edge. But the one gag that struck right home with me, and which matched the view perfectly, was when Captain Rod came to discourse on the old Ministry of Transport buildings in Marsham Street. 'Those three big blocks to the left of Parliament,' he said, 'are now part of the Department of the Environment and are scheduled for demolition, because everyone agrees that they're an incredible eyesore. It's a bit ironic, really, when you think that were the Department to consider their planning application now, they'd definitely reject it.'

Ho-hum, I suppose so. But am I in a minority of one in not finding the Marsham Street buildings to be that much of an eyesore at all? Perhaps it's just another aspect of the way I experienced the Eye as a colossal revolving madeleine – like Proust's famous cake, each metre of its progress released another inundation of recall – but I've a certain fondness for these monoliths. I well remember going, ten years ago, to interview some wonk in the old transport ministry for an article about the Westway flyover. Even then the congruence between the offices' brutalism and the brutalism of the subject under discussion struck me as a fruitful one. When I got home from the Eye, I felt impelled to ring the Property Adviser to the Civil Estate and discover what they were going to do with the Marsham Street site. The old buildings are so imposing it's hard to imagine Westminster devoid of them. Watch this site – and I'll tell you what he said next week.

Building Design, May 2000

107

I ran into David Marks at the reopening of our local adventure playground in Stockwell. To begin with I didn't know it was Marks, and when a tall, blue-eyed, dark-haired man of smooth good looks accosted me thus: 'Hi, Will, how're you doing?' I had no alternative but to wade in with 'Not so bad – and yourself?' hoping that I could discover his identity in the course of conversation.

We went on thus for a few exchanges, until I realised we were reaching that fine juncture in badinage where anonymity would no longer suffice. I tried a gambit: 'So what're you up to?' 'Up to' is a good catch-all; it covers the activities of serial killers or politicians, the idle rich or the idle poor with commensurate ease.

'Looking for work at the moment,' came the reply.

Hmm, my interlocutor didn't appear to be dole fodder, but then I surprised myself with my alacrity: 'What kind of thing are you after?'

'I'd like to do some housing,' answered the good-looking one, and then the rusty wards ground into configuration and the mnemonic key fitted: this was David Marks, the architect, who together with his partner Julia Barfield had built the London Eye; this was the fair Ferris-builder himself. 'Not,' he continued, 'that I have much choice in the matter. I'll just have to see what comes along.'

And then we got on to other, more local concerns, like whether the reopened adventure playground (which is being charitably funded) will get an extension on its lease from Lambeth Council, or whether the powers-that-be-crap will see fit to sell the prime package of building land off to a developer, as they've done with so many other chunks of the borough. All around us small boys and girls tooled their BMX bikes through the recently threshed undergrowth, while still smaller boys and girls trundled happily along recently refurbished aerial wooden walkways. It was a most convincing scene of the urban bucolic, and my hatred of anything that smacks of 'village London' was kindled when Marks told me that he'd lived in a house immediately abutting the playground for nigh on twenty years – in fact, ever since he was a student. Then it was all but ignited when a stately lady hove into view, who it transpired was Marks's mother. I had to get away – I craved alienation.

Still, Marks's words about 'looking for work at the moment' stuck in my mind, and were revived by an interview with Norman Foster I heard on Radio 4's *People You Know* later in the week. Foster was asked about what he'd wanted to build as a young man – and he spoke about how the architect is offered only a limited set of opportunities upon which to impose his 'values'.

It struck me as strange that these two colossi of contemporary architecture should feel so trammelled by traditional demarcations between commissioner and commissioned – especially given that it was Marks himself who created the whole context within which the London Eye was built. Still, I suppose there are two ways of looking at these demarcations. One is that they allow architects, engineers, developers and financiers to divide large projects into suitable chunks of endeavour; the other is that they allow for responsibility for a botched job, or a structure disparaged by the public, to be similarly doled out – or even altogether avoided.

When I probed Marks about the instabilities of Foster's millennium footbridge, it was interesting to note that while to begin with he said he'd guessed it would have that certain swing, he none the less refused to condemn Foster or Ove Arup for not spotting it on the drawing board.

Arguably, it's in part the unquestioning acceptance of this division of architectural responsibility that's allowed for the erection and demolition of large-scale public projects in Britain within the space of a few decades, while the constructors' community remains largely unrepentant. We might choose to see the débâcles of high-rise housing, or Bull Ring-style shopping centres, as the result of vaunting modernism yoked to headstrong post-war expansionism, but perhaps much of the building boom that's currently under way will itself become a transitory object, and its buck will be just as efficiently passed.

Maybe architects should consider joining in partnership, at the training stage, with people who can really facilitate their vision, rather than with others of their kind? Then architectural 'values' could amount to a bit more than simply ensuring that the Reichstag is eco-friendly.

Building Design, June 2000

108

Book review: Natural Born Killers *screenplay*
by Quentin Tarantino (Faber & Faber)

I've never sat through a Quentin Tarantino film and I have no intention of ever doing so. I don't want to make great claims for my perspicacity in this matter, but the fact remains that as regards this so-called *auteur*, I find myself in the reverse of the normal situation regarding popular cultural phenomena.

It often happens that you pick up on some new artist, early on in their career, before the media have wallpapered the empyrean with their likeness. Once this has occurred you feel your enthusiasm for them falling off. Every time someone says, 'Oh, aren't they fabulous . . .' you feel like saying, 'I know, and what's more *I* knew long before types like you began to leap on their bandwagon.'

With Tarantino and me, exactly the opposite has occurred. I went to see *Reservoir Dogs* on its release. I appreciated the snappy quality of the dialogue in the opening scenes of the film, and I understood – or at least thought I understood – what the writer/director was aiming at when he bedded Tim Roth down on a futon of blood for the next thirty minutes of action, following the unsuccessful heist. But when I got to the torture scene involving the ear and the cut-throat razor, I balled up my popcorn, dumped it on the floor and quit the cinema.

It may have been the supposedly ironic counterpoint of the backing music – Stealer's Wheel doing 'Stuck in the Middle with You' – or it may have been the threat of steel on cartilage, but most probably it was the fear that the conjunction of the two would make me puke my guts out. Not, in my opinion, an aesthetic reaction worth experiencing.

True Romance managed to pass me by. By now the chatter concerning Tarantino's 'post-modern' and 'iconic' attributes was becoming a babel; and although I attended the London première, I couldn't quite manage the crawl from bar to screening.

Some time later Miramax Films sent me a copy of the screenplay of *Pulp Fiction*, with some suggestion that I might be interested in novelising the film. In a way the idea amused me. It pointed up the real possibility of film finally eclipsing literary fiction as the dominant narrative medium. Of course, novelising screenplays is nothing new, but for someone such as me – who regards the integrity of the form I work in extremely highly – to undertake such wilful unoriginality would have been to cede the high ground to the *cinéastes*.

In the event this wasn't an issue. I thought the screenplay hackneyed, exploitative and crass. The brouhaha that surrounded the film's release left me cold, and it wasn't until it eventually cropped up locally (at the Leiston Film Theatre – 'Suffolk's Oldest Cinema') that I got round to attending. I lasted all of ten minutes on this occasion, before walking.

Thus I have the rare distinction of having been way in the avant-garde of the Tarantino backlash, which I'm glad to see is now ponderously getting under way. When the offer came to review the screenplay of *Natural Born Killers*, I balked. Would I have the emotional wherewithal to attempt a showing of another Tarantino-scripted film? Predictably the answer was no. After five minutes of the thing I decided that as I was witnessing a film dedicated to displaying short lives, I was justified in arguing that life was too short to bother with it.

As for the screenplay itself, well, while it's egregious to quote back-cover blurb, in this case Faber & Faber have so delightfully distorted the truth (and English syntax) that I feel I must: 'This script is of special interest as a map of Tarantino's original intentions of the film,' they write. 'Much tauter and leaner than the completed film, Tarantino's mesmerising gift for language creates an impact that is as unsettling as it is poetic.'

Well, obviously I cannot comment on the divergences between Tarantino's screenplay and Oliver Stone's direction, but what I can say unequivocally is that *Natural Born Killers* exhibits absolutely no poetic language whatsoever. Indeed, it could be argued that if the screenplay has any virtue at all it is as an anti-style guide, a set of instructions on how to prevent even the meanest poetics from getting into film dialogue.

As for 'tauter and leaner', I will say this much. It took me all of fifty minutes to read *Natural Born Killers*, and for that I am profoundly grateful.

Of course, the first point that needs to be made about the screenplay is how blindingly unoriginal it is. The romanticism of the outlaw on the run, racing from location to location in a hail of bullets, is a perennial theme in American popular culture. It's no accident that Mickey Knox – Tarantino's 'outlaw' – refers to *Butch Cassidy and the Sundance Kid* when contemplating a shoot-out to the death with the deputies guarding the penitentiary. And, of course, the same kind of themes have been dealt with in numerous other films, most notably Arthur Penn's *Bonnie and Clyde* and more importantly Terrence Malick's *Badlands*.

Indeed, *Badlands* foreshadows *Natural Born Killers* in almost every respect: the pathological 'love' of the two protagonists for each other, the parricide that sets them off on their killing spree, the obsessive attention of the media that encourages popular hero-worship. But whereas the former film is tense, elegiac and haunting (summed up by the use of Orff's *Carmina Burana* on the soundtrack), the screenplay for the latter is mere slapstick, Looney Tunes for perpetual adolescents. And there's nothing new about the American cinema examining the extraordinary popular delusion of the press – one thinks unhesitatingly of *Sweet Smell of Success* or *Ace in the Hole*.

Some people affect to find the endless referentiality of Tarantino's screenplays evidence of his deep and meaningful absorption in his craft (what among writers is termed 'intertextuality'). I find it merely irritating. When Wayne Gayle – the television journalist who wishes to scoop an interview with the eponymous anti-heroes – is razzing his team up with the prospect of comparing it to other, similar *coups*, Roger, the soundman, quips, 'This is Raymond Burr witnessing the destruction of Tokyo by Godzilla.'

This is reductionist irony: something potentially important being en-mired in the trivia of reference to the ephemeral. It's basically the same gag when in this script – as in all of Tarantino's others – the characters maun-der on endlessly about fast food. In this one we are treated to the rich irony of the television crew's obsession with chocolate-cream-filled doughnuts.

It's no wonder that Tarantino's most strident acolytes are those who wish to democratise culture by yanking the low up to the status of the high. Having educated themselves by lying on couches watching afternoon television reruns, they wish to drag the rest of us down to their potato-level. The idea that this screenplay represents a moral condemnation of the media's role in the promotion of murder-as-mass-entertainment is another piece of flummery. Tarantino's imagination is too much of a plateau to provide the necessary vantage point from which to see this truth. Thus *all* of the characters in the story are unredeemedly awful – and worse, stupid.

What else to say of the fact that Scagnetti, the top cop who is meant to be taking the Knoxes to their final incarceration in a secure mental hospital, enters Mallory Knox's cell unarmed? Naturally he, like Gayle, the television journalist who commits the same folly in respect of Mickey, gets attacked. Tarantino may imagine he is portraying the hubris of law enforcement and media respectively, but to me it just seemed implausible. Stupidly implausible.

There are also irritating errors of continuity in the screenplay. Initially it is said that the Knoxes will be lobotomised at the mental hospital. Latterly, they are only to be subjected to ECT. Which is it? There is a flatness about the speeches that means they don't serve their purpose. Thus, Neil Pope, a film director who has made an exploitational feature about the murderous duo, and who is 'interviewed' about it in the documentary-within-this-feature (ha-ha! How post-modern), says of the Knoxes' story, 'Yet amidst the violence and murder and carnage, you've got the structure of a Wagnerian love story.'

Two pages later, in the context of the same 'documentary', the psychiatrist Dr Rheingold says, 'Basically, the very thing that makes them most lethal is the exact same thing that captures the public's hearts and minds – Mickey and Mallory's operatic devotion to each other.' The feel of both phrases, as well as the content, is exactly the same.

And if it is the characters of Mickey and Mallory themselves that are meant to redeem the script, by providing language that justifies our belief in them as almost supernatural characters, *Übermenschen*, then here again Tarantino fails. He avoids having to make much of Mallory's dialogue by having her refuse to do anything but sing old pop tunes throughout. But with Mickey, Tarantino has more of a problem. Here's his climactic, self-justifying speech: 'Everybody thought I'd gone crazy. The cops, my mom, everybody. But you see they all missed the point of the story. I wasn't crazy. But when I was holding the shotgun, it all became clear. I realised for the first time my one true calling in life. I'm a natural born killer.' Wow! What a gift for poetic language!

Sight and Sound, November 1995

109

Restaurant review: PizzaExpress, 29 Wardour Street, London W1

You can get few clearer perspectives on the enormous social changes that this country has witnessed over the past thirty years than by surveying our restaurant-going proclivities and eating habits. Within this purview (a kind of victual reality) the pizza provides us with a lens-shaped (albeit opaque) device with which to examine in greater detail how we have become what we are.

Thirty-one years ago when the first PizzaExpress outlet was opened by Peter Boizot in London's Wardour Street, the pizza was almost unknown in Britain. Sure, the idea of a roughly circular, essentially farinaceous base upon which successive layers of cheese, tomato purée and miscellaneous savoury gobbets would be overlaid did have some theoretical currency, but as far as practicalities were concerned we lagged woefully behind other European countries.

The first four pizzas ever to be imported to Britain were seized by Customs and Excise at Heathrow. The courier (a dermatologically-challenged youth, riding a moped and wearing a hip-length nylon jacket) was interrogated for days, but turned out to know nothing – about anything. Some things don't change.

The pizzas were handed over to the government laboratory at Porton Down, where scientists attempted first to project one (fooled by their circular shape into believing they might be some novel form of film spool); secondly to fire one from a large-barrelled artillery piece (believing it to be some phenomenally snub, but highly calibrated new Soviet ordnance); and only thirdly to eat one. This was not a success, as the principle of removing the pizza from its cardboard housing was yet to be discovered. The final pizza was handed over to the Duke of Buccleuch, who for years employed it as a spare tyre on his marvellous vintage Hispano-Suiza. And this despite the fact that it was only a nine-inch with a thin crust!

Now, of course, pizzas are everywhere. I don't need to remind readers that the largest pizza in the world is not so much 'in' the Warwickshire town of Nuneaton, as the Warwickshire town of Nuneaton is *in* the pizza. Since pizzafication, the town hall is to be found beneath an 80ft-high mound of chopped onion, while the sports centre is effectively hidden by discs of pepperoni sausage the size of hayricks.

And only last week came the welcome news that the Millennium Fund has agreed to the construction of a gigantic pizza Ferris wheel on London's Battersea embankment. The pizza Ferris will be 6,000 inches high, but still have a light, thin crust. It will take twenty minutes to get half-way round the rim, and from the top of the pizza it will be possible – on a clear day – to see Nuneaton.

However, until this wonder is upon us we can do a lot worse than visit one of the 100-plus PizzaExpress outlets that have blossomed since the original Wardour Street joint opened. PizzaExpress is, as I have had cause to remark in this column before, to my mind far and away the best pizza chain in the country. At Pizza Hut there is always the sinister fear that as you remove a slice from your pizza, the mozzarella cheese will resolve itself into the uprights and obliques of a recognisable inscription, like some hideous, low-rent version of Belshazzar's feast. 'MENE, MENE, TEKEL, UPHARSIN!' the cheese striae will read. 'You are weighed in the balances, and are found wanting.'

At Pizzaland, by contrast, the atmosphere is considerably less Old Testament. However, I've never managed to forgive this chain its decorative excesses of the mid-1970s, when the outlets all had murals of alpine scenes that looked as if they had been painted by that tried and tested technique of coating a bull with Artex and then letting it run amok.

The PizzaExpress restaurants are by contrast usually light and airy. The original Wardour Street outlet has changed over the years but now exhibits the same tile floors, marble-topped tables and clean white walls as the majority of the others. Enzo Appicella was involved in the design of the Coptic Street branch (behind the British Museum, the second restaurant in the chain to open) and has continued to have an input to this day.

I'm particularly fond of my local branch, off Shepherd's Bush Green, where the colourful Appicella mural provides a charming, fantastical view of the Côte d'Azur ('The further off from England . . .' and all that jazz).

I shudder to think just how many pizzas I've eaten at PizzaExpress restaurants since I first started regularly attending the Hampstead branch in the early 1970s. Four thousand Four Seasons, perhaps? And certainly enough Venezianas to ensure that the 25p optional levy, added on to the price of the pizza as a contribution to the Venice in Peril Fund, ought by now to have mounted up sufficiently to winch the entire city some twenty feet above the lagoon.

The thing I like best about the PizzaExpress pizza is its consistency. In a world of bewilderingly rapid change (there have been three presenters of *Desert Island Discs* since the 1960s!) it's reassuring to bite into a PE pizza knowing that the dough is still made centrally to the original formula at their depot in Camden Town (where they also have a world-beating collection of pine kernels).

PizzaExpress did go into franchising in the mid-1970s, but since floating the core business as a PLC some four years ago, it has bought back most of these franchises, ensuring group-wide quality control – although, this being noted, PizzaExpress does not see itself as in any way a 'corporate' outfit. When I asked the restaurant chain director, Ian Eldridge, to what he attributed this consistent high quality, he remarked, using typical management-speak, 'A lot of old hacks like me buggering about in the restaurants.'

PizzaExpress employs properly trained pizza chefs, who make a great spectacle – especially for the children – as they flip their diskettes of dough in full view of the diners.

One aspect of the chain that I have – lamentably – yet to experience is its involvement with jazz. It sponsors its own combo and has regular gigs at many outlets. But hell, jazz was still trendy in 1966, and in 1996 it's trendy again. I'm sure that the pizza is now here to stay as well, proving the literal truth of the French apophthegm '*Plus ça change, plus c'est la même chose*,' or 'What is round, comes around.'

Observer, May 1996

I IO

Restaurant review: Alastair Little, 136A Lancaster Road, London W11

Wittgenstein memorably remarked, 'It doesn't matter what you eat as long as it's always the same thing,' by which I think he intended to bolster up his argument concerning private language, rather than call our attention to the bewildering variety of canned tomatoes now available in supermarkets.

Wittgenstein was not, after all, exactly a gastronome. When asked by Bertrand Russell what his favourite snack food was, the great Viennese sage and wiseacre thought for some time, before answering, 'That Welsh rarebit over there in the corner of your study, I admire its square asperity.' Russell was perplexed by this, because *there was no* Welsh rarebit in the corner, merely a biffed-about Pot Noodle container, with which the author of *Principia Mathematica* had missed the bin.

Late that night Russell wrote to his inamorata Lady Ottoline Morrell, 'I had a trying time with my young Viennese today. He continued to insist that it was by no means a certain thing that there was no Welsh rarebit in the corner of my room, despite my grabbing him by the nape of the neck and grinding his face into the carpet. Eventually I persuaded him to go out to KFC for some hot wings and fries, but he became hugely agitated in the Cornmarket, crying out that it was futile for us to be eating fast food while the central problems of metaphysics remain unsolved. I fear I may have to let go of him if he persists with such fervid idealism.'

All of this came to my mind last week, as I strolled up Lancaster Road and confronted the façade of Alastair Little's new restaurant. For Little's gaff *nouveau* has no name on it; it is a restaurant without ascription, de- – as it were – signified. Was this, I wondered, an indication of Little's preoccupation with semiotics? On entering the establishment we were confronted with an interior of Bauhausian purity that would have gladdened Ludwig; and there, up on the wall, by way of a referent, was a large, wooden, letter 'a'.

Was this lower-case 'a' a fragment of symbolic logic, I wondered, part of a truth table rather than a dinner table? I didn't have to speculate for long, because Little himself appeared at this point. I've been on nodding terms with Alastair for some years now. At a meeting of the Philosophical Society, he was good enough to refer to my article 'The Eschatology of the Escalope' as 'utter cack'. The originator of the tiny dish of olive oil for bread-dipping and one of the most aggressively intellectual of the new breed of British chefs, Little was hobbled by a cast on his foot – the result, he told us, of dropping a volume of Frege on his big toe.

'Nah,' he said, 'the "a" is for Alastair, and as for the lack of a sign out front that's because we ran out of dosh. All I really want to have out there is a blue plaque saying that [the mass murderer] Christie used to have breakfast here, because years ago this was the St Remo café.'

Besides being near to the street formerly known as Rillington Place, the new Alastair Little's is no more than a few short propositions away from the restaurant where Little started out, 192.

Not that Little himself is doing the cooking at the Lancaster Road branch; this is largely the preserve of Toby Gush, and a very fine job he does too. Little comes in occasionally to oversee. He has made the point in recent interviews that it's ridiculous for the punter in one of his restaurants to imagine that it is the great man himself who is making free with the Sabatier out back. As ridiculous, one might say, as imagining that it's Damien Hirst who actually puts the calf in the formaldehyde, or that it is I who really write this column, rather than a number of assistants I have trained up for the job, and who work in a special atelier in Dollis Hill.

I'd clocked the opening of the new Little's, but hadn't yet managed to go, for the very simple reason that for the past few months the press of other restaurant critics in the place has been oppressive. People have told me that it's barely possible to get a sprig of radicchio to your lips without falling foul of Nigella Lawson's elbow, or Adrian Gill's impressive embonpoint. But now the dust has settled, it's possible to obtain rental of a brace of the thirty-eight covers, without having to file a thousand words.

On the evening we were there, the clientele was what one would expect: international, eclectic, upper professionals. To one side of us sat two Germans, speaking business German. To the other sat some English, speaking English as if it were business German. The waiting staff displayed an elaborately casual kind of courtesy. They replaced ashtrays with great ceremonial, as if taught to do so by a master of Noh theatre. Their leader was a young man with such an avant-garde growth on his chin that I surmised he must be an archimandrite of the Goatee Support Group, rather than a mere member.

As dusk kissed the darkling tarmac outside the door, the woodblock floor became lustrous, illumined by the grid of lighting panels on the ceiling. The gentle clink of metal on ceramic provided me with a steady rhythm with which to punctuate my musings. I had eaten asparagus with Parmesan and eel with new potatoes. My companion had had the Spanish ham with artichoke and a brill. We had washed the lot down with a bottle of Rioja. But how could I describe it all accurately? How could I be sure that the words I used to breathe life into these flavours would really be understood by my readers? In one of his later works, *Remarks on Yoghurt*, Wittgenstein stated that 'a true food criticism' was an impossibility, the result of a conflation between two symbolic orders.

I set my assistants to work on the problem. They laboured for days until the Dollis Hill atelier was adrift with crumpled sheets of paper. Eventually they arrived at a description of the cuisine, which, albeit written in standard English, still seemed to skirt what P. F. Strawson has described as 'the bounds of sense', while also providing a clear value judgement: 'Very good.' My companion, however, had made a more trenchant, un-Wittgensteinian remark. On confronting my eel she said it made her feel 'rather Bobbity'. Watch this space.

Observer, May 1996

I I I

Like other prominent public figures I have been grappling with my homosexuality over the past couple of weeks. I know it's not a pretty sight – witnessing someone grappling with any aspect of their sexuality – but in this day and age of tolerance, open-mindedness, compassion – the virtues so embodied by the late Princess of Wales, which is presumably why she was the fag hag *ne plus ultra* – I feel I must have it out in the open, for all to see. They can refuse to lower the age of consent for homosexuals, they can reject the repeal of the repugnant Section 28, but New Labour remains the party of New Honesty as far as I'm concerned. Tony – what a liberal guy!

In truth, my homosexuality has always been a somewhat evanescent thing. There was the regulation mutual masturbation at the prepubescent stage, along with naughtily nude frolics, but it was understood by all – except Richard, who went on to run a ninety-two-bed 'travellers' hotel' in Amsterdam – that this was just a stage. Although if it was a stage, I'm a bit disappointed with the lack of mutual masturbation and naughtily nude frolics in the heterosexual phase that's followed. In my late teens I had a very brief liaison with a man who's now a prominent barrister. I'd out him here and now – something we're rather good at at *The Times* – if it weren't for the fact that he's been as flagrantly queer as Dick's hatband all his working life.

And then there was my latest experience: an impassioned snog with

333

the restaurant critic of this very magazine. Yes, Meades and I locked on to each other like eels mating in the Sargasso Sea. I can't remember who suggested it, but once we'd docked I was surprised by the immense size and power of his lingual apparatus. It reminded me insistently of Stephen Jay Gould's essay 'The Flamingo's Smile', in which he points out that the reason flamingos' tongues were such a delicacy in Ancient Rome was that, unlike other birds' tongues, they are designed to effect the continuous, vigorous pumping action required to sluice up vast amounts of nutriments, and are thus immensely big and thick.

Since then, nothing. Not a card, not a phone call – a girl just feels used. My friend Paul Burston, the editor of the gay section of *Time Out*, and author of *Queens' Country*, took pity on me the other night and invited me out for an evening's 'discovery' clubbing. 'We'll start off at Helmet's Slang,' he said. 'It's one of the newer Soho club nights, very fashionable with the younger set. It'll be lots of posing, fun, frolics . . . not really a cruising place at all.'

'So, um, it won't be, like, exclusively gay?'

'Oh no, not at all. Lots of straights go to this kind of thing nowadays. You wouldn't get a second look.'

'I was rather afraid of that – couldn't we go somewhere a bit more *intense*?'

'You mean more gay . . . well, that's difficult – with bars like the Edge and West Central licensed until three, exclusively gay clubbing has taken a bit of a knock. Everyone in town drinks until late and then goes on.'

'But what if we did go to an exclusively gay club – I bet it would be pretty heavy, right?'

'There are cruisier joints like Substation and the Hoist –'

'The Hoist – that sounds fairly intense.'

'Oh it is, but you wouldn't get in there, not without the right kit. They're very proper about that on the fetish scene. Mind you, you *could* be a leather queen – you can be a leather queen at any age, and no matter how little care you've taken of yourself. Even Ron Davies could be one.'

'Thanks very much. But am I to take it that in at least some of these places there would be open homosexual acts and conspicuous drug-taking?'

'Well I should hope so – it wouldn't really be a scene if there weren't.'

'And the police don't do anything about it?'

'Well, they raid places occasionally, but on the whole I suppose they're rather pleased this kind of thing is kept off the streets.'

There was silence for a time, while my mind, like the little engine that couldn't, struggled to comprehend the dynamics of the liberated gay scene. 'Well, it doesn't sound very exciting or dangerous to me. Perhaps we could go cruising on Clapham Common – it's just up the road.'

'Hmm, well, I don't *think* so. I used to monitor the cruising scene up at the Common – keeping an eye on police activity – and contrary to what the media are saying it's a very small, very discreet set-up. Nothing blatant about it at all.'

'Not the place to find a warm, black, male body.'

'Oh no, there are clubs where you can meet gay black men now – there's no need for that.'

I was driven into inertia by Paul's remarks. Instead of going clubbing we watched the box. In such circumstances it was difficult to imagine why anyone needed to deny their homosexuality – unless, that is, they wished to be part of a regime that denies equal rights to homosexuals. Now that really would be a kick. I turned excitedly to Paul. 'Is there a club for gay men who want to be part of a regime that denies equal rights to gay men?'

'Oh yes, the Labour Club – there's quite a few of them round here.'

The Times, November 1998

112

I want to find out what the new weaponry is going to be like, the stuff aimed at You Know Who. Last time round the sandpit we had some pretty nifty new theatre weapons (love that 'theatre weapons' – *so* theatrical!); you remember good ol' Cruise, but there was funky Patriot too; and those 'smart' bombs you remember, the ones that elided warfare and television completely with the deployment of 'bomb-cams', so that we could sashay vertically down Iraqi ventilation shafts, deeply in tune with our leaders' war aims.

As I say, I want to find out – but I can't stand weaponry of any kind. When the police last held an amnesty I handed in my nail-clippers; nasty, big, aggressive things they were. If someone waves a water pistol in my general direction – I surrender. People often ask me if I'm sorry that I never met the American writer William Burroughs, who died a couple of years ago. I'm not. He loved guns and hated women – I'm entirely the reverse.

I needed an intermediary, someone to stand between me and the vile, death-dealing phalluses. I called Jane's Information Group, the mighty collator of all military facts, and was put through to a Claire Bruhaus in the press office. 'I want to find out about new weaponry,' I snapped, 'stuff for the Gulf.'

'You need Paul Beaver, our group spokesman,' she snapped back. 'Here's his mobile number.'

I called it, and to my surprise got him immediately. 'I want to find out about new weaponry,' I snappily reiterated, 'stuff for the Gulf.'

'There'll be more accurate AFs – those are air-launched Cruise missiles from B52s. They've ironed out a lot of the bugs with Patriot –'

'Look, that's great, but I couldn't meet with you in person, could I –'

'Now!'

'Not now – tomorrow?'

'I've got a surface-to-air missile conference at the Grosvenor Hotel. Meet me there at three o'clock.'

The whole conversation had taken seconds. Was this how everything was done in the world of weaponry? At great velocity and with pin-point accuracy? It made a strange kind of sense. And Paul Beaver's gruff eagerness to impart – what was that about? Was arms all tough, tough toys for tough, tough boys? I quivered in my black silk *cache-sexe*.

At the appointed hour I arrived at the Grosvenor Hotel. Now owned by Thistle (prickly name – thorny business), it's a perfect venue for anything that has the remotest ring of the clandestine about it. The hotel actually constitutes the wall of Victoria Station, so that you can dodge any number of men wearing trench coats who're pursuing you. Or, alternatively, rendezvous with any number of men wearing trench coats who you're pursuing. There's an excessively woody bar, and numerous large reception rooms through which ancient American women drag wheeled suitcases, as if they were on their way to some bizarre, personal Calvary.

In the main lobby I approached a porter with maximum tact: 'Um, I see you've a number of conferences on here today.'

'Yes.'

'There isn't one to do with . . . um . . . to do with . . .' – never had a euphemism appeared more acceptable – '. . . the defence industry.'

'Up there in the Gallery Suite. You can wait over there.'

I waited on a banquette, holding a copy of *The Times* so that Beaver would recognise me. Everyone who traversed the lobby looked like a potential arms dealer to me. Anxiety – as it always does – induced bigotry. Swarthy men with attaché cases were carrying anthrax; black men with attaché cases were porting automatic rifles; white men with attaché cases were weighed down with anti-personnel mines and fragmentation bombs. Vicious bastards! And here, in the heart of London!

When the conference session let out it was easy to tell the real arms-industry types. They were all carrying thick ring binders, prominently labelled 'Weapons Conference'. Most of them looked pretty sweaty and shifty – but not one tall, urbane figure, who detached himself from the group descending the stairs and strode over. 'Will Self? Paul Beaver.' A handshake and we were ensconced – and he was off:

'Yeah, they've got an accurate and much cheaper Patriot. Patriot was far worse than Cruise in the Gulf – far more collateral damage. It's true – they wanted to see if these weapons were "as advertised" – and they weren't. But this time Tomahawk will be more accurate as well – far more bang for your buck. They've also got things called – you'll love this – "penetration weapons". They hit things called "point targets" – bunkers and so on. The thing is the statistics. In the Gulf there was 45 per cent accuracy for smart weapons; by the time they bombed the Serbians in 1994 they'd got this up to 85 per cent. Now, when they hit those targets in Sudan and Afghanistan – no matter that they weren't the right ones – they were better than 90 per cent accurate.'

'Wow –'

'Wow indeed. They'll be confirming this. With new smart bombs, with something called CACLEM, air-launched from B52s. They've got these penetration weapons which travel on flat trajectories – up, then down – for greater –'

'Penetration?'

'Exactly. It's all being talked up by American congressmen.'

'Republicans? Democrats? Corrupt men whose election campaigns were paid for by arms manufacturers?'

'Oh no,' he laughed, 'not that crude, but these guys want all major operations to be launched from the continental USA by the year 2010.'

'So, traditional American isolationism?'

'Exactly. Excuse me – I'll have to go.'

And he was gone; our rendezvous hadn't even been long enough for us to exchange a microdot. I was left with an impression of elegance, humour, self-deprecation. Not exactly what you expect from a weapons expert. Perhaps it was love. Perhaps it's time we should all stop worrying – and learn to love the bomb.

The Times, November 1998

113

Television review

Isolation and solitude fascinate me. I like nothing better than to read about Shackleton and his men, marooned for years on the slowly revolving pack ice of the Weddell Sea. They ate a lot of seals, you know, and 'Shacks' (as his loyal drifters styled him) banned all smutty talk, on the principle that it was pointless to dwell on what you couldn't have.

When they finally emerged from the pack and floated their frail vessels on the treacherous waters, Shacks deposited the bulk of his men on a desolate rock called Elephant Island, before sailing on with a few companions in an open boat, across six hundred miles of the roughest sea in the world, to fetch help from South Georgia. It was on the final leg of this epic journey, when the party was traversing the treacherous, unmapped spine of the island, that Shacks thought he felt 'a fourth presence', another man, who trudged beside them, willing them on with quiet, paternal assurance. It was talk of this numinous being that inspired Eliot to write, in *The Waste Land*, 'Who is the third that walks always beside you?/When I count, there are only you and I together/But when I look ahead up the white road/There is always another walking beside you . . .'

Fourth man – third man; it's not the numbers that count, it's that 'other', that elusively supportive man we travellers into the uncharted wastes yearn for. Certainly Matthew Parris would have been overjoyed to encounter another man on one of his bone-numbing treks across the icy wastes of Desolation Island, treks we endured with him for the sake of his soul and a four-month video diary (*To the Ends of the Earth: Dreaming on Desolation Island*, Channel 4). And if that man had been gay, then so much the better. But would *any* gay man have done? Suppose, when Parris was tramping through a white-out, he'd felt a ghostly presence at his side and discovered, on closer examination, that it was Peter Mandelson? 'Peter!' Parris might've exclaimed. 'How amazing! What brings you to this astonishingly remote place almost entirely devoid of cocktail parties, although blessed with staggeringly low property prices?' But what if Mandelson had only stared at him balefully through the blizzard, and pronounced the awful enquiry, 'Why did you out me on *Newsnight*?'

I suppose Parris was only being reasonable when he dwelt on the issue of his sexuality during his sojourn through Antarctic winter. After all, what are diaries for? And parked at a French scientific base on Desolation Island (or Kerguelen as the French tediously insist on calling it, simply because some geezer by that name pitched up four years before Captain Cook), Parris was entirely alone save for fifty-six Frenchmen and two Frenchwomen. And when there was homophobic banter, or stir-crazy drag acting out, he 'just grinned' and pretended it didn't matter.

It was a form of 'deception by silence' that didn't make him feel comfortable, although in the end the harsh exigencies of life in this *ultima Thule* made him realise that it was, quite simply, beside the point. Indeed, after all, look at the arithmetic – if all the men and both women were heterosexual, any sexual activity whatsoever could only heighten tensions unbearably. But what I prefer to believe is that most of the French were in fact as camp as a row of explorers' tents, and that Parris's sense of isolation was ruthlessly compounded by a fiendishly sustained Gallic practical gag. Every day Parris stood in the canteen queue with rugged hunting types called things like Thierry and Lionel, who the minute his back was turned began tittering, and saying to one another in impenetrable dialect French, 'Ho, ho! Outed Mandy on *Newsnight* – and now he has to stay in on Desolation Island!'

I digress – but only a little, because beyond the issue of his sexuality, we gained little insight into the whys and wherefores of Matthew Parris, beyond the fact that he's feeling his age (fifty), and that he found that Kerguelen itself 'refused to be real'. But in fairness to Parris, although he confessed to a mid-life crisis, and a need to escape the persiflage-for-pelf that constitutes his métier (or as he put it rather well, 'sneering for a living'), he never said he was going to Kerguelen to find himself, or any such hippie twaddle. No, Kerguelen had fascinated him since boyhood, and why shouldn't it? This archipelago, marooned down in the roaring forties of the southern Indian Ocean, is the size of Wales, has a coastline the same length as France's, and boasts a unique flora and fauna, while being devoid of human population beyond the above-mentioned *blagueurs*.

Parris said goodbye to Austin Mitchell and Michael Fabricant on the terrace of the House of Commons. Blimey! Imagine that – if I had to spend two minutes with Michael Fabricant I'd happily undertake to do a video diary from Devil's Island for a twenty-year stretch. Parris flew to Mauritius and then on to Réunion, where he experienced a wildlife preview in the form of a vast colony of penguins which reminded him of New Labour – 'Their proximity breeds hostility; while they co-operate they don't like each other' – and some elephant seals which reminded him of Tories – 'great big uncouth things wrestling together in the slime'. But from there on, as the ship took him two thousand miles further south, Parris's way with words steadily fell behind in its wake.

He did manage one good line over the next four months. When fearing for his life, he ruminated on how corpses on Kerguelen became 'human beings in kit form, held together by Gore-Tex'. However, for most of the time his schoolboy French was matched by his schoolboy English. When one of the Frenchmen, Jackie, was shot in a hunting accident by Joel, the base's senior doctor, Parris averred that his journalistic instincts were 'completely inappropriate'. How true, but some of them wouldn't have gone amiss in his coverage of the rest of this unique beat.

Wherever Parris pointed his video camera he came up with astonishing footage of a land where waterfalls blow up in the sky like fire hoses, and that sky is traversed by sun after snow after rain within minutes. Yet still we came away knowing little of either his companions or their forlorn fiefdom. Instead we were treated to a couple of brave-verging-on-foolhardy journeys into the interior, one of which aimed at circumnavigating – at Parris's bequest – Mount Ross, an impressive ziggurat of rock and ice which is Kerguelen's highest peak. Parris trained up for this to no avail. After being blown over countless times, and suffering a soaking sub-zero bivouac, he conceded, 'Kergeulen is nature's way of telling me to slow down.' Poor island, to be known only as Parris's pathetic fallacy.

On the way back home, Parris told us that he wouldn't have minded staying, and that he'd have to 'persuade myself it all mattered again'. I say: don't bother, Matthew, turn around. And while you're at it, there are a fair few political commentators who could usefully accompany you. But next time, don't bother with the video diary – there's a good chap.

Independent on Sunday, December 2000

114

Schadenfreude is one of the English's least attractive national characteristics. I say 'English' advisedly – for this propensity for laughing at the misfortunes of others seems to be the province of nations who consider themselves to be superior to the common weal of experience. At its simplest, *schadenfreude* expresses itself in the involuntary guffaw expelled in the face of a pratfall. 'You silly fool,' the laugh says, 'you can't even manage to walk along the road without encountering a banana skin, whereas I inhabit a more ethereal plane where such things could never happen.' But at its most sophisticated, this crass emotion encompasses the fate of whole peoples subjected to the imperial boot: 'You daft indigenes,' proclaims nationalist *schadenfreude*, 'how could you be so stupid as to fight our wars for us, render unto us your raw materials and the sweat of your labour, let alone learn to play cricket!' Is it any wonder that *schadenfreude* is one of the few national characteristics that the English indisputably share with those other Hegelians of the joy buzzer – the Germans?

On the face of it, this has been a vintage week for those of us such as myself who, in the ordinary course of events, would no sooner laugh at the misfortune of others than we would inflict it. The news that the Prime Minister's son, sixteen-year-old Euan, was found drunk and incapable, lying by some railings in London's Leicester Square, should've given me the opportunity for a righteous fit of merriment at the expense of a premier who has given every indication, since his ascent to power, that he considers his example – as parent, as moralist, as pedagogue – to be the one that all we adult children should rigorously adhere to. Yes, this was a heaven-sent opportunity for me to visit the sins of the child on the sanctimonious father, and see him hung high on his own hoisted petard.

And yet, even at this point of maximum payback, why is it that I, who have every reason to want the stretched elastic of the Prime Minister's convictions to snap back in his face, find myself unable to let go? Is it because, in truth, there's nothing to be gained politically by anyone who wishes to put a spin on young Euan's case of the spins? What we have here is harsh evidence of the fact that we live in a society where the socially acceptable way for young people to celebrate a milestone in their cephalisation is for them to put large portions of their forebrains to sleep with a toxic, sedative substance.

I don't doubt that Euan Blair is, as his father says, fundamentally a 'good lad'. But there are masses of 'good lads' out there who lose control over alcohol every night of the week. With increasingly liberal licensing laws, and a plethora of sugary alcoholic drinks on the market, rituals of intoxication in our culture are just another zone of unfettered capitalism. If there was one thing that Old Labour *did* understand, it was the virtue of a bit of social drinking – while with New Labour it's the antisocial variety that's gaining ground.

Today, BBC Radio 4, July 2000

115

I had nursed a strange ambition to walk to the end of Britain. Not, of course, the *whole* way; any old fund-raiser on a tricycle can manage that. But the last little nub end – the End end. Few people seemed really to know where the end of Britain was. It certainly wasn't at John O'Groats – even though this stretch of chomped, northern coastline is itself deliciously under-imagined.

This Endism had been broiling inside me while I hung out in Glasgow for a few days last summer, but when we headed north I began to simmer over with the notion. I've been heading up to Orkney now for some five years, for R and R and for serious peace and quiet within which to write. I have a friend who has a beautiful, early-nineteenth-century dower house, which looks across the sound from the northern isle of Rousay, to the mainland of Orkney. It's possibly my favourite place in the world.

But this trip to the far north was going to be different. We were going beyond Orkney – itself a most under-oriented place (friends in London can't even pin its tail on the British donkey) – extreme as that might seem. We were going to Britain's true *ultima Thule*, the long, crooked finger of land that stabs towards the pole – Shetland.

As an adoptive Orcadian I was sceptical about Shetland. The landscape was said to be far rockier, the people more insubstantial and, inevitably, the weather worse, the winter days shorter. In the event I was ludicrously charmed. From our precipitate landfall – the little Shorts inter-island plane dropping like a stone on to the runway that slopes down from the vast, encephalitic, Sumburgh headland – we entered a green Arcadia. Everywhere the sheep-cropped turf was covered with a pointillist carpet of wild flowers; everywhere the blue seas scintillated; and everywhere we went there was the excellent infrastructure that is born of exceedingly healthy oil revenues.

Not only that, but there was also the infectious hospitality only possessed by those who have always been friendly to strangers, and who are now enjoying a windfall season of cosmic proportions. No wonder the Orcadians speak dourly of the place; the Shetlanders – for the time being – have got it made.

We had three days to drive the seventy-odd miles up through Shetland. The days remained sunny – if not exactly fit for basking. (This may have been mid-June, but we were as far north as Bergen in Norway.) We stayed at a marvellous manse-style hotel near Walls, where, after a bibulous dinner, I backed my hire car off the ha-ha. 'Oh my God!' I said to the proprietor. 'I feel incredibly embarrassed . . .' 'No matter,' he replied; 'you get to bed and let me sort it out.' And he did – I heard him and a posse of the other guests bodily shifting the vehicle in the small hours.

Further north we stayed at a 'traditional Shetland croft', full of such traditional elements as a massive satellite dish, and a landlady who had her own web page. She described her hostelry as offering a 'warm Shetland welcome', but really this was a gross understatement – the welcome was positively incandescent, with food provided non-stop in simply gargantuan helpings.

On the efficient inter-island ferry we departed the mainland and headed north, first to the island of Yell, known chiefly for being an enormous peat bog, and then, on another short ferry crossing, from Yell on to Unst – the final island in the Shetland group, and, of course, the end of Britain.

We were scheduled to stay with the Laird of Unst, who, things not being what they were, has been reduced – along with his good lady wife (can 'Lairdess' possibly be correct?) – to running a bed and breakfast out of their manse, near the settlement of Buness. The Laird, who flew for the RAF for many years, and had the balding, avine appearance of your serious fly-bird, is the lineal descendant of a batch of famous Shetlander naturalists; one of these fellows saw fit to campaign for the protection of the great skua, a particularly noisy – 'Aaark-Aaark!' – and aggressive gull of vast proportions. The bird is known locally as the bonxie, because of its quite understandable desire to bonk you on the head with its beak if you trespass upon its nesting sites during the breeding season.

The principal breeding ground of the skua is the northernmost part of Unst, which is also the northernmost part of Britain. You can park about four miles short of the final landfall, and walk up and over the rugged moorland, until you achieve the End. This – I announced to the company (the Laird and Lairdess and a couple of fearsomely spry retired doctors from Edinburgh) – was what I intended to do after dinner. They didn't attempt to dissuade me.

After all, as Shetlanders never tire of telling you, the nights are so light here at this time of year that you can comfortably read a newspaper outside – as long, that is, as it's printed in 32-point Helvetica extra-bold. For the dusk may never fade to black, but it still gets very dusky in these parts come midnight.

I left my pregnant and long-suffering wife in the last car-park in Britain at about 12.30 a.m. and set out on the steep path leading up to Herma Ness. To my right the ground fell away steeply into Burra Firth, and on the peak of the hill on the other side I could see the lights of the radar station, Saxa Vord, twinkling eerily.

As I gained the moor, two brown, whirring shapes lifted aloft from the heather. They were aaarking furiously. They were bonxies. I had brought a handy stick with which to fend off the gulls, but even so their sudden appearance shocked me – I've never been that wild about birds, especially not large, aggressive ones. Inadvertently I shouted out, 'Bugger off, you bonxies!' and then suddenly some thirty pairs lifted off from the surrounding heather. I had forgotten the magnificent work of the Laird's twitching forefathers: this was the breeding season – and this was the nesting site.

I walked the seven miles there and back whirling the stick around my head, as bird after bird attempted to plant its beak in my forehead. Despite this, the end of Britain lived up to expectations. The bonxies served only to crank up a sense of overweening isolation. As I gained the high point of the headland I could see the land fall away towards the north, and there, beyond the final cliff edge, was a final skerry, with a final lighthouse upon it.

For a while I was the last man in Britain, standing in the gloaming, whirling a fence post around my sweaty head. Somehow it felt absolutely right.

Sunday Telegraph, November 1997

116

So, the Oxford University Press is relaxing rules on the use of split infinitives, the use of 'but' at the start of sentences, and the use of mono-sentence paragraphs. Bully for them.

Naturally this will engender a backlash from those who see their role in life as defenders of that notorious oxymoron 'correct English'. As if correct English were to the language what 'full English' is to the breakfast: a comprehensive, wholesome, national repast, which will keep you regularly using the right syntax and grammar throughout the day.

Of course, the problem here is that any such prescriptive rules – telling people what should and shouldn't be done with a language – will utterly fail to generate more English sentences, whether 'correct' or not. And the only way to discover if a piece of English is truly grammatical is to go and ask the people who use it if they understand it. YerknowhatImean an' that?

The whole industry of language correctness has become the preserve of a group of prissy conformists, whose attempts to bolster the *status quo* are as transparent as those of censors in any other medium.

The notion of 'correct English' belongs to the eighteenth century and the rise of British imperialism, when it began to be believed that English should aspire to the regularity and (alleged) clarity of Latin. But Latin was already, by this time, a dead and codified language, no longer subject to the ceaseless change and mutation that mark a living tongue.

Another key factor needed for language correctness is a desire to impose class and ethnic differences, by reinforcing a hierarchy of acceptable usage. Looked at this way, the drive towards 'correct English' is to class divisions as the Académie Française is to French cultural isolationism: a great support.

However, the written language does not exist in isolation, it is continually fertilised and synergised by foreign languages, argot, patois and slang. This occurs at the level of utterance, when the multifarious semiologies – body language, accent, gesture, tone, touch – are simultaneously braided in the act of understanding.

Looked at this way 'correct English' is dry, dead English; the language with which one would converse with a computer, not a lover.

Of course, there is a need for people who write English with the intention of conveying complex ideas to have a close understanding of how to accurately parse a sentence. But this is not analogous to the need a fine artist has to be a proficient draughtsman. Too many of the rules followed by the writer are, in fact, meta-rules. These rules about rules are a limiting constraint. They help the writer to easily express, solely, what can be easily conceived. They are, therefore, part of the problem to which the only solution is the neologism and the wilfully misapplied rule.

Thus.

Independent, August 1995

117

If you're a novelist – which I profess to be – one of the most favoured questions for people to ask is: do you mind criticism? Why novelists should be either immune from, or consumed by, criticism any more than anyone else is beyond me. If I tell a plumber that his ball isn't cocking, or an accountant that her tax returns deserve an indefinite run, I'd expect both of them to respond with the appropriate ire or joy – we all like to be told that what we do, we do well.

Still, the position of the writer is perhaps a bit more complex, given there are myriad possible critics of any given piece of work, and that not all of them equally affect the reading public's overall perception. It's usually assumed that the critics the novelist most fears are the newspaper and other media pundits, who allegedly pore over the text on publication – but this isn't so. Any writer who's worth his Biro knows that these effusions – whether positive or negative – are ephemeral. No matter how much a newspaper critic dislikes a book, she cannot be on hand, day after day, in the bookshop, to impress upon the consumer that they really ought not to buy it.

The bookseller, on the other hand, is the critic whom the writer needs must respect and fear. The bookseller has the power to stock a book, and the authority to recommend it. The bookseller can make or break a writer's career. All of this explains why, during the emotionally draining weeks that have seen the publication of my latest novel, the most depressing piece of criticism has come not from any scion of Grub Street, but from the board of Waterstone's the bookshop chain, who, in their infinite short-sightedness, have seen fit to fire Robert Topping, the manager of their branch in Deansgate, Manchester.

Over the years Topping has consistently bucked the growing tide of corporatism in the chain, which has seen the steady erosion of its founder's concept of individual branch buying policies, and commensurate profit-sharing. At Deansgate, Topping and his staff proved that you could stock a plethora of titles and still turn a profit. While never neglecting to order the mass-market books that people know they want to read, he also made sure there were others available to extend his customers' literary range. He's been a true friend – and by extension generous critic – to every writer he's elected to champion. When he told his staff the news of his dismissal – they wept.

While the notion that the market should dictate to the retailer may hold true for sellers of widgets or winkle-pickers, in the realm of creative properties such a policy will only result in wall-to-wall pulp. Without any retail outlet for serious or diverse writing, will there be any possible incentive to create it? The on-line bookselling operations may make it easier for people to purchase, but they, like all the dot-com companies, represent the growing anonymity of retail exchange.

No, to sell books properly you need the personal touch – not just the mouse's click. In the looming world of corporate globalisation, it seems some won't be content until one size of book is made to fit all. It'll be their own damn fault if it turns out to be one by Jeffrey Archer.

Today, BBC Radio 4, June 2000

118

I wonder if museum curators can get quite as emotionally blind and negatively protective of their work as restaurateurs? I only mention it because I'm about to deliver a bit of a slap to the people responsible for the new Earth Galleries at the Natural History Museum in South Kensington, and I'm keen to avoid being barred.

I admit, the idea of some epicene type in bifocals, their flannels flapping, and their Oxford tones quavering, 'You're barred from the ammonites!' isn't likely to strike fear into my ample bosom. It's hardly on a par with some of the threats I received during my time as a restaurant reviewer, when on one occasion a disgruntled *patron* sought to have me smeared in the press. Luckily the press seized up – but it was a close thing.

At the time, a friend remarked that I had to appreciate that receiving a tough review for any creative enterprise could be emotionally devastating – the nerves of the artist and all that crap. After all, how did I feel when I'd got a panning for a book I'd written? Not good, I concede, but I'm not subject to charging around the world seeking out people who might be reading the offending text and tearing it out of their resisting fingers. Indeed, it strikes me that the whole onus of the genuinely creative contract is *caveat emptor* on all sides.

I hope these curators understand this. Or are they – as their work might seem to imply – rather more spontaneous, even aggressive, artists? The *pièce de résistance* at the Earth Galleries is a mock-up of the interior of a convenience store in Kobe being shaken by a tremor. It has to be the first and last time in my life that I'll get to witness small children running towards an earthquake. The high style of bad taste involved in this pseudo-catastrophe, which trades on the screaming obliteration of thousands of Japanese people for the screeching titillation of thousands of museum-goers, defines a new nadir – and suggests equally direct ways of conveying other human disasters in exhibition contexts.

Why not a chance for visitors to the London Transport Museum to apprehend the forces involved in the Moorgate tube crash, when they step inside the realistic simulator (a train)? Or a prick in the arm when you visit the Wellcome Institute galleries? It'll make you violently ill for a couple of hours so that you can experience the beginnings of an Ebola outbreak!

But I'm running away with myself here – which is what I also like to do in museums. Let's face it, they're there for a good stroll on a Sunday afternoon when it's pissing outside. The only people who take a close interest in the exhibits themselves are either rejects from Larson cartoons (usually walking hand in hand) or children. A good museum should be a profoundly ambulatory and equally didactic experience. Old-fashioned exhibits involving *tableaux vivants*, panoramas, and things kids can crank, turn and press, are just dandy. Alternatively there's nothing wrong, when you've got something worth showing, in simply putting it on show.

The problem for the modern museum, which the Earth Galleries perfectly exemplify, is that it feels it has to compete with contemporary ideas of modern kids' entertainment. Thus, when you come in from Exhibition Road you're confronted with an entire four-storey atrium, dominated by an escalator which slowly sweeps you up into the interior of a colossal globe. The walls are midnight blue and painted with constellations. At the base of the escalator stand statues of six emblematic figures, kicking off with Blake's old, bearded Creator – if you like, a kind of Blake's Six. As you ascend into the globe you are treated to inspirational slogans projected on to the buckled walls of its heavy industrial interior: 'How Does the Earth Work?'; 'Can We Predict the Earth's Future?' Horribly New Labour – I wouldn't have been surprised if 'Ecosystems Will Be Smaller' had come up.

It's a sad attempt to reduce the grandeur of nature to the status of an arty evocation of the entrance to the Epcot Center at Disney World, or some such kitsch – and it's purely a function of assuming that contemporary youth can't get over the not-so-special effects provided by computer and video graphics. When you get to the top of the escalator you're treated to a glass cabinet containing a television on which Trevor McDonald intones news of the 1991 Pinatubo earthquake in the Philippines. Fantastic! History as it's made.

Besides the teasing notion of 'exhibiting' VDUs (watch out Bruce Nauman and all other installation artists – you have competition), there's the compulsion these wayward curators have felt to trick out each of the galleries as if it were another set from a science-fiction film of the past – here is *Babylon 5*, there's *Star Trek*, up above you can see a really quite striking *Blade Runner*, while down there is *Beneath the Planet of the Apes*.

There's nothing to arrest the progress of the foreshortened attention span, so the kids charge on. There are only a few things that require more interactivity than pushing a button – dribbling water over sand and gravel so as to demonstrate erosion is one of them – and they are appropriately busy. Otherwise all was onward march, except for a minute in the false Kobe, watching cans reassuringly rattle – but not fall – on the shelves and listening to the charming cries of young people being educated. Oh – there is one other piece of unusual cultural diffusion: all around the broad stairwell to the rear of the galleries wafts the pungent aroma of fish and chips, courtesy of a superb Leith's cafeteria. Truly earthy.

I suppose the problems of the exhibition designers are, quite literally, monumental. They have to set the immemorial within the context of the ephemeral and somehow make it last. I think they've cocked up, and the Earth Galleries will look as laughable as a pair of loons in twenty-five years' time. But then I and many other cultural commentators can be wrong. In the early seventies J. G. Ballard launched his book *Crash* by holding an exhibition of crashed cars. People called him sick and deranged. Now there's a quake-crushed Mitsubishi on show in South Ken – how the world turns!

On second thoughts, scratch that image of the flannel-clad Oxbridge twerp; any curator who can do that to a perfectly good family car is on the edge.

The Times, April 1998

119

The astonishing X1 button radio – from only £7.50.
Only the size of a 10p coin, it offers the full performance of a VHF radio, yet with its unique design fits discreetly in your ear. Only available from Sinclair Research – can you think of a more exclusive Christmas gift to give?

Well, put like that – no. I've always been a fan of radio, and the smaller the better, but the Sinclair X1 is actually a Hindenburg zeppelin of a miniature radio, crashing to the ground in great gouts of gaseous incandescence. It is *truly* astonishing – astonishing that Sir Clive is still at it after all these years, pumping out products with absurd, Dan Dare-style serial numbers ('Good evening gentlemen, let me introduce you to the L9 Erection Enhancer'), and astonishing that they're still utter crap.

After all, this was the man behind the C5. The C5 was such a turkey of a vehicle that far from its contributing to a major reduction in urban traffic density, the only one of the *bijou* pods I can ever remember seeing in service, in London, was on the roof of a Volvo parked outside a fitness centre in Hampstead, acting as a stand for an advertising hoarding. Every time I drove past the place I used to feel sorry for Sir Clive – until the advent of the X1, that is.

Sir Clive has taken years to recuperate from the débâcle of the C5, but eventually he has emerged from his sequestration to bring us the X1; and astonishingly, as the C5 is to small-scale passenger transit, so is the X1 to small-scale radio listening: an utter failure. I couldn't resist the display advert in the papers, which shows a grinning Sir Clive with one of the button radios held up against his spectacle frames. As if that weren't enough to disabuse me, there was also an 'actual size' picture of the X1, and beneath it the wholly beguiling offer that I could purchase six of the little buggers for a mere £45.

Without more ado I made with the ancestral cheque book and waited for the self-styled 'master of innovation' to post me my cache of X1s. The box arrived from Sinclair Research in Wellingborough and I ripped it open. It wasn't that hard to fit the lithium battery into the X1, and it certainly wasn't difficult to turn it on and tune it in, but getting the thing inside my ear proved quite another matter.

I don't know whether Sir Clive modelled the X1 on his own ear, or that of a relative, or that of some unsuspecting worker, or another sort of creature altogether, but whoever it was they had enormous ear-holes. I'm not exactly petite, but even after I'd removed the foam surround from the ear-piece of the X1, I had as much chance of getting it into my ear as I would a fair-size turnip. I could have hammered at the thing with a rubber mallet and it still wouldn't have lodged. The master of innovation claims that the X1 has 'unique sure-grip ear design'. He's bonkers in the nut – the only way you can get the X1 to grip in your ear is by risking the perforation of your ear-drum.

Actually, this foible of the X1 was almost worth the £45. I had hours of fun just sitting there with an X1, and whenever anybody came into the room I'd say, 'Do you want to try the astonishing X1 button radio?' Then I'd collapse in undulations of the most delicious *schadenfreude* as they intimately wounded themselves. Unsurprisingly I wasn't at all popular for some weeks. But they think they suffered? I actually had to road-test the X1. I managed to get one lodged in my ear, manipulated the hideous little plastic knobbles so that I could hear John Humphrys duffing up some unsuspecting junior minister, and ventured forth into the city.

Yes, it was all as Sir Clive – that master of innovation – promised me: I could walk down the street, sit on a bus, or a train, and no one about me could tell that I was listening to the radio. Actually, I could hardly tell I was listening to the radio either, because the volume of the X1 is pitched so low that the bloody thing is completely inaudible unless you're squatting in a soundproofed room. As I strolled down the street John

Humphrys was reduced to the merest of background murmurs. If you elected to gain your impressions of the world from the astonishing X1, it would be like permanently overhearing life rather than listening to it; the world as a species of cosmic Muzak.

Yes, the only intimation I had that I was porting the X1 – 'weighs only half an ounce' – was the acute pain induced by mashing the thing into my poor lughole. Sir Clive generously provides a year's guarantee with the X1, but it's entirely unnecessary, because I can guarantee that you won't be wearing the thing for more than a few minutes. This radio is a novelty – and then it's a useless piece of plastic tat.

Not that I feel disappointed or in any way cheated by the master of innovation. The X1 has provided me with hours of febrile tittering – and I've given the other five to friends who also have lamentable senses of humour. Having waited so long to see what Sir Clive would come up with after the world-beating fiasco of the C5, I can honestly say that the X1 is no let-down whatsoever. It also introduces the teasing prospect of what the self-styled master of innovation will be up to for the millennium. A food processor the size of Milton Keynes? A vacuum cleaner inside its own bag? A mobile phone with a cord? An enormous dome in Greenwich?

Well, whatever it is – it's bound to be astonishing.

The Times, March 1998

120

As an agnostic I'm not at all sure that I should be saying anything at all about the Christian festival of Easter. We are living through paradoxical times as far as religious beliefs are concerned. Indeed, when it comes to considering Easter I find myself screwed to the sticking-point of what my 'agnosticism' actually means. It's all very well hiding behind 'I don't know' when it comes to the large-scale metaphysical underpinnings of religion: does God exist? (I don't know.) What happens when we die? (I don't know.) Are we brought into this world for a transcendent purpose? (Once again – I don't know.) However, at the level of everyday ethical decisions – should the whereabouts of sex offenders be made known publicly? Should government seek to influence the nature of the family? – such 'I don't know's really do become offensive to the properly religious – of all stripes.

'When you're lost in the rain and worries and it's Easter time too/And your gravity fails, negativity don't pull you through . . .' Bob Dylan a.k.a. Robert Zimmerman – the secular Jew-turned-fundamentalist Christian-turned-orthodox Jew, whose Zen grappling with religion and religiosity lies as near to the core of the poetics of the post-bomb twentieth century as any other body of literature – speaks for me in this cold, awful, vernal equinox, as he voices for us all the unnaturalness of the rest of the emotional year: 'I've never seen spring turn so quickly into autumn.'

I hate Easter time – and by extension I hate Easter. Not that I really know anything of Easter itself at all. There's a Venn intersection between Radio 4, the laity of the Church of England and the rest of what laughably calls itself the fourth estate in this country, which means that the rituals of the organised and semi-state-sanctioned religions receive a vastly disproportionate amount of consideration. At the very exhausted fag-end of a century that has seen so many human lives snuffed out in such physically obliterating ways – conflagrated to ash, gassed to ordure, machine-gunned to pulp, exploded to inhumanly less than the sum of their parts – it would seem to me that to seek redemption in the forty extra days between Easter and Pentecost putatively allotted, two thousand years ago, to a self-proclaimed messiah is – how can I put it with even a scintilla of respect for people's beliefs? – utterly ridiculous.

What should a Lenten discourse really concern itself with here? Perhaps the history of the cartography of egg hunts? Or the provenance and eschatology of the Easter Bunny? Which, for those of you at home, I have respectfully capitalised. No, I'm not being remotely facetious here – I'm absolutely confident that for those non-listeners, those uncomfy non-communicants, the tale of Jesus Christ's trumped-up 'trial', barbaric execution, clandestine interment and then jack-in-the-box reappearance was quite simply the most *Star Trek*-like episode of the dumbed-down Biblical fables we were retailed as we sat, cross-legged, serge-shorted or -pinafored, on that primarily important, herring-bone parquet.

Which is not by way of implying for one second that the religious observance of Easter is solely the preserve of the bourgeoisie; avocados are not the only fruit. It's just that you out there in radio land are unlikely to be working-class churchgoers (small 'c', small 'c'), tent-peggers, adopters of strange undergarments, wacko or Waco sympathisers. No, I see you

353

gently chortling along with *The Vicar of Dibley*, fully paid-up subscribers to a faith which has – let's face it – joyfully auto-destructed: 'Devil-worshipper? Jolly good, come along to the Vicarage on Saturday, we're having a little coffee morning for newcomers to the parish.'

I've now been to Golgotha. Been to that Unholy Land. There's nothing more risible and historically disorientating about the environs of Jerusalem than those road signs that read 'SODOM 20 KM'. And there's nothing more destructive of the *Star Trek* view of the Resurrection – a peculiar scenario involving a being with amazing powers marooned on a remote, backward planet – than a stroll around that cramped quarter wherein Jesus spent his final mortal hours. In the *Star Trek* view Jesus is, of course, Caucasian. Pilate has a toga and a laurel-style eyeshade. The temple priests – the quisling Klingons of their day – have exaggeratedly curled and perfumed beards; unctuous and unguent in one. And everyone observes the most important convention which renders this outlandish primitivism endlessly relevant: they speak standard – RP, even – English.

The cross is plywood – and a criminal from central casting, complete with standard-issue off-white dhoti, gets to carry the thing. The Way of the Cross is like any picturesque stroll through an ancient medina; the stations are spiritual time clocks; the Crucifixion itself is mercifully televisual – when the sign is placed above His head with the dreaded ascription 'King of the Jews', it's more in the manner of a title sequence than a grotesquely abusive, cosmologically evil singularity.

To complete the teleplay, the garden of Gesthemane is just that, a municipal-cum-Olympian agglomeration of miniature cypresses, gravel paths and well-tended ornamental beds. The womenfolk, who're beautifully, cleanly attired in freshly laundered blue robes with white borders, arrive to make that epoch-creating discovery. Now at this point in the gospels it's easy for us cross-legged 1960s late-baby-boomer, Vietnam-as-TV-spectacle-witnessing kids to understand how it should be that the rock placed at the mouth of the tomb has been rolled to one side. Clearly, like all those bits of other worlds that are forever being hefted around by the crew of the starship *Enterprise*, this alien stone is made from polystyrene, or foam rubber, or moulded plastic. Suffice to say – even a flabby Kirk could've thrust it aside, and we know what a demigod he is.

Yes, I hate Easter, and the very movability of the feast makes it still more hateful – for I never know, in any given year, when it will heave into view, freighted down with its groaning cargo of unpleasantness. It's not the Council of Nicaea that bothers me – although as a half-Jew with Catholic children from my first marriage, I would seem purpose-built to respond to doctrinal disputations. Even that half-Jewishness requires some clarification -- I mean, is it strictly *possible* to be half-Jewish?

The Jews might well claim me for their own, as my mother certainly was Jewish. But so intent was she on making her entire life a performance act of deracination that I was uncircumcised, not barmitzvahed, and only ever went to synagogue in my early teens, accompanying thoroughbred schoolfriends in order to get in with them. On the other hand my philosophically-inclined, Anglican father – 'I think of Jesus as a remarkable personality, rather like Plato' – did make a claim on my soul. I was christened – as was my brother before me – by the fantastically ancient vicar of All Saints, Hove, the Reverend Bickerstaff.

Throughout my childhood our father would take us two, squealing, atheistically-perverted (courtesy of my Jewish, anti-Semitic mother) brats along to whatever empty, prayerful barn happened to be in our vicinity when either Christ's birthday or His death day fell. What a thankless, graceless task it was for him. Try as he might to enthuse us with the sonorous beauties of the King James Bible, as declaimed by middle-class, middle-aged men in dresses, it was far too late. We had already been claimed by the split infinitives of *Star Trek*, were already preparing to boldly go into a world where ethics, so far from inhering in the very structure of the cosmos, was a matter of personal taste akin to a designer label, sewn into the inside lining of conscience.

My mother *died* at Easter. She who thought all religion was an out-and-out con, in that beautifully wiseacre fashion only a native New Yorker can achieve. She died in the Royal Ear Hospital of lung cancer – an irony she might have appreciated, were it not for the fact that in dying my mother was fearful, alone, angry and devoid of any humour, no matter how black.

She said to me a few weeks before her death, 'The greatest thing about being a pessimist is that you're always starting off on the race of life with the understanding that you're bound to lose.' Whether this was intended to give any comfort to either her or me I've no idea – since it certainly did neither. In the event, her pessimism was of no use anyway; she died utterly unconscious, shoved deep beneath the meniscus of sentience by barbiturates and opiates.

They had admitted her to University College Hospital where her oncologist was the consultant, but – wasn't it ever thus – there were no beds available, and my brother and I had to follow her prone body as it was pushed through the subterranean passageways that connect this central London necropolis, until we rose up in a lift to the Royal Ear. This process was, on reflection, my mother's crucifixion: the cruel, iron trolley they wheeled her on was her secular cross; in place of the vinegar that was thrust into Christ's mouth by the disciples, nutriments were fed into Mother's arm via a transparent drip; and instead of the Roman legionnaire's sword, thrust into Mother's side were the increasing dosages of diamorphine that ensured that for all time she would remain dead.

In mourning my mother – whom I loved very deeply – I went through all the recognised stages of anger, denial and eventual acceptance. Like the disciples, in the days and weeks immediately succeeding her death I would see 'fake' mothers wandering the streets of London much as she did in life. However, since neither of us believed remotely in the existence of personal immortality (and she in no kind of transcendence whatsoever), these visitations were mute and hazy. If Mother had felt driven to communicate anything to me from beyond the grave, it would doubtless have been a sardonic remark about the cost of her cremation.

Like so many of the most important and resonant facts about our lives I have opted to block out the exact date in April when it was that we stood in the plastic cubicle and watched the mutant cells finally push Mother out of her own head and into oblivion. So Easter is, for me, for the rest of my life, that time of the year when death comes to visit for a while. Western death: painless, medicalised, and about as ethical as a tooth extraction. It's a pity there are false messiahs – just as there are false teeth.

Yes, there will be no resurrection for Mother, just as there will be no resurrection for all the millions upon millions of dead souls which clutter this world of ours, like so much psychic lumber. Yes, they're gone – and they're not coming back.

So it is that I suppress my memory of the date my mother died and I never know the date upon which Easter is going to fall. As winter fades, a council quite as doctrinally hair-splitting as that of Nicaea begins its first convocation of the year.

Lent talk for BBC Radio 4, February 1999

121

As I walked towards the St Stephen's entrance to the Houses of Parliament it became clear to me that something was not so much afoot, as underfoot. It looked like red dye, but presumably it was meant to resemble blood. Mixed in with this slurry, as if they were the ingredients of a bizarre, alfresco salad, were crude photocopies of banknotes. From the angled barriers, where docile tourists shuffled and lowed, to the Gothic portico of the Mother Legislature, this stuff was smeared across the flagstones. Burly policemen stood about with their arms crossed in that way that only burly police can effect: as if it were the very hand signal of authority itself.

And inside the portico, surrounded by more crossed arms, were the tossers of the salad; a small posse of anti-arms-trade demonstrators. Some police with uncrossed arms were wearily removing them one by one. 'Mind your step, sir,' one of them cautioned me as I entered; 'it's very slippery,' while one of the demonstrators chipped in as well, 'Don't support the bloody arms trade . . .' – it wasn't so much an exhortation as a mild appeal. The scourge of the international arms dealers and their log-rolling parliamentary buddies was speaking more in sorrow than in anger; and as I proceeded to the formidable battery of metal detectors it struck me just how suitable it was that his accent was so resolutely Oxbridge, impeccably upper-middle-class.

For class is what the House of Lords is *really* all about; and I was visiting Parliament to see the Lords in action – if that isn't a contradiction in terms – and speak with Lord Conrad Russell, the Liberal Democrat Social Security Spokesperson, scion of whiggery, third of his line and a man firmly committed to undermining the ground of his – and his descendants' – very existence.

But before I could get to Lord Russell I had to negotiate the Pantagruelian corridors of power and peek into the chamber itself. Inside the Houses of Parliament people of all stripes walk with an extra spring to their step, as if they were on their way to do something of monumental, but not manifest, importance, such as photocopy the Zinoviev letter. There is this air of substantive bustling, and there is also the sheer size of the joint – everything seemingly constructed for a race of Victorian giants with dreadfully kitsch, neo-Gothic taste.

Turning right from the vast central lobby, I entered the Lords with no need of any ceremonial. After all, they are lords, I'm a commoner; their very ascription implies suzerainty – mine subjugation. But even a minor, middle-class hack such as myself gets a regal welcome from the tail-coated major-domo in the Lords' lobby. I picked up my press card, and after ascending staircases with the air of being backstage to a poorly-attended performance that has been on a centuries-long run, I entered the chamber itself.

From the press gallery you look down on a scene that is essentially mock-sacerdotal. The House of Lords is constructed in the form of a church of bespoke-suited cardinals, who sit on red leather banquettes with microphones dangling over them. At the far end there is, of course, a throne, and this is divided off from the body of the house by a railing analogous to a rood-screen, in that it symbolically marks the break between kingly priest and noble suppliants.

Despite the microphones, the glutinous burble of the noble Lord's voice was hard to decipher. This might well have been Viscount Astor, asking Her Majesty's Government what progress had been made in the review of Independent Television Commission programme sponsorship, but it was hard to tell. Perhaps if the Viscount had been wearing a real coronet, of the form to which he is entitled – sixteen silver balls on stalks – then I would have been able to identify him. As it was I found myself unable to do anything but agree with Walter Bagehot's famous assessment of the actual business of the Lords: that the best cure for admiring it was to go and take a look.

Over the last few weeks, and most notably in the last issue of the *Statesman*, the advance guard of the Labour Government-in-waiting has been rehearsing some of its proposals for stimulating this impotent mausoleum. In fact, Blair's proposal to abolish the right of hereditary peers to sit in the Lords may be his most sensible policy thus far. It's a simple and effective blow against ancient privilege, and it obviates the need for *a priori* constitutional change of the kind that would become a morass of committee speechifying.

But does Labour really understand what's involved? Are they fully aware of what it means to bat all those balls about? Titles have a resonance and meaning that are well capable of infiltrating and perverting the egalitarianism of the most committed democrats. I vividly remember having the misfortune to sit at a literary lunch next to the wife of an ennobled former Labour minister. When I challenged her as to why she was allowing herself to be addressed as 'Lady —', she replied that she only used her title in public contexts – which rather raised the question, what other possible context *could* you use a title in? 'Oh, by the way, my Lady, would you pass me the butter?' springs to mind.

The bewildering gyroscope of potential constitutional change in which we currently find ourselves, where sovereignty is compromised by a supranational as well as an internal dimension of instability, may be blinding us to the extent to which we still pay attention to the balls. The recent defence proffered by Viscount Cranborne (also entitled to sixteen silver balls) of the hereditary peerage as 'coming to represent the common man in Parliament' may be logically laughable, but that such a notion could even be entertained gives the lie to just how little faith we have in our parliamentary system, and how fundamentally we are affected by the balls.

I myself experienced this on descending from the press gallery and lingering in the lobby while Lord Russell (eight silver balls on stalks, alternating with eight gold strawberry leaves), chatted to Lord Callaghan (six silver balls) and another noble lord whose ball count was uncertain. I, who would have been altogether comfortable being cop-handled out of St Stephen's gate, my hands smeared with red dye, found myself suffused with a most unpleasant deference. Even the sight of the Marquess of Bath (four strawberries alternating with four silver balls), tripping past in trademarked velveteen suit and matching shoulder bag, failed to jerk off my culottes.

This unaccustomed deference persisted over tea and tea cakes ('I think you'll find them quite excellent') with Lord Russell in the Lords' tea room. Lord Russell talked eloquently of the history of the House – something that, as a historian, he was more than entitled to do – and rebutted some of the lower balls that are tossed at the balls. No, there wasn't a lavish attendance allowance available to the backwoodsmen, just thirty quid for expenses and thirty for secretarial help – less than social security if it were viewed as a wage. No, he couldn't in all conscience defend his privilege; after all, his own wife pointed out that he had no more right to sit in the House than she. But the Lords, he felt, still had an important role, and the hereditary peers had a vital, if numinous, connection with it. The Lords were an arena in which non-partisan opinion could be represented; in the Commons they played to the gallery, or would be responding to the upheld Blairite red card, while in the Lords there could still be an opportunity for meaningful dissent. The role of the legislature had to be to check the power of the executive, and in this the Commons were already notably deficient, and there was no reason to imagine that a government of a different stripe would make much difference.

Lord Russell was compelling and frosty. At one point in our conversation he said, with absolutely no trace of irony whatsoever, 'When my great-grandfather passed the Reform Act . . .' and I didn't bat an eyelid, because for the last forty minutes or so I had really been charmed by the balls. Charmed by my host's erudition – in discussing the perverse attitude of the English to the Act of Union with Scotland, he described the English nation as 'a confirmed bachelor with a penchant for visiting prostitutes' – and paralysed by his deployment of that most deadly of class weapons: perfect manners.

Labour governments traditionally have a hard time on coming to power. The civil service can be institutionalised and obstructive, the very machinery of administration can gum up. But there's another deadly source of inertia: the very exact, frosty manners only ever fully achieved by those, such as Lord Russell, who seem to contain, encoded within their psyches – as if they were some kind of sentient, politico-cultural DNA – the living history of our polity.

I would argue that if you want to abolish the right of hereditary peers to sit in the Lords, you're going to have to strike profoundly at the class system itself, all the way up to its method-acting apex, the future monarch. And frankly, even I find it hard to believe that good-quality suits and nice haircuts can really substitute – in the popular, collective imagination – for all those balls.

New Statesman, December 1996

122

Restaurant review: Café de la Mer, 124A King's Road Arches, Brighton, East Sussex

For me the most perfect gastronomic moments are almost always alfresco. There's something about confining walls that detracts from any eating experience, and if they're restaurant walls all the more so. I recall a fantastic golden evening many years ago in the Dordogne when we discovered that a famous Parisian chef had gone to ground at a farmhouse in the vicinity. We trolled over there, and on trestle tables set up in a yard were served with a kingly meal. There was a whole chicken roasted in pastry, there was *foie gras* from a goose personally known to *le patron*, there was a lot of rough cider. Later, we played circular ping-pong using vacuum-cleaner attachments as bats.

And then there are the illimitable grazing precincts of Bangkok, where you can wander from stall to stall, having a fried fish stuffed with garlic at one and a plate of sweetmeats at the next, assembling an entire meal in a picaresque fashion.

Another great open-air eatery is the Djemaa el Fna, the main square in Marrakesh, where kitchens are set up amidst the dust and heat and you can eat your tajine within venom-spitting distance of a snake-charmer while arguing the finer points of theology with a Sufi mystic. (These will come up with the most unexpected throwaway remarks. When I was last there one shouted at me across a café in accusatory mode, 'Did you pay the poll tax!')

After all, if you're going to eat in public, you may as well be among the generality of mankind or the verdancy of nature, rather than having to listen to some fraught couple dissect their relationship alongside their fish dinner and confusing the bones of one with those of the other.

Which brings us rather neatly to Brighton on a baking hot Saturday afternoon. The stretch of the front at Brighton between the Palace Pier and the charred, buckled remainder of the West Pier becomes something quite special when the temperature soars. The crowds of day-trippers are noticeably more polyglot and urbane than you find at most seaside resorts. Hair is peroxided, earrings and tattoos are multiple, funky youth is in the ascendant: the air scintillates with pheromones.

Behind the beach the great bank of buildings – the Grand Hotel with its balconies and turrets, the concrete boxiness of the Metropole, and towards Hove, the Celesteville-style Regency terraces – waves and distorts in the haze. Sweep your gaze from the leaden pan of the sea across the crowded beach with its press of flesh to the townscape behind, and for a moment you could be on the tiered banks of the Ganges rather than the shingle shore of the Channel, so Babylonian is the impression of massed humanity, massed buildings and pious pleasure-seeking.

Even poor Madeleine, who was running something of a fever on one of the hottest days of the year, was awed by this prospect. She urged me on through the crowd using the simple expedient of sitting on my shoulders, pulling my hair and chanting rhythmically, 'I want to go on the bouncy castle!' The castle was duly attended, and then we looked for somewhere to eat.

Brighton has a lot of good places to eat at, but not many where you can just slide in and trough on a Saturday lunchtime without a reservation. And besides that, neither of the children could have been dragged away from the beach without a fight.

We stumbled on the Café de la Mer, tucked into one of the arches under the front itself. It looked perfect. It was licensed. It offered various, simple fish dishes. It had two ranks of tables, one set atop the hutment the cooking was done in, the other spread out along the tarmacked lane in front. There were artfully-sited tubs of geraniums. We could put ourselves down under one of the Brighton Corporation beach umbrellas (done in royal-blue and white stripes) and vicariously experience the ongoing promenade.

We decided on up rather than down. From the terraced level the mirrored ball, revolving on top of the Palace Pier, lanced rays into our eyes. Even from this distance we could see the gaping mouths of the screamers on the rollercoaster. Tucked behind this, there was some still more terrifying ride that seemed to involve being strapped into a giant hammer and tossed into the air. The West Pier, on the other hand, presented a sorry spectacle in contrast to this priapic promontory of adrenalin.

Long defunct as an amusement arcade, some years ago it was severed from the mainland to prevent more vandalism. The pier now hovers offshore like some dilapidated ghostly reminder of lost childhood. In my youth I far preferred the West to the Palace Pier. It was more homely and still had those mechanical tableaux, where if you dropped an old penny in the slot Mary Queen of Scots was beheaded, or the butler saw something (although you didn't).

The first bouncy castle ever to be erected in the British Isles was on the West Pier. A primitive thing, made from an inflated whale's bladder, it was much patronised by the notables in the 1871 season. Queen Victoria gave it a try but soon retired, remarking, 'It jiggles me in a most unseemly fashion.'

We ordered a bottle of Butterfly Ridge chardonnay from a waitress wearing slinky shorts with a corkscrew belt, and some juice for the children. Both arrived with pleasing alacrity. In a concrete area abutting the beach, a karaoke session was under way. A bald man was on stage singing along to the Detroit Spinners, and doing it not at all badly. In time he was replaced by a blues guitarist who essayed 'After the Thrill Is Gone' and then to my delight 'All Along the Watchtower', which for me is the heat-haze track *par excellence*.

The food came. The menu was nothing special at the Café de la Mer: fish and chips, moules and chips, burgers, baguettes, Greek salad and various jacket potatoes with fillings. The claim that the fish on offer was fresh struck me as dubious. Not even the fish that are alive in the Channel at the moment can be meaningfully described as fresh, let alone those removed from it. My sardines were all right – but I'd wager they came from somewhere like Portugal. The cod was truly grimbo, though; the batter had the consistency of grout – and so did the flesh.

But the chips were fine, and what more does one need than a chip, a glass of Australian chardonnay, and a runny-nosed three-and-a-half-year-old sitting on your lap, looking like a walrus with two tusks of snot? '*Et in Arcadia ego*,' I said to my companion. 'Who's an arsehole?' she replied, absent-mindedly.

Observer, June 1996

123

Restaurant review: McDonald's, 49 King's Road, London SW3; La Tante Claire, 68/69 Royal Hospital Road, London SW3

How to end it all? That was the problem. How to finally put down my eating irons, hang up my bib and resign this column in the same spirit that it has been written for the past couple of years? The answer came after deliberations between editors, consultants and various illustrious fatties of my acquaintance. Finally it was Christopher, my wayward architect buddy, who came up with the solution: 'You should eat at McDonald's on the King's Road, and then proceed on foot to La Tante Claire, where you should attempt to match the McMeal in every respect with items from Pierre Koffmann's notoriously rich, Gascon cuisine.'

He was right, of course; what greater contrast could there be than that between one of the only three Michelin three-star restaurants in London and the biggest restaurant chain on the planet? At La Tante they wear their stars on their window – at McDonald's they tend to be on the lapels of the staff's shirts. And in traversing the bare half-mile between the two establishments, I would in a sense be striding from one half of our divided nation to the other: from high-carbohydrate meals designed to bloat the bellies of the lumpenproletariat, to high-protein repasts engineered to tighten the collar studs of their rulers. If you wanted to make the ultimate assay of public British eating in 1997, this would have to be it. My only concern was – would I be able to cram it all in?

There may be no such thing as a free lunch, but in Christopher's peculiar case there were now two in the offing. We met at McDonald's at 12.30 sharp. Both of us had abstained from breakfast and from dinner the night before. We were ravening. From the outside you can tell the King's Road McDonald's is a flagship of the enterprise. The expanded wooden façade on Royal Avenue – which caused a collective aneurysm among local residents when it was built in the late eighties – has a Rennie Mackintosh feel to it, and the giant chrome 'M's that underpin the bench tables facing out from the windows impart a thirties-in-nineties feel of design mishmash. This was one of those McDonald's outlets that poncy local residents campaigned to put a stop to on aesthetic grounds. Needless to say, ten years later the joint is crammed with little Georginas and Edwards, being fed Happy Meals by blue-blooded Norland nannies.

I don't think there's any need to refresh your memory as far as the menu in this restaurant is concerned. With a McDonald's being opened somewhere in the world about every seven minutes, it seems only a matter of time before children are actually *born* knowing the price difference between a fillet o' fish and a McCroissant. We approached the distinctly up-market-looking counter, and from Isabela ordered a plain hamburger and regular fries, six chicken McNuggets and regular fries, and two regular Cokes. The food was ready in a trice (it was already ready), and as she plonked it down in front of us Isabela intoned, 'Burger and fries, McNuggets and fries, two Cokes . . . That'll be £4.97 please . . .'

It was quite crowded upstairs so we adjourned to the basement. Here an absence of windows was made up for by a lot of pink neon tubing which circled an egregious central pillar. The walls were coated with bevelled mirrors, the anchored tables covered with what appeared to be encapsulated, ancient, institutional lino. Over the PA a disc jockey with an irritating cod-American accent warbled about how much money had been raised by McCustomers for Help a London Child. We dug into our food.

Christopher was surprised to find his nuggets tasting of chicken at all – even if the flavour was effectively a reminiscence, a kind of '*Où sont les nuggets d'antan?*' experience. The fries even more pleasantly surprised him by being crispy, not fatty, and ready salted. As for myself? Well, I have young children and have eaten more McDonald's in the past five years than I care to think about. I am a walking, breathing incarnation of Ray Krock's philosophy of food Fordism. I exist to eat these glutinous patties.

Time was getting on, and with a passing nod to the idea that this odd décor might, in twenty-five years or so, become as quaint as the interiors of the old Lyons Corner Houses which finally closed down in the early eighties, we took our leave of L'Oncle Ronald, and headed in the direction of La Tante Claire.

The atmosphere at this exclusive restaurant has been described as 'intimidating' and 'reverential'. The cuisine is the highest of the high – dishes to span the empyrean. In the vestibular waiting area there is a transparent lectern on which reposes one of the Master's cookery books, as if it were some arcane religious text in an inner sanctum. But naturally, what struck Christopher and me most were the similarities to McDonald's. La Tante like L'Oncle boasts a décor that can at best be described as anachronistic and at worst as banjaxed.

The dining area is a single room, about the same size as the basement of 49 King's Road. As at McDonald's, what dominates is the ceiling. This, Christopher informed me, had been machicolated and coffered to the hilt. Also as at McDonald's there were uplights, but at La Tante the sconces were of smoked rather than black glass. In common with the fast-food joint, La Tante has seating oddly suggestive of bondage. But while the McDonald's chairs are anchored to the floor, La Tante's are bound into an odd, tangerine-coloured corsetry, buckled at the back. Indeed, as the clientele somewhat resemble furniture dressed as people, it seems only fitting that the reverse should also be the case.

A *maître d'* of uncompromising deportment seated us and menued us. He rematerialised some minutes later and asked us if we had 'perused it enough'. We goggled at him – neither of us had done *any* perusing at all since the mid-nineteenth century. Actually the menu was getting to us a bit. All right, granted, there was a set *déjeuner* at the absurdly low price of £27 for three courses, but – *Côte de boeuf sauce vigneronne*? I could feel my belly bulge dyspeptically just reading the words. Christopher wasn't looking too happy at the prospect of this ultra-rich food either, but I chivvied him into ordering, from the à la carte, a teasing dish entitled *Marbre de foie gras, gésier de canard aux pistaches et salade d'haricots verts truffés* – an absolute snip at £22.

I had the *Bisque d'homard et ravioli* to start, then the dreaded hamburger substitute; Christopher stuffed down his pâté so fast he might have been a kind of meta-goose, intent on repeating the process of its production at a higher level. I stared at my bisque. It was intense. It looked so thick and creamy, more like the surface of Neptune than a soup. I took a sip – it was as if I'd eaten five lobsters in one mouthful. This wasn't just rich – it was a Sultan of Brunei of a potage. I barely managed to get through half of it. I would wager that the ravioli alone had more nutrition in them than the average family meal for four.

We had ordered a bottle of Côte Rôtie Chapoutier '83, which was, at £58, as Ribena to the rest of the wine list. Our cheapskate status was underscored by the fact that whereas all the other diners had their wine brought to them in some peculiar metal contraption, the *sommelier* merely decanted ours.

I don't know whether the staff at La Tante had got some whiff of L'Oncle off us, but they did do us the service of saying – just as Isabela had an hour or so before – the name of the food they were presenting us with. '*Canard à la presse aux herbes sèches, petits maïs et brocolis,*' one of these archimandrites intoned as he plonked an enormous pile of duck flesh in front of Christopher. 'Golly!' the stuffed architect replied.

I managed about half of my beef. As I glooped my way through the potatoes *dauphinoises* that accompanied it, I meditated on how well McDonald's had done its job. The carb had swelled in my gut and I had absolutely no room for this fantastic food. Not only that but the richness of the flavours was making me feel queasy. As for the ambience, well, if you've followed this column for long enough you'll know that the sight of wealthy people eating rich food turns me on about as much as an outbreak of Ebola.

Christopher drank a Calvados that had been distilled during the General Strike. I wearily picked at the smallest madeleine I'd ever seen in my life – *à la recherche d'une milliseconde perdue.* The bill came to a stonking £194.20 – inclusive of service. As we were ushered out, I mused on the experience. True, La Tante had been expensive, but we still had some change out of two hundred quid – and we'd eaten *two* lunches.

And as for all you moaning minnies who've written in complaining about these ridiculously overpriced meals the *Observer* has been paying for me to eat, I'd like to take this opportunity to inform you that in this instance I paid for the McDonald's myself.

Bon appétit!

Observer, March 1997

124

Massive trade fairs. I mean mass-ive. I mean the kind of trade fairs – remember my sojourn at Frankfurt's Book Babylon last year – where entire integrated transport systems are required to bring vendor, product and buyer together. Even the most prosaic of human manufactures becomes oddly glamorous when quantities of it are assembled together for furlong upon furlong, within halls so large that a Boeing 747 could comfortably execute a three-point turn without biffing the skirting boards. I can quite conceive of attending the World Rawlplug Fair, or the All-Asian Hostess Trolley Monster Rally for that matter – here, as with so much else that revolves our mortal coil, it's size that matters.

In this weight-nary-watched garb Olympia never really dissatisfies. While others may carp at the downside of this Hammersmith, west London, location – no good restaurants, unless you're the kind of Mandy who eats at the River Café, no hospital (I feel personally aggrieved about this as my son was born there) and no good shops (unless you count King Street, one of the capital's busier, homicidal thoroughfares) – I love the place. This is an exhibition hall and two more halves. It's a bewildering agglomeration of thirties-through-nineties architecture, of such vastness that it has at least three putative 'grand' entrances, and its own underground and overground stations.

I've been to Olympia for the London Book Fair (eurgh, yuk!) on a number of painful occasions, usually to sit on panels discussing the state of the novel, or the novel of the state, and a few years ago – together with an adult male friend whose relationship with my young son I later had to abruptly curtail – I visited the Model-makers' and Modellers' Fair. But this outing was different and my most Olympian to date. My wife's and my friend Elaine Finkeltaub (crazy name – crazy woman; she isn't Jewish, nor is she married to a Jewish guy) had taken a stand at the British International Toy and Hobby Fair, in order to launch a fantastic new board game she's dreamed up (together with her friend – board games are, after all, the preserve of the amicable) called In the Know, of which more later.

What a great gig! We get to visit the Toy Fair in order to provide someone with moral support. Wild! Naturally this meant we were entitled to treat the whole thing as an excuse for an infantile jaunt. I just about managed to drive over from our house in Vauxhall without wilfully yanking the wheel about so as to sideswipe other motorists off the road. Then, when we'd parked, press registered, and cantered into Olympia, we insisted on trotting all over the place, gawping, pointing and making silly remarks for ages, before we realised that in truth we were lost. Then it took us at least another half-hour of gawping, pointing and making silly remarks (for some reason asking for directions at a vast toy fair always makes me break out in silly remarks) before we located Elaine.

Part of the reason was that it was tremendous fun juxtaposing the seriously suited toy-makers and even more seriously suited toy-buyers (no Stu from *Rugrats* on view here) with the products they were pushing. In colloquy after colloquy we would observe greyly intent, businesslike faces, only to draw closer and discover that what they were contemplating was a foam-rubber caterpillar: 'Gentlemen, I give you Stumblebugsy, the future of puppetry!' Of course, with some of the more constructive and mechanical toys it's possible for businessmen – and businesswomen – to look as if trafficking in them is a mature enough affair; but with anything soft, cartoon, under-five, or simply fun, it's downright impossible.

I found this so diverting that we wandered 'midst a host of Darth Vaders, Teletubbies, Muppets and the like for quite a while during which I only scrawled a single word in my notebook: 'Tooberzotoo' – and I'm not even sure that's spelt right, nor whether it refers to the toy that was attracting the most kiddie action (a constructor toy which – as its name possibly implies – utilises bendy tubes to make just about everything from masks to creatures), or the beautifully-made wooden castle that we thought of buying for our toddler. When we enquired of the serious businessmen on the wooden-castle stall where we might purchase one, they were most discomfited: 'Ve are . . . how you say . . . exhibiting for the first time here . . .' they gutturalised. 'Germans,' said my wife as we skipped on, 'they make the finest wooden toys in the known universe.'

But eventually we found ourselves ensconced with Elaine, in her booth (which she was sharing with a group of amicable board-gamers under the loose umbrella 'Upstarts'), and playing In the Know. Now, I think this game is a sure-fire winner, although not chiefly for the reasons Elaine has assembled for her promotional literature. Yes, I grant that it comes in an attractive tubular format which allows for the handy removal of question cards and obviates that age-old, drunken Trivial Pursuit problem: 'Wish end youse taken the cards from?'; yes, I allow also that In the Know focuses on those most *Zeitgeist* of preoccupations jigsaw-making (as beloved by HRH the Queen) and celebrity trivia – but none of this, absolutely not one scintilla, makes this game as attractive to me as the fact that the fifty-four jigsaw play pieces (nine per celebrity) come in an attractive, velveteen, drawstring bag.

Come on, let's face the facts, it's these drawstring bags that make all these board games so appealing. Where would Scrabble be without its drawstring bag? In the remainder pile, that's where. And what is it that we love so much about the drawstring bags? Come on, come on . . . let's not fool ourselves, we're all adults; it's the fact that jumbling apparently solid objects within a rumpled manifold reminds us – at some nearly-conscious level – of fumbling genitals. Yup! That's it – genitals. Fumbling genitals!

One minute I was expressing this unorthodox – but for all that heartfelt – opinion, and the next I was being expressed from Olympia by two burly security men. It took a long time, this expressing, given the size of the exhibition hall, and the security men had plenty of time to tell me what they thought of perverts of my ilk.

Mind you, once I'd been fully expressed they were also good enough to tell me the dates for the next Model-makers' and Modellers' Fair, where I'll be guaranteed to find plenty of drawstring bags – velveteen or otherwise.

The Times, February 1999

125

So, I'm lying under a snooker table in the Groucho Club horning with my egregious brief, when some kind of fucking goateed pixie wearing an immaculately pressed white apron pokes a telephone down to me. '*New Statesman* here,' says a woman's voice. 'We want you to do a piece on the influence of gonzo journalism to commemorate the twenty-fifth anniversary of the publication of Hunter S. Thompson's *Fear and Loathing in Las Vegas*. There's fuck-all in the way of a fee, no expenses and certainly no soundproof suite booked at the Flamingo.'

I hung up abruptly and passed the information on to my brief, who was massaging his temples with two snooker balls while still horning. 'Jesus! The *New Statesman* – as your lawyer I'd advise you to put a serious drug collection together for this one. With this kind of a commission you're going to need everything you can get your hands on that will make the enterprise even remotely enjoyable . . .'

Fear and Loathing in Las Vegas. For years it was embarrassing to admit what an influence this slim text had on me. I must have been around sixteen when I first read it – I loved the book so much I bought a T-shirt with Ralph Steadman's astonishing cover drawing on it. Together with friends I assembled a serious drug collection: fifty amphetamine blues, a bottle of amyl nitrate, a sheet of blotter acid and two ounces of red-seal Paki black. We went careering around the country in a Triumph Toledo, playing punk music and doing routines from the book. Its picaresque sense of the frontiers of the psyche had an instant appeal to adolescents like us, and as for the narcotics, they were merely a slalom of toxicities, to be negotiated with an effortless switch of youthful, epicene hips.

Even at that age I think I did perceive some of the very serious themes that run behind the acidic, surreal, slapstick routines which make up Thompson's excoriating attack on the reality of the American Dream on the far cusp of the sixties. And coming back to the text now – and listening to a hilarious new CD adaptation of it – I find that it has acquired still more resonance.

The tale of Raoul Duke a.k.a. Dr Gonzo a.k.a. Hunter Thompson, his Samoan attorney, two trashed hire cars and a kitbag full of seriously mind-warping drugs is really one of the many recastings of Voltaire's *Candide.* Thompson is the Panglossian figure, endlessly optimistic behind a veneer of cynicism: 'The Circus Circus is what the whole hip world would be doing on a Saturday night if the Nazis had won the war.' The superficially hostile and deranged Samoan attorney – who significantly remains unnamed, opaque – is in fact a noble and innocent savage, whose justification for eating an entire sheet of acid blotters and forcing Thompson to throw a radio into the bath with him, as Jefferson Airplane's 'White Rabbit' 'peaks', is that he 'just wanted to get higher'.

Thompson, like many of the real definers of the sixties, was in fact old enough to have been hip when the decade began and hipper when it ended. He had witnessed the acid tests in Haight-Ashbury in 1965 and '66 first-hand. He had written his seminal work of 'new journalism' (Tom Wolfe and E. W. Johnson's 1973 anthology coined this term – retrospectively – to explain the plethora of new directions reportage was headed in during the late sixties and early seventies) *Hell's Angels*, and he was heartily sick of the whole shemozzle. What's so notable now about *Fear and Loathing* is not how ephemeral it is, but how wise it is. As Thompson says in the text, he could see the high-water mark where the great wave of cultural revolution had broken and flowed back. *Fear and Loathing* is located in the very wrack of that tidemark.

Thompson's 'gonzo' method of reportage, in which a fictionalised authorial persona is introduced into the text as a character, was also practised by other contemporaries. The extravagant persona is a vehicle for Thompson to introduce a fictive immediacy to his material; others of the 'new journalists' – such as Wolfe himself – used different techniques. In Wolfe's *The Electric Kool-Aid Acid Test*, the 'journalist' becomes an omniscient eye, able, like some steadicam of the psyche, to penetrate floors, walls and minds.

Really, the ego to *Fear and Loathing*'s anima was Michael Herr's *Dispatches*, another text in which the author featured as a character, another picaresque array of routines. In Herr's book there is no need for the baroque, however – this *is* war. But Thompson's book was about Vietnam as well, insofar as all serious writing in America at this time was about Vietnam. Naturally the country itself is barely alluded to, but when Thompson describes Las Vegas as 'a society of armed masturbators', we know what he's talking about.

The significance of Thompson et al.'s recasting of that perennial genre docufiction is that it has had a lasting but diffuse influence. Much of the technique has been passed on to the mainstream press. Even the most asinine and self-regarding 'columnist' may employ gonzo techniques in the process of baring his or her emotional breast in public. It is far more acceptable now to pass satire off as reality – even if both are banal. Perhaps this is the counterpart – in terms of reportage – to J. G. Ballard's observation that the job of fiction writers has become to invent reality, because reality itself is so fictive.

But at a more prosaic level, Thompson's *meisterwerk* has had hardly any direct or serious heirs – certainly on this side of the Atlantic. And that's because an absolutely essential component of the Thompson satiric armoury was the ingestion of large quantities of mind-distorting drugs. However warped, twisted and cynical Thompson's perception of drugs and their effect, the fact remains that at the time he was writing the ingestion of illegal, mind-altering substances still had a social revolutionary cachet. That's why Thompson ends his coverage of Nixon's re-election campaign in 1972 with a portrait of himself sitting, shooting smack, at the end of a jetty sticking out into the ocean, while various colleagues pass by to ask if he's feeling OK.

Thompson, as he pushed the plunger home, could doubtless scry in its barrel a future in which presidents younger than him didn't inhale, and prime ministerial candidates with formerly shoulder-length hair had had nary so much as a whiff of giggly Oxo. Drugs are yuppie now, mainstream. The political realities of their illegality remain the same, but they no longer possess much potential for torque, for a clarifying lens to be held up against the culture that refuses to tolerate them.

And are the illegal drugs essential to the gonzo methodology? Well, you could remove them from *Fear and Loathing* altogether and still somehow conjure up an evocation of those same states of mind, but on the whole, given the available options, drugs do really seem to be the best one. Large quantities of stimulants and hallucinogens produce quite delightfully awful states of paranoia. Chuck some high-proof spirit into this boiler of toxicity and you have a conflagration on your hands. Add in some heart-pumping, anus-dilating amyl nitrate into this mix and then you'll really be taking your medicine.

Of course, what this allows you to achieve is the condition of a harassed, strung-out war reporter, working for a wire agency that might not pay him, or even support his accreditation, crouching in a shell crater, while in fact you haven't even quit the bathroom of your soundproof suite. The drugs both enhance and synergise with the feeling that many reporters get when they're exposed in front, by the story they're covering, and exposed behind, by the news service they're representing.

As is famously noted by Hesse concerning his book-within-a-book *Der Steppenwolf*, this book is emphatically 'not for everybody'. Thompson himself, in an almost unbelievably lucid recent interview with P. J. O'Rourke, is sound and objective about the downside of using drugs for writing. But he acknowledges their usefulness. I just don't see too many journalists around at the moment who are prepared to get themselves into a state where they see their dead grandmother crawling up their leg with a knife in her teeth, and – damn it all! – still file.

New Statesman, March 1997

126

My mission: to divine as much as possible about the city of Naples in forty-eight hours. Who but an absolute ass – as my dear old dad would've said – would dream of accepting it? But it's a lobster-pot of ingress – this business of boundless enthusiasm and total confidence; every time someone calls to ask me about the Naples trip, I come out with the same blather: 'No, no problem, I'll hack it. I'll get to the core of the place; I'll suss it out.' I inch forward into the labyrinthine task, with no possibility of retreat without ripping off my wavering antennae.

As the jet slumps from air pocket to air pocket, and the burnt lip of Vesuvius curls back below to reveal first a carious city and then the blue gullet of the Bay of Naples itself, I feel death enfold me with its nauseous presentiment. That's what we get with the passage of three and a half centuries; Goethe looked to arrival in this city as the summation of his aesthetic – but for me it's the confirmation of a phobia. After the short day of enlightenment comes the long, crepuscular period of neurosis. I grope at my steadily receding hairline, hoping to find the edge of my Will Self mask, so that I can peel it off and assume a more intrepid visage. No dice.

The city is fantastically, cavernously depopulated. As I'm hustled in from the airport by a malevolent Spirito di Punto, whose driver attacks each vaunting hyperbola of a flyover as if it were a mortality rollercoaster, I see more people on the advertising hoardings than I do on the streets. The entire population has quit town in appropriate class moieties: the bourgeoisie to the Amalfi coast, the working class to Ischia; and the trendies to Capri. Even the poor, who inhabit the notorious *bassi* of Naples – one-roomed homes carved out of the geological slums – have to be winkled out of their dwelling places.

Of course, to undertake the impossible mission I must have a guide, and my controller, Bernardo, has lined up Vittorio, who's a nervy, wiry, wholly engaging native Neapolitan photographer. Unfortunately he has only that afternoon and evening to spend with me. Tomorrow – horror of horrors – he has to go to Turkey to photograph contemporary Anatolian architecture. 'It is very boring,' he tells me as we sup espresso in Gambrinus, an art nouveau café on the edge of the vast Piazza Reale.

373

'I do not like reality much; the work I do for myself is mostly fantasy.'

I don't have any time to quiz him on how it is that he manages to photograph fantasy, because we're off, up the Via Toledo, past the cavernous aorta of the Galeria Umberto I (a late-nineteenth-century shopping mall of Kennedy Space Center proportions), and coursing through this hardened artery into the diseased heart of the city.

To our left the alleys of the Spanish Quarter mount the hill towards the Castel San Elmo, each one a six-storey rampart of laundry and impacted humanity. 'Naples is simple,' says Vittorio; 'you only have to remember that there are two ways: up the hill to the castle, and down the hill to the sea. This part of the city is a grid system, laid down by the Romans.'

It's true that while I can see the whole length of Via Toledo everything seems simple, but Vittorio soon demolishes this facile fantasy by dragging me off to the right, and we plunge into a confusion of piazzas and churches and convents and alleys and palazzi. Not only is there the tortuous street plan – reminiscent of the folds and lumps of a solidified lava stream – but there's also the riot of architectural styles and periods. A Greek wall is surmounted by a Roman one; a Gothic arch contains a baroque piece of *trompe-l'oeil*; in the courtyard of a sixteenth-century palazzo a tiled platform has been carefully dovetailed to hold an immaculate Lambretta, as if it were the scooter of the Lord. In the immediate environs of Naples, Homer found the gateway to the underworld, the Sibyl prophesied, and the Sirens sang. Sod the absence of people – the streets of the city throng with mythological figures, who easily outnumber the tourists.

It isn't too many minutes before my confidence begins to slough off me like the carapace of that figurative lobster – but my enthusiasm still bowls me along in Vittorio's wake. I may not be able to discover Naples with my wavering antennae, but there's no backing out of the mission. As for photographing fantasy – that I begin to comprehend as well.

Building Design, August 2000

127

I wonder how many of the hundreds of thousands who gathered along the River Thames to witness the humungous fireworks display that ushered the third millennium into this ancient burg really appreciated why this year was so special? Special, that is, for anyone who fancies himself as a dandy, or a wit, or a bon viveur, or a boulevardier. Special for any of us who is an *homme du monde* – let alone a *fille de joie*. Special for the aesthetic – although certainly not for the ascetic. Special for the classicist, the neo-classicist and the defiantly modern. Special for the straight, the gay *and* the Janus-assed. In Times Square they had a New Year's Eve jollification that would've appealed more than mere fireworks to the man I choose to regard as the presiding spirit of this year. I refer to the traditional dropping of the Waterford crystal globe.

Appealed more because like my hero, Oscar Wilde, the crystal globe originated in Ireland. Appealed more to him because of its scintillating impermanence – and appealed to him more because, like dear Oscar, the globe was beautifully constructed simply to be destroyed.

Oscar Wilde died on 30 November 1900, in Paris, France. He was just forty-six years old – but what amazing years they'd been! The doyen of his Oxford generation, a prodigious classical scholar, Wilde won the Newdigate Prize for poetry and charmed the English academic establishment, despite his habit of dressing excessively showily, compulsive non-attendance, and running up huge debts with local tradesmen. Needless to say he 'went down' (marvellous expression that, signifying – one is tempted to imagine – a headlong descent from the ivory tower of the university to the flesh pots of London) without a degree.

But what need had Oscar of mere paper qualifications? He embarked, more or less immediately, on a hugely successful career as a public lecturer in America. His declaration to customs officials on his arrival at Staten Island of 'nothing but my genius' is probably apocryphal, but little else about his sojourn was. It was all written about fulsomely in newspapers of the day. And written about, and written about, and written about. Wilde tracked back and forth across the country giving lectures on the 'House Beautiful' and the Aesthetic movement. He appeared in costumes of his own, highly aesthetical devising. Velvet knee-breeches, a fur-trimmed overcoat, a quilted smoking jacket. Tom Wolfe – eat your heart out, you're so *passé*.

Many flocked to hear this dandy speak without realising that their fascination was provoked by witnessing tomorrow's cultural news today: Wilde – the harbinger of the styles and modes of the twentieth century, an era to be rendered dyspeptic with the gorging of its own decadences. Not only that, he has to be one of the few great writers to have played Peoria and received rave notices. For while Wilde may have been an intellectual and aesthetic élitist, that was the only élitism he espoused. He was no social snob – something Americans understood intuitively.

Wilde initially chanced his arm at high-flown theatrical pieces of almost stultifying impenetrability, and turned to the supreme comedies of timeless manners, for which he is remembered, only as a nice little earner. What delicious legerdemain! If only a fraction of today's poetasters could achieve such consummate insouciance! Still, the reason I'm making Wilde my man of the year isn't simply that it's the centenary of his death (an anniversary that, unlike the millennium itself, is cross-cultural and indisputable), it's that here in benighted Britain, his memory is still under the most pernicious of threats.

A couple of years ago, a statue of dear old Oscar was finally unveiled in the lee of St Martin-in-the Fields, hard by London's Theatreland – the only realm he ever aspired to dominate, and the one he does to this day. The statue, by Maggi Hambling, portrays the artist reclining, smoking one of his trademark opiated cigarettes, and staring towards the West End. The caption on the base of the statue sums him up in his own words: 'We are all in the gutter, but some of us are looking at the stars.' The idea of the piece – which is a kind of granite sarcophagus from which Oscar's head and gesturing arms emerge – was that people could come and sit on his chest and chat to him. Indeed, Hambling's title for the piece is *A Conversation with Oscar Wilde*.

The ribbon was cut by the current British Minister for Culture, Chris Smith, a man who shares with dear old Oscar none of the artist's most important characteristics – to wit, wit, wisdom, immaculate prose style, effortless sartorial style and iconoclastic socialism – and only one of his most salient ones: being openly homosexual. Needless to say, despite being our first uncloseted gay minister, Smith received the attentions of demonstrators during the unveiling – demonstrators who wanted to know what the New Labour Government would be doing about Section 28. This is an infamous piece of legislation introduced by that drag queen of darkness Mrs Thatcher, which makes it illegal for British schools to in any way educate children as to the whys and wherefores of same-sex relationships.

In fairness to Tony Blair and his merry men, the abolition of Section 28 is now under way – but only with tremendous resistance being incurred from every homophobic institution in the land (which is just about all of them with the exception of the Royal National Theatre and the night-club Heaven). But where does this leave dear old Oscar? I'll tell you. Passing by Hambling's statue the other day, on my way to purchase some green lilies in Covent Garden, I was appalled to see that it's been encased in what – for want of a better word – can only be described as a little wooden cottage. If you wanted to have a conversation with Oscar, you'd have to break inside.

The cottage has been put there because the statue kept being vandalised. Yup – it's the solid truth. A hundred years since the man died, his health broken, after a two-year sentence of hard labour for 'gross indecency', the really gross indecency of defacing a memorial to him is being perpetrated.

Well, I for one won't stand for it. One of my projects for this, the year of Wilde, is to finish writing a new movie version of his classic *The Picture of Dorian Gray*. I shall dedicate it to my hero. In the draft I've done so far, I've updated the action from the end of the nineteenth century to the end of the twentieth. *Plus ça change?* – as dear Oscar might say himself. Well, not much. Of course, in the original, the buried metaphor-that-wasn't-really-a-metaphor was syphilis – which Wilde himself suffered from. And in my version it will be Aids. Other than that, the observations of social mores, the melodrama of debauched morals and the superlative epigrams, which apotheosise *everything*, all remain as fresh as the day they were penned.

Indeed, it's the epigrams that have dated best of all. So, it's Oscar's own words that serve best to debunk the freaks who would dare to attack him today – just as they did a hundred years ago: 'A man cannot be too careful in the choice of his enemies.'

Have a Wilde year, everyone.

US GQ, February 2000

128

Is shopping the new food? And concomitantly, are domestic interiors the new restaurants? People ask these things – just as they used to aver that brown was the new black, or witter that Clerkenwell was London's 'new' Soho. The answer is, of course, an emphatic 'yes' on all counts, because, you see, the nineties – it's transpired – are the eighties revisited, with painless gentrification now taking place in all styles, modes and locations. They've been the eighties without bad feeling; the eighties as *fait accompli*.

Of course shopping is the new food, but it's also the new shopping – and the old shopping for that matter. Nothing better exemplifies this than the Swedish furniture and household megastore Ikea. Ikea is *so* eighties, from its aluminium, blue-and-yellow-cladded exterior to its modular 'warehouse' interior; from its crowded car-park to its overly child-friendly restaurant (overly, because you can't help feeling that it bears some relation to the low birth-rate in those climes). And naturally, in the car-park stand two mighty factory chimneys, all that is left of the pathetic secondary manufacture, before the tertiary, retail industry oozed its way in. Two brick dolmens, ringed around at their summits with the yellow-and-blue standard.

(But it must be stressed, the eighties in Sweden *were* the nineties, just as the nineties here *are* the eighties. It does follow that the nineties have gone on for eighteen years in Malmö; however, we needn't let that bother us.)

What we need to concentrate on is the shopping experience as a species of praxis; a union of action and reification which nullifies traditional Marxist categories of surplus value. At Ikea we are instructed to take tape measure, pad, and leaflet; to note the items we wish to purchase as we advance, zigzagging, through displays of modular good living. Kitchens of birch-fresh antisepsis, living rooms of beech-warm sociability, bedrooms of cherry-beech consanguinity. Everywhere there is helpful signage, and sales assistants who are standing at plinth-borne computer terminals.

The prices – as long as you, like me, are incapable of adding two two-digit numbers together in your head – seem ludicrously low. I begin to entertain fantasies of completely reordering my life around timelessly

378

modern, Swedish furniture and home furnishings. Winters spent in the far north, cocoa mugs resting on warm beech; I only venture out when the local maniac chainsaws another sheep to pieces. Then spring. The long journey south with my daughter-in-law driving me in my customised fifties Volvo (dashboard of birch-fresh antisepsis), with only the occasional roadside break for temporal hallucinations. Then autumn with Liv Ullmann in a cherry-beech, split-level house on a southern islet. As I chop cauliflower on a solid beech chopping-board (a snip at £16), she remains resolutely silent. Winter again. Death plays me at chess and wins repeatedly; although at Pictionary I continue to reign supreme.

We gain the restaurant and I opt for 'regular' meatballs, while my companion goes for the large ones. It's so nice here at Ikea. The spaces broad, the vinyl neutral, the lighting diffuse, the signs discreet but plentiful, and the meatballs a-bobbing. I glance around at my fellow diners, these scions of a year of social democracy – how are they faring in this temple of Scandinavian rationality? They're certainly looking great – somehow taller, straighter of limb, more open of expression, and – dare I say it – *blonder!?*

Yes, blonder. Saving that rubicund old fellow over there, hale and hearty in a sensible windcheater, his back-combed ruff of white hair rendering him typically Nordic. It's true, so omnivorous is the Swedishness of Ikea that it actually makes shoppers in its own image. Even Asian and Afro-Caribbean visitors go a bit Abba in the aisles. And a Norwegian friend of my wife's comes here when she feels homesick.

Refreshed, and entertaining notions of large-scale eugenics programmes, we rejoin the human travelator on the *Generation Game* finale that is life. I am reminded, poignantly, of a graffito I once saw on the wall of Safeway in Yate: 'SHOP, CONSUME, DIE'. We leave the flatpack zone and pass down into the bowels of the building. Here all is wear – bed, table, garden; and naturally, as we load our extra-wide trolley, my companion and I begin to tear.

The fissure at the core of our relationship widens and flames spew out. And this in the duvet-cover section. Ostensibly the argument is about colours of said linen, but really it nets in everything: sexuality, aims, ideals, norms, honour, aesthetics, teleology, guitar bands. We are as painfully enmeshed as any two people can be, which is absurd as my companion is my neurologist, Dr 'Big' McFee of the Glasgow Royal Infirmary, who's only accompanied me to Ikea to buy some oven gloves.

It's a wonder we make it through to the final section emotionally intact, but we do and we're rewarded with a vision of the high temple of the late nineties: a mammoth hall, divided into aisles by mighty shelves of mutant Dexion, and to the rear, the maw of a still larger warehouse, its hissing lifts and whining forklifts debouching flatpacks with mantric consistency. McFee and I wander these aisles, marvelling at the huge chattel stacks, and wondering how the hell we'll get anything down from a shelf forty feet up without the assistance of a giant hornhead.

We make it back from Ikea, and McFee assembles my two, new, sub-Bauhausian armchairs with commendable speed. (He finds them a doddle compared with psychosurgery.) Then he tries to seduce me in one of them. 'Isn't this a little unethical?' I say. 'I don't know about unethical,' he replies, his accent gruff with lust, 'but it's arguably quite Swedish, very decadent, and absolutely contemporary.'

It was my first time at Ikea.

The Times, March 1998

129

On Holywell beach in Cornwall we sunbathers and surfers and loungers disported ourselves, our slightly frenzied yawps of pleasure clear evidence that we were determined to suck the last few fervid drags from the dying butt of the August sun. Holywell beach is magnificent – a great sweep of sand, backed by pink granite cliffs and hundred-foot-high dunes. There's a salt-water tidal creek, there are offshore rocks, there's a caff. Among the thousand-odd holidaymakers the morphological strata of body forms were exposed between the tidemark and the waterline. At the top of the beach there were Michelin men and women who wouldn't look out of place on a Donald McGill postcard; further down there were the stick figures of anorexic teenagers sunning their shrunken embonpoints; and in the surf, the neoprene-suited surfers lunged up to catch waves of such a domestic size that they couldn't quite be called breakers – more fractures in the sea's silky surface.

A series of stentorian notices and flapping flags indicated the area of the beach the coastguard advised swimmers to occupy, and the vast majority of them complied with this. Further flags showed where surfers might go, and these free spirits once again obeyed. A coastguard station, right on the beach, was manned by athletic-looking types sitting atop all-terrain buggies. We took the notices and flags to be suggestions only – the sea was, after all, about as anfractuous as a municipal paddling pool – and trudged off down to the far end of the beach, away from flags, bathers, caff and all. My wife and the ten-year-old daughter of our friend went in to the sea and holding hands leapt over the chest-high waves. One of the buggies came speeding across from the coastguard station within a matter of minutes. Its rider told my wife – in the nicest possible way – that he'd be obliged if she would confine her pleasures to the flagged zone, along with the rest of the lemmings. 'We've only had one drowning on this section of coastline all summer,' he said, 'and that's something we're proud of.'

Indeed, as a society we're proud of preserving life at all costs – and make no mistake about it, cost is the operative factor here, what with helicopters being regularly scrambled for errant windsurfers – and if we can't preserve our lives indefinitely, we wish to lose them painlessly, drugged up to the eyeballs in high-tech hospitals, not floundering in some primal element. About 90 per cent of the healthcare expended on the average individual in Britain takes place during the last six weeks of his or her life. It follows that we elect governments on the basis that they'll provide us with a painless death. It's long been the policy in the NHS to make quality-of-life decisions on the allocation of beds: if a patient is a mere sentient blob then why not swivel the stopcock of budgetary apportionment? But really, rather than allowing nice men on all-terrain buggies to shepherd us into swimming pens, shouldn't we retain some quality-of-life decisions for ourselves? After all, as Maynard Keynes so sagely observed, 'In the long term we'll all be dead.'

Today, BBC Radio 4, September 2000

Index

brown rats 23, 26, 283
Brown, Cedric 149
Brown, Divine 275
Brown, George Mackay 10
Brown, Gordon 110
Brown, Jackie see Jackie Brown
Brown, Ron 278
Browns (night-club) 134
Brynner, Yul 93
Buccleuch, Duke of 328
Bunny, Easter *see* Easter Bunny
bunnykins 34 *see also* Easter Bunny;
   rabbit(s); Welsh rarebit; White
   Rabbit
burgers 4, 15, 63, 363, 364, 365
Burr, Raymond 178, 326
Burroughs, William S. 12, 70–6, 142–4,
   171, 216, 336
Burston, Paul 61, 334–5
Burton Ale 107 *see also* Newcastle
   Brown Ale
Burton, Decimus 301

cake 3–5, 34, 64, 163, 259, 292, 321, 359
   see also madeleines
   beef- 234
   cheese- 14
   crab 17, 226 *see also* crab(s)
   pan- 163, 193, 252 *see also* make-up,
      pancake
   potato 195
camel-hair hats 203
Camelot 149
Camels 231
camels 97, 123
Campbell, Alastair 187
Campbell, Malcolm 164
Camus, Albert 233
Carroll, Lewis 174–6, 302 *see also*
   White Rabbit
cartoonists 317, 318
cartoons 33, 57, 119, 155, 156, 186, 317,
   348, 368
Castaway (BBC1) 96–8, 207
catch-phrases 51, 54, 176, 187, 231,
   235–6, 274

Caxton, Mr 80
Charing Cross Road 13–14, 15, 60
Charles, Prince of Wales *see* Tampon
   Apparent; Windsor, Charles
Cheddar 62, 192 *see also* Brie; goat's
   cheese; Welsh rarebit
cheese footballs *see* footballs, cheese
cheeses, big *see Fromages, les Grands*
chimpanzees 42–3, 138 *see also* apes;
   gorillas; monkeys
Christmas 8, 9, 60, 114–15, 225, 227, 284,
   287, 288, 350
churlishness 219, 263, 293
clicking mead horns 295 *see also*
   locking antlers
co-ordinated foot- and sockwear 267 *see
   also* matching socks and shoes
Coca-Cola 132 *see also* Coke
cocaine 23, 132, 143, 215–16 *see also*
   coke; horning; snow
cod 191, 192, 363
cod surrealism *see* surrealism, cod
coke 131 *see also* cocaine; horning;
   snow
Coke 61, 364 *see also* Coca-Cola
Colin the Canadian 86–9
Commons, House of 1, 271, 309,
   340, 359
conceptualism 43, 76, 77, 79, 131, 183,
   185, 186, 246, 270, 315–18
Conran, Jasper 161, 162, 164
Conran, Sebastian 162, 164
Conran, Shirley 162, 164
Conran, Sir Terence 161–2, 162, 163
Conran, Tom 162
Conran, World of 162, 164
conundrums 174, 176, 264, 266
crab(s) 17, 27–9, 33, 117, 226
Cronenberg, David 70, 183, 216
Crowley, Aleister 281
crystal(s) 7, 20, 34, 375
Crystal, Billy 260

Dalglish, Kenny 99, 100, 102
Daumal, René 281
De Quincey, Thomas 71, 228